Table of Contents

113015

From One Medium to Another

---○---

Basic Issues for Communicating the Scriptures in New Media

Edited by Paul A. Soukup
and
Robert Hodgson

Co-published by

Sheed & Ward
Kansas City

AMERICAN BIBLE SOCIETY
NEW YORK

Sheed & Ward™ is a service of The National Catholic Reporter Publishing Company.

Library of Congress Cataloguing-in-Publication Data pending.

ISBN 1-55612-968-8 (Sheed & Ward version)
ISBN 0-8267-0034-9 (ABS version)

Published by: Sheed & Ward
115 E. Armour Blvd.
P.O. Box 419492
Kansas City, MO 64141-6492

To order, call: (800) 333-7373

From One Medium to Another

Introduction

Overture

Introduction

An Urgent Need:
God's Word in a Post-Literate World

It's one sign of our times that traditional forms of literacy such as reading and writing are declining while new forms of literacy, sometimes called "secondary orality" (Ong, 1982), are emerging. This new literacy results, in part, from that permanent fixture in American homes, the television, and, in part, from the increasing portability and ubiquity of computers, popular music, and electronic games.

Another sign of our changing times is our increased awareness of the ways in which culture, theology, and communications interact one with another. We have come to see this interaction particularly at the places where the Church transfers its theological content, for example, its Holy Scriptures, into a particular culture and then communicates that content in the forms of the host culture—forms such as electronic and screen technologies. The American Bible Society (ABS) has long wrestled with the question of communicating and translating the Holy Scriptures in and for particular cultures and language groups. Since the 1960s it has communicated the Scriptures to and through English-language cultures via a translation theory called functional equivalence, an approach to translation that transfers the meaning of a source text into close, natural equivalents within the language of a target text (de Waard & Nida, 1986). Its most recent formulation of the question inspired this volume and the Symposium upon which it is based: *How can the message of the Holy Scriptures be faithfully translated and communicated from one medium to another?*

Practical Theology and Applied Communication

While this question may be newly posed, the problem is not. For centuries, Christian artists have moved the message of the Holy Scriptures from its oral form to icon, mosaic, stained glass, and painting, as well as to highly illuminated written and printed texts. For their part, preachers have turned printed texts into homilies and pulpit sermons whose oral and illustrative nature explicates difficult biblical passages, making them culturally accessible to church laity. In our century, we see the transfer of the Scriptures to radio, film, television, and now the Internet and World Wide Web. The move from one medium to another has become part of the practical theology of the Church. People do it, and members of local and universal churches judge the results.

Consider two cases in point: Protestant evangelist Aimee Semple McPherson and Roman Catholic bishop Jacques Gaillot. McPherson, who virtually invented radio evangelism in the 1920s, used commercial broadcasting to help launch worldwide Pentecostalism, thus embedding the Scriptures in a new technology and forever changing the form and content of evangelism and religious discourse (Blumhofer, 1993a). Gaillot, bishop of Evreux near Paris, suffered the displeasure of the Vatican and on January 13, 1994 was reassigned to the North African diocese of Partenia. There bishop Gaillot created in January 1996 Roman Catholicism's first virtual diocese when he put his See on the World Wide Web with its own home page accessible under http://www.partenia.fr. Like McPherson, Gaillot has inculturated the Gospel in a new form and created a communications network to proclaim the Good News.

The ABS Multimedia Translations Project, which will be described more fully later in this introduction, also forms a good case study since it shows theology at work in cultural production. As it continues, the project will be evaluated by the community of believers. Along with this will come academic evaluation—something that we begin here.

How did the ABS come to do this? We find a clue in its history, origins, and character.

A Visionary Organization: Origins and Character of the American Bible Society

John Jay (1745-1829) and Elias Boudinot (1740-1821), along with some 55 other Federalists, founded the ABS on May 10, 1816, after meeting for three days at the South Reformed Dutch Church on Garden Street in Manhattan (Lacy, 1977, p. 1). In so doing, they established an institution and benevolency that played two roles in early 19th century American social and religious history.

In the one role, ABS helped define and direct the Second Great Awakening, a period of 19th century social and religious history that witnessed not only the rise of the Bible Movement but the advent of the Sunday School and Tract Movements as well. As a result of the Great Awakening, there emerged "a period of theological ferment based on new notions of human perfectibility...an era of millennial optimism" (Wosh, 1994, p. 3).

In the other role, ABS acted as a Federalist voice and outpost during a period of Jeffersonian and Jacksonian populism—a movement whose free-wheeling spirit of rationalism and dissent contrasted with a Federalist vision to reform and rally the national moral character around respect for patrician values and established religious authority. The Federalist reform program drew heavily on the Bible for form and substance, and in its view, "Placing the Good Book in every household, in the minds of many, might lay the foundation for a common Christian social consensus" (Wosh, 1994, p. 13). Today, the ABS has evolved into a broad-based and non-sectarian Bible publisher. But this Federalist zeal for "placing the Good Book" still permeates all that ABS does.

With civic duty and religious conviction molding its corporate character, ABS took up this mission with great energy. Article 1 of its 1816 Constitution made the mission public:

> This Society shall be known by the name of the AMERICAN BIBLE SOCIETY, of which the sole object shall be to encourage a wider circulation of the Holy Scripture without note or comment. The only copies in the English language to be circulated by the Society shall be of the version now in common use. (Lacy, 1977, p. 10)

This outlay of energy on behalf of the Bible Cause was matched by a spirit of innovation and research that, within a few years, pushed the ABS to the forefront of print publishing houses. In 1817, ABS engaged printer Daniel Fanshaw whose print technology included the latest steam-powered Treadwell presses and a stereotype printing process. By the 1820s ABS Manager Amos H. Hubbard was supplying ABS with mass-produced paper from his Fourdrinier paper making machines (Wosh, 1994, pp. 17-20, 22-24; Burke, Wosh, & Goostree, 1992, pp. 18-19; Boomershine, 1993b, p. 181).

The earliest record of a research grant notes that Dr. S. G. Howe received $1,000 in 1835 for experiments in the field of "research for some type of printing that could be read by the blind" (Bonnell, 1935, p. 154; Chamberlain, 1935, p. 155). Using Howe's research results, ABS published in 1843 "the whole of the Bible, in raised Roman letters" (Bonnell, 1935, p. 154). In this century, ABS has helped underwrite translation studies, including the research of Eugene A. Nida (1952, 1964, 1969).

Experimenting with new electronic and screen media, ABS circulated stereopticon slides in the 1920s. In 1922 it broadcast its first radio program; in 1948, its first television program. The first ABS motion picture ran in 1935, and in 1945 the ABS created a Visual Materials Department that by 1966 had produced 29 films (Zimmermann, 1968). Most recently, the ABS has supported prototype development of a reference Bible on CD-ROM, as well as the experimental work of the Multimedia Translations Project (Hagedorn, 1991).

A Timely Response: ABS Multimedia Translations Project

While the previous efforts of the ABS to use electronic media and technology focused mainly on raising public awareness about the work of the ABS and only to a limited extent on Bible programs, the Multimedia Translations Project (MTP) had a different goal. Launched in 1989 as an experiment to test the limits and possibilities of translation, it boldly claimed that screen and electronic technologies could transfer and inculturate the very message of the Holy Scriptures and do so with faithfulness and integrity. The ABS selected teenagers as its primary audience, reasoning that, while they might not read a Bible in our post-literate world, they might well come to know the Word of God by means of translations and presentations in new media formats (Burke, 1993, p. 102).

To initiate the experiment, the MTP sought and received approval for 13 prototypes that would constitute a series entitled "Jesus in the Gospels." Each prototype had as its subject a Gospel passage that a team of scholars translated from the original Greek. This same team also drafted an encyclopedic text base that contained background and foreground material. The background material consisted of historical, cultural, and exegetical studies that shed light on the passage. The foreground material provided a selective overview of the art, music, and film inspired by the passage over the course of history.

By the time of the Symposium in September 1995, all participants had had an opportunity to view the three prototypes completed at that time: "Out of the Tombs" (Mark 5.1-20), "A Father and Two Sons" (Luke 15.11-32), and "The Visit" (Luke 1.39-56). Each prototype featured a 7-10 minute music video translation housed on a VHS tape, together with a companion study help—housed initially on a laser disc, but later, as technology evolved, on a CD-ROM. For a description of these programs, please turn to the back of this book (pages 381-382).

The three prototypes caught the attention of the film and multimedia industries, earning some of their highest accolades. In 1996, the video translation "A Father and Two Sons" won a special prize for artistic excellence at a film festival sponsored by the International Catholic Organization for Film and Audiovisual (OCIC). Two years earlier, in 1994, the Council on International Nontheatrical Events (CINE) bestowed its top prize, the Golden Eagle Award, on the video translations "A Visit" and "A Father and Two Sons." In 1992, the video translation "Out of the Tombs" garnered a Golden Eagle Award from the Council on International Nontheatrical Events (CINE). At that time, this prize qualified films for the Academy Award nomination process.

At the 1996 Intercomm Festival the jury presented the "Out of the Tombs" CD-ROM with a Gold Plaque, signifying outstanding artistic achievement. That same year, "The Visit" CD-ROM took First Prize in the OCIC festival's multimedia competition, while "A Father and Two Sons"

CD-ROM earned a Silver Award at the Houston International Festival. A year earlier, in 1995, "The Visit" CD-ROM won a Bronze Apple from the National Educational Media Network.

A leading trade publication, *Multimedia Producer,* named the director, Fern Lee Hagedorn, as one of the U.S.'s top 100 multimedia producers for 1995.

A Challenge for Today:
Devising and Creating Multimedia Translations

At ABS, the term "multimedia" has been used primarily in connection with Bible translating. But even in this limited context, the term has been remarkably fluid and its meaning at ABS has evolved in recent years. Factors that have played a role in this evolution include a changing understanding of media, the rapid growth of technology, and the ability of digital technology to support ever more sophisticated computer-based communications systems. It should come as no surprise that at ABS and elsewhere, "multimedia" has connoted different things to different people.

When the MTP began in 1989, "multimedia" was virtually synonymous with "synchronized slide show." Later, ABS came to use the term as a marker for the "multiple media" (for example, text, image, sound, movement, and color) that translators and artists have used over the centuries to convey the meaning of biblical narratives. Thus, an English-language music video translation of the parable of the Prodigal Son (Luke 15.11-32) with Spanish subtitles would be "multimedia" or "audiovisual" in the sense that it depends on these traditional media to build a translation.

Such a video is "translation" because it faithfully transfers into the target language of film and video the meaning of a source text, though it does so using not just the words of the source text, but also the contemporary sounds and images that are invited by that text (Burke, 1993, p. 105).

By the early '90s, however, as the computer industry was at last able to provide affordable computers with CD-ROM drives and "multimedia" capacity, the term "multimedia" also came to connote at ABS a very specific application of this new technology: the development of interactive pilots and prototypes housed on CD-ROMS.

The evolution of the term "multimedia" at ABS reveals the breadth of the mission of the MTP: to test the limits and possibilities of Scripture translating. On the one hand, "multimedia translations" can refer to existing prototypes such as the video translations and their companion CD-ROM study helps. On the other hand, the term can refer to not-yet-existing prototypes and pilots presented on interactive video, virtual reality systems, or the World Wide Web.

However the term "multimedia" is defined, there are certain features that characterize this approach to translating the Bible. It is communication, just as traditional print translation is communication. It is thus a process involving at the most basic level a source message with its codes, a target message with its codes, and a channel for transferring the message from source to target. In new media translating of the Bible, the source message is contained in the ancient Greek or Hebrew text, the target message in the modern performance with its words, sounds, and images. Among the source codes are the grammars of Greek or Hebrew language as well as the grammar of ancient manuscript and codex culture. Among the target codes are the grammars that structure film and CD-ROM production, modern English language, and the gestural and tonal cues that are essential aspects of spoken and performed language.

Although multimedia and print translation are both forms of communication, multimedia translation begins where print translation leaves off, engaging with issues that print translation never needs to face or resolve. Print translation focuses necessarily on the linguistic and denotative meaning of words along with the larger rhetorical, grammatical, and lexical units that words form. When print translation wishes to go beyond denotative meaning and work with elements of connotative and associative meaning—elements such as historical, cultural, performative, sonic, imagistic, and aesthetic information—it must place these elements in footnotes, maps, graphs, and charts. Print study Bibles are the result.

Multimedia translation, no less than print translation, faithfully transfers the denotative meaning of words from source to target, creating what is referred to within the ABS project as a "wordtrack." But thanks to a sociosemiotic approach to translation (see below pp. 15-16) coupled with the power of digital media, it can reproduce more than just rhetorical, grammatical, and lexical meaning. With careful historical-critical research, with sensitive treatments, with collaborative story-boarding, and with controlled approaches to production, it can also faithfully translate in a functional equivalent way other aspects of meaning, for example, the images and sounds, together with the cultural, historical, aesthetic, and performative information that also constitute the meaning of biblical discourse.

Consider a hypothetical translation of Psalm 92.1-3 in a new media format:

> How good it is to give thanks to you, O LORD,
> to sing in your honor, O Most High God,
> to proclaim your constant love every morning
> and your faithfulness every night,
> with the music of stringed instruments
> and with melody on the harp.

Today's English Version

Translation would begin with a functional equivalent rendering of the Hebrew text. At the same time, it would also want to provide contemporary functional equivalents for other elements that make up the meaning of these verses. For example, the title of the Psalm ("A Song for the Sabbath Day") gives performance information, indicating that this ancient text is a song and thus suggesting a modern musical setting. The references to stringed instruments provide clues to how we might realize a modern treatment. Linguistic and cultural data embedded in the Psalm indicate that Psalm 92 is a song of praise that an individual sang or chanted in the Jerusalem temple (Brown, Fitzmyer, & Murphy, 1990, p. 542). These data also provide clues to the sounds and visuals that might make up a translation of Psalm 92.

New media translation is a collaborative effort, and in this respect it mirrors trends in print translation. But a new media translation team collaborates in ways that have no real analogy in print translation. First is breadth and scope. Members must acknowledge and engage the expertise of authorities in areas that print translators are free to ignore: for instance, art and music historians, graphic artists and composers, scriptwriters, filmmakers, software designers, and communications and media experts. Second is accountability. Here multimedia translation marks a departure from contemporary patron-artist relationships in which an artist is free to play a lonely but inspired genius, accountable to no one but his or her own muse. Multimedia translation draws upon collaborative artist-patron traditions that predate the more isolating work patterns that began to emerge after the Enlightenment. Essential qualities of this vision are the full engagement of all parties, mutual respect, healthy criticism, and joint decision-making (Goethals, 1996).

New media translation, like print translation, is normative, operating at every point on the basis of translation theory (Burke, 1993, pp. 105-109). In the ABS project, functional equivalence, also known as dynamic equivalence, provided an initial theoretical framework. More recently ABS has recognized the need to develop this print-oriented translation theory in ways that are appropriate to non-print translation, for instance, along lines suggested by a sociosemiotic approach (see below pp. 15-16). Multimedia translation looks to theory to provide broad *a priori* norms, for example, faithfulness to the biblical message, closest natural equivalence, relevance, and audience sensitivity. Such norms provide tools for measuring the adequacy of a translation. Theory also provides specific principles and guidelines that inform research and production decisions. One principle states that "Each specific multimedia translation project will deal appropriately and responsibly with the various tensions involved in translation from original language texts to an audiovisual version" (Burke, 1993, p. 106; Thomas, 1994, p. 45). Another determines that "Each selected passage of biblical text must be a unit of discourse which is recognizably complete in itself" (Fry, 1987, p. 59).

Several years of production experience have resulted in a set of practical guidelines. One provides that biblical experts must be involved not only in research and development but also in every phase of production, thus assuring the fidelity and integrity of the translation. Another states that the success of a multimedia translation can only be judged after the fact. In other words, you don't know if you have done it right until you have had a chance to step back from a production and see what you have created.

New media translation is also descriptive and shares a number of features with descriptive translations studies (Toury, 1995, pp. 9-19), for example, a commitment to research and a need to work functionally. It must not only study and research the passages to be translated, but it must also research and study itself and similar translation processes and prototypes in an effort to better describe and improve all of the elements that make up multimedia translation. It is functional because it must produce translations in their target languages and among their target audiences that actually function as translations at the level of word, sound, and image.

When the MTP translates functionally it follows precedents set by translators as diverse as Jerome and Luther (Stoerig, 1963). Modern print translators work functionally as well, for example, when they take into account reader and audience sensitivity at Isaiah 7.14, translating a Hebrew word as "young woman" for one target audience, but as "virgin" for another (Bratcher, 1995, pp. 439-440). Those who work on multimedia translation projects make the same kind of functional decision when they, for example, take the modern performance genre of the music video as a functional equivalent for the ancient performance genre (chant) of a passage such as the Gerasene Demoniac (Mark 5.1-20) or the Prodigal Son (Luke 15.11-32).

Discussion, Debate, and Directions:
A Record of the Symposium Presentations

Responding to the emerging new literacy as well as to the success of the MTP's experiments and prototypes, the ABS convened a Symposium around the question *How can the meaning of texts, especially biblical texts, be translated and communicated faithfully into media other than print?* Entitled "From One Medium to Another" the Symposium met on September 7-9, 1995 at Bible House in New York City and brought together key experts from a variety of disciplines. These experts presented and responded to 17 papers addressing theoretical and practical issues assumed by the question.

In this volume each paper is preceded by a précis of its contents. To assist the reader, the editors have grouped the papers into three logical categories that do not necessarily reflect their sequence of presentation at the Symposium. The first group, "Theoretical Approaches," includes those papers that center on key conceptual issues. The second, "Case Studies," presents a look into several studios and workshops to help us see creative and interpretive processes at work and to watch artists and other professionals apply the guidelines and principles that shape their processes. The third, "A Look to the Future," points to paths down which technology may take translation in the 21st century. By way of preparation, Gary Rowe's paper on "Publishing Words and Images" sets the tone for the overall discussion. Ronald Roschke's "Summary and Synthesis" integrates remarks and reflections made during the course of the Symposium and serves as an apt and inspiring summary of all that transpired.

Part I. Assessing the Challenge: Theoretical Approaches

In "Recent Developments in New Testament Hermeneutics," Moisés Silva surveys New Testament interpretation since the beginning of this century. He underscores the single-minded devotion to philological and historical/critical analysis that characterized scholarship in the early 20th century. By the end of the 20th century, however, there is no single dominant approach, but rather a multiplicity of models for New Testament interpretation. Silva regards such multiplicity as necessary, and he helps us understand why multimedia translation is timely.

In "Problems and Challenges of Translation in an Age of New Media and Competing Models," José Lambert addresses theoretical and practical issues that translators face as they not only work with modern screen and electronic technologies but also with diverse and often competing models of communication and translation. He underscores the need for all partners in the translation process to find a common working language, and he makes a strong case for more research into translational theory and phenomena.

Patrick Cattrysse combines semiotics and systems theory in "Audiovisual Translation and New Media" to suggest a polysystems approach to translation and translation studies. For Cattrysse, translation is a process of communicating culture. But it is also a product whose form and content are necessarily shaped by the systems and norms that make up source and target cultures. By way of example, he uses *film noir* adaptations of American detective novels to demonstrate the value of a polysystems approach to communication and translation.

Paul A. Soukup reviews audience analysis studies in "Understanding Audience Understanding" and suggests a model for assessing how audiences understand mass media products and how they participate in the meaning-making process of such products. His communications-based research dovetails neatly with descriptive translation studies that ask both how translations function within an audience, and why audiences expect such translation criteria as readability and audience sensitivity to be honored in the construction of translations.

The hermeneutics of Hans-Georg Gadamer provides the subject for "The Seriousness of Play: Gadamer's Hermeneutics as a Resource for Christian Mission," Fred Lawrence's contribution to this volume. Lawrence finds in Gadamer's thought a mode of being and a model of interpretation called "game-play." In game-play, humans structure their being-in-the-world as they appropriate art and literature. In the act of translation, game-play comes to the fore as humans transfer meaning from a source to a target culture and engage that meaning for their own lives.

Part II. Accepting the Challenge: Case Studies

In these essays we meet several practitioners who explain how the meaning of narratives is transferred from one medium to another.

The section begins with a look at the past. Aimee Semple McPherson was the most successful woman evangelist of this century. Edith Blumhofer examines McPherson's life and work in "Tuning In: A Historical Look at Evangelicals, Pentecostals, and Electronic Media" and describes how McPherson almost single-handedly invented radio evangelism. Even though she shared the distrust of worldly media that was typical of turn-of-the-century evangelicals and pentecostals, she developed a principle that enabled her to work with them: Let worldly media save the world!

In "Telling a Story in Dance," Elizabeth Keen covers the process by which a choreographer translates a story into dance. Keen takes as her case studies three well-known ballets: George Balanchine's *The Prodigal Son,* José Limón's *The Moor's Pavane,* and Martha Graham's *Night Journey.* She shows how in each case key principles (speed, focus, compression) guided the choreographers as they moved the story from the medium of text to that of dance.

In "Installation Art: Sacred Places in Secular Spaces" Jennifer González presents three case studies that introduce the installation art of Amalia Mesa-Bains, Renée Stout, and Jenni Lukač. Each artist has created a sacred space with shrines and altars, and González shows how these sacred spaces rely for their effect on principles of classical rhetoric such as persuasion and praise.

"Film Language and Communication: From Cecil B. De Mille to Martin Scorcese" is Jayne Loader's look at the Hollywood tradition of Bible films from the vantage point of the many languages that films speak. She analyzes, for instance, the visual language of the director and cinematographer and the verbal language of the screenwriter. Out of this virtual Babel of messages and languages, she retrieves two principles that have characterized the Hollywood tradition: return-on-investments and entertainment.

Alice Bach writes about the biblical figure of Eve in "Out of the Garden and into the Mall." Bringing feminist and audience analysis to bear on popular culture, she follows Eve through various incarnations in film and advertising. She aims to illustrate how popular culture has reduced the archetypal woman Eve—and thereby all women—to a single role, namely, woman as companion for man.

J. Ritter Werner wrote "Musical *Mimesis* for Modern Media." He surveys Hebrew and Greek musical traditions, revealing how even ancient performances combined many media, including mime, dance, and dramatic movement. Unifying factors for such performances were the principles of *mimesis* ("imitation") and *harmonia* ("harmony").

In "Multimedia Images: Plato's Cave Revisited" Gregor Goethals analyzes the visual side of the ABS Multimedia Translations Project. She illustrates how the ABS's approach to art and artist has revived older views of art as a portal to the transcendent and the artist as a member of a creative fellowship. This approach challenges contemporary notions of art as personal mystique as well as an older romantic notion of the artist as a lonely seer.

Writing from his perspective as a software developer, Reg Pettus also studies the ABS project in "Programming Issues in Multimedia Design." He demonstrates that even at the technical level of software programming, the principles of collegiality and collaboration must guide the work. Pettus describes a typical production team, identifying roles and responsibilities of each member.

Part III. Accepting New Challenges: A Look to the Future

"From Scriptural to Virtual: Bible Translation, Hypercommunication, and Virtual Reality" comes from Gregory Shreve who charts one future scenario for translation. He sees virtual reality technology with its computer-generated contexts and settings as a powerful delivery system for translating biblical texts into new media formats. The implications of a virtual reality approach to translation are far-reaching, bearing on such questions as the authority and canon of the Bible as well as the nature of religious faith and communities.

For her paper "Stories as Dynamic Adaptive Environments" Glorianna Davenport drew on the work of Vannevar Bush, an early champion of computing and hypertext. Davenport illustrates how recent experimental work at MIT continues to build on Bush's insights. For the future, Davenport predicts the emergence of more programs with predictable feedback loops and immersive participatory environments. Such loops are already available in prototypes of interactive video.

New literacy, computer-mediated culture, and the emerging media ecology are the focus of Phil Mullins's reflections "Media Ecology and the New Literacy: Notes on an Electronic Hermeneutic." Some important features of this new literacy and ecology are hypertext, random and instant access to information, a blending of traditional notions of writer and reader, and a reassessment of concepts such as text, meaning, and canon. This is the environment and ecology in which translators of the 21st century will find their home.

Conclusion: Contemporary Currents

By way of conclusion, we may note that a symposium volume on translating the Bible into new media formats catches up many currents flowing through contemporary theological and biblical studies. We have mentioned two at the outset of this introduction: the new literacy and our growing awareness of how communications, culture, and theology interconnect one with another. Here we may note two more: the fluid, dynamic state of modern translation theory and practice, and the "digitalization" of theology.

Translation is communication across cultures, and as such it evolves along with the cultures in which it is located and across which it is practiced. Today, this evolution is occurring simultaneously on several fronts. In part, this is due to advances in communications and computer technology that are daily shrinking our global village; in part it is due to languages and cultures that were once considered unworthy of serious translation efforts, but now are taken as serious objects of translation and translation studies.

On one front, we see the very definition and concept of translation expanding beyond traditional notions of "literary translation" with its classical canon of standard works such as Homer and the Bible. Today, *Kleinliteratur*—for example, occasional pieces such as travel guides, brochures, and advertisements—has its place in the practice and study of translation. Additionally, such activities as film dubbing and subtitling, along with simultaneous interpretation have broadened the concept and definition of translational activity. Such a redefinition challenges Bible translators and theologians to face old questions in light of new cultural realities. For example, how do we retain the sacredness and authority of the Bible and remain faithful to the biblical message while transporting the Bible and its message into new media, using new technologies, and submitting them to new and more diverse translational activities?

On a second front, we note that translation has developed descriptive and pedagogical approaches that complement the traditional and more familiar normative approach with its focus on producing actual translations using theories and norms such as formal and functional equivalence. We see the pedagogical side of translation in the growing number of programs and institutes devoted to training translators, dubbers, subtitlers, and interpreters. The descriptive side of translation has been developed by theorists, researchers, and practitioners who have in common

> a view of literature as a complex and dynamic system; a conviction that there should be a continual interplay between theoretical models and practical case studies; an approach to literary translation which is descriptive, target oriented, functional and systemic; and an interest in the norms and constraints that govern the production and reception of translations, in the relation between translation and other types of text processing, and in the place and role of translations both within a given

literature and in the interaction between literatures. (Hermans, 1985, pp. 10-11)

For Bible translators and theologians a descriptive approach means that research into existing translations is not a luxury, but a necessity. Among other things, such research reveals the cultural, theological, and media-specific rules and norms that have made established translations and translation processes a success (or a failure), thus leading to a better understanding of how to translate and inculturate the message of the Holy Scriptures.

On a third front, we see that translation has become increasingly interdisciplinary. Of all the fields that promise to enrich translation let us cite one that, as we have noted above, has already proved helpful in developing theoretical and practical approaches: semiotics or the study of signs and the way signs create meaning. Print translators have long recognized the importance of semiotics:

> A sociosemiotic approach to meaning seems particularly useful in Bible translating in view of the following: (1) semiotics is the most all-embracing system for the analysis of signs, (2) a sociosemiotic approach to the meaning of verbal signs always involves the total communication of an event within the social context; in other words, a text cannot be isolated from its context....A sociosemiotic view of signs involves the interpretation of signs in terms of the structure of which the signs themselves are a part. (de Waard & Nida, 1986, p. 73)

Among the most promising tools in a semiotic approach to meaning and signification are those originally developed by Charles Sanders Peirce (1955) who, along with Ferdinand de Saussure, is credited with founding modern semiotics. One of these tools is a principle stating that we always interpret and translate signs (including words) in terms of other signs, sometimes mixing and matching classes of signs, as when we raise our hand in greeting and someone takes that gesture to mean "hello." A second tool is provided by the observation that signs always depend on established codes, rules, habits, and patterns of behavior for their signification. Thus, when someone interprets a hand gesture as a sign signifying "hello," they rely on a convention or rule determining that such a gesture is a friendly greeting and not a threat. Greek and English grammar also function as codes whose rules allow words to take on meaning suitable to their context.

The division of signs (including words) into the categories of icon, index, and symbol provides a third tool. The justification for such a division lies in the differing relationships that signs have to their referents. Icons (for example, a photograph as a sign of a person) physically resemble their referents, while indexes (for example, smoke as a sign of fire) have a cause-effect relationship with their referents. Symbols (for instance, the algebraic notation of π) have only arbitrary and culture-specific relationships with their referents.

Semiotics not only helps translators uncover the linguistic, imagistic, and sonic meaning of a source text (to name just three of the possible levels of information embedded in texts). It also offers them clues for transferring such information to a target text, and for determining what range of linguistic, sonic, or imagistic signs might offer faithful functional equivalents. For example, semiotics makes it possible to assign words, whole discourse units, and even the codes and rules that organize such words and units, to the categories of icon, symbol, or index. If we treat a word or a discourse unit as an iconic sign, then we would look for iconic functional equivalence. We would look for symbolic functional equivalence if we took another word or unit to be a symbol. In short, a semiotic approach to new media translation creates an additional way to understand functional equivalence.

We have already noted at the beginning of this introduction how culture, communications, and Christian theology condition one another. Christian reflection on this conditioning is at least as old as the apostle Paul. His Corinthian correspondence, for instance, testifies passionately, if somewhat cryptically, to a first-century perception of the interplay between the culture of letter writing and the message of theology (1 Corinthians 2.1-5; 5.9-11; 7.1-8.13; 12.1-31; 2 Corinthians 1.13-14; 2.1-11; 7.8-13). Today, Christians increasingly take for granted this state of affairs that Paul intuited and for which Marshall McLuhan's "the medium is the message" and Walter Ong's "secondary orality" have become verbal icons. Our efforts now go to tracking this relationship and working out its implications for the study of culture, communications, and theology.

One clear implication is that modern theological and biblical studies will become increasingly "digital" (Negroponte, 1994) as they compete for our attention in the 21st century. They can no more insulate themselves from the coming (and already present!) millennial shift in media and communications than could first-century preaching of the Good News insulate itself against the shift away from oral proclamation to letter and Gospel writing. This does not mean that we have only theological and biblical eye candy and sound bites to look forward to. But theologians and Bible experts must face squarely the prospect of going increasingly "online" if they are to remain relevant. For the theological process the millennial shift will change the way we exercise the analogical imagination; for the biblical process the shift will affect the dominance of the historical-critical method. For both it means rethinking and revising traditional roles as gatekeepers of protected intellectual properties.

Ong has summarized this evolution within contemporary theology as a "shift away from a basic orality in theology, an orality with profound historical roots hitherto never bared, to a multimedia theology in which the almost total communication ambitioned in electronic technologized culture interacts vigorously with the theological heritage" (1992, p. 162). How is this multimedia theology being done? Paul Soukup has identified six prominent communications models that will provide its structure: linguistic, aesthetic, cultural, dialogic, broadcast/mechanical, and theological (Soukup, 1983, pp. 31-73). Where is multimedia theology being done? Many places, but perhaps most strikingly on the World Wide Web in the home pages of local and global churches.

Visit, for example, the Lutheran Church of the Redeemer in Atlanta, GA at http://www.redeemer.org; or the Central Assembly of God, Columbia, SC with its audio devotionals, daily Bible readings, and online counseling at http://www.scsn.net/users/central/. Or stop by and spend time at a Benedictine community in the New Mexico desert at Christdesert (http://www.christdesert.org/pax.html). You can even drop in on the Vatican at http://www.vatican.va/ whose official documents concede the change that is approaching:

> Within modern society the communications media play a major role in information, cultural promotion, and formation. This role is increasing, as a result of technical progress, the extent and diversity of the news transmitted, and the influence exercised on public opinion. (*Catechism*, 1995, p. 658, par. 2493)

In the spirit of collaboration inherent in new media productions and as explored in the discussions of the Symposium itself, the ABS has been delighted to combine skills and forces with the talented editorial staff at Sheed & Ward to prepare this volume. To accommodate the divergent audiences that each publisher is accustomed to serving, two separate editions of this volume have been prepared. The ABS edition, appearing in the Society's general catalogue, will go out to a broad denominational readership. For these readers the volume represents an in-depth look at the emerging field of multimedia Bible translation theory as well as a study in the relevance of the Bible in and for the 21st century, thus continuing a discussion already opened at the ABS's 175th anniversary symposium in Philadelphia in 1991 and summarized in the publication, *The Bible in the Twenty-First Century* (Kee, 1993).

The Sheed & Ward edition, aiming for an academic readership, treats the symposium as a case study in the larger field of communications and theology. It appears in the series, "Communication, Culture, and Theology," whose purpose is to publish historical and thematic studies that bring together questions of communications and theology in order to show how these two fields help define religious self-understanding, Christian attitudes toward communication, pastoral uses of communication, and ethics and advocacy issues (Soukup, 1983, p. 13).

Acknowledgements

Any symposium can only be successful when all invited participants have mastered their areas of specialization, researched and prepared their presentations, scrutinized the work of their colleagues, and arrive ready to engage in lively discussion. Such were the experts who gathered for the ABS Symposium "From One Medium to Another." The American Bible Society gratefully acknowledges their commitment, enthusiasm, and thoroughness. A brief biography of each of the participants can be found at the end their chapters.

In addition, as convener of the symposium and co-editor of the volume (along with Paul Soukup, S.J.) I would like to acknowledge the vision and support of the American Bible Society's Board and officers, especially as expressed by Eugene B. Habecker, President of the ABS, and Maria I. Martinez, Vice-President for Scripture Publications.

Various publishers and copyright holders have graciously allowed us to reprint materials. I acknowledge them and offer thanks:

The University of Chicago Press for excerpts from Lanham, R.A. (1993). *The electronic word: Democracy, technology, and the arts.* Chicago: University of Chicago Press.

Lawrence Erlbaum Associates, Inc., for excerpts from Bolter, J.D. (1991). *Writing space: The computer, hypertext, and the history of writing.* Hillsdale, NJ: Lawrence Erlbaum, Associates, Inc.

The University of Pittsburgh Press for excerpts from *Word perfect: Literacy in the computer age,* by Myron C. Tuman, © 1992. Reprinted by permission of the University of Pittsburgh Press.

Educational Technology Publications, Inc., for excerpts from Rowe, G. (1994). "Education in the Emerging Media Democracy." *Educational Technology, 34*(7), pp. 55-58.

Taylor & Francis, Inc., for excerpts from Rowe, G. (1992). "Multimedia Technology as a Catalyst for a New Form of Literacy." *The Information Society, 8*(2), pp. 83-90. Taylor & Francis, 1992, used with permission.

The Assemblies of God Archives for the photo of Aimee Semple McPherson.

The Balanchine Trust for the photo of a scene from *The Prodigal Son.*

Amalia Mesa-Bains for the photo of the Dolores Del Rio Shrine.

Nicholas Whitman for the photos of Renée Stout's and Jenni Lukač's works.

Turner Entertainment Co. for the still from *King of Kings.*

Twentieth Century Fox Film Corporation for film footage from *The Story of Ruth.*

The MIT Media Lab for the images from *Water* and *Dogmatic.*

Gregor Goethals, Scala/Art Resource, NY, and the American Bible Society for the image of Christ, the Pantocrator.

Gregor Goethals for the image of the mall.

Gregor Goethals and the American Bible Society for the image of the nautilus.

The American Bible Society for the images from the CD-ROMs, *The Visit* and A *Father and Two Sons*.

It takes many minds, hearts, and hands to create an environment where creative thinking can flourish. Essential to that process were ABS staff members David G. Burke, Director of Translations, and Fern Lee Hagedorn, Assistant Director for Translations, along with ABS special consultant Paul A. Soukup, S.J. They in turn join me in thanking the large company of colleagues who gave generously to the planning and execution of the Symposium and the Symposium volume, in particular Estér B. Vargas-Machuca, Barbara Bernstengel, Charles Houser, Rachel Corfield, Nancy White, Pamela Meyer, Deborah G. Atkinson, Christina Murphy, and Juliana C. Moseley at ABS; Robert Heyer and Sarah Smiley at Sheed & Ward; and Elwood Mills, Chimene Pollard, and Connie Ricc at Santa Clara University.

Robert Hodgson

Overture

Publishing Words and Images: Schools and Learning in the Millennial Shift

Gary R. Rowe

Wishful thinking informs much contemporary analysis of media—analysis that often refers to television as a "vast wasteland." Such thinking ignores technological advances, television's societal role, its rationally-driven audience preferences and, most importantly, the profound and accelerating information shift that is underway. Reflection on the emerging information world needs instead to take clues from its first explorers, our children, who are opening the first settlements in the next millennium. The speed and acceleration of this information shift profoundly affect the Bible, biblical scholarship, and biblical translation in this age of rapid change.

The Education Problem

A group of middle school students in Georgia willingly returned to their classroom over the summer months to learn geography in an untried—and unapproved—new way. Using software designed for emergency management professionals, not for children, they eagerly explored exacting simulations of widespread flooding in the river systems, tributaries, and flood plains of south Georgia. They also managed crowd flow, parking gridlock, and emergency evacuation plans for a Super Bowl Game. When asked about their excitement for learning in this new way, they exclaimed that their textbooks are like "baby food" and that the computer simulation is "real life"!

Sections of this essay first appeared in G. Rowe. (1994). "Education in the Emerging Media Democracy." *Educational Technology, 34*(7), pp. 55-58 and G. Rowe. (1992). "Multimedia Technology as a Catalyst for a New Form of Literacy." *The Information Society, 8*(2), pp. 83-90. They are reprinted with permission of the author and editors.

21

At least four things are at work in this real life scenario. Children willingly appropriate the tools of the adult world without inhibitions. These same children widen the dynamics of formal learning by expanding the time and energy they are willing to devote to it. They are also happily unaware of the levels of complexity and thought required for their work. Such concerns are subordinated to the elements of fun and shared excitement possible with the manipulation of multimedia tools. Most noteworthy, however, is their disdain, when interviewed, for the confinement and homogenization of the information typical to ordinary classrooms.

None of these students is especially "gifted" in academic study. Unlike many high achieving students who are quite happy with traditional schools because they have solved the formulas for success in them, these students define a new mainstream that has radically shifted away from what schools used to offer. They form a new majority culture. Why don't adults understand what can happen in our schools? In a tortured quest to "reform" education, adult concerns are wrong-headed, obsolete, outmoded, and irrelevant. Adults want to improve the old model, not discover a new one. Adults share a slowly vanishing minority culture, the culture of the book.

Printed books are slow. It takes a lot of time to read a book or to find information in libraries of books. Printed books are narrow. The "bandwidth" of the printed page contains no sound, no motion, and no easy way to connect to other books. Printed books are solo performances. They project the statements of an individual or small collaborative group and create a mental feedback loop confined in most cases to the reader's mind alone.

In a culture of television, computers, and telecommunications traveling at the speed of light, the industry that serves schools with textbooks has no future. As each day goes by, more and more teachers and schools will organize themselves around the idea that they are using a defective product. Children already have.

A new vision of learning has emerged in schools willing to use more non-print media and the written word housed in new media devices. To begin to understand the future, we must think about words and stories no longer captured on a page, no longer bound in books, but reanimated with sound and vision. We must think about how rich and dense a book can be if it is delivered over a wire or is stored magnetically or optically until the user needs the information.

Our traditional schools, built for the industrial age, are bound to printed books. They reward most those who can decode and learn in this confinement. Schools will change only when the curriculum no longer shows up on the loading dock but comes over wires and through the air, when it can be updated every day and can be customized by the user.

This book is about multimedia in the context of biblical translation and the work of the American Bible Society. But it is not about multimedia alone. It is about a new worldview. Perhaps our children more ably capture the worldview because they willingly live in a world saturated by multiple media. In their behaviors, in their wants and needs, they challenge the comfortable enclosures of conventional thinking. In order to look forward, this chapter will look back and look around. What is the world like now? What possibilities for learning show up on the horizon? This chapter reviews information resources, television, and learning problems before presenting an outline of what ought to be.

The Information Economy

Not every household can have gold, land, power, or money in abundance. But the world of the next century will feature a new economy in which all can have untold and unprecedented wealth defined in a new way.

If there is an economic "story" to human life and commerce, it is a story about struggle and pleasure in a world in which scarcity defines the significant measures of wealth. Economics based on agriculture, on land, on military power, on money, on industry are all limited by the relativity of abundance and scarcity. The economic household, whether defined by the microcosm of the individual or the macrocosm of the nation-state, whether defined by the tribe, the neighborhood, the city, or the international alliance, exists in a finite, limited circumstance. But the *homo oeconomicus* of the postmodern world will exist and act in a sphere of choices and decisions radically different from the precedents defined by classical notions of economic behavior and its aggregation of individual choices.

What happens when wealth can be seemingly limitless? The wealth of the emerging multimedia culture is a wealth based not on guns or gold, not on land or industry; it is a wealth based on information and the basis of its power is the common currency of "dirt." What, after all, are the mineral values contained in a silicon chip? Human design and engineering inscribe its value, not the intrinsic costs of its manufacture. Such costs string out along a continuum of mass production that continues to exponentially raise the power and speed of computation and storage and exponentially lower the costs of doing so.

Common expectations about the silicon-based economy today center on the computer and its costs. This view is too narrow. People don't accept high technologies; they adopt useful appliances. The closer a computer gets to a common gadget in cost and ease-of-use, the more common it becomes. A solar-powered television set in the outback tuned to CNN is a source of information, not a technology. A battery-powered Walkman, a digital satellite dish, a cellular telephone, and a microwave oven all share the common currency of household appliances, each earmarked by a once sophisticated and expensive technological innovation now made unbelievably inexpensive compared to its first real-world prototypes.

This staggering change is, as yet, ill-defined and little understood by economists or politicians. It has incalculable implications for things we now take for granted: national sovereignty, military power, political popularity, mass culture, educational attainment, and self-esteem, to name a few. In his prologue to *The Gutenberg Galaxy,* Marshall McLuhan anticipates the dislocation represented by this change in our world by taking the measure of dislocation in the 16th century:

> We are today as far into the electric age as the Elizabethans had advanced into the typographical and mechanical age. And we are experiencing the same confusions and indecisions which they had felt when living simultaneously in two contrasted forms of society and experience. Whereas the Elizabethans were poised between medieval corporate experience and modern individualism, we reverse their pattern by confronting an electric technology which would seem to render individualism obsolete and corporate interdependence mandatory. (1962, p. 1)

Imagine *homo sapiens* in the remotest part of the planet carrying a device that is cheaper and smaller than a book, runs on solar cells, and contains vast libraries. When it is built, if it contains simple interconnecting telecommunications too, then we have the beginning of the global tribe, a corporate community unbounded by the limitations of agrarian, industrial, and nation-centered economies.

Beyond Minow's World

In 1961, the newly appointed chairman of the Federal Communications Commission, Newton Minow, looked out over a sea of perplexed faces at the National Association of Broadcasters' Convention and invited industry executives to sit down in front of their own broadcast signals for a day to behold what they would inevitably see. "I assure you that you will observe a vast wasteland," said the chairman (Barnouw, 1970, p. 197).

Minow's critique has been a dismissive benediction about television in the minds of cultural leaders ever since. But a critical perspective from nearly 35 years ago is insufficient to account for the radical transformations of television, and by means of television, of us, in the intervening years.

Television is the principal medium that redefines human experience in unprecedented ways. Whether we take notice or not, it prepares us for life in the new millennium. Its glowing presence prepares us for a new form of literacy just as certainly as it has changed our perceptions about the nature of the world we inhabit, for better and for worse.

We must put aside our cursory notions about television and develop a mature understanding of what it is, what it does to us, what we can do with it, and what it means. Television has given us the beginnings of a borderless world. It is not merely the dissolution of geopolitical borders that will make passports seem less meaningful to restive travelers. Already, the daily judgments of money markets on nations and their governments supersede traditional definitions of sovereignty, commercial activities, military strategies, and political debates with blinding speed.

It is important to start with the recognition that people do not perceive television as a "technology." It has been a home appliance for nearly half a century. Contemporary developers of multimedia take little note of this reality to their own peril. Eager to exploit the fashion of computers as high technology and to celebrate interactive communications on the high altar of elite discourse, they miss the dramatic paradox in the rhetorical question of television's beginnings: "Who sold more TV sets in the 1950s, RCA or Milton Berle?"

There may have been a brief moment when television emerged as an icon of high tech. Filmmaker Barry Levinson parodies such a moment in his film *Avalon* (1990) when he portrays the extended family of his characters gathered nearly mute in front of the test pattern displayed on the new television set. But ever since prime time filled up with its pastiche of diversions, television has been less an objective thing and more of an amorphous culture subtly shaping everyone in the path of its electromagnetic reach.

Minow could blame a wasteland on network executives in 1961 but not today. Two things have changed television in the past 15 years: the expansion of programming options and the possibility of personal control. Remote programmers no longer call the shots. Consider that the VCR is now the logical extension of the television set just as the ubiquitous cable channels and the video store extend the range of answers to the question, "What's on TV?" If it's a wasteland, the finger of blame points not to the programmer, but to the viewer.

Television doesn't belong to broadcasters anymore; it belongs to everyone. The content of television is no longer limited to a broadcast schedule put together by individuals or committees at headquarters. Those people aren't in charge of television anymore. The viewer is. The modern tools of the "program executive" are the remote control and the VCR.

Television is changing the world—has *already* changed the world—in radical ways. No armies marched to tear down the Berlin Wall. It was vaporized by television signals, information no dictatorship could hold back. International diplomacy was changed irrevocably by the war in the Persian Gulf. Every world leader was tuned into the same information at the same time. Feedback loops created by cellular telephones and fax machines supported the 1989 student revolt in Tiananmen Square.

Consider the things television is and does that require us to totally redefine it. Television maps its own culture. Television does not mirror the traditional or the given. It is not subject to the same constraints as the culture in which it originates, and its impact is not fully or finally controlled by cultural elites, the authority of sovereign states, or their agents. The behavior of the students in Tiananmen Square was authorized by the culture of television, not by Chinese custom or the state.

The world of television has porous boundaries. The culture that television maps respects no political boundaries. It is possible to limit and regulate broadcast signals but it is not possible to limit and regulate television, that is, what is on television, what arises from the conventions of television, and the effects of what your neighbors may be saying about you on their televisions. The students in Tiananmen Square built an analog of the Statue of Liberty, not because they were ready to become Americans but because the world's cameras were there and events were best expressed in the form of symbols rather than argument.

Television works in collaboration with other media. Television no longer exists in isolation from other media, and the information carried on television has to be measured by the effects of many media. Chinese students in America were filing detailed reports of American news coverage of the demonstration in Tiananmen Square back to the students in that square only moments after the reports appeared on American television.

No area of the world can expect immunity from the presence of television. The technology of television has made it ubiquitous because new technologies have made it so portable. The CNN transmission from Tiananmen Square, and from Baghdad, occurred on a complete earth station and uplink/downlink that packs into only 22 suitcases and can go anywhere on an airplane as excess baggage. Consider the camcorder—cheap, portable, and easy to use. During the invasion of Panama, with military censorship restricting access to the story, CNN gathered footage from citizens who were covering the invasion of their own country using camcorders.

Never before in human history has there been such a powerful tool as television to overcome the barriers of time and distance in communication from one point to many points. Never have so many individuals had the opportunity to make a personal appliance out of such powerful technology. And this personalization will accelerate. The cost of a color camera that will produce technically perfect images is now four percent of the cost of its equivalent 20 years ago.

The Millennial Shift

The growth of electronic communications has bred talk of a powerful "media shift" in contemporary society. There may be risk of inflation, but it is probably not making too much of what is occurring in our world to nominate a new phrase for the media shift. I prefer to call it a "Millennial Shift" in the sense that what is transforming our world is so monumental in its current inscrutability, its power for epochal change, and its fundamental redefinition of human life, that it will make the next millennium unrecognizable from the view of the former.

The Millennial Shift eludes a concise definition. To give it attributes is to leave its description incomplete. To give it dimension is to see it with the limited fuzziness of a moment in time. By its nature, it transcends a mere moment. To give it structure is to invent a grammar for a language no one has quite heard or spoken. Whatever it is, it deserves to have this descriptive phrase attached to it, if only to provoke vigorous debate about the radical transformation of our worldview and, if not ours, the worldview of those practitioners of the culture of television known as children.

The segments which follow try to give the Millennial Shift tentative attributes, dimension, and structure by using the example of what might happen in the learning environments of schools when the options for publishing, storing, and using information exist in a multimedia world, not a book-bound world. This new learning world will displace our present ideas of authority, it will involve more learning styles, and it will re-invent the textbook.

The Displacement of Authority

A friend's granddaughter ended her first day of kindergarten with the pronouncement, "I'm never going back there. Do you know, they don't even have a single computer? How do they expect me to learn anything?" Observe the abilities of many children to manipulate media devices—computers, VCRs, game machines, telephones—and the manipulation is not the point. The expectation is. These facile users live with a set of expectations about controlling information, controlling the content of the screen with a personal ability to exercise power. There may be slight danger to children from the discoveries possible on the Internet, for example. But a far more subversive phenomenon is represented by the mere fact of the Internet and a child's using it. Any child comfortable in this ocean of information is living testimony to habits of learning outside the discipline of parental or pedagogical authority.

The formation of educated minds prior to the 20th century occurred in an environment radically different from our own. Our forebears, armed with the proper tools of classical languages, must have believed that a lifetime of devotion to the great books and a knowledge of rhetoric and basic science were the necessary ingredients to mastering the scope of human knowledge. No such optimism can possibly support us today. We live in a much less friendly neighborhood of facts and ideas. The boundaries of knowledge have long since expanded beyond our individual horizons. Granted, there is a slippery gulf between what is defined as "knowledge" and the mere "data" that comprise "information." Without exception we cannot thrive as a learning self without interdependence on the collective knowledge of a wider circle of "knowers" and learners. Even the products of the individually-inspired intelligence in art or science are the realizations born from the collisions of a noisy, vibrant, and irritating social culture.

Remember, if possible, the mind of a child on the first day of school. The mindscape remembered by today's mature generation must certainly contain a greater certainty about school as a place to master a "quantity" of information leading to maturity in the adult word. In this view, the chronology of passing through the grades of school, if not achievement, would still confer credentials defining a useful space in the economic household.

If it is also possible, imagine the mindset of a contemporary child on the first day of school. Surely, this mind must at least dimly perceive a different scale of what it is possible to know and what is necessary to learn. Such a child cannot be aware of an information explosion because there is no benchmark of conscious experience to measure against. Nonetheless, children today are born into a media-saturated and information-saturated world. They are no more and no less than awash in this great sea of stimuli, and they live in its different sets of expectations. No adult knows what this is like and certainly can't, from any previous experience, remember anything like it.

The issue of "authority" is a fundamental problem to be addressed in discourse about new modes of learning. The parent, the practitioner, the professor, are displaced in the multimedia culture by the availability of ubiquitous alternatives. Options abound. The scale of knowledge shifts from knowing "all" to knowing "little" of the all there is to know.

But this displacement may be highly justified. The book culture has given us models of learning that are linear, hierarchical, closed, chronological, limited, and incomplete. Developmental psychologists like Howard Gardner (1983) argue the case for multiple "intelligences" that broaden not only our definitions of learning but of the resources required to support it.

We learn with what Gardner describes as linguistic intelligence and logical-mathematical intelligence. These two forms are neatly inscribed by Scholastic Aptitude Tests. But there are at least five other ways we learn that are ignored in traditional academic testing. Humans also learn by spatial intelligence, musical intelligence, bodily-kinesthetic intelligence, interpersonal intelligence, and intrapersonal intelligence, Gardner argues. This list begins to suggest that books can, by definition, play only a limited role in learning compared to the varieties of images, sounds, actions, simulations, and interactions that create a holistic environment in education.

A minority of students truly excel in our schools. A minority actually read books for information, fewer still for personal enjoyment. A minority go on to higher education. A minority continue to actively pursue learning opportunities for the rest of their lives. From the perspective of the Gutenberg world, the world inscribed by the culture of the book, this is not alarming at all. It's how we define human differences and how we affirm the arduous, non-pleasurable tasks of learning. Only the truly talented, hardworking, determined, and inspired individuals really make it.

It isn't saying much for learning bound in books to acknowledge that it leaves out the majority of people who are meant to learn in its domain.

If there is a radical idea to be discovered behind the encrustations of an academic world defined by books, it is the notion that *all* people can learn at a high level of energy, commitment, and enjoyment if we can provide the resources that connect, at least at one point, with the phenomenal varieties of how we learn. Everyone can go to college if college is ready to be something much grander and more magnificent than it has ever been before!

From Object to Experience

A planning and design group of media specialists, educators, and wildlife biologists at Zoo Atlanta is currently grappling with the same issues faced by the American Bible Society's multimedia translations project in its early stages: how to organize the rich possibilities of storage, access, and presentation afforded by a multimedia device to entertain and educate young people. As one of the nation's newly prestigious institutions in the forefront of species conservation and public education, Zoo Atlanta wants to use its work in the conservation of gorillas as a means to provoke thinking about the broader issues of habitats, population pressures, human and animal interactions, and the geographical and political barriers to successful species preservation in the wild.

A solution to the daunting task of appealing to the imaginations and interests of young people was solved in the first planning discussion with the wisdom that the design must avoid teaching "about" gorillas. The clever possibilities with multimedia are realized if the application is designed to let a child "be" a gorilla. In other words, let the user understand the issues from the inside, from the intimacy of the connections made between who we are as humans and what the animal is in our world. If all goes according to plan, the application will allow a child to identify with particular gorillas, learn to "speak gorilla" in the imitation of their sounds, to "be gorilla" in mimicking their movements, and to see the interplay among the individuals in a gorilla family including the rearing of newborns. All of the tools used by scientists in gorilla observation, both in the wild and in controlled environments, will be available to the user, allowing the child to not only be a gorilla, but to be a scientist who studies gorillas.

There is a new standard at work here in the very act of creating new learning resources. Rather than didactic or merely objective views of a subject, the learner is allowed to develop personal intimacy with the subject and a rich array of information that makes learning a matter of experience, both cognitive and emotive. True mastery of information requires resources that can overcome the minority culture of the book alone.

Traditional learning begins in a presentation prison. Inside the four walls of a classroom, unconnected with the wider world, based largely in silent reading with linear text, the learner remains detached from a multi-dimensional experience of a topic or an issue. The book is a very small "house" for containing the information that promotes learning. A new form of literacy is required.

New Expectations of Publishing

Innovative teachers have created for themselves new expectations about what it means to "publish" information. They have created a respected place for the value of television as a teaching tool, a publication of vital information. The world of the traditional school built on the core of printed, bound textbooks is no longer sufficient. While a great convenience to the traditional teacher, the textbook is a lame contrivance for today's media savvy learners.

Textbooks are creations of the analog world. They are linear, chronological, and finite. If we learn to perceive in the digital world—as our children are prepared to do—and throw off our captivity to analog thought, we will measure the value of information in new ways just as innovative teachers are already doing.

Consider what a textbook can't do. Its images don't move, it makes no sounds, it accepts no new information, it connects easily to nothing else. It confines the learner to written language and silent reading in solitude. It ignores the benefits of talking and listening, collaboration with other learners, experimentation and simulation, and the knowledge discovered through personal curiosity and exploration. Yet good teachers are desperate to make these things occur in classrooms more easily. Businesses want to hire workers who are trained to think, not just follow orders.

Why can't a "textbook" make sounds, display images, connect to a vast array of resources, and provide a seemingly limitless quantity of information, including whole libraries of text? The answer is, it can. A "textbook" can be built to do these things. Using a combination of videotape or optical storage media, broadband pathways like cable television, and simple home appliances, schools can begin to have comprehensive curriculum products fashioned from the resources of television, software producers, on-line services, and print publishers. The key challenge is creating the management tools for the information.

Consider the impact interactive multimedia can have on learning. Why would any learner want to memorize the formula for a chemical reaction without an opportunity to actually see the results? Why stop at merely reading *Macbeth* when the finest actors can portray its drama right in the classroom? Why let human liberty be a mute abstraction when the "book" could feature everything from freedom songs to the Federalist papers?

American schools already pay up to $2.5 billion a year for textbooks that few students want to read and that are often obsolete before they leave the bindery. Constructive dialogue with educators clearly reveals an interest in shifting resources away from textbooks if a better alternative is available.

Visionaries are eager to discover willing customers for multimedia, users of interactive services, and applications that take advantage of technologies and broadband spectrum capacity. Educators are desperate to find new ways to engage learners in an educational system that really works. Our children understand intuitively that learning occurs faster and more effectively when they can break through the limitations of the printed page alone and use the rich resources of sound and image, of unlimited libraries, of collaborators in the real world. There isn't so much a crisis in education as there is an imperative to begin to take real advantage of assets of the Millennial Shift.

Listening to Teachers

The design work of multimedia begins best with inference, not deduction. What are the critical needs of a learning challenge and what benefits apply from the integration of many resources easily used in collaboration one with the other? The critical question is not what a technology can do. The American Bible Society had it right from the beginning. Multimedia doesn't present the opportunity to be slick; it presents an opportunity to reach a new audience, an audience ready for information delivered in new modes.

So far, many traditional publishers are approaching the traditional classroom with multimedia assets configured in the ways that books work, not in the ways that media work. There is a seeming distrust, not of multimedia, but of the multiple senses that can come into play in learning. This is not unlike the inelastic distrust of the senses grounded in the radical extremes of Reformation theology, when postures taken over the meanings of words displaced spiritual sentiments and existential passions.

It takes a very self-confident human being to be open to the pleasures of entertainment in the pursuit of learning. The revulsion against pleasure in learning is the plague of the Gutenberg world. The humorless tasks of taking in information and regurgitating a synthesis of that information on a test make the task of the teacher easier but not necessarily that of the learner.

In the traditional academy, learning with the head alone is the provincial metronome of the book culture. A teacher or professor here and there might actually expect visceral reactions of fear and pity in the reading of *Hamlet*, of *Silas Marner*, of Prufrock, of Yosarian, or of Portnoy. Comments from the spleen are not, however, the common currency of the test scores that prove mastery in the classroom.

The success of new enterprises to build learning resources for the multimedia culture is predicated, in the short term, on what professional educators are willing to accept. These are the gatekeepers of what is permissible in the classroom. Will acceptance extend to sources of information presented in an entertaining and engaging way? Will pleasure become an ingredient in the speed and the success of learning? What do teachers say they want? What can be discerned about the meaning of what they are saying that reveals what they really want? What barriers, both semantic and bureaucratic, must they hurdle to attain what they want? What are the differences between listening to the future and listening to the past? Some teachers are creating the opportunities for new enterprises to succeed. Some are merely marking time and will never join the ranks of the innovators. To what degree might there be a critical number of innovators who may, in turn, lead others in sufficient numbers to make a true market?

The best feedback is provoked by innovation. Substantial business risks and investments necessary to launch new products and services for school classrooms require a stamina uncommon to less enterprising corporations, but the yield may well prove to be pervasive and profitable. New forms of publishing require the risk of investment and production to coax meaning out of the school market. Enterprises that subordinate their own creativity to safe bets alone will not invent the breakthrough opportunities that build success.

The American Bible Society's multimedia translation initiative is framed by this bold leadership. Theorizing about a multimedia translation proves a useful intellectual exercise but it takes on meaning only when such a translation is actually produced for an audience to experience.

Public education in America may be the one sector of society poised for the most radical innovations in the emerging multimedia culture because it rests currently on such extremes of abject failure and public discontent. There is no stronger animating force for change than nearly universal agreement that the old ways just aren't working anymore!

Concepts for a Textbook of the Future

A "Textbook of the Future" is a useful metaphor to describe a product and service built by an act of multimedia publishing. It is a multimedia-based learning system built on the power of images and sound to motivate learning in today's generation of students. It is integrated with text, graphics, online services, and multimedia libraries. It features internal, user-friendly navigation, perhaps software-based, that can be customized to the needs of the learner by individual teachers, built on commonly accepted learning standards, even indexed to national curriculum standards. It features dynamic assessment tools and diagnostics to track student progress toward skill competence and subject mastery. Unlike a textbook-based learning system that excludes the learner from careful tracking of progress, assessment tools in this system *include* the learner.

A prototype of such a "textbook" should set out to prove four principles: using a combination of many media saves time for the learner and the teacher; models of classroom practice are changed and personalized; learning is accelerated across all styles of learning; and using information in this way actually lowers the real costs of instruction.

Building such a prototype takes into account the integral nature of the media shift that denotes the Millennial Shift, making the case, in fact, for the degree of radical change that merits the nomenclature. It is not about the technologies per se but the fundamentals behind the devices that characterize their nature. These include the miniaturization of media machines with the attendant attributes of portability, interchangeability, low cost, and easy replacement; the falling costs of information storage and retrieval including the nearly geometric rates of change in the capacity versus cost ratios, in other words, the high tech capabilities of low cost appliances; and access to low cost networks that are virtually "citizens band" electronic pathways reaching global availability.

A growing constituency of youthful enthusiasts are masters of making high technology disappear behind common, everyday use. The world of school is rapidly proving to be a fertile ground for the first systemic proof that multimedia is a viable new market forming around its potential customers and those, like their most talented teachers, who are eager to serve them. The whole paradigm is shifting—away from a regimented school built for the industrial age and toward an environment of information options that can take advantage of multimedia and make instruction more effective and learning more fun.

While this chapter doesn't presume to present a blueprint for a prototype, it is worth noting that a "Textbook of the Future" may have many features never found in a printed, bound textbook. These include playback capability like a VCR for both images and text; user capability to originate "telecasts" of images and text and send them to others; voice and data communications capabilities, both inbound and outbound; quick retrieval of any digital information and the capability to access or design elaborate experiments or simulations of phenomena in the real world and provide utilities to construct new ones; testing and competency measurements built in so that learning assessment can be managed by both the teacher and the learner by faster and more comprehensive means; writing and publishing utilities, including the ability to publish from point to multipoint simultaneously; telecommunications software that can work with images, graphics, *and* text; records storage for keeping a personal library of knowledge and notations; and, perhaps most important, a utility to identify, capture, and file daily information updates.

All of these functions should be housed in a device that is truly interlinked to not only teachers, but other learners, even if they are all in the same room. It is a community of learners that is at the heart of the design.

These radical departures from the norm, when tested in sketchy fashion with teachers, never fail to evoke the response, "When can I have it?"

Many students have a more dynamic reaction: "Why don't I have it already?"

Respectful Beginnings

The ideal purpose of this book should be measured by the lasting effects of this dialogue of essays, presentations, and discussions. If we can yield anything of value, the very first should be a continuing dialogue arising from a new community of thinkers, a community willingly and eagerly addressing the new, the unknown, and the dimly perceived, willing to take every risk of the imagination to win new understanding and perspectives in service to humans who are groping for new ways to communicate with each other.

We must approach the continuing work of the Symposium from which this book comes with a respectful acknowledgment of the vast distance required for our travel from a world that has been to a world that is yet to be. For it is more than a mere human conceit that the turning of the second millennium into the third marks a challenging and nearly unfathomable transition we can only dimly comprehend.

It is not that we are ignorant of what is happening in our world. It is not that we are without history and, with our history, able to exercise its precedents to measure what might come. The change we describe is really that epochal as to require a new vocabulary.

Let our words include respectful silences. Let's pause to give acknowledgment that we are only beginning the work that many others will have to join to give it full form and scope.

Johannes Gutenberg didn't change the world. His technology of printing with moveable type changed the options people had to receive information in a new way and *those* changed the world. Our children are making a similar revolution out of media. Watch children watch TV. They see television as a very personal appliance, not a technology. They possess the unstated expectation that they are in control of its content and they interact accordingly. To them, television is not just a form of theater in which a viewer is a mere spectator.

In learning environments of the 21st century, we will take for granted the truth in the cliché, "a picture is worth a thousand words." But we will realize an even greater truth. The mastery of information, the words and images, will belong to the learners themselves. The enterprises that serve their information needs with respect for this will prosper.

The key to the information society emerging out of the history of the industrial society is about this personal power. A new *animus populi* leads this shift and it is in our best business interest to follow the leadership of the innovative teachers and students we discover in our schools. Information technology is transforming the nation-state, rearranging the relevance of international boundaries, and democratizing human commerce in new communities of interests. It will change our schools irrevocably. It will, and it is, changing each of us.

Gary R. Rowe is President of Rowe, Inc., an educational multimedia publishing and production house. He serves as media consultant to the American Bible Society's multimedia translations project and advises Cable in the Classroom on educational technology issues. Formerly, Rowe served as Senior Vice President of Turner Educational Services, Inc. (TESI), a division of Turner Broadcasting System, where he led the development of CNN NEWSROOM, a multimedia daily newsprogram designed for schools and Turner MultiMedia, the first Peabody Award-winning educational product line.

From One Medium to Another

———————— ⬤ ————————

Part I

Theoretical Approaches:

Assessing the Challenge

Theoretical Approaches: Assessing the Challenge

How is it possible to translate from one medium to another? Most reflection on translation considers moving across linguistic lines rather than across modes of expression. Within biblical studies, the work of Eugene A. Nida (1952, 1964, 1969) marks a certain theoretical sophistication with its emphasis on functional equivalence. Little comparable effort—with the possible exception of Marshall McLuhan's "probes" (1962)—has addressed the equivalence of media. Yet the fact remains that humans have continually expressed similar themes, crossing from one medium to another: epics take form in Greek drama; sculptors and painters fashion pictorial representations of stories; filmmakers retell novels; television producers even recreate the news in docudrama.

This section begins this volume's exploration of cross-media translation with theoretical contexts and explanations. Since our concern is biblical translation, we begin with Moisés Silva's review of New Testament hermeneutics: What current trends govern how people interpret the New Testament? What can contemporary practice contribute to the effort of the American Bible Society to develop guidelines for translating the Gospels into non-print media?

The section then examines a relatively new scholarly area, one not well known outside of its European home—translation theory as it applies to non-traditional materials like advertising, simultaneous translation, and travel guides. José Lambert's essay describes the current state of the question and suggests some directions. Following on this, Patrick Cattrysse presents an overview of polysystems theory, another attempt to apply translation theory to complex "texts" like film, which consist of multiple elements of meaning (language, music, nonverbal behavior, and editing). His descriptive work lays the groundwork for a continuing theoretical project.

Paul Soukup takes a different direction. Drawing on communication research into the audience, he calls attention to the ways that people interact with the media to construct meaning. How much "meaning" resides in a complex "text" and how much comes from the situation of the audience members? Translators should make themselves aware of these interactions, which can influence whether people will accept a given translation across media.

This first section concludes with Fred Lawrence's extended examination of one of this century's most powerful theories of interpretation, that of Hans-Georg Gadamer. Gadamer argues that the hermeneutic process must involve game play, or interaction. His theory suggests that the medium of communication does matter, but that it forms just one part of a complex web of exchange in which meaning is constituted.

This inaugural section has as its purpose the setting of a context in which to consider how translating from one medium to another works. We know people do it, but we have relatively little conscious reflection on the process.

1

Recent Developments in New Testament Hermeneutics

Moisés Silva

The last quarter of the 20th century has seen dramatic changes in New Testament interpretation. To appreciate these, we need to understand early 20th-century biblical scholarship with its optimism, historical criticism, distrust of the allegorical method, and accent on ascertaining original meanings. This approach, however, downplayed issues of relevance and theology. Key figures in the development of 20th century hermeneutics include theologians such as Karl Barth and Rudolf Bultmann, literary critics and philosophers such as Hans-Georg Gadamer and Paul Ricoeur, and scientists such as Thomas Kuhn. These figures challenged the objectivity of interpretation, leading Bible interpreters to rethink questions considered settled.

The attempt to summarize contemporary currents in the interpretation of the New Testament is fraught with many difficulties, not the least of which is defining what should come under its purview. For example, should we include the results of exegetical investigation? If we were to do so, one issue that would come immediately to mind is the renewed assessment of first-century Judaism.

The work that is usually regarded as having caused this shift is by E. P. Sanders (1977). Disturbed by what he perceived to be a prejudicial treatment of Jewish sources on the part of Christian scholars, Sanders sought to show that those sources placed great emphasis on divine grace and thus could not accurately be described as "legalistic." In some respects, Sanders brought out very little that was new, but his massive research and vigorous protests had a great impact on New Testament scholarship. For one thing, students of the Gospels have had to reconsider their understanding of the Pharisees and, by implication, of Jesus' message.

Even more significant is the "new look" on the apostle Paul. After all, if Judaism were not burdened by a works' righteousness religion, then Paul must have been attacking something else, and that in turn would mean that the Reformers were quite misguided to use the Pauline writings to develop their doctrine of justification by faith and not by works. Some publications have taken issue with this new approach and shown that the conclusions derived from it are quite premature (for example, Westerholm, 1988; Thielman, 1994), but it is also clear that our understanding of the New Testament message requires greater nuancing than we have been used to in the past.

The reassessment of Judaism, however, is only one among hundreds of important changes that have recently taken place in New Testament interpretation. And even if we had the space to describe them all, it is doubtful whether such a survey would give an adequate picture of the discipline. An alternate approach that seems especially appropriate for the present volume is, first, to focus on general interdisciplinary developments that affect biblical hermeneutics directly; and second, to address one of the most fundamental questions facing exegetes, namely, How do we arrive at the meaning of the text?

Interdisciplinary Approaches

Perhaps the most obvious interdisciplinary effort is the growing use of general linguistics in exegesis (Silva, 1990). Toward the end of the 19th century, the study of language was dominated by the historical approach of comparative philology, and prominent biblical scholars generally kept abreast of that discipline. During the 1920s and '30s, however, so-called "modern linguistics" came into existence, a discipline characterized by such principles as (a) the priority of "synchronic" over against "diachronic" or historical description; (b) the priority of speech over against written forms of language; and (c) the understanding of language as a structured system.

These and other changes in linguistics were almost totally ignored by biblical exegetes. It was only in 1961, with the publication of James Barr's influential book, *The Semantics of Biblical Language*, that the guild of theological scholarship became aware of the great distance separating the typical use of language by exegetes from the generally accepted analysis of language in modern linguistics. It would be many more years, however, before this gap was to be narrowed significantly. Even today, most New Testament exegetes show little genuine familiarity with the field, but there seems to be sufficient awareness of the pitfalls to make scholars more cautious. Moreover, the current generation of younger scholars includes a growing number of researchers who seek to integrate biblical exegesis with a sophisticated use of general linguistics.

A second, and related, interdisciplinary development involves the self-conscious study of the New Testament text as literature. This approach can take many forms. For example, straddling the boundary between linguistics and literary criticism is the field of discourse analysis, a somewhat elastic concept that has served as an umbrella for such diverse tasks as (a) close readings of syntax, focusing on conjunctions and other means of relating propositions to one another; (b) analyses of larger units of language, especially the paragraph; (c) studies of thematic development; and (d) broader semantic analyses of texts.

The concerns of discourse analysis often overlap with those of rhetorical criticism (Kennedy, 1984), which in the strict sense deals with the application of ancient rhetorical categories, though in fact many of its practitioners have a broader set of interests. One important consequence of these developments is the growing tendency to look at texts as literary units rather than as composites. For example, strict adherents of the historical-critical method often view Paul's Letter to the Philippians as a merging of two or more distinct documents, whereas those who approach the letter from a literary perspective emphasize the unifying threads that argue for the integrity of the document.

Literary approaches are especially common in the treatment of narrative. The Gospel according to John, for instance, has been subjected to the kind of narrative criticism developed for the study of modern novels (for example, Culpepper, 1983). The results have been both interesting and controversial. It is certainly debatable whether the biblical books were written for aesthetic purposes and thus whether it is fully appropriate to describe the Bible as "literature." (C. S. Lewis had serious misgivings about that.) Further, many of the techniques developed by literary critics were intended for application to the study of fiction, hardly the most accurate label to use with reference to the Gospels and Acts. Moreover, some scholars have challenged the validity of ignoring the prehistory of the text and the value of using complicated and questionable theories when simpler methods prove adequate (Ashton, 1994, pp. 141-65). Nevertheless, it can hardly be denied that the Gospels and Acts do have artistic qualities and that at least some of the methods of narrative criticism, if used with care and moderation, can contribute significantly to our appreciation of the text.

A third interdisciplinary area of interest is that of the social sciences. Modern historical exegesis has always been concerned with the need to bridge the cultural distance between us and the biblical text. In the last two centuries, accordingly, much effort has been expended on the task of rediscovering the ancient world. It is also clear, however, that most of us find it very difficult to recognize, much less shed, our modern "eurocentric" preconceptions. Indeed, our tendency is to filter any new knowledge about ancient culture through the spectacles of our assumptions. Many publications during the last couple of decades have sought to reverse that tendency (Meeks, 1983; Malina, 1993). Important insights, unfortunately, are usually mixed with highly questionable interpretations of specific passages, and there is a need for a more careful integration of the new methods with the more traditional approach.

The Historical Method and Textual Meaning

During the past couple of decades, new perceptions about the nature of meaning have led to profound changes in the interpretation of the New Testament. Any genuine attempt to describe the current status, however, must look at those changes not in isolation from the past but as developments that are organically related to previous advances.

We need to keep in mind that biblical scholarship, as it entered the 20th century, was characterized by optimism. It is possible, I suppose, that this positive outlook had something to do with contemporary religious thought, since the dominant theological system in the Protestantism of the time was what we now refer to as "classical liberalism." This label must be carefully distinguished from the more popular and general term "liberalism," which is sufficiently vague to be used in a wide variety of contexts and can easily become a slur-word. According to "classical liberalism"—whose most distinguished exponent was Adolf von Harnack—Jesus was a great moral teacher who preached the universal fatherhood of God and the ethic of love. Convinced of the essential goodness of man (in those days no one spoke of the goodness of woman, or even of persons), many theologians and religious leaders at the turn of the century devoted themselves to preaching the Sermon on the Mount, for they believed that its application in modern society would usher in nothing less than the kingdom of God. As is generally recognized, World War I and its later repercussions shattered this dream, though certain basic commitments of liberalism would have long-lasting effects, even to our own day.

Whatever the connection, if any, between this religious movement and the confident spirit of biblical scholarship at the time, we need to appreciate that there were very good reasons indeed for New Testament specialists to feel optimistic. In particular, the second half of the 19th century had seen the full flowering of historical criticism. This label too has become rather ambiguous, but a special effort must be made to understand its significance.

At the simplest and least controversial level, historical criticism may be understood as more or less equivalent to grammatical-historical exegesis. Biblical students of all stripes—Jewish and Christian, Protestant and Catholic, liberal and conservative—have acknowledged the foundational importance of this method. It is a recognition that the Bible needs to be understood in conformity with its original character. Our interpretive work must be "grammatical" in the sense that it should conform to the meaning of the original languages of Scripture—as opposed to depending totally on a translation. And it must be "historical" in the sense that it should take fully into account the original setting of each passage—as opposed to reading into the text cultural assumptions tied to our modern situation.

Directly or indirectly, the emphasis on grammatical-historical exegesis was a polemic against the allegorical method, which in a variety of forms had played a prominent role in the history of biblical interpretation. This point is crucial, especially if we want to appreciate more recent developments. Proponents of the historical method in the 19th and early 20th centuries took it for granted that the only viable approach to interpretation focused on authorial meaning. They did not always use the label, but that is obviously what they meant. Frederic W. Farrar's influential *History of Interpretation* (1886) is a gallery of what the author regarded as well-intentioned but confused students of the Bible. With a few partial exceptions, such as John Chrysostom and John Calvin, interpreters throughout the history of the church are perceived as Christians who twisted the biblical text because they simply were not sensitive to the meaning intended by the original writers. By the 19th century, however, this problem had been solved: The champions of allegorical interpretation had been vanquished, and a new era had begun.

From a more technical perspective, grammatical-historical exegesis could boast some truly astonishing advances. Archaeological discoveries were shedding light on numerous biblical details, while the development of the comparative method in historical linguistics revolutionized our knowledge of the ancient languages. Perhaps the most enduring monuments of this classic period are two sets of commentaries. One of them, the Kritisch-exegetischer Kommentar über das Neue Testament, was started in the middle of the 19th century by a pastor, Heinrich August Wilhelm Meyer, whose extraordinary exegetical powers are evident on every page of the many volumes he contributed to this series. The other set, the International Critical Commentary, covering both Old and New Testaments, was produced by British and American scholars. Both series continue to be published, with revised editions of individual volumes (in effect totally rewritten works) appearing from time to time.

However, the label historical criticism implies much more than the use of the grammatical-historical method of exegesis. The very term criticism, which can be used innocuously enough ("the scientific investigation of literary documents," says *Webster's Collegiate Dictionary*), reflects a post-Enlightenment commitment to the priority of human reason. With that commitment as a starting point, the application of the critical method to the Bible was normally built on three, closely related, assumptions: (a) The Bible must be investigated "like any other book"; (b) biblical scholarship must be practiced more or less independently of church pronouncements, theology, and personal faith; and (c) the critic must evaluate, and therefore pass judgment on, the biblical text.

Not every scholar, of course, would have subscribed to these tenets—one thinks especially of such luminaries as J. B. Lightfoot and J. Gresham Machen—while those who did were not always consistent in applying them. In general, however, mainstream New Testament scholarship was learning more and more to operate by such criteria. Especially illuminating in this regard is the classic history of New Testament scholarship by

W. G. Kümmel (1970/1972, pp. 29-31 and *passim*), who explicitly defines a "historical" approach as one that accepts the reality of contradiction in the biblical record.

One can therefore understand quite easily why the serious study of the New Testament was split along so-called conservative and liberal lines. Anyone committed to the unique inspiration of the Bible—let alone its infallibility—could hardly be expected to use the historical-critical method as we have now defined it. Toward the end of the 19th century, and even into the first decade or so of the 20th, a significant number of scholars who had a strongly conservative bent continued to be "players" in mainstream biblical scholarship, but certainly by the 1920s things had changed dramatically. In the case of the United States, the modernist-fundamentalist controversy played a major role in these developments.

Remarkably, there were still broad areas of research where these differences did not prevent conservatives from making use of, and even contributing to, the field of biblical scholarship. Part of the reason for this situation is the crucial point already mentioned: Both sides shared the fundamental assumption that exegesis is supposed to uncover the original, historical meaning of the text, that is, the meaning intended by the biblical author. Undoubtedly, for someone who regards God as the ultimate author of Scripture, the question of "divine meaning" comes into play, and this factor complicates the process of interpretation. Even in this case, however, it was normally assumed that the divine meaning must be tightly related to the human meaning, and so historical exegesis was held to be indispensable. In short, the exacting philological and scientific labors of the historical-critical method (with or without an abandonment of the doctrine of inspiration) reigned supreme at the beginning of the century.

Enter Karl Barth. Writing his famous commentary on Romans right after World War I, Barth (1918/1968) was not only addressing a devastated Europe, where the hopes of classical liberalism had been shattered; he was also taking on the biblical and theological leaders of his day, many of whom (in Barth's judgment) had compromised their principles during the political struggles that had just ended. Moreover, during his early years in the pastorate, Barth had found that the theological teaching he had received failed to prove its relevance in the life of his congregation. The technical scholarship of the critics tended to treat the biblical text as a fossil, and a new approach to interpretation was needed. This cry for relevance would set in motion a revolution in hermeneutics that could not possibly have been foreseen by Barth or anyone else.

It should be kept in mind that Barth did not wish to reject the role of historical criticism. His own commentary on Romans made little use of the method and, in the opinion of many, contributed hardly anything to our understanding of what the apostle Paul intended to say in that letter. But Barth continued to affirm the value of rigorous criticism while arguing for a return to classical theology. In his case, the maneuver consisted of drawing a sharp distinction between the *historisch* ("historical") and the *geschichtlich* ("historic"): The former term refers to that which is observable and subject to scholarly investigation, while the latter pertains to the realm of faith. This move had been made possible by Kant's phenomena/noumena dualism, a perspective that informs almost all forms of modern thought, though one must question whether it is at all compatible with the biblical message. Indeed, in a curious twist that seems to turn upside down and inside out the most cherished beliefs of the biblical writers, modern theologians routinely affirm that a concern for objective historical evidence undermines "the risk of faith" because such a desire reflects a flight to worldly security (see Robinson, 1959, p. 44; contrast, for example Luke 1.1-4; John 19.35; 1 Corinthians 15.14; 2 Peter 1.16).

Be that as it may, Barth's work appeared to open up a new way. Biblical scholars could pay attention now to matters of relevance and theology without having to give up historical-critical analysis. The most distinguished practitioner of the new approach was Rudolf Bultmann (1960), whose early career had some significant points of contact with Barth's. The further development of Bultmann's thought—such as his radical application of the history-of-religions method, as well as his appropriation of Heidegger's existentialist philosophy—created a serious rift between him and Barth. Nevertheless, Bultmann's scholarly output became a paradigm of 20th-century hermeneutics over against the earlier, arid exegesis that Barth had so fiercely attacked. Moreover, Bultmann's disciples played a major role in the development of the New Hermeneutic in the 1950s and 1960s, though this movement is less germane to our concerns than its name might imply. (The New Hermeneutic was in effect a way of doing theology rather than a new method for exegeting the biblical text.)

Just about this time certain developments were taking place in other scholarly disciplines—literary criticism, philosophy, and even the sciences—that would leave their mark on biblical interpretation. The movement known as the New Criticism, which had been all the rage some decades earlier, affirmed the autonomy of the text as such and thus redirected the reader's attention away from authorial meaning. Later developments, such as structuralism, reader-response theory, and deconstruction, have further eroded confidence in the older historical method, which assumed the priority of original historical meaning in the hermeneutical process.

In the area of philosophy, we have space to mention only two very influential figures. H.-G. Gadamer (1976), hoping to raise the level of respect enjoyed by the humanities (vis-à-vis the sciences, which claimed to give objective truth), argued for the value of "prejudice." While the scientific method seeks to eliminate prejudice, the humanities can flourish—indeed, can produce their own brand of truth—only by making full use of the prior commitments that arise out of the tradition. Paul Ricoeur, for his part, picking up on the concerns of literary criticism, suggested that written texts have a "surplus/reservoir of meaning" that transcends authorial intention (1976; 1980). Ricoeur's development of this theme, as well as of other rich concepts, has had a notable impact on many biblical interpreters.

But the "hard sciences" came under fire as well. Thomas Kuhn, among others, began to raise questions about the objectivity of the scientific method. The history of science, he argued, makes clear that so-called scientific truth is largely a matter of interpretive consensus (1967; Poythress, 1988). In the course of time, a reigning "paradigm" will be replaced by another one—although the change sometimes waits for the death of scientists who refuse to give up an outdated paradigm. In other words, scientists tend to hold on to an interpretive framework even when such a framework, undermined by a growing number of anomalies, is no longer able to account for the available facts.

These and other developments conspired to cast serious doubts on the objectivity of biblical hermeneutics. The question of relativity in interpretation has therefore been a driving concern for New Testament scholars during the last quarter of the 20th century. We should reiterate, however, that these changes have occurred in reaction to the historical method, and the results have been rather ironic. For example, when Ricoeur (with the agreement of many others) tells us that a written text "escapes the finite horizon lived by its author," so that "what the text means now matters more than what the author meant when he wrote it" (1976, p. 30), one wonders whether we are returning to the allegorical method that modern scholarship had fought so hard to vanquish. Or again, consider that the term *eisegesis* (reading into the text what is not there), which had been a term of opprobrium referring to the absurd opposite of historical exegesis, has now been proudly adopted by at least one popular biblical scholar as the way to do interpretation (Croatto, 1984, p. 73).

It is difficult to assess just how much influence these views have had on mainstream New Testament scholarship. Articles and books that adopt some form of reader-response criticism are not uncommon, but the vast majority of scholarly publications (even when they pay lip-service to contemporary approaches) reflect the standard methods of historical criticism. Writers who do seek to exploit the role of the reader in the production of meaning characteristically adopt radical interpretations that ignore or even contradict the historical meaning—and most interpreters instinctively perceive that the failure to do justice to that historical meaning entails doing violence to the text. On the other hand, scholars who wish to preserve the priority of the historical meaning while acknowledging the role of the reader usually fail to integrate these two perspectives.

Though only time will tell whether a coherent method will develop, it is clear that biblical interpretation will never be the same. One can hardly deny that any reading of any text engages a person's presuppositions—that it is impossible for us to understand anything without in some way "adding" to what we read from the store of our experiences. Yes, such a process appears to relativize interpretation, but experience also teaches us that this is by no means an insurmountable obstacle. Social interaction, for example, shows us that all communication includes plenty of checks and balances preventing us, in the vast majority of cases, from taking off in unacceptable directions. The fact that misunderstandings are possible does not paralyze us in our day-to-day living. None of us fails to deposit money in the bank because we are afraid that our instructions to the cashier could be subject to wild interpretations, such as "Burn all this cash, please." Similarly, there is no reason for us to give up biblical interpretation, or even to worry unduly about its "objectivity," since there are adequate ways of verifying whether or not our reading is proceeding along appropriate lines.

To be sure, in the case of an ancient written text, especially one that has religious authority, we have something else to worry about—tradition. To what extent have readers throughout the centuries "added" to the text? How much of that history have we accepted unconsciously? And once we have identified these "additions," should they be rejected outright, or may we use them in a positive way? Contrary to what many people seem to think, these questions are not easily answered, and much more work needs to be done before we can reach consensus. Even after taking these concerns into account, however, we would be unwise to reject the priority of authorial meaning in biblical interpretation.

The proliferation of theories and methods in biblical scholarship can prove confusing and discouraging (Silva, 1994). And undoubtedly, the increase in our knowledge means that greater time and effort must be spent in sorting through the data. On the other hand, we should remember that this very phenomenon also increases the reliability of our conclusions. A prior generation may have "felt" more secure about some of their convictions, but not because they had a firmer basis on which to stand. It's just that ignorance can be very comforting.

Born in Havana, Cuba, **Moisés Silva** earned a B.D. (1969) and Th.M. (1971) at Westminster Theological Seminary and studied Semitics at Dropsie University (1968-1970); at the University of Manchester he earned a Ph.D. The Mary F. Rockefeller Distinguished Professor of New Testament at Gordon-Conwell Theological Seminary, his publications include *Biblical Words and Their Meaning* (1983; 2nd ed. 1994); *Philippians* (Baker Exegetical Commentary, 1992); *An Introduction to Biblical Hermeneutics: The Search for Meaning* (1994; with W.C. Kaiser). From 1982-1995 Moisés Silva edited the *Westminster Theological Journal*.

2

Problems and Challenges of Translation in an Age of New Media and Competing Models

José Lambert

The main goal of this paper is to call attention to the problems and challenges of translation by (1) connecting the question of Bible translation with research on translation (in this case called "translation studies") and (2) to connect translation with media communication, in particular with the question of translation in media communication.

The Rules of the Debate: Terminology and Discourse

It is quite difficult to discuss any topic in a scholarly manner without certain prior agreements. Thus the origin and status of our discourse, that is, the kind of terminology and concepts we will employ forms an initial problem for us. When entrusting ourselves simply to the words and discourse adopted in everyday language or even in the language of dictionaries (assuming direct linguistic equivalents exist for such everyday language and for such dictionary language), we assume from the beginning that the topic under consideration is not really problematic and that our language appears to have universal relevance. As any dictionary can illustrate (Lambert, in press a), the phenomenon of translation is first of all a problem of everyday language. Without a consensus on the concepts, and one that is certainly more than a consensus on terminology, we may be trapped from the beginning if we simply assume that our own discourse as such could be viewed as neutral and scientific.

Another problem to be solved is the question of scholarly discourse. After all, scholars cannot even discuss "scholarly discourse" without having first reached an agreement on the kind of language, terminology, or concepts to be used. It is thoroughly possible, though, to expect that agreements on the status and goals of our scholarly language may lead to a systematic approach, whatever differences between languages may exist, even when a topic such as translation is at stake. In fact, other disciplines such as linguistics or intercultural communication have to overcome similar difficulties. What's more, if we assume exactly the opposite, namely, that communication beyond language barriers is not possible at all we would face an *ex absurdo* starting point. And from the moment international audiences understand that language differences may reduce international understanding, they may have solved the problem. In short then, any scholarly discussion of translation—or any other topic—would be simply absurd if not supported by a basic and preferably explicit agreement about the discourse to be used.

What Kind of Agreements May Be Called For

As a starting point, we suggest agreement on a negative consensus that is not necessarily shared by all experts in the field. This consensus states that many theories cannot serve as a basis for the discussion of translation as a cultural phenomenon, since they do not (all) define "relevance" as a concept based on empirical research, but rather on the basis of normative evidence. In other words, they deal with an idea of translation rather than with the features of actual translational phenomena.

We further suggest that there are no solid grounds for revising in 1996 the assumptions underlying Gideon Toury's quest for norms from 1975-1976 (Toury, 1978)—a quest whose first formulation of concepts goes back as far as 1975 and whose first public discussion took place at the Leuven Symposium on "Literature and Translation" in 1976 (Holmes, Lambert, & van den Broeck, 1978; Toury, 1980). There are still a large number of different views on translation and many different theories, many among them claiming a scholarly status. Even so, not all are (totally) compatible with each other since among other things they often aim at very different goals. Hence the only way to avoid chaos and to talk with each other in an understandable language lies in the search for "norms" and "models" that make interaction, dialogue, cooperation, and discussion possible, although in many cases dialogue and cooperation are not even possible.

Without a satisfactory encompassing theory, scholars ought to test the validity of various approaches in two ways: by a confrontation of the various approaches among each other; and by a confrontation, in empirical terms, of their relevance with respect to the topic(s) under discussion. The only way to make such scholarly operations possible is, of course, to work out common rules for discourse. This is the first meaning of the "norms" concept as worked out by Toury (1978, 1980) along the lines of principles borrowed from other disciplines like sociology and sociolinguistics. Toury notes that speaking about translation would be quite utopian if we had no conventional or even hypothetical tools that make possible systematic discussions among scholarly partners.

A second function of the norms concept refers to the features (regularities) of the phenomenon studied and (often, but not always) called "translation" and "translating." It would not be possible to work out general models for the study of such a phenomenon if we did not assume from the beginning, and in a hypothetical way, that at least some common features do occur. But it may turn out that the first hypotheses in terms of norms and models need to be revised afterwards. Anyway, rather than prestige and power, research and (empirical) evidence are needed, even when different approaches claim to have provided already some (partial?) evidence in favor of their concepts.

Whatever the confusion and contradiction between the various approaches, scholarly discourse on translation does not necessarily face chaos. Several partial or even conflicting theories may have a certain relevance, and some would-be global theories may have their relevance under certain conditions. But, here arise questions. Does our first consensus about our own scholarly discourse give rise to counterproductive consequences? Do we even have the right tools and instruments for comparing and confronting the different theoretical approaches if we do not define the exact topic under observation? How could we have any parameters that allow for a confrontation of the various approaches when we cannot circumscribe the topic itself?

The only or first possible exit from this vicious circle is probably to assume that our scholarly discourse can at least be compared and discussed on the basis of some common concepts and goals. Whether they have any empirical relevance, that is, whether they allow for the analysis and explanation of translation or translational phenomena will depend on further rules and agreements. The inevitable attempt to put some order into translation theories has enormous consequences because several theories do not aim at achieving scholarly goals and hence do not have any scholarly status. From the moment we require empirical evidence in real-life situations rather than simply evidence that exists in the mind, it will be much more difficult to reach an agreement with many so-called theoreticians. Some among them, together with their theories, will be excluded from our discussion. They may hold interest for extremely different reasons, for instance as expressions of a remarkable individual or collective approach. But there are no grounds for taking them into consideration if we want to deal with translational phenomena in culture, that is, in real life, and in historical space and time. After all, they do not aim to account for actual phenomena. On the other hand, several apparently very different theoretical utterances and concepts may be compatible though dealing with very different aspects of translation, or only with part of them.

Before any real dialogue can occur, we need a comprehensive theoretical-hypothetical model in order to observe and to explain (all) translational phenomena, from all ages and times. Partial theories may be relevant without being sufficient. This has enormous consequences for our definition of the object of study. Narrow definitions exclude some aspects of translation, or particular translations and "adaptations" on the basis of *a priori* definitions. Marginally, we may note that the question of "adaptation" is a real hobby horse for the advocates of descriptive translation studies. And it provides an interesting test for our concepts since it reminds us of the necessity to question the concept "adaptation" rather than the term. The phenomena referred to with the aid of "adaptation" are not necessarily different from what others call "translation." It is easy to imagine how such distinctions may apply to many other terms (like "imitation," "parody," but also "copywriting"). What is at stake is our very idea of translation. No scholarly discussion is possible when assuming that "translation" itself is an unproblematic word and concept.

As long as no satisfactory general theory is available, only open, hypothetical theories can be accepted, theories that can be revised and corrected. This implies that the theories needed are meant to stimulate observation, analysis, explanation. They ought to be research-oriented, and they cannot offer any basis for the evaluation of translational phenomena before a better descriptive knowledge and mapping of translational phenomena has been provided. Hence the start of descriptive translation studies in the mid-'70s and its success since the 1980s. Theories that have other goals are not necessarily wrong or uninteresting, but they serve purposes other than research.

Bible Translation and/or General Translation

Long before Eugene Nida started his pioneering work, many considered Bible translations a key area of translation in general, and in most cultures (Frank, 1994; Nida & Taber, 1969). Evidence of the cultural impact of Bible translations comes from a fascinating conference held in Toronto in 1994 and devoted to the development of writing in Korea. There the role of Bible translation appeared to be central for the development of cultures in east Asia. Although in most cultures explicit academic discussions on translation have generally occurred less frequently than the practice of translation, the question of Bible translation has provided a privileged area for the confrontation of translation concepts and ideologies, as may be illustrated by the cultural history of England, France, Germany, Holland, Korea, and Africa. We assume that translational practices and oral discourse on translation occur in all cultures, and that written comments are much more exceptional, while remaining also inevitably implicit. One expects scholarly discourse to be as explicit as possible but knows that it can never be fully explicit.

The question arises, however, whether we should reduce the question of translation to Bible translation as such. Nida and Taber (1969) claim that hardly any kind of translation is lacking in the history of Bible translation. But is it really accurate to say that the Bible contains all possible kinds of text genres and that, even if this were so, we would have a sufficient argument in favor of a biblical approach to translation in general?

Without answering such a basic question on the legitimation of our models, I would rather stress how particular and limited is the point of view that Nida and Taber adopt in their discussion. Even if Bible translation were indeed the best possible synthesis of translation types in general, we still have not shown that the Nida-Taber approach to Bible translation can represent all possible approaches. There are indeed strong indications that in this particular case the theoretical aims are linked to quite particular circumstances, options, and goals. Moreover, not all translators of biblical texts want to fulfill a religious function. Some may rather be inspired by literary motivations.

In fact the distinction between Bible translation and other kinds of translation is only one of the many possible and current distinctions accepted nowadays by experts in translation studies. While generalizations in scholarship as well as in everyday life are hard to avoid, the fact is that in scholarship they have to be justified by empirical evidence. And as long as the opposite has not been demonstrated, we may assume there is no satisfactory universal model for approaching the translational phenomena. Before it even makes sense to discuss relevance, we must examine the very possibility of making distinctions as well as the criteria (norms, models) for such distinctions.

From an historical vantage point, the first real attempts to develop translation studies as a scholarly discipline go back to the beginning of the 1970s (Holmes, 1972). One of the main results of these attempts was that a growing—though still limited—agreement was reached on some basic points and that a growing institutionalization of translation studies took place on the basis of such agreements. One of the illustrations of this institutionalization has certainly been the distinction between research on translation and professional and didactic translational activities of many kinds, including for instance the production of translation as such, translation teaching, criticism, and machine translation. The use of new labels such as "translation studies," or "descriptive translation studies," though too often mixed up with "translatology" (where no such distinction is being made), is another strong indication of the establishment of a scholarly tradition (Lambert, 1991; Lambert, 1995a).

Distinguishing between Translation as Skill, Art, Science and Object of Research

The categories, oppositions, and distinctions used so far do not at all originate in the naive belief that we can directly grasp an object of study. They reflect rather the state of the art, more or less institutionalized by publications and by research. Without claiming to be the only possible or existing distinctions or to have any monopoly position, they refer to positions that scholars have gradually accepted in publications, conferences, and manuals.

Although translation is one of the oldest professions on earth, and although an impressive number of intelligent books have been devoted to translation, the beginning of a scholarly approach to translation is a rather recent phenomenon. Not unlike many other intellectual and professional activities, those responsible for its production have first analyzed translation. The first theoretical explanations owe a heavy debt to a particular group of agents in the translation process: those who have produced translations.

Practices of all kinds have always preceded theoretical thinking. Most academic and scholarly disciplines from medicine and law to economics and philology have first developed with the aid of the expertise accumulated by professional practitioners and then by theoretical thinking. Theoretical thinking on medicine, on society, on language, and on translation has developed gradually, first among those involved in health care, in politics, in language teaching or in translation, and only much later by people and groups not involved in any action. For this very reason, theoretical thinking on these various disciplines has closely followed the perspective of those who produce, along the basic principle: *Fecit cui prodest.* The very idea of independent research is of course rather young in our western societies.

In fact, throughout the ages and various cultures translation practice has been much more widespread than discourse on translation. Until this very day, many consider it a technical skill (Lambert, in press b) rather than a matter for intellectual discussion, unless heavy cultural values, as for example, those embodied in the Bible or Greek classics, were at stake.

Little by little, people rejected the idea of translation as an art since no one could reach agreement on how to judge the quality of a translation. Even the distinction between a good and a bad translation or between (good) "translations" and "adaptations" remained problematic. The conflicts and hesitations due to matters of translation have gradually generated some independent and more general discussions in most cultures. Among these discussions, some have acquired a sufficient general scope and have gained standing as statements with a more general value, or even with a scholarly status, about one of the most complex among all human activities.

Given the lack of an established tradition, people or groups already involved in the translation process initially produced most of the discussions. Hence some may generally consider them as interesting but ad hoc discussions, or as philosophical considerations rather than as scholarly contributions. Just like many literary treatises, they have often functioned as apologies (for example, Du Bellay's *Deffense et illustration de la langue française*), or as philosophical treatises (for example, many 18th century German books). But they were not scientific, not even for practitioners and users, and hardly ever for scholars. *Nemo iudex in propria sua causa.* We are well aware of the ambiguity of all historiography. Most scholars would like to rewrite the history of their discipline according to their own parameters. In this case I borrow explicit criteria from Holmes, Toury, and descriptive translation studies, distinguishing between Nida's "Science of Translating"—which is older—and Holmes' "Translation Studies" on the basis of their goals: One tries to promote a systematic translation methodology, the other wants to organize scholarly discourse.

The idea that independent people and agencies were needed in order to approach the translational phenomenon had hardly ever been formulated explicitly before the 1970s (Holmes, 1972; Toury, 1978). Today, however, it has been formulated very systematically and in a redundant way within descriptive translation studies rather than in translation teaching (Vinay & Darbelnet, 1958; Hönig & Kußmaul, 1982; and Newmark, 1981) or in the linguistics-based tradition (Nida, 1964, 1969; Koller, 1972, 1979; Wilss, 1977; Vermeer, 1971, 1983; Snell-Hornby, 1988). Rather than providing here the rich bibliography of this tradition in translation theory and translation training, I refer to some of the recent key books like Snell-Hornby (1988) and Pym (1992). In fact this differentiation in the options of the various theoretical models is not strange at all. One can understand quite easily that the development of the program and the goals of "a discipline" had systematic links with the academic or unacademic position of the various experts. It seems too that many disciplines with a rich academic tradition (such as linguistics or literary studies) have developed in a similar way, and that the (weak) institutional position of those dealing with translation has had enormous consequences.

Translation was first taken seriously only after the Second World War, and then by private companies in need of quick and efficient translation services. At that moment, linguistics, literary studies, and other disciplines turned translation over to technical institutes where by definition, training and education came first and where conceptualization was supposed to be counterproductive. At that time, only "practice," experience, and efficiency supposedly were needed, while all conceptualization and the very idea of research were judged irrelevant. Hence "theory" stood in opposition to "practice," but not in opposition to "research," as could be exemplified by many books published between 1960 and 1990. On the other hand, the academic world itself had excellent reasons for keeping its distance and for not taking seriously the question of translated discourse. First, it considered translations secondary texts, that is, texts subordinated to the (holy) "original(s)." Second, it felt that second-rate intellectuals produced translations. Third, the structure of the academic world map of languages (and literatures) favored a systematic exclusion of translation because it was not compatible with the idea of homogeneous western and written languages (Lambert, 1989, 1994).

Until this very day most of the famous linguists and most of their
handbooks deal with translation haphazardly and in an intuitive way and
hardly ever on the basis of any empirical research. One of the other consequences of this situation is that discourse on translation remains in the hands
of very dispersed and isolated groups representing often the professional
world with its didactic traditions, as well as its money, rather than in the
hands of intellectuals. In sociological terms, these various groups often work
in isolation. But, mainly since the 1980s the institutionalized publications
and conferences indicate a growing trend of interaction, cooperation, and
even common planning. For example, publishers have created very important
new channels such as book series in various countries as well as scholarly
journals and newsletters. In these publications as well as during the many
conferences of experts from the various traditions (teachers, literary scholars, linguists, media experts, even "machine translation"), the level of cooperation has improved since the 1970s, when even contacts between the sub-
groups were rather exceptional.

It is fascinating to notice how research on interpreting slowly follows
more general trends. For instance international copyright rules, which support those who defend the profession against research, represents one of the
last remnants of an old monopoly which established that discourse on translation is a matter for those who produce it, and not for those who observe or
study it, nor for those who study or observe language and communication.

In recent years, in fact since Holmes, Toury, and several others began
to publish in the mid-'70s, the dominant trend in research on translation has
redefined the very goal of research and theoretical models while disconnect-
ing them from didactics and from applied research. Rather than trying to
answer the question "How to translate (well)?"—which seems to imply a
normative and ideal(istic) view of translational phenomenon—contemporary
research wants to solve first more basic questions such as "How does translation work exactly?" and "Why is disagreement on translation so systematic?"

On the basis of this new paradigm I assume that any discussion of
translation will fail as long as the role played within such a discussion by
the various partners, for instance translators, their audiences, their sponsors,
their distributors, intermediaries, and critics has not been made explicit. It
will also fail if people allow only a normative approach to the theory and
practice of translation. The best way towards a better understanding of the
various points of view will first make clear the goals and the position of
those who take part in the discussion and second will examine to what extent goals and positions do condition their basic norms.

Since Toury (1978, 1980) worked out the concept of norms, the distinction between prescriptive-normative and descriptive perspectives has
been more and more accepted, and the very idea of research has become
common, even within institutes for translation training. The orientation of

conferences in some of the most experienced countries such as Germany, Canada, and Finland clearly illustrates this. There empirical research on the behavior of the target audiences, as well as research on cognitive aspects of the translation and interpreting process represent the common trends. Twenty years ago one had to stress that translation studies needed a descriptive branch, to be distinguished from the prescriptive point of view. Nowadays the opposition with the normative-prescriptive options has become largely familiar and the need for a label like "descriptive translation studies" has become less obvious, simply because the danger of confusion with a monopolizing didactics-oriented approach is not that common anymore.

Toury's work on norms has led to the establishment of several other distinctions and to an abandoning of a unilateral perspective on translation from the point of view of those who produce or generate it. Today most accept that not only translators take part in the translational process, but also their recipients, and their target and source traditions. Translators and their business and media partners believe more or less that translation and translational equivalence are possible (the equivalence postulate), but on the other hand they realize that their target audience(s) or those who use translations may have quite different considerations. In terms of scholarship this implies that there is no perfect communication (neither in translated communication nor in other kinds of communication) and that research may help to locate the communicational difficulties and conflicts. Those who produce translations want to know how to guarantee "quality" although in fact they often accept that "quality" simply refers to "efficiency" and not at all to any kind of metaphysics. And many realize that quality does not necessarily coincide with the idea of a perfect original model. Those who study translations have learned that no ideal reproduction of an original is possible, if wanted at all, since the very idea of "sameness" or "symmetry" is incompatible with communication. The systematic distinction between the various points of view of the different partners does not imply at all that interaction and cooperation cannot exist. Rather, questions and goals have become pragmatic and functional. What's more, translation itself is no longer always confused with scientific research on translations, as it was in the Vinay and Darbelnet tradition. Today, most believe that translation research supports translation. Even computer-aided translation has dropped the idea of any perfect mechanical activity or product. Strangely enough, computer-supported translation suddenly gathers new chances and energies from its improved cooperation with the human world.

Although both theory and research have demonstrated that "quality" as such does not exist, but rather quality exists for somebody in given circumstances, translation practice, translation didactics and translation research (theory and historical-descriptive study) may very well go hand-in-hand as long as they understand each other's aims and positions. Quite a new insight (borrowed unofficially from marketing research) holds that one may describe and even predict the relationships between particular strategies (options) and the expectations of the recipient. However, the conviction that translation itself might constitute a science results from a confusion of the levels to be distinguished: the object of study on the one hand and the approach to the object on the other hand.

Some main positions have developed out of several theoretical traditions. These positions describe only a state of the art along dominant and research-oriented perspectives and have their origin partly from within the so-called discipline, and partly within neighboring disciplines. Plainly, translation studies cannot be a discipline in its own right since translation does not seem to have clear specific features and since it seems to function within other discourses, often without being identified as a specific type of discourse.

As long as the opposite has not been demonstrated we may accept that:

(1) Translation is supposed to be an activity. (Is it really a particular kind of activity?) As an activity, it no less than other kinds of communication reflects (most of) the complexities and paradoxes of human behavior as observed and analyzed by psychologists and sociologists. This implies that it is a socio-cultural activity whose behavior may vary according to socio-cultural parameters. This also implies that it can never be a totally individual matter since partners must be involved. Hence one of the key questions will always be the identity of the different partners, their role, and the location of that role in the activity (Bourdieu, 1994).

(2) Translation is also a (particular?) kind of verbal, but never strictly verbal communication, in which (most of) the basic rules of communication are supposed to be relevant. As a form of communication, translation involves inevitably complex intentions, never sufficient for the full comprehension of the communication since there is no communication beyond the intended or real perception on the side of the target partners. This implies that observers, scholars, and critics who attempt to understand a given communication event will have to reconstruct the entire communicational situation and context.

(3) Translation is also a (particular?) (kind of) textual phenomenon and a kind of textual communication, which again implies that it submits itself to (most of?) the rules of language, text, and textual traditions such as genre, distribution, and audience.

We assume in the three definitions that translation is a norm-bound and culture-bound phenomenon. We could not even speak about translation without using principles such as the ones labeled here as "norms." The three complementary definitions imply that:

- Practice and theory are linked within the translational activity itself, but practice should precede theory in most cases.

- Theoretical considerations and utterances are generally speaking not systematically explicit; they often remain oral rather than becoming written.
- Written reflections on translation occur much less frequently than translational activities; historical-descriptive research has already formed strong hypotheses about the situations in which such reflections occur.
- Due to the rules accepted or rejected, most of the written utterances on translation, whatever their claims, do not function like scholarly discourse; they often have links to protectionist or polemical positions.
- Even very systematic and scholarly discourse can never be totally explicit; hence discourse on translation will never fail to remain at least partly implicit.
- It is even hard to assume that any of the various possible statements, even the scholarly ones, could ever be totally individual (what is it to be individual after all?); according to the situations and degrees there will always be a part of unconsciousness involved.
- One of the requirements of scholarly discourse, however, will be that explicit and systematic thinking are not just possibilities any more; they have become requirements.

Back to Definitions: What Is Translation after All?

Given this hypothetical starting point of translation research, we have constantly to reconsider our definitions, which in fact only manifest a state of the art. If we knew what translation was and how it actually worked no research would be needed.

In descriptive translation studies we begin with the idea that we do not know what constitutes the components and features of translation. Translation is supposed to be the kind of text (activity, process, communication) called so in a given target culture. How given cultures approach the phenomenon, how they change their definitions and distinctions is a matter for discussion and research.

Such a starting point is narrowly conditioned by an attempt to avoid any normative and *a priori* definition of what translation is supposed to be. At the same time, it remains open to some doubts and criticism. Certain texts may be viewed as translations since they simulate them. These are called pseudo-translations. The fact is that often texts and activities seem to have many features of translation without ever being treated so: advertisements, copywriting, business letters, adaptations, quotations, and text fragments. Hence the category of "translation" may need to become much larger and more open. This is even more obvious if we do not postulate from the beginning that "a translation" or "translated phenomenon" can only be complete texts. On what basis would we do this anyway? After all, even the most famous translations in the history of humankind are never entirely translated since they contain non-translated words, patterns, and structures. What's more, our "normal" discourse always uses items borrowed at some previous point from other languages. Many contemporary companies sell their imported products in the target language of their customers without indicating at all that both product and discourse have been imported!

If we reserve the label "translation" for autonomous texts rather than for text fragments, and if we tolerate the quite common tendency in contemporary business and media life to conceal the foreign origin of texts, we implicitly ignore an enormous quantity of texts that are not called translations but that in fact play a key role in our contemporary societies. It looks more and more relevant then to take seriously the following tautological definition: "Translation is a phenomenon that cultures consider to be translation." As good and important as this definition is, it is not a sufficient kernel for a definition of translation since one feature of cultures is to refuse to consider certain translational phenomena as translation. The characteristics of such phenomena and the reasons for refusing to consider them translations should be studied to determine their relevance for the whole question of translation.

Translation and/as Language: Verbal and Beyond

Due to the development of the descriptive branch of translation studies, it has become possible to redefine translation(s) in culture and to redefine the links with linguistic, moral, social, and (many) other norm systems. One of the consequences is that the role of language, whether written, oral, standardized or non-canonized, has been redefined in relation to other sign systems. Neither in contemporary society nor in previous ages has the translational phenomenon ever been a purely linguistic one, though verbal communication has always played a crucial role. The dominant view remains the verbal one, however, as can be attested in dictionaries.

Several other factors explain why translation is, generally speaking, no longer universally supposed to be a language phenomenon. First of all, research on translation began worldwide in centers and departments for applied linguistics. The growth of translation training, however, has gradually stressed the need for a larger, interdisciplinary approach in which the monopoly of language and linguistics has been questioned. The success of more functionally oriented approaches such as skopos theory (worked out, for example, by J. Holz-Mänttäri, H. Vermeer, and C. Nord) and a polysystems approach has presented the phenomenon of translation as a communicational and a cultural one in which language plays a key role (Lambert, 1995a). Also, due to the particular implications of audio-visual communication and research on communication, the systematic interactions and interferences between verbal and non-verbal communication have gradually been recognized. In a way similar to research on literature and cinema, functional-systemic models have dealt with media translation and even with film adaptation (Cattrysse, 1992a). Not only Even-Zohar's polysystems theory (1978, 1979, 1990), but also and especially S. J. Schmidt's (1991) systems theory envisages literature as one of the media. Semioticians, literary scholars, and specialists in translation studies realize that even in poetry, in theater, and in prose, traditional text strategies do not necessarily reduce written texts to their language component. The semiotics of space and gesture plays a key role in translated communication as soon as the representation of a real or possible world is involved. The idea of texts in communicational frames has been redefined again and again in recent years by semioticians, in particular by J. Lotman and the Tartu school.

Second, since the hypotheses borrowed from a functional approach to translation seem to be relevant to the case of cinema adaptation and even to the case of dance (Lambert, 1995a), we no longer have sufficient grounds for limiting translation to the level of verbal communication, or to the realm of language. As a symptom of the hesitation between the two main heralds of the polysystems theory in the mid-'70s we may note that Toury has left the discussion of transfer theory to his master, Even-Zohar, who has written some basic studies on the question of transfer between sign systems from a semiotic perspective. The relevance of the concepts of "equivalence" and "translation" for explaining transfer phenomena between non-verbal sign systems appears simply a question of generality. How general exactly are the transfer phenomena that occur when translators move from one linguistic and socio-cultural tradition into another one? The thesis that in such cases the rules of intersemiotic relations are also a matter of prestige, dominance, and strategies, obviously makes much sense, as does the position that their success depends upon the perception and the traditions of the recipient. Expanding the concept of translation in this way involves much more than a simple metaphor, as can be illustrated by usage. Intellectuals and societies need to adapt to the idea, but this is exactly what happens all the time through history.

Whatever scholars may say nowadays on the basis of their sophisticated contemporary models, culture itself has never had any hesitation. Although the main definition of translation has always linked it with languages, most dictionaries and many sciences also recognize that there are translations in mathematics, in chemistry, and in biology. It would be hard to call such implicit definitions nonsensical when we take seriously the tautological definition "translations are what cultures accept as translations."

Third, the absurdity (!?) of an exclusively linguistic approach to translation is strengthened by the crisis of a reductionist view on language. Media translation has revealed how easy the shift is from oral into verbal discourse and vice versa. Movies can be "translated" into written subtitles or rendered as dubbing or voice-over versions. Various new techniques of speech recognition make it possible to transfer speech from written into oral texts, or from oral into written formulation. Institutes for translation training have discovered how important this new area is for their education programs. At the same time they also have learned how the borders between other disciplines are being revised. Within translation curricula worldwide, the distinction between interpreting and translation has generally been taken for granted. Since dubbing and subtitling have become part of daily life, the shift from oral into written codes has become more and more common, and digital television as well as distance learning oblige us to test out new combinations. Translating for the blind and the deaf also comes into the new media landscape, together with monolingual written versions and monolingual subtitles (!) of spoken communication. Translation appears everywhere, but the differences between national languages are not any more the key difficulty of media communication.

However, given the very international framework in which these new media are used and produced, the relativity of the various national standard languages is also at stake. It appears that languages do not simply exist as autonomous systems, but rather as the result of institutionalization. The new media world simply pushes us into new experiments with verbal and communicational borderlines. Oral, written, standardized, and experimental discourse are constantly submitted to reshuffling in our media world, and it is not clear where innovations will stop. The crisis of the exclusively written language is also the crisis of standard language and the crisis of verbal language. Behind the language crisis, the traditional instances of canonization are at stake. Obviously, the question of translation is never only nor simply a question of translation.

In a contemporary world that tends to become more global, it is not clear any more how metaphorical the extension of language to the whole world of communication still is. Anyway we may suppose that the kind of strategies, norms and conflicts that can be observed empirically in the case of translation appear in communication in general. And if this view is correct, the question of research on translation is directly linked with the problem of metaphor: Is it a metaphor at all to assume that translation is a matter of communication and not just of language? It is much easier to answer "No" than with a simple "Yes" since we cannot know what our language of the future will mean exactly.

The Future: from Translation Studies into Media Studies

One of the strongest tendencies of contemporary research on translation is to refuse the subservient role. Neither translation research nor translation theory are undertaken in order to offer a *deus ex machina* solution to translation and/or communication problems. What is possible, however, is to observe better what is going on and to offer better predictions. The analysis of conflicts, difficulties, and options may allow for a certain predictability in a quite new area, and we may learn from research how predictions can be worked and tested out.

Who is going to benefit exactly from a better understanding of the enormous question of media transfer? First of all, society itself since language and communication shifts are never just language or communication shifts. They affect society as such, and the development of self-consciousness ought to enrich decision processes and social organization. When contributing to the growing autonomy of societies in their decision process, translation studies has better chances to get out of the ghetto. The main problem will remain an institutional one however. Who is going to plan and organize interdisciplinary research in our contemporary academic world where interdisciplinarity is constantly promoted in principle but hardly ever put into practice? The trouble could be that private research will take up the challenge. But how will it escape being normative?

José Lambert is professor of Comparative Literature at the Catholic University of Leuven (Belgium), where he heads the Leuven Research Center for Translation, Communication and Cultures (CETRA). He is also a founder of TRANSCETRA, a European-wide distance learning program, and an officer in the European Society for Translation Studies (EST). Ilis research and writing focus on descriptive translation studies as well as on media translation. The International Encyclopedia of Translation Studies (de Gruyter, Berlin) counts him as one of its editors.

3

Audiovisual Translation
and New Media

Patrick Cattrysse

As new forms of international and intercultural communication appear, new forms of translation and adaptation arise with them, and traditional concepts have to be updated. This chapter proposes a functional-historical definition of translation or adaptation that stems from the so-called polysystem theories of translation. It leads to a number of interesting new questions about translation and adaptation research and training.

This study of audiovisual translation is based on a research project that started near the end of 1985 and dealt with the development of a theory for film adaptation studies. The project experimented with some specific theories of translation studies, called the polysystem (PS) theories of translation, on the hypothesis that there are important similarities between film adaptation and translation. These similarities appear not only on the level of the transfer process, but also on the level of critical approach. Since the completion of the project, film adaptation and translation studies have evolved along their own lines, and several publications in each field of work have appeared. This study reviews some of the results achieved in the field of film adaptation studies in order to examine a couple of methodological repercussions affecting adaptation and translation studies in general. In this chapter, I also briefly point out some of the major programmatic points of the PS approach, adding along the way remarks on certain topics that remain controversial, even within the PS discussion. One conclusion of the present study is that continuing changes in the field of communication may bring adaptation and translation studies quite close to each other, maybe closer than some scholars would like them to be.

Some Methodological Polysystem Principles

The polysystem (PS) approach starts from the hypothesis that communication does not occur arbitrarily. After all, if everything could mean anything, there would be no communication. The PS approach thus adopts the hypothesis that communication must follow some rules, which it defines as "norms" and "systems" and takes as two key concepts of the PS approach. Furthermore, the PS hypothesis differs from previous translation and adaptation theories by its target-oriented approach as well as by its descriptive nature. As a consequence, the concepts that are studied on an object level are labeled in a functional way.

Norms

The concept of a "norm" may be defined as "an energetic principle that determines behavior in a non-idiosyncratic way." Each time that a norm is supposed to have determined semiotic behavior, that behavior follows similar options in a similar situation. Such norms are descriptive norms, because they refer to actual behavior. In this respect, they differ from normative norms that relate to wishful behavior.

The distinction between normative and descriptive norms is very useful, as I have demonstrated in a study on the impact of the Hays Office in film noir adaptations in the 1940s and 1950s (Cattrysse, 1990, pp. 270-72; Cattrysse, 1996). Normative norms do not always correspond with descriptive norms. Sometimes, both types of norms relate to quite opposite types of behavior. Elsewhere (Cattrysse, 1992b) I have explained how from the 1920s on, a reactionary formula emerged in the field of the literary detective genre: A tough guy private eye variant revolted against the classical "Whodunit" formula. In that study, I observed how an ever larger number of normative norms were published as "Rules of the Game" (the "game" referred to was, of course, the classical whodunit formula) as the tough guy private eye variant grew more successful and deviated more and more from the traditional whodunit formula. The more that normative norms took the field, the more that descriptive norms deviated from those normative regulations.

Normative norms are often put in writing. We find them in classical grammars, indicating the so-called possibilities of semiotic systems. In such grammars, they refer to future, possible, and often expected, preferable, or "correct" options within a semiotic system. Descriptive norms appear in actual behavior. As a consequence, we can detect them only after the fact. What's more, descriptive norms are not the same as the verbalizations that paraphrase such norms in positive and negative ways (for example, an order or a prohibition). To put it another way, the positive or negative character of a norm refers more often to the verbalization of the norm than to the norm itself.

Norms can function in a more or less strict way. That is why Toury (1995) places norms somewhere between idiosyncrasies and absolute rules. One of the observations I made during my analysis of the Hays Office showed an interesting correlation between the normative and descriptive norms on the one hand, and the potency of these norms on the other. The correlation showed that the stricter the normative norms were (for example, in matters of nudity and sex), the more these norms were respected in practice and the more they then corresponded to the descriptive norms. The correlation also showed that where normative norms were more tolerant or hesitant, for example, in matters of alcoholism or violence, adaptation policy was ambiguous and descriptive norms deviated from those normative norms.

The distinction between normative and descriptive norms puts a regularly recurring question in a new light: Can norms be broken? In his new book, Toury (1995, p. 55), quoting Hermans (1991, p. 162), repeats that "non-compliance with a norm in particular instances does not invalidate the norm." Non-compliance on an individual scale does not invalidate a norm, whether descriptive or normative. Non-compliance in a general way, however, does invalidate or change a descriptive norm, and it is exactly in this way that descriptive norms can start deviating from normative norms, and eventually change the normative norms, or turn back towards compliance with the older normative norms, or find some evolutionary way in-between.

Sometimes, norms are presented as constraints situated between absolute rules (de Saussure's *langue* or the sum total of possibilities offered by a semiotic system) and idiosyncratic practices encountered in the working field (de Saussure's *parole*). This definition of norms seems to confuse two aspects of norms that might better be distinguished: the power of a norm and its reference to actual or wishful behavior. It is on the first level that Toury originally distinguished absolute rules from idiosyncrasies. According to him, absolute rules do not refer to the *langue* or the possible options offered by a semiotic system. They refer rather to a type of constraint that has powerfully determined a corpus of semiotic devices in a general, absolute way (see Bakker, 1995, p. 33).

Systems

When descriptive norms function systematically, they constitute a system of communicative behavior. Norms and systems are thus two sides of the same coin we call communicative behavior. Now while it is true that the concept of a "system" is controversial (even within PS studies), and that communicative practice is not completely systematic, it is also true that the concept of a system is a useful one.

The concept of system refers to open systems and not to closed ones. By open, I mean that not all features of an analyzed communicative behavior occur necessarily in a systematic way. The system concept also refers to a heterogeneous and dynamic entity. And finally, a system is always a conglomerate of norms identified and constructed by scholars after the fact and as an act of interpretation. A system can thus contain different types of constraints as well as different types of semiotic devices. One consequence of such an open and dynamic view of a system is that it is often hard, if not impossible, to distinguish for example, between "purely" literary and "purely" filmic components within a literary or filmic system. The fact that systems are dynamic means they change through time and space while still being recognized as, or presenting themselves as, the same systems.

Because systems are open, dynamic, and the result of an interpretation act, they challenge the views of some PS scholars who claim that PS theory provides an empirical science and actually predicts communicative behavior. While PS theory may have an empirical and predictive capacity when dealing with very general principles (for example, in postulating that, when a film or literary genre starts losing public interest, it will either change or disappear), predicting communicative behavior on a more microscopic level is somewhat hazardous, in as much as communicative behavior is not wholly systematic.

A Target-Oriented and Descriptive Approach

Finally, I want to mention two other revolutionary innovations brought about by the PS theory of translation and adaptation: (1) an orientation to the target rather than the source and (2) an approach that emphasizes the description of translation and adaptation phenomena. Traditionally, critical and scientific discourse on translation and adaptation was, and sometimes still remains, source-text oriented. Translations and adaptations were studied, sometimes even defined, on the basis of predefined ideas of adequacy with a particular source text. The PS approach turns this procedure upside down. Its

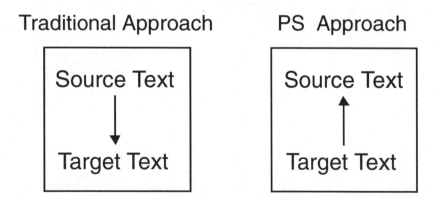

Figure 1

starting point is the translation or adaptation as a finished product and functioning in a particular target context (see Figure 1). Whereas traditional discourse on translation and adaptation focuses on faithfully reconstructing a source text, the PS approach starts from the target text, and explains that, apart from the source text, other norms and models, situated in the target context, may have played a role in the production and perception of the translation or adaptation.

A Functional Approach

The PS revolution implies a redefinition of some concepts. We can no longer define translations or adaptations on the basis of *a priori* determined adequacy conditions. Therefore translations and adaptations are redefined in a functional way and take as their starting point the target culture, allowing us to say that translations or adaptations are phenomena that function as such in the target culture. The term "function" is a theoretical concept that for the purpose of research means "to present itself and/or to be perceived as." The functional definition of "translation," "adaptation," "film noir," or "western" for that matter, is thus "every phenomenon that functions as such," that is "that presents itself and/or is perceived as a translation, an adaptation, a remake, a film noir, or a western." As a consequence, a functional definition turns out to be more of a historical description of how phenomena have functioned in a particular context. New subsequent questions are therefore: Who decides what is translation and adaptation in a certain community? And on the basis of what criteria?

Such redefined questions and concepts show that the functioning of translation and adaptation concepts and phenomena is much more complex than we had imagined. At the same time, it enables research to present a more subtle and historical account of the functioning of those phenomena. Closed questions yield to open questions such as "Do these movies function as film adaptations in this particular historical context?" A simple Yes or No does not answer the question since a detailed description and explanation is needed. This observation explains why film adaptations or translations that are approached in a functional way do not represent "observable facts." The act of describing how phenomena function is an act of interpretation. On the other hand, the need to interpret phenomena does not imply that the functional approach is in any way arbitrary.

Comments on a Functional Approach

A functional approach has helped the study of film noir and film noir adaptations in many respects. For example, one of the chronic problems within film noir studies was generated by an *a priori* definition of the term "film noir" and the use of this definition in film studies. Approaching the film noir discussion in a functional way, however, has helped to solve the definition problem by showing that the concept is not static but dynamic and changing ever since its conception in 1946.

A functional approach to the definition of translation and adaptation has also helped the study of film adaption by freeing it from pointless discussions about terminology. What's more, this approach has given film adaptation studies and translation studies a much enlarged field of study, and at the same time, raised new and interesting questions about aspects of film adaptation no one had even raised before. In this larger field of study, for example, pseudo-translations or unfaithful adaptations of popular and even semi-literary texts could now also be researched. New questions arose, asking about possible systemic relationships between the function of a finished translation or adaptation and the transfer process.

Does this mean that a functional approach has solved all possible problems? No, of course not. One remaining problem has to do with the question of how we study translational phenomena that do not function as translations or adaptations. Two other problems have to do with the confusion between discourse about translation on an object-level and discourse on a meta-level, and the clear distinction between research that is concerned with a normative approach and research that is descriptive.

Translational Phenomena that Do Not Function as Translations

A functional definition of translation presents one major problem. If translation or adaptation is defined as any phenomenon that functions as such, how can we study phenomena that show clear traces of transfer processes and relationships, but do not function as translations or adaptations? In one study (1992a), I have suggested how we can recover those phenomena by postulating a distinction between an object of study and a working field (see also Cattrysse, 1994a; Lambert, 1995b, p. 171; and Toury, 1995, p. 33). An object of study refers to the phenomena that function in a particular way in a particular context. The working field represents every part of reality that may be relevant for the analysis of the object of study and that may be studied as a semiotic device. And these semiotic devices are not studied in the abstract; they are examined within and in relation with their respective historical contexts. In short, a working field may be extended to reality as a whole.

Placing an object of study in a larger working field permits us to recover those phenomena that present similar features to the selected object of study, but function in a different way. It also helps us to analyze how and why different phenomena function in a similar manner. For example, in the case of the film noir, quite different types of movies function as film noir within the one genre. And to give another example, not all movies adapting the story of a novel function as filmic adaptations of novels.

Level		Attitude
Object-level	Object of study	Functional or descriptive attitude
	Working field	

Meta-level	Theory	Normative attitude

Figure 2

Object-level versus Meta-level and a Descriptive versus a Normative Attitude

A second problem is more tenacious, and results from scholars who confuse two things. On the one hand, they confuse discourse on a so-called object-level with discourse on meta-level; on the other hand, they confuse a descriptive approach to research with a normative approach (Cattrysse, 1992a, p. 62; Cattrysse, 1994a, p. 73). To adopt a functional approach means that on the object-level, that is, on the level of the object of study and the working field, a researcher has to adopt a functional, that is a descriptive-explanatory and historic approach. On the meta-level, that is on the level of theory or descriptive apparatus, the researcher must adopt a normative and ahistoric approach. Schematically, this agreement can be represented as in Figure 2.

Descriptive versus Normative

A descriptive or functional approach implies that researchers relegate definitions and labels to the object-level and no longer advance their own criteria and definitions. Instead, they describe how, and explain why, certain phenomena have functioned the way they have in a particular historical context.

Critics may say that the distinction between a descriptive and normative approach is untenable, that in the end, every approach is necessarily normative since researchers cannot but decide themselves how to define or verbalize phenomena. My reply is that, however real this objection, there still remains a difference between these two approaches. In a normative approach, scholars formulate their own criteria in order to identify and define objects of study. In a descriptive approach, they decide to identify and define an object not on the basis of their own criteria, but rather on the basis of criteria applied explicitly or implicitly by other users in a particular historical context. Obviously, in both approaches, researchers take the initiative; in both approaches, they make their own decisions. But in the normative method, they decide to make their own decisions without taking into account historical uses, while in the descriptive method they decide to accept, describe, and eventually explain the decisions made by others. Since in both approaches they make their own decisions, the difference is not one of nature, but rather one of degree. In a normative approach, scholars foreground themselves; in a descriptive approach, they are less inclined to do so, because a descriptive approach creates "distance" between the researchers and the phenomena they are describing and explaining. Bakker (1995) calls this the "meta-leap." I prefer to call it more modestly one meta-step-back from the object level. Taking this one step back permits the scholar to be less subjective.

Descriptive versus Objective

Keeping a clear distinction between the object-level and meta-level permits us to maintain a clear distinction between a descriptive and a normative approach. These distinctions enable a functional PS approach to raise its scientific standards by adopting a descriptive approach where possible, and a normative one where necessary. As indicated in Figure 2, a distinction between object-level and meta-level allows us to research less subjectively and more descriptively with regard to the object of study and the working field; at the same time, it permits us to place a more subjective, normative attitude on the level of theory or descriptive apparatus.

I purposely avoid the term "objective" because it is clear this meta-step-back does not provide the PS approach any assurance of objectivity. Research into any object of study in any working field is always colored by the theoretical tools that are used to make the analysis. In this respect, it is important not to treat descriptive translation or adaptation studies as objective studies. Scholars always remain part and parcel of the world they are studying, and they can never step outside this world. Even if they could, they would always approach that same world from one particular point of view, since it is impossible to perceive this world from all points of view at the same time, let alone describe it that way. Since absolute impartiality in research is impossible, the most honest procedure is to make as explicit as possible the points of view that we are adopting during an analysis.

In this respect, it is interesting to notice how results vary according to the point of view that is taken. A brief experiment with students analyzing a group of recent American movies has shown some interesting results. If a film adaptation is considered from the point of view of the literary source text, many omissions are noted, and the film adaptation seems reductionist and a simplification. If however, the film adaptation is analyzed from the point of view of photography, setting, design, or music, the analysis reveals many additions and elements that complete the literary source text in as many ways. Clearly it is important to change perspectives from time to time, not only to learn more about the adaptation process, but also about the relativity of the "observations" that were made previously.

It is therefore prudent not to put too much stress on the so-called objective or empirical status of descriptive translation and adaptation studies. After all, whatever the position one takes, the object of study remains a construct resulting from an act of interpretation. Since sensory perception passes through many filters before leading to a mentally constructed perception; and since human knowledge, even in the natural sciences, is indirect and determined by intermediate factors such as linguistic competence and theoretical and methodological approaches, it is better to speak about factors diminishing subjectivity or idiosyncrasy, rather than to suggest that total objectivity is possible.

In this regard, I would also refrain from calling translations or adaptations "observable facts" (Toury, 1995, pp. 23-25), given the problems with so-called "facts" and historical research that many epistemologists have often dealt with (Lorenz, 1987, pp. 24-26). On this point, I agree again with Bakker (1995), who urges a collaboration between descriptive translation studies, which are sometimes too empirical, and certain deconstructionist approaches (Cattrysse, 1992b).

Theory and Terminology at the Meta-level

By theory or descriptive apparatus, I mean the theoretical concepts and the methodology that are used to examine an object of study and a working field. By contrast with the descriptive and historical labels and concepts that are used at an object-level, the theoretical concepts are necessarily defined in a normative and ahistorical way, for example, analytical tools such as focalization. These theoretical concepts are necessarily put forth in a normative way because researchers have to define their analytical tools and agree on certain labels and concepts in order to communicate their findings to each other and to their academic community. The theoretical concepts are ahistorical in as much as they function in a "here and now" situation. Of course, this does not imply that theoretical tools are created once and for all as invariable, static terms. They are analytical tools and they are used for scientific analyses. These analyses provide feedback about the viability of the analytical tools, so that some tools may prove to be very practical, whereas others may prove to be useless or in need of adaptation.

In translation studies, many researchers have pleaded for a coherent and scientifically founded method. In film adaptation studies, seriously developed methodological proposals still remain hard to find (Cattrysse, 1994b), even though the use of a coherent and systematic methodology and terminology is absolutely necessary. If there is no systematic theory, researchers proceed in their own idiosyncratic way, using personal terminology and methods with no possibility to coordinate, accumulate, or even compare research results. Also, there is no way to avoid overlapping efforts and leaving gaps in a research program.

It seems to me that, if a new discipline such as descriptive translation studies or film adaptation studies is to be accepted as a full-fledged academic discipline, it will have to standardize its scientific terminology, although such standardization will probably be difficult, if not impossible, without resorting to some institutional organization(s), the competence of which is commonly accepted by the academic community. It is in this kind of organizational forum that, in a democratic way, any theoretical and methodological discussion about the definitions of analytical tools should take place. It is in this forum also that researchers should debate the viability of their analytical tools, and the need to fine-tune them (Rey, 1995, pp. 32-34; Lambert & Robyns, in press.)

Some Confusion

Confusion results when research on the object-level does not clearly distinguish between a normative approach and a descriptive approach, just as confusion results when research fails to distinguish between an object-level and meta-level. The first type of confusion has existed practically from the beginning. For example, in the article where Toury proposed a functional definition of translation as a final product, he also defined the translation process as:

> an act (or a process) which is performed (or occurs) over and across systemic borders. In the widest of its possible senses it is a series of operations, or procedures, whereby one semiotic entity, which is a [functional] constituent (element) of a certain cultural (sub)system, is transformed into another semiotic entity, which forms at least a potential element of another cultural (sub)system, providing that some informational core is retained "invariant under transformation," and on its basis a relationship known as "equivalence" is established between the resultant and initial entities. (1986, p. 1112)

The purpose of Toury's definition was obvious, of course: to account for the enlargement of the object of study and the working field due to the functional definition of translation as a product. A true functional definition of the translation process, however, would have been: any process or phenomenon that functions as a translation process. A similar approach to the study of the film adaptation process has revealed, for example, that not all transfer processes function in the same way. Some function as adaptation processes, while others, and even similar transfer processes, do not.

A second type of confusion stems from an uncertainty about terminology. Is it being used at an object-level or at a meta-level? Sometimes, the distinction is easy to see, for example, when we use technical terms that differ clearly from everyday language. Terminology can become problematical, however, when everyday, common language words like "translation," "adaptation," and "genre" are used for scientific purposes, such as in classi-fications and typologies. The problem arises because those words were never meant to fulfill a scientific function since they were never designed accord-ing to scientific or academic criteria. When we researchers use terms and definitions, we must ask ourselves: Are we referring to an object of study or are we referring to theoretical tools for analytical purposes? If we talk about "translation" or "adaptation," are we referring to phenomena that function as translations and adaptations, or are we referring to our own definitions and analytical instruments for theorizing about translation and adaptation? As an example of a problematic definition of "translation," I quote the global and hypothetical definition by Lambert and Robyns, "We may...define translation in the largest sense as migration-through-transformation of discursive ele-ments (signs), a process during which they are interpreted (re-contextual-ized) according to different norms, codes, and models" (in press, p. 11).

This definition raises a number of questions: Who is defining "transla-tion" and on what level? "We may...define" suggests a normative definition on the part of Lambert and Robyns and a normative approach suggests that the discussion is situated on a theoretical meta-level. On the other hand, "translation in the largest sense" suggests a descriptive approach on the ba-sis of which researchers study a large number of phenomena that have or have not functioned as translations in different historical contexts, and then inductively reach a generalizing statement about those phenomena. This ap-proach becomes problematic if the historical corpus that supports this induc-tion is not made explicit.

Other questions that critics raise include: Does such enlarging the con-cepts of translation and adaptation not lead to a metaphorical use of these terms? Does an extended research definition of translation or adaptation that does not coincide with the common usage of these concepts present a prob-lem? If we can no longer distinguish "translation," "rewording," "adapta-tion," "condensation," and related operations, do translation and adaptation studies have a future? Or will they merge into one large, generalist field of intertextual or intersystemic studies? These questions remain unsolved be-cause it is not clear whether the definition is descriptive or normative. How-ever, we can help resolve these questions by a simple technique of reformu-lation. For example, Lambert (1995b, p. 171) replaces the concept "translation," which often refers to a single, unified text, with "translational devices," thereby eliminating all confusion about whether terminology is situated on the object-level or meta-level.

In any event, a clear distinction between object-level and meta-level voids any criticism that the concepts "translation" or "adaptation" are used in two disparate meanings; or, that researchers' definitions of translation or adaptation show little or no resemblance to the concept that is used in every-day language. When new terms are created or old ones redefined and explicitly posited on the meta-level, everybody is clear about what is meant by what, since object-level language and meta-level language now represent different languages, and similarity or dissimilarity between the two becomes irrelevant.

Precise Terminological Discussions

When we clearly distinguish between discussions on an object-level and those on a meta-level, we must also clearly distinguish between the terminology used on these two different levels. By doing so, scholars can place their meta-terminological discussion on a theoretical level, where rules proper to theoretical discussions are respected. Another benefit of such precise terminological discussions is that terminological discussions would not obstruct practical historical research. We would, in short, help solve the problem about which Toury complains: "rejection(s) of somebody else's concepts on the grounds that they are untenable within one's own frame of reference" (Toury, 1995, p. 24).

Pending a meta-terminological standardization, practical historical research can proceed without delay on the object-level. What's more, while researchers organize and finalize terminological discussion on the meta-level, other findings realized in the meantime on the object-level can only help researchers develop, construct, and correct their meta-terminological discussions. It should be evident that the demand for a clearer distinction between object-level and meta-level does not mean that theoreticians should proceed without knowing practical research, nor that historical scholars should conduct their research without methodological expertise. As I have elsewhere explained (1994a, p. 73), both types of activities complement each other, and the distinction is not meant to divide historians as mere consumers of theory from theoreticians as mere providers of theory. Both groups of researchers have to provide feedback to each other. Only then will theory be up-to-date, and only then will practical research proceed in the most efficient way.

Descriptive Definitions and Universals

When we distinguish between an object-level and a meta-level, we throw fresh light on some recurring questions, for example, whether we can define translation or adaptation once and for all as universal concepts, outside any specific context. The answer to this question is: Yes, of course, since it has been done. After all, general rules taken from large corpora can lead to descriptive, historical, and at the same time very general definitions. The aforementioned definitions by Toury (1986) and Lambert and Robyns (in press) offer good examples. Such general definitions have the advantage of showing some fundamental characteristics common to all the phenomena that at one time or another, and in one place or another, have functioned as translations and adaptations. One disadvantage, of course, is that such definitions can become too abstract to hold any concrete meaning. Another is that they may present translations or adaptations as static and homogeneous phenomena that are defined in a normative way. This is especially true when the specific corpora that have led to the definitions and rules are not explicitly mentioned.

Another interesting point about "universal" definitions concerns their purpose. Are they supposed to describe inductively all phenomena that have ever functioned as translations and adaptations? Do they aim at identifying a static idea about what translation or adaptation should be, in order to ignore those phenomena that do not correspond to the prescribed definition? Or, on the contrary, do they rather serve to indicate a larger working field, the analysis of which might show even more fundamental characteristics of a defined object of study? The latter seems, at least partly, to be the purpose of the above mentioned definitions by Toury and Lambert and Robyns: to suggest a larger research program during which researchers can recover more translational phenomena than have been studied traditionally in translation studies. By stressing "in the widest of its possible senses" (Toury, 1986, p. 1112), or "translation in the largest sense" (Lambert & Robyns, in press), the authors want to describe a new and wider working field and prevent any *a priori* exclusion of relevant phenomena.

Binary versus Multilateral Approach

A functional approach to the adaptation process (as opposed to the approach that views adaptation as a final product) of the American film noir has led to an interesting observation: These film adaptations generally process more than one source text at a time. Whereas so-called film adaptations of novels "use" novels and adapt their narrative material—that is, main happenings, main characters, and eventually some of the main narrative characteristics—they are also determined on other levels by other modeling material. For example, the acting style might follow or react against some method acting conventions based on Konstantin Stanislavski or Lee Strasberg; photography may adapt still photography, other photographic conventions in cinematography, or even drawing or painting; or, film music may again follow or not follow previous filmic and non-filmic musical conventions. As a consequence, film adaptations generally show many types of transfer relationships with a wide variety of modeling source material. This observation has provoked the suggestion that it might be more appropriate to replace the binary approach of one source text (modeling semiotic device) and one target text (cf. Figure 1) by a multilateral approach (Figure 3).

In this star-like model, the different T1 sources (modeling semiotic devices) refer to many different types of modeling source material: narrative, acting style, setting, photography, music, and sound as well as the surrounding cultural, political, and social norms and conventions. All of these source materials may have determined the production and reception of the final T2

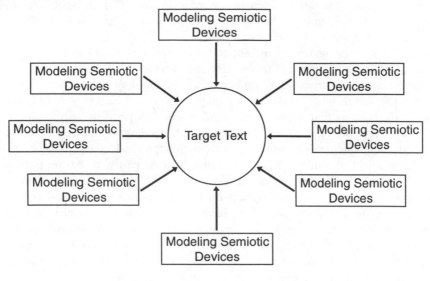

Figure 3

(target text). The fact that arrows only point in one direction suggests that a scholar can only adopt one point of view at a time. Of course, it is possible that influences go both ways, as in the case of the film noir adaptation history. But in that case, research adopts another perspective. Another point about this star-like approach is that it opens up a new series of interesting issues, for example, the target text shows traces of many transfer processes and relationships, but not all the processes and relationships function in the same way.

Taking up the case of the film noir adaptation again, it is clear that here some types of transfer process are made explicit, sometimes even advertised, and perceived as such by the public. Others, however, remain quite hidden and present that aspect of the adaptation as "original." These hidden aspects of adaptation are thus generally not perceived as adaptational by the public.

Adopting a functional approach to the study of the adaptation process leads to a greater awareness of both visible and hidden adaptations and to an interesting question: Which types of transfer processes and relationships function how, and why do they function in that specific way? I have explored this question elsewhere and explained how, for example, film noir remakes use transfer processes that are similar to adaptations of non-filmic material, but function quite differently (1992b, pp. 67-69). One advantage of this line of research is that it introduces film adaptation studies (and translation studies?) into the larger field of comparative film (or literary) studies. This move, however, will not go unchallenged since traditionally, west European universities separate translation studies from comparative literature. At the same time, the lack of any similar institutionalized specialization in the field of film studies could present an advantage.

Consequences of a Comparative or Intersystemic Approach

A multilateral and functional approach to the adaptation process has a number of consequences with respect to some traditional translational concepts. I will limit my discussion to three of these: intermediate translation, the concept of original, and the concept of pseudo-translation.

Intermediate Translation or Adaptation

The concept of intermediate translation (Toury, 1995, pp. 129-130) represents one instance of the binary model shown in Figure 1 and implies that translations translate single texts as whole texts. By placing T1 (source text), T1', and T2 (target text) on a single line, the concept of intermediate translation misleadingly suggests that the T2 could only be determined by the T1 via the intermediate T1'. In a multilateral approach (Figure 3), the so-called T1 is initially put next to the so-called intermediate T1'. But at the same time, T1 is studied next to many other types of T1s. After all, many relationships may (pre)exist between the different types of T1s that have functioned as a model for the production and perception of the T2. This hypothesis is not presupposed, but remains a question to be examined. Furthermore, the different T1s do not refer to entire texts only; they can also stand for parts of texts or groups of texts. That is why we consider them "modeling semiotic devices." The purpose of the analysis consists in examining how different models and norms have determined the production and perception of the translation or adaptation.

Putting the T1, T1', and T2 on a single line also perpetuates the binary representation of a source system that is totally separated from a target system. The PS study of the film noir adaptation has shown that this is not necessarily true. The American film noir and the novels which they adapted, for example, were both part of the same American popular cultural system, and some parts of the filmic and literary systems clearly overlapped. When we represent *a priori* a source system and a target system as hermetically separated, we can obstruct the study of features both systems may have in common.

For these reasons, I believe the "star" model is more helpful. Among other things, it corresponds better with the Peircean idea of semiosis or meaning-making as an infinite chain, regressing into the past. Within this line of thinking, every "original" constitutes some sort of "intermediate" text or semiotic device that has led to some kind of "translation," which in its turn, has been processed into a new type of target message (Lambert & Robyns, in press).

The Concept of an Original

A multilateral approach also involves consequences with respect to the traditional notion of an "original." On the basis of film noir adaptation study, it is plain that every film noir shows traces of transfer processes and transfer relationships, although these processes and relationships do not always function as such. In these films, for instance, parts of scores come back, photography shows influences from specific German expressionistic models, and the mere presence of actors evokes memories of previous and later movies. Most of these links, however, do not function as adaptational relationships. Still, we could not tell any difference in nature between these relationships and the explicit adaptational ones with the processed novels. Some movies (or aspects of movies) functioning as originals (or as original aspects) appear therefore to be pseudo-original, just like some adaptations or translations have appeared to be pseudo-translations or adaptations.

The concept of a pseudo-original puts some traditional translational terms in a different perspective, and has prompted Toury to note that "An interesting field for study is therefore comparative: the nature of translational norms as compared to those governing non-translational kinds of text-production" (1995, p. 61).

The distinction between translational and non-translational norms corresponds with my own distinction between operational and transformational norms (1992b, pp. 37-38). Both distinctions are, however, equally problematic. If originals actually represent pseudo-originals, how can we distinguish non-translational text-production (Toury, 1995, p. 59) from translational text-production? Again, only a functional approach seems to offer a way out. On a meta-level, translational and non-translational phenomena are therefore probably best defined in an historical way as phenomena that at one time or another and in one place or another have functioned as such.

The Concept of Pseudo-Translation

Finally, what has been said about the pseudo-original applies *grosso modo* to the phenomenon of pseudo-translation. Toury defines pseudo-translations as "texts which have been presented as translations with no corresponding source texts in other languages ever having existed—hence no factual 'transfer operations' and translation relationships" (Toury, 1995, p. 40). Disregarding the fact that translational phenomena do not always represent whole texts, we may say this: If every semiotic device that functions as an original device actually shows, or better, hides translational or adaptational relationships that may or may not be detected afterwards through analysis, there are no pseudo-translations, or at least the definition of pseudo-translation has to be adapted. If, as Toury argues, pseudo-translations pretend to present translational relationships with previous modeling material, which they actually do, they are not pseudo-translations but simple translations.

Of course, this is not what the "pseudo" in "pseudo-translation" actually refers to. The "pseudo" refers to modeling source material that does not exist or has not functioned in the way it is presented by the pseudo-translation and perceived by the public. On a meta-level, we may conclude that pseudo-translations (or adaptations) are phenomena that, for some reason, not only hide or leave implicit part or all of their modeling source material (which all translations and adaptations do), but even make alleged modeling source material explicit in a misleading way. As a consequence, transfer relationships are presented and perceived under false pretenses.

New Types of Communication and Translation

New types of communication bring along new types of message processing. If we accept a functional approach to translation and adaptation and the concept of a large working field, these new types of message processing can also be studied within translation and adaptation studies. These phenomena may not necessarily function as translations or adaptations, but a comparative analysis with phenomena that do function as translations or adaptations may be highly instructive. From a functional perspective, two key questions are: how and why these new types of message processing function the way they do in their specific historical context.

A Functional Approach to Audiovisual Translation

Although some traditional translation scholars still think of translation as a purely linguistic concept rather than as a complex amalgam of socio-semiotic devices, contemporary descriptive translation studies with its functional approach realizes that we can no longer isolate the traditional linguistic factor from the surrounding communicational and contextual components of the total communication. The shift from the study of written translation to the analysis of oral interpretation already suggests that linguistic communication cannot be studied in the abstract and that many nonverbal elements surround so-called linguistic communication, as the study of subtitling and dubbing (which launched the concept of audiovisual translation) has shown.

This observation leads me to return to a thesis I defended several years ago (1990). There I made a plea for linguistic, literary, and translation studies to collaborate more closely with communication studies. Whereas the former disciplines have generally neglected the importance of nonverbal semiotics, the latter have generally underestimated the importance of verbal components in international and intercultural communication. Furthermore, content analysis has never been a strong point in west European communication studies. A closer collaboration between translation studies and communication studies would not, as some fear, lead to the disappearance of the verbal component in the field of study. On the contrary, it would lead to a study that puts all communicative components in their proper relationship to each other.

Dubbing

In order to demonstrate the importance of an integrated communicational approach, I'll discuss briefly the study of dubbing. The use of the term audiovisual translation suggests that the verbal component constitutes only one integral part of the total audiovisual communication. The example of dubbed dialogue in feature films is a case in point. Writing dialogue is a speciality, and not all screen writers are equally adept at dealing with dialogue. Some writers specialize in plot development, others in character development, and many others manage both specialities very well. Dialogue writing, however, is often a speciality offered by one person who does not do anything else.

In a classical narrative screenplay, dialogue often fulfills several functions at the same time. Above all, dialogue is action: It furthers the narrative and defines the characters at the same time. Not only what characters say, but how they speak or do not speak are important and significant. Dialogue is always part and parcel of the action, since people say and do things at the same time. What people do when talking is called counteraction, a technique that serves to complement not only verbal speech but the whole act of communication as well.

The study of screenwriting and dialogue ought to interest translation scholars and trainers. The latter are not necessarily concerned with strict originality, as historical research has amply shown. So, the original situation of a dialogue writer might be interesting to those trainers who are concerned to render a so-called faithful translation. And when training translators in dubbing, it might be advisable to insert aspects of screenwriting into the training program. The former profit from a comparison between the respective situations of an original screenwriter and a translator of the dubbed version. Some research questions are: To what extent are dubbing translators trained in screenwriting, dialogue writing, and/or writing for spoken language in general? Is there a significant difference in dubbed versions made by translators who are also screenwriters? In what way?

New Types of Communication and Translation

New technologies enable new types of communication, and in the new world of media communications, the buzzwords are multimedia, hypermedia, interactivity, and Internet. In this new world, old boundaries disappear, global communication becomes a norm, and new types of international and intercultural communication bring new types of translation, adaptation, and message processing. These new phenomena may not function as translations or adaptations, but they can surely be studied in a functional approach within translation and adaptation studies, since a functional approach starts precisely from the hypothesis that forms of communication evolve in time and space.

New types of communication bring new terminological difficulties, since new technologies result in new ways of organizing work and competencies. Consequently, traditional translation tasks are modified, old concepts are changed, and new ones invented. This is why not only translation research, but also training is adapting to new situations.

Multimedia Production

Multimedia productions offer a clear example of how traditional approaches to linear video production, graphic design, copywriting, and programming are being modified, and how different specialists work in new ways to produce interactive multimedia programs. A traditional writing function no longer exists. Writers are information designers, who know how to communicate with sound and moving image, how to lay out text with graphics, and how to copy-fit words for the screen design. For many traditional (screen)writers today, new and complicated technical requirements and skills make it difficult to find work in the interactive multimedia production process.

A query at a very productive screen writers' discussion group on the Internet about their experiences with writing for interactive multimedia provoked responses about the great difference between writing for interactive media and writing for linear programs. Among other things, the former demands too much technical knowledge to be able to compete and collaborate with engineers, programmers, designers, and technicians. Part of the problem lies with the way professional authoring systems are designed. These authoring tools generally make little or no distinction between the scripting process and the process of media assembly. As a consequence, writers and information designers find themselves standing before a dilemma: Either they get acquainted with an authoring tool in order to keep control over their project, or they have to rely on a programmer early on in the preproduction process. This situation explains probably why very often computer specialists and programmers sometimes take over the construction and/or writing process from the writers. Needless to say, this production situation influences the content of the interactive programs that are made. Translating and adapting this material across language and culture barriers implies similar shifts in task and competence organization. Actually, this is one of the major problems confronting the multimedia industry in Europe today.

Hypermedia

Hypermedia and interactivity allow new "genres" to be born. For example, some interactive hyperfiction has already been developed and led to the development of a body of research. Well-documented publications in print and on the Internet have come from Charles Deemer, Stuart Moulthrop, George Landow, Greg Ulmer, Jim Rosenburg, and V. Balasubramanian. A good introduction is Deemer (1994). For an extensive bibliography, see Harpold (1991).

Most of these publications and related conferences are ignored by translation and adaptation scholars, although some of these publications and conferences deal with the topics of conversion or adaptation. For example, Balasubramanian (1994) deals with several conversion issues, such as converting into hypertexts and vice versa. The author also deals with the problem of translating hypertexts into other hypertexts.

Even a brief look at these new forms of translation and the research they are producing shows many similarities with the traditional normative approach to translation. First, the point of view taken is that of the adapter or translator, not that of the researcher. Research is done in terms of "how to." In this respect, we must also conclude that a PS approach to translation and adaptation studies has largely gone unnoticed by hypertext and hypermedia scholars. Consequently, Balasubramanian and others mix a descriptive approach with a normative one, as we see when the conversion from linear text to hypertext and the classical question of translatability come up:

> Printing a branching [hypertext] document in a linear fashion poses both technical and conceptual problems....It is easy to linearize a hypertext document having a strict hierarchical structure by performing a depth-first tree traversal, by printing the first chapter and its sections and moving onto the next chapter and so on. However, in the general case where the hypertext document is a highly connected network without any special order, it is very difficult to produce a good linear document. (Balasubramanian, 1994)

Adherence to a normative approach to translation probably explains why one writer concludes that "hypertext cannot be translated into print" (Moulthrop, 1995). Similar statements reveal the well-known normative definition of translation, based on *a priori* adequacy relations with one source text.

With respect to the conversion from one hypertext system to another, it has been said that most current hypertext systems are closed systems: "Material created in one system cannot be transferred or integrated with material created in another system because of proprietary document formats and storage mechanisms. Conversion programs are difficult to write since the formats are not disclosed by organizations" (Balasubramanian, 1994).

This citation illustrates that translation occurs on many different levels, and that, with the coming of new technologies, new challenges await the translation and adaptation scholar with respect to knowledge in matters of hypertext systems such as *Storyspace*, Hyper-Text Markup Language, and other software packages that allow writers to add interactivity to their communication. Manuals like Balasubramanian's remain interesting, however, because they provide normative norms. At the same time, researchers will want to check if and how these normative norms have determined actual adaptational and/or translational behavior, and in doing so, whether they have become descriptive norms.

Internet

With the Internet, boundaries of all kinds disappear, while at the same time, more global and more individual communication is made possible. The public access to the Internet and the electronic nature of its messages also have consequences for copyrighting and protecting intellectual property. Information that is put on the Internet can easily be copied or stolen. Even traditional references for notes and quotes no longer work with hypertext, since hypertexts do not use traditional page numbers, and they are regularly updated. It therefore becomes very hard to recover the original version to which a document is referring. After all, in the meantime, it has been adapted, rewritten, and modified, and all traces of previous version(s) have been erased! The deletion of previous electronic versions of messages powerfully illustrates that in a functional approach, traditional concepts like original will have to be adapted or redefined.

Conclusion

New types of electronic messages and especially a hyper-mode of communication involve new types of intertextual relations. Since translations and adaptations are largely determined by specific types of intertextual and intersystemic relations, these new technological evolutions will affect the study of translations and adaptations. On the one hand, we find ourselves in a revolution; on the other hand, some changes are not as revolutionary as we might think.

A hypertextual mode of text production puts the traditional concept of intertextuality in a different perspective. Whereas originally, the concept started from the hypothesis that a reader approaches a text with previous readings of other texts, hypertexts and hypermedia continue the same idea, but they add links with other texts which, through "hot spots," knobs, or other audiovisuals, are made explicit in the text, and by the author(s). This practice implies a number of interesting consequences:

- The study of markers in an intersystemic approach (Cattrysse, 1994a) becomes more varied and somewhat more complex.
- Interactive hypertexts may stress the activity of the reader or viewer, but they do not imply the death of the author; quite the contrary.
- The linear versus the non-linear nature of hypermedia is a relative concept since non-linearity refers often more to the production side than to the reception side. As Deemer (1994) explains, presenting hypermedia as non-linear may be misleading. "Any individual path through hypertext is linear, of course; the reader is still reading or viewing or hearing items in sequence, which is to say, one after the other, linearly. What makes hypertext hypertext is not non-linearity but choice, the interaction of the reader to determine which of several or many paths through the available information is the one taken at a certain moment in time."
- Examples of adaptations of so-called flatland novels into hyper-novels, or linear movies into interactive ones, suggest that our cultural tradition of storytelling will be challenged in many respects. What, for instance, will come of our narrative tradition with a main character, and a beginning, a middle, and an end? These hyper-adaptations suggest at the same time that the adaptational category of transfocalization (Cattrysse, 1992b, pp. 161-163) will become an important tool to describe these new types of adaptation. Also, hyper-adaptations from flatland novels or linear movies seem to show many similarities with traditional adaptations of short stories into long feature films. The category of the "addition" seems to play an important role here.
- Study of the American film noir adaptation has shown that genres are important factors in adaptational policy. This observation suggests that the coming of new genres such as hypernovels, hyper-drama, hyperpoems, and interactive television or movies, will result in new generic conventions, which in their turn, will largely determine translational and adaptational behavior.

Our overall final conclusion must be that translation and adaptation scholars will have to be flexible. Concepts as well as methods will have to adapt to the new forms of communication, and to the new forms of reality. If not, reality will pass them by, unnoticed, and the scholars, not reality, will be ignored and forgotten. This could hardly be the purpose of any type of scientific research.

Patrick Cattrysse is currently head of the postgraduate program "Culture and Communication" at the Catholic University of Brussels (Belgium). He lectures on comparative Film Studies, Film and Literature, Screenwriting, and Film Production. Since January of 1995 he has directed the Flemish Script Academy. Cattrysse earned a Ph.D. in Communication Studies from the Catholic University of Leuven (Belgium) with a dissertation on film adaptation as translation. Major publications include *Handboek Scenarioschrijven* (Garant, 1995) and *Pour une théorie de l'adaptation filmique: Le film noire américain* (Lang, 1992).

4

Understanding Audience Understanding

Paul A. Soukup, S.J.

Communication study has approached the issue of audience understanding of messages from the perspective of the message and from that of the audience. On the one hand, the "powerful-message" construct paints the audience as passive recipients of the meaning presented in the media. On the other hand, the "active audience" construct places most interpretive power in the audience, stressing their selectivity of messages, their use of the media, their social positions, and their ability to generate new messages based on the media. A middle position sees audience understanding emerge from an interaction between messages and audience members.

The American Bible Society's Multimedia Translations Project provides an interesting case study for reflection on the process of communication. By combining biblical translation with new media formats, it cuts across several boundaries of communication study—concern with and for the text, message formation, technical skills, and audience analysis. While communication research might legitimately contribute to each of these areas, this chapter will review only something of what we know about audiences.

The study of audiences intersects the study of messages. In fact, when dealing with these two areas, communication research tends to swing between two poles: powerful messages and powerful audiences. Currently, the research outlook suggests an interaction between the two, with audiences exerting some control over messages (White, 1994). To give at least an introductory sense of how communication researchers understand audiences and conceptualize how audiences understand messages, I will first review some of the materials from the perspective of powerful messages and then look at things from the perspective of powerful audiences, noting cognitive, behavioral, and emotional effects of the media. I will conclude by posing some models for understanding audiences, seeing how these might address questions of translation.

Powerful Messages

A focus on the power of media messages entered communication research early on. Most people now know the story of the "powerful effects" research tradition. Beginning from a theory of mass society in the 1920s, scholars conceptualized the audience in this way:

> Messages could be sent to every person to be received and understood more or less uniformly. Presumably, such messages would appeal to emotions and sentiments and sway the thinking or actions of each recipient in much the same way. Thus, the mass society concept yielded a theory of mass communication effects in which the media were seen as powerful, and their effects both uniform and direct among the members. (Lowery & DeFleur, 1983, p. 23)

Anecdotal evidence, particularly from advertising, fueled this theory. For example, a young William Paley left his family's cigar business to direct CBS after seeing sales skyrocket in his native Philadelphia when he placed radio ads on local stations.

The powerful messages/powerful effects pole of communication audience research contains several theoretical strands that still appear in later years. As implied above, the theory sees audiences as aggregates rather than as individuals. The theory further tends to regard audiences as passive recipients of messages and focuses on what Thomas Lindlof has termed "presented meaning" (1988, p. 84). In addition, while not denying their cognitive or emotional effects, it directs attention primarily to the behavioral effects of messages. Finally, the powerful messages construct builds on what James Carey (1989) has described as a "transport model" of communication in which the whole communication process is geared to delivering messages from sources to receivers.

Mass society theory increased the likelihood that communication researchers would think of audiences as aggregates. Survey research, whether for academic purposes or for agencies, reported data in terms of population segments; with a population as large as that of the United States, a market share could refer to millions of people. Communication research and marketing research soon became accustomed to charting the program preferences, voting patterns, buying habits, and other behaviors of social blocks. Improved sampling techniques led companies like the Gallup and Nielsen organizations to predict national trends in voting or viewing from relatively small groups of people. How audiences specifically understood messages did not matter as much as how audiences acted—or as much as how far the message reached. The prevailing assumption held that if the message was sent and the audience was exposed to it, it would have the intended effect.

In general this tradition regards audiences as passive. They understand messages primarily by receiving the messages. In its strong form, such a view becomes the "hypodermic needle" or "bullet theory" of communication, in which a message is shot into an audience. "Communication was seen as a magic bullet that transferred ideas or feelings or knowledge or motivations almost automatically from one mind to another" (Schramm, 1971, p. 8). This theory held particular strength in the war years:

> At that time, the audience was typically thought of as a sitting target; if a communicator could hit it, he would affect it. This became especially frightening because of the reach of the new mass media. The unsophisticated viewpoint was that if a person could be reached by the insidious forces of propaganda carried by the mighty power of the mass media, he could be changed and converted and controlled. (p. 8)

No one holds this strong view of the passive audience today; by the late 1940s some scholars demonstrated audience resistance to messages (Cantril, 1940). Why, they asked, did only some radio listeners of Orson Welles's 1938 War of the Worlds broadcast panic? Why did some believe the program and others switch channels? Hadley Cantril and his associates concluded that audiences do not passively accept everything broadcast by the mass media but bring various resources to their listening or viewing. Some compared information from station to station; some simply resisted the suggested plot, being naturally skeptical; others closely attended to the internal references of the broadcast.

This last group highlights the ability of audiences to evaluate the presented meaning of a program. Here, the nature of programming itself offers some clues to how audiences understand. "Presented meaning" forms the message intended by program creators; many regard it as a fairly straightforward idea, though some question whether meaning should ever be objectified and treated as an artifact (Lindlof, 1988, p. 84). Whatever the status of that debate, the powerful messages research pole accepts meaning as a given and as something that can be presented more or less powerfully through rhetorical forms. In evaluating the concept of message power, both Roland Barthes (1970/1975) and Umberto Eco (1979) have argued that texts can constrain or encourage readers. We can apply these ideas to radio and television programming by treating that programming as a "text." A "closed text" (Eco) or a "readerly text" (Barthes) falls close to the pole of powerful messages because it allows only one meaning. John Fiske spells this out:

> The concepts of open and closed texts are useful, particularly when we ally them with the notion of a struggle for meaning. We can then characterize the television text as a site of struggle between the dominant ideology working to produce a closed text by closing off the opportunities it offers for resistive readings, and the diversity of audiences who, if they are to make the text popular, are constantly working to open it up to their readings.

> Barthes's (1970/1975) categorization of texts into the readerly and the writerly has some similarities with Eco's into the closed and open. A readerly text is one that approximates to what MacCabe calls a "classic realist text," that is, one which "reads" easily, does not foreground its own nature as discourse, and appears to promote a singular meaning which is not that of the text, but of the real. (1987, p. 94)

Closed texts act to limit the interpretive action of their readers/listeners/viewers and steer their understanding and behavior in specific directions.

Strong theories of presented meaning or closed texts also appear in film study and, from that origin, have influenced thinking about audience understanding. Auteur theory stresses the role of the director in constructing messages; for such a theory to have any validity, the audience must be able to perceive the presented meaning of the director and accept it at face value. A different branch of film theory, arising in the British publication *Screen* in the 1970s, proposes that "realism" positioned audiences in ways that allowed them no room for any negotiated meaning. The cinematic "real" was so obvious and beyond question that audiences could only accept the meaning. Shaun Moores terms this the "textual determinism of screen theory" and goes on to note that "It appeared...as though the subject is always-already successfully interpellated, or positioned, by the text" (1993, p. 15). If the program/text can position the audience to perceive it in its own preferred way—from one given perspective—then the writer or director has succeeded in conveying a presented meaning.

Another form of the "presented meaning" construct that favors message content over audience understanding shows up in supporting roles in a number of other media theories. One, which stresses the potential of the message to arrange or present a world or worldview, posits an ordering or structuring role for the message strong enough to determine meaning. Donald Roberts describes it this way:

> We can conceive of messages as providing *prestructured* information—information organized such that certain relationships and associations are salient (and often such that others are not) in the hope that a receiver's interpretation of those prestructurings will influence his image of the environment, hence his behavior. (1971, p. 362)

Lindlof analyzes the same phenomenon, noting that audience members seldom consciously avert to it:

> This perspective posits at least one level of meaning that is systematically organized "beneath" a more overt and conventionally acceptable level. These deeper logics operate at psychological or ideological levels and may motivate behavior in ways that serve the interests of content designers. Moreover, this type of meaning is often thought to exert its intended effects with greatest efficacy if persons approach a media encounter assuming a conventional or transparent meaning. (1988, p. 85)

In both views the message gains power from its role in describing the world and thus offering the audience a shortcut in its attempt to understand. This view of the powerful role of presented meaning is assumed in the theory of agenda setting, which argues that the news media set the public agenda or "tell us what to think about." By reporting certain issues and stories, they shape the public mind and influence political debate, for example. These media then become what Klaus Jensen has termed "institutions-to-think-with." In other words, the "media institutions...serve to bracket reality and place it on a public agenda" (1991, p. 21). In this the audience passively accepts the picture of the world it sees.

The presented meaning and passive audience constructs also enter in as assumptions in George Gerbner's various cultivation studies. Concerned with the effects of violence, Gerbner and his colleagues argue that depictions of violence do not directly cause aggression in viewers but do affect how people perceive the world. Frank Biocca (1988, p. 56) has culled some representative statements from cultivation theory:

> Gerbner [Gross, Morgan, & Signorielli] (1986) write: People are born into a symbolic environment with television as its mainstream.... Television viewing is both a shaper and stable part of certain lifestyles and outlooks. It links the individual to a larger if synthetic world, a world of television's own making.... The content shapes and promotes...dominates their sources of information...continued exposure to its messages is likely to reiterate, confirm, and nourish (i.e., cultivate) their values and perspectives. (pp. 23-24.)

Gerbner and his colleagues have shown that heavy television viewers are more likely to think that the television world accurately represents the external world than do light viewers, that violence is more common than it truly is in their cities, that television values reflect majority values, and so forth. In all of this the audience understanding (or basis for judgment) is shaped by the message content and construction.

A final area in which the strong message construct appears is in studies of learning from the media. Most agree that the mass media can succeed in teaching, but direct learning depends somewhat on audience activity. However, message effects show their strength in indirect teaching—when people don't expect to be learning—much as Gerbner and his colleagues have argued. Studies conducted as early as the 1920s indicated that mass media images influenced children's play and adult clothing fashions (Lowery & DeFleur, 1983, pp. 47-49).

The powerful messages/powerful effects pole of communication research has conceptualized the audience as relatively passive consumers of messages that influence their behavior and understanding in predictable ways. In this scenario, originators of messages need to take care with message construction and with message saturation. Audience understanding will follow more or less automatically. (See Figure 1)

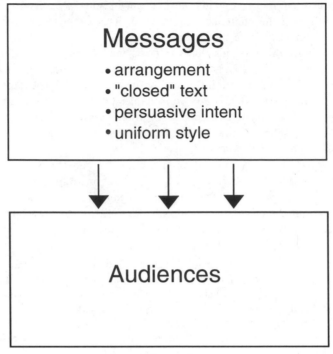

Figure 1

Active Audiences

The second pole of audience research examines audiences more closely, placing a great deal of emphasis on what people do with messages. Researchers have credited audiences with more and more power. According to Robert White, "During the 1970s, the study of media audiences moved from an emphasis on media effects to a focus on how audiences select media programs....Since the mid 1980s there has been yet another move toward an analysis of how audiences actively construct the meaning of media" (1994, p. 3). This latter swing has moved communication research more firmly to the camp of powerful audiences.

The notion of audience activity towards media messages encompasses several different approaches. Some originally appeared as limitations to the powerful effects/powerful messages construct, noting that different audiences react to messages in different ways. Another approach goes under the generic name of "uses and gratifications" research, examining how audience members use particular media in order to gratify personal needs. A third approach examines how audiences construct meaning from their media experiences. Finally, another looks at what audience members do with media "texts"—how they extend those texts into other areas of their lives.

Limitations on Media Power

The idea that audiences differ in their response to messages is not new. As noted above, Cantril and his colleagues began exploring the causes of differential media effects shortly after 1938. Without crediting specific audience activity, Hastorf & Cantril (1954) chronicle how supporters of different teams viewed a football game differently. What people bring to their viewing (for example, attitudes, emotional involvement, and prejudice) determines the audience's interpretation: A "good hit" for one viewer is rough play for another. The ultimate but indirect conclusion of their study is that a mass audience does not exist. Individuals do different things with media messages. In this early work Cantril's group approached their conclusion from the perspective of the individual, particularly examining psychological variables.

While some early scholars, notably Herta Hertzog (1944), investigated people's motivations in using programming (or the needs fulfilled by different programs), audience research did not focus closely on audience activity until the 1970s. Uses and gratifications research led to an ongoing effort to classify exactly how audiences utilize the media. As opposed to Cantril's psychological work, uses and gratifications research has its foundation in functionalism, an approach that combines demographic and psychological characteristics. The assumption in this research is "that the member of the audience is not a passive but rather an active part of the mass communication process. Such active participants seek content selectively, commensurate with their needs and interests" (Lowery & DeFleur, 1983, p. 374). The audience's understanding arises from the specific uses to which they put the media, for example, information, relaxation, and social contact.

Other theoretical constructs of the active audience also find a place in communication research. In a review of these, Biocca arranges active audience studies into five groups. First, audience activity is defined as selectivity. Audience members select which programming they will listen to or view; in addition, some theories also include selective perception and selective retention. Activities here do not have audience members doing much more than making an initial choice. For example, one might ignore advertising completely. Second, audience activity is defined as utilitarianism. Here the audience member uses the media much as a "self-interested consumer" and is active insofar as making rational choices to satisfy conscious needs. For example, one might view advertising for information regarding a purchase or one might view the ads purely for entertainment. Third, audience activity is defined as intentionality. This activity is primarily cognitive and refers to the schemas and structures that individuals use to make sense of media content; as such, it shows individual personality and motivational traits. For example, one might view advertising with suspicion, even when it offers needed product information. Fourth, audience activity is defined as involvement. Researchers in this part of the tradition look to affective arousal or para-social interactions in which the audience members "interact" with mass media characters. For example, one might identify with a particular character in an advertisement or on a show. Finally, audience activity is defined as imperviousness to influence. This definition refers to a kind of negative activity in which the audience members resist the influence of the mass media. The audience is active in choosing not to believe a message or in choosing not to buy a product (Biocca, 1988, pp. 53-54).

Uses and Gratifications

The uses and gratifications approach solidly established the idea of an active audience, demonstrating how the audience members understood and used the media. As a theoretical grounding, this approach allowed researchers to explain both why media messages did not always work and how audiences resisted categorization as an undifferentiated mass. The approach indicates that audience understanding hinges on audience members' needs and decisions to fulfill those needs.

Researchers, particularly those whom Biocca would class as examining the intentionality aspect of audience activity, have developed some fairly sophisticated theoretical ideas about how audiences actually understand messages. Collins (1981) and Mandler (1984) represent a group that describes mental functioning in terms of schemas that audience members use to construct meaning from the stream of images, words, music, text, and experiences that come to them. Hastie defines a schema as "an abstract, general structure that establishes relations between specific events or entities" (1981, p. 41). Such schemas allow the audience to make pragmatic sense of the message fairly rapidly by integrating it into their own mental categories.

Carey (1989) proposed a parallel theoretical move to the uses and gratifications model by suggesting a distinction between transportation and ritual models of communication. The former focus on moving a message through a communication system while the latter look to the role that communication plays in people's lives. The ritual model of communication considers what audience members do with communication—at the role television plays in family life, for example. James Lull's extensive television viewing studies (1980, 1988) confirm the distinction and extend the ritual use of television to both structural and relational acts:

> Under the category of the structural, [Lull] included the employment of the medium as an "environmental resource"—"a companion for accomplishing household chores and routines...a flow of constant background noise which moves to the foreground when individuals or groups desire"—and as a "behavioral regulator" that serves to structure domestic time, punctuating daily activities and duties. (Moores, 1993, p. 34)

In his category of relational acts, Lull includes the use of media content to facilitate interpersonal relationships by, for example, giving topics for conversation, allowing an excuse not to talk with someone, and providing common referents outside the home. In this ritual view of the media, the audience understands media products as part of their repertoire of behaviors and environmental resources, without too much concern for the intention of the message creators. The media messages merely fit into a pre-established routine of the audience members and their households.

Meaning Construction

Besides this account of how and why audiences use the mass media, significant theoretical progress has occurred in terms of how audiences understand messages. The last 15 years have seen communication researchers move away from a concentration on the presented meaning of a text/program to a concern with the "constructed meaning." Constructed meaning arises from the interaction between audience members and texts and presumes that audiences hold the balance of power:

> Meaning that is person controlled is created out of an entire range of sources: the person's ongoing needs, beliefs, and attitudes; social affiliations and reference groups; cultural memberships; language use; the resources and artifacts available in the settings of human activity. Central to constructed meaning is the idea that significance comes into being *in the articulation of a specific person-medium encounter* (which may occur after the media reception event that precipitates it), but only within the terms of a form of social reality. (Lindlof, 1988, p. 86)

This notion of meaning arises somewhat in reaction to earlier emphasis on the presented meaning. Analysis of audience reaction to television and film led a group in England at Birmingham University's Centre for Contemporary Cultural Studies to challenge the ability of powerful messages to situate audience members or to determine meaning:

> The Birmingham group strongly contested *Screen's* model of text-audience relations, putting an emphasis on readers as active producers of meaning and on media consumption as a site of potentially differential interpretations....While recognizing the text's construction of subject positions, the Birmingham group pointed to readers as the possessors of cultural knowledges and competences that have been acquired in previous social experiences and which are drawn on in the act of interpretation. (Moores, 1993, p. 16)

Audience members, then, created the meaning of texts/programs based on their experience rather than on the presented meaning of the media source.

This re-thinking of audience understanding of meaning appropriated through the media has generated a great deal of scholarly effort, some of it overlapping, some of it borrowed from related disciplines, particularly semiotics and literary study. Barthes's and Eco's ideas of a writerly text and an open text, respectively, provided a theoretical basis for seeing media products as open to multiple interpretations:

> The writerly text...is multiple and full of contradictions, it foregrounds
> its own nature as discourse and resists coherence or unity. None of its
> codes is granted priority over others, it refuses a hierarchy of dis-
> courses. The readerly text is a closed one, the writerly text an open one.
> (Fiske, 1987, p. 94)

The qualities of the text allow the audience to actively construct a meaning.
Rather than assign power to the message creator, this outlook shifts it to the
audience members.

A number of communication scholars have tried to apply this to television narratives in particular. Working from people's responses to television
news reports, Stuart Hall at Birmingham first proposed an "encoding/decod-
ing" model in which audiences develop three kinds of meaning: the dominant code, which is the creator's preferred or "intended" meaning; the negotiated code, which recognizes the intended meaning but resists it by posing
exceptions; and the oppositional reading, which contradicts the intended
meaning. In the latter two, audience members assert their authority over the
message by filtering it through their own experiences. For example, a news
report on a labor union's strike might lead business executives to approve
policing tactics while simultaneously leading workers to protest police bru-
tality (Hall, 1980).

Fiske (1987) qualifies Hall's work and argues that audience understanding arises primarily from three forces: the nature of the text, the mode
of reception, and a social determination. With open or writerly texts capable
of many meanings, the audience activity takes on even greater importance.
On the one hand, he claims that how audience members experience televi-
sion/text influences the meaning they ascribe to it. As Lull showed, television is a domestic medium and its audiences watch with varying degrees of
attention; with other household activities going on; and with constant negotiating about program choice, family authority, and even gender roles (1987,
p. 72). "Television, to be popular, must not only contain meanings relevant
to a wide variety of social groups, it must also be capable of being watched
with different modes of attention" (p. 73).

On the other hand, Fiske notes, "Meanings are determined socially:
that is, they are constructed out of the conjuncture of the text with the socially situated reader" (1987, p. 80). Social groupings position viewers/read-
ers vis-à-vis the program/text: Thus, audience understanding flows partly
from audience identity. But this undercuts the very concept of the audience:

> There is no stable entity which we can isolate and identify as the media
> audience, no single object that is unproblematically "there" for us to
> observe and analyze. The plural, audiences, is preferable—denoting sev-
> eral groups divided by their reception of different media and genres, or
> by social and cultural positioning. (Moores, 1993, pp. 1-2)

Communication researchers have begun to look at the social factors that
situate audiences. Among these are gender (Brown, 1994), social standing,

economic value, and political or ideological beliefs (Moores, 1993). However, these positionings of the audience members do not have to remain stable. A working parent may shift viewing position from parent to worker, depending on the program. Everyone belongs to more than one audience situation. (See Figures 2 and 3)

Lindlof has recast these groupings and named them interpretive communities. Such communities guide readers/viewers/listeners to ranges of meaning possible in the program/text. "The individual's actual reception of mediated content represents a social performance mandated by the role structure operative in the reception setting" (1988, p. 82). From this perspective it is the community that guides meaning by giving its members a set of interpretive tools or genres with which to decode media content. "The criterial features of any interpretive community consist in the modes, meaning constructs, and frequency of its internal messaging in using media technologies and content" (p. 82). Audience understanding happens as a function of group identity.

Audience Activity with the Text

Another part of audience understanding arises after the encounter with the text. Audiences also understand pragmatically. What do audiences do with the program/text? Newcomb & Hirsch (1984) offer the concept of cultural forums in their description of the media. In these forums, meanings, audiences, and media institutions interact with each other to raise questions and constitute new social groups. The measure of audience understanding

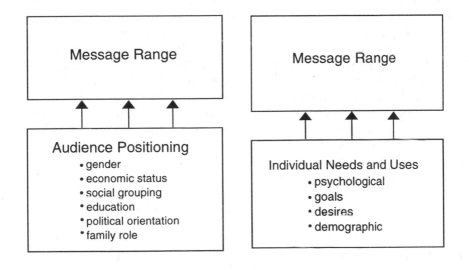

Figure 2   *Figure 3*

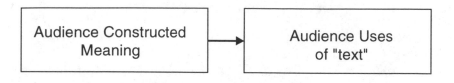

Figure 4

becomes what audiences do with the program/text. For example, they might treat a television program as a metaphorical place (or forum) to listen to alternative views of society.

Audience members also act to construct their own discourse from the meanings they make of media content. For example, television involves audiences because its narratives find a place in popular culture, which is still largely an oral culture. In other words, television works as a part of the culture because people talk about it and incorporate it and its stories into their conversations (Fiske, 1987, p. 105).

In a similar way, some audience members extend the discourse of the mass media by finishing its stories and adding their own. These audiences are among the most powerful because they do not allow the media producers to control either their programs/texts or the circulation of those programs/texts. Jenkins sees this group epitomized in fan clubs. He "proposes an alternative conception of fans as readers who appropriate popular texts and reread them in a fashion that serves different interests, as spectators who transform the experience of watching television into a rich and complex participatory culture" (1992, p. 23). Fans understand programs/texts by commandeering them for their own purposes, as "Star Trek" fans do when they write their own scripts based on the series characters. Understanding only begins with the interaction with or viewing of a program. What matters is what the audience does after their viewing. (See Figure 4)

The powerful audience pole of communication research sees audience members as actively choosing what to do with communication products. They select programs. They resist some cognitive, affective, and behavioral appeals and succumb to others. They experience communication products from defined (but sometimes shifting) positions. They determine the meaning that they attach to the program/text. And they re-make the program/text as they wish through conversation, interaction, and even play.

Ways to Understand Audiences

The two poles of communication audience research represent extreme positions. Undoubtedly, neither the message nor the audience holds all power when it comes to understanding mass media products. The two poles do clearly illustrate, though, the forces that act upon messages and people. They also show that many of the constructs used in communication study link it to other interpretive disciplines. While the issues raised by audience interaction with programs/texts may be new to communication, they are not completely new for the humanities. This appears especially in three areas: interpretation, interpretive communities, and the nature of texts.

Hans-Georg Gadamer (1960/1991) has explicated a hermeneutical model that proposes that meaning results from a "fusion of horizons" of the text and the reader. Both bring something to the meaning, which comes to its fullness only in the interaction of the two. Among other things, that interaction includes a kind of back and forth rhythm between text and reader; no interpretation is final, though some interpretations may be privileged and gain wide acceptance. This model seems particularly apt for describing what happens when audiences receive mass media products: Meaning results from the actions of both. Programs/texts do carry meaning, meanings which their creators did in fact intend. Audiences for their part do actively negotiate meaning, based on, for example, their positioning, their prior experience, and their needs. Where two audiences may perceive and receive a program/text differently, they still have some common areas. Unlike Lewis Carroll's Humpty-Dumpty, one cannot make texts mean whatever one wishes them to mean—there still remains both a text and a community of interpretation to put a brake on unlimited interpretation and to reject unwarranted claims.

Communities of interpretation offer another means to understand audience understanding of programs/texts. Audience positioning occurs because people bring particular shared tools and common mental constructs. They learn some of these explicitly in schools; they appropriate others from families and social organizations. And they assimilate concepts of relationship, value, and utility from their own community organization and structure. All these things affect their dealing with mass media products; at the same time mass media products become part of the mix of community organization and structure. Brian Stock describes a similar experience in what he calls "textual communities" in his exploration of the rise of literacy in the Middle Ages (1983, pp. 88-240).

Stock notes that textual communities, which first arose among dissenters, "demonstrated a parallel use of texts, both to structure the internal behavior of the groups' members and to provide solidarity against the outside world" (p. 90). The groups' reliance on texts (or on those who could read the texts) conditioned the ways they conceptualized their world. The text rearranged the patterns of the world for members of these communities: The familiar was a text; the outside world, beyond the text. The text also changed the group. Because all the members knew the text, even if they could not read it, they shared a common base:

> As a consequence, interaction by word of mouth could take place as a superstructure of an agreed meaning, the textual foundation of behavior having been entirely internalized. With shared assumptions, the members were free to discuss, to debate, or to disagree on other matters, to engage in personal interpretations of the Bible or to some degree in individualized meditation and worship. (p. 91)

The medieval textual communities allowed a certain freedom vis-à-vis the defining tradition and fostered an individuality within the bounds of the group. Much the same thing happens within the interpretive communities shaped by the mass media. The common outlook fosters going beyond the program/text while making the program/text absolutely indispensable to the group.

The text itself must have some essential characteristics if it will function for communities of interpretation. Briefly, it must be interpretable. Eco's and Barthes's distinctions between open (writerly) and closed (readerly) texts point out that people can create texts with greater or lesser scope for audience interpretive activity. In addition, texts interact with one another and this too makes them suited for interpretation. Fiske adapts the literary construct of intertextuality to define this aspect of the television text:

> The theory of intertextuality proposes that any one text is necessarily read in relationship to others and that a range of textual knowledges is brought to bear upon it.... Intertextual knowledges pre-orient the reader to exploit television's polysemy by activating the text in certain ways, that is, by making some meanings rather than others. (1987, p. 108)

Like the audience members' communities, the mass media's programs/texts prepare them for interpretation.

From these things we can construct a model for understanding how audiences understand mass media products. (See Figure 5) First, media messages and media audiences interact. Second, audience members' communities position them to construct certain meanings over others, within the range of possible meanings of the text. Third, media messages are constructed to define a range of meaning; the narrower the range, the more powerful the message and the more directed the audience's understanding. Fourth, audience members also respond to their own needs and goals; even as members of an interpretive community, they have individual motivations and needs, some of which will drive their understanding of the mass media through selectivity, involvement, or resistance. These audience members extend and clarify their understanding through incorporating the media message in daily talk. Thus they give new life (and new form) to the message by

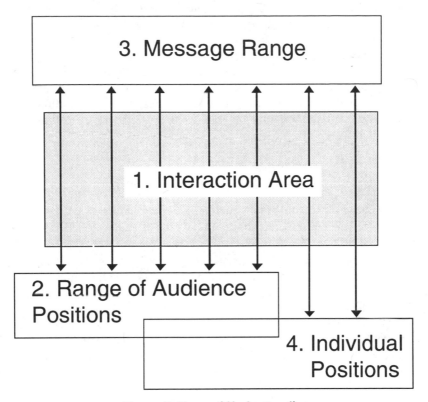

Figure 5: Zone of Understanding

transposing it into their oral culture. These factors combine to create a "zone of understanding" in which the message and audience come together.

One final factor, which is well known but little understood, also influences audience understanding: technology. The ubiquity of communication technology leads us to take it for granted even as it promotes the ubiquity of media messages. Technology does make a difference, apart from any concern with media and message (McLuhan, 1962) or with media and thought (Ong, 1982):

> It is also necessary for us to ask about the ways in which that technology serves to "mediate" between private and public worlds—connecting domestic spaces with spheres of information and entertainment that stretch well beyond the confines of family and locality. Communication technologies have...played an important part in the symbolic construction of "home"—whilst simultaneously providing household members with an opportunity to "travel" elsewhere, and to imagine themselves as members of wider cultural communities at a national or transnational level. (Moores, 1993, p. 70)

At minimum, technology adds to audience understanding by extending the audience's world and helping to shape that world. People become part of interpretive communities and approach media content in specific ways because of communication technologies.

Understanding technology demands a separate essay; let me just note here that the technology makes possible most of what this essay describes. In this way it directly influences audience understanding. Its indirect influence extends to habits of thought, modes of expression, use of time, and household arrangement.

Towards Multimedia Translation

Given what we know about audience understanding, what should multimedia translators do? Using the model sketched out above, I will suggest six possibilities.

- Admit the power of the audience in shaping its own understanding. Because audiences are active, the translator/communicator should accept that and build on it, both in text construction and in text arrangement (through use of multiple media, for example).

@BULLET = Know the psychological and social needs of the audience. Audiences both choose and respond to communication in terms of their needs—and those needs differ from one person to another and among groups. Understanding the audience helps the communicator position the message within the desired zone of interpretation.

- Foster closed texts for greater control of the message, but foster open ones for greater participation by audience members. The translator's goal will affect how one constructs the message. If fidelity to a text ranks high, then the translation should produce a closed text; if one desires to have the audience members appropriate the text, then the translation should induce audience activity.

- Direct the uses of the product so that audience members let the translation become part of their oral culture. It should become something talked about and shared with friends. In this, the translators should merely facilitate how the Scriptures normally become a part of the culture of any people.

- Create a community of interpretation. By incorporating the Scriptural text into the oral life of the people, the translators take the first step toward connecting their readers/viewers/listeners with a community of interpretation. The Christian community itself and all of its local churches form a community of interpretation. For a multimedia translation to be successful, it should connect back to that community.

- Take advantage of technology. The multimedia translation project has already taken advantage of technology, but it should go beyond its initial use of the technology and take advantage of the ways in which communication technology shapes and interacts with its audience. The project teams should look again at how technology affects the audience and adjust the project to take full advantage of this.

Finally, as a kind of postscript, let me also suggest that multimedia translation look at models of understanding drawn from their own studies. For example, relevance theory addresses how people make sense of complex verbal messages. Gutt explains:

> Communication works by inference. The communicator produces a stimulus from which the addressee can infer the communicator's informative intention. This process succeeds as well as it does because of a universal psychological principle—the principle of relevance. The addressee can assume that the first interpretation consistent with this principle is the one intended by the communicator:
>
> One of the entailments of this principle is that, in order to be communicable, the informative intention must yield adequate contextual effects for the addressees. (1992, p. 35)

Gutt's summary indicates that people attempt to make sense of messages as they receive them, according to their experience and background—an active audience principle. Relevance theory also echoes the notions of a community of interpretation and the balance between open and closed texts.

The many areas of overlap in audience studies and between audience study and other approaches to understanding should remind us that, when it comes to understanding audience understanding, we need as many tools as we can manage.

Paul A. Soukup, S.J., has explored the connections between communication and theology since 1982. His publications include *Communication and Theology* (1983); *Christian Communication: A Bibliographical Survey* (1989), and *Mass Media and the Moral Imagination* with Philip J. Rossi (1994). In addition, he and Thomas J. Farrell have edited three volumes of the collected works of Walter J. Ong, SJ, *Faith and Contexts* (1992-1995). This later work has led him to examine more closely how orality-literacy studies can contribute to an understanding of theological expression. A graduate of the University of Texas at Austin (Ph.D., 1985), Soukup teaches in the Communication Department at Santa Clara University.

5

The Seriousness of Play: Gadamer's Hermeneutics as a Resource for Christian Mission

Fred Lawrence

German philosopher Hans-Georg Gadamer's philosophical hermeneutics has synthesized the foundations for the third stage of the development of hermeneutics initiated in the 20th century by Karl Barth and Martin Heidegger. In this stage the premodern hermeneutics of consent and the Enlightenment hermeneutics of suspicion are sublated into an integral hermeneutics in which the game-play structure of human existence provides the critical grounding for faith seeking understanding in a way that is neither fideist (eliminating the role of critical rationality) nor rationalist (eliminating the light of faith). In game-play human beings come into their own in discerning response to the supervening event of meanings and values moving in and through history. The game-play structure illuminates language-games, conversation, understanding, interpretation, and translation. But it also casts fruitful light upon the Christian Scriptures as *Urliteratur*, and the Christian message as testimony, as eminent text, and as sign.

Gadamer and the Contemporary Revolution in Hermeneutics

Hans-Georg Gadamer, who was born in 1900, is one of our century's most important philosophers even though he became world-famous rather late in his life. But his reputation had been sufficient to permit him to be called to a professorial chair in Heidelberg in 1948 as the successor to the great Karl Jaspers who had moved to the University of Basel (where Bachofen, Burckhardt, and Nietzsche had taught in the past). At that time, the presiding figure in Basel was another great hermeneutic revolutionary of the 20th century, Karl Barth.

Gadamer, whose reputation was based on his seminars, especially on Plato and Aristotle, became renowned among the students at Heidelberg, forming many future holders of chairs of philosophy throughout the German university system. His reputation suddenly became worldwide with the publication in 1960 of his fundamental work, *Wahrheit und Methode* (*Truth and Method*) (1960/1991). Gadamer says he finally forced himself to write that book after so many years because whenever his students had spoken proudly of having been formed by him, they were invariably met with the puzzled question, "Who?" For years they had begged him to let the wider world know the teacher they had experienced in those seminars first in Marburg, then in Leipzig (where he had also been rector under the communist regime), briefly in Frankfurt, and finally at Heidelberg (Gadamer, 1975/1985).

Gadamer spent the vacations of the better part of a decade writing this book based not just on research, but upon his long experience as an interpreter of what in America have come to be called "Great Books." Instead of writing a theory of interpretation in the abstract *de jure* style of post-Kantian continental philosophy—and in the manner of his contemporary from the Cassirer school of neo-Kantianism, Emilio Betti (1962)—Gadamer grounded his theory on his factual and phenomenologically ostensible practice of interpreting texts, doing history, and appreciating works of art.

His hermeneutic philosophy also grows out of and is a radicalization of the phenomenological movement in continental philosophy. As such, it is also located within the trajectory of the 20th-century hermeneutical revolution that marks the third great turning point in the development of hermeneutics in western culture (Gadamer, 1968; Grondin, 1991/1994). Its founders were Barth in theology and Martin Heidegger in philosophy. *Truth and Method* became its fundamental text.

The first turning point in the development of hermeneutics in the West came after the emergence of both the canon of sacred Scripture and the dogmatic creeds of the great ecumenical councils. In his *De Doctrina Christiana* Augustine of Hippo articulated an approach to interpretation that shaped the world of Christian learning throughout medieval and early Reformation theology. This approach was rooted in liturgical practice, especially Baptism and Eucharist, and in the Christian praxis of love, and took a dogmatic theological context for granted. We can speak of this approach as the hermeneutics of consent.

The second great turning-point in western hermeneutics arose with the Enlightenment and was indelibly marked by Baruch Spinoza's *Theologico-Political Treatise*. In time and through the offices of Karl Marx, Friedrich Nietzsche, and Sigmund Freud, its basic approach has come to be called the hermeneutics of suspicion. From the 18th century to the present this approach has presided over historical method and the critical retrieval of historical texts, of church history, and of the history of dogma outside the auspices of ecclesiastical authority. It transformed the relationship between the contingencies of history and the truths of faith into "a gaping abyss," as Gotthold Lessing called it. This historical-critical method was governed by the usually latent presuppositions of Enlightenment epistemology as formulated by such early modern thinkers as René Descartes and John Locke: The "gaping abyss" mirrored the subject/object split and the so-called "problem of the bridge": How does the subject "in here" really reach the real object "out there," or vice versa?

Later on, Immanuel Kant's search for the limits of reason in order to "make room for faith" or "eliminate faith" (the word *aufheben* in the *Vorrede* to edition B of *The Critique of Pure Reason* is ambiguous) seemed to provide a philosophical support for the classical Protestant doctrines of *sola fide, sola gratia,* and *sola scriptura.* But in fact Kant also opened the way for liberal Protestantism's difficulties with relativism, for instance, Ernst Troeltsch's "Christ without absolutes" (Coakley, 1988); with historicism, for example, the so-called quest for the historical Jesus from David Friedrick Strauss through Adolf von Harnack and Albert Schweitzer to Rudolf Bultmann, and after (Neill & Wright, 1988; Meyer, 1989); and with subjectivism, for instance in the dependence of the theologies of Albrecht Ritschl and Wilhelm Hermann upon "religion within the limits of reason alone" as a matter chiefly of imagination and morality. These tendencies culminated in that *Kulturprotestantismus* against which Barth, the young Swiss Reformed pastor, rebelled on the eve of World War I (Busch, 1975/1976; Frei, 1992).

To be sure, when Barth saw that the great theologians and teachers he had admired were signatories to blatant nationalistic propaganda he was provoked. But the underlying perspective is deeper and goes back to the writings of Søren Kierkegaard, a Danish Lutheran student of the old Schelling then being translated into German. From his invective against the bourgeoisification of the Danish Lutheran Church, through his critique of Hegel, to his depiction of the existential plight of the New Testament interpreter in *Concluding Unscientific Postscript,* the books of Kierkegaard were causing a sensation throughout the world of German-speaking philosophy and theology.

Kierkegaard profoundly influenced Barth's early dialectical theology. In the hermeneutic revolution initiated in Barth's 1919 *Epistle to the Romans* (especially as documented in the prefaces he wrote for successive editions of that commentary), the key term—almost a slogan—that would recur in the ensuing theological discussions regarding the mediation of truth in history is the German *Sachkritik* (Robinson & Cobb, 1964). The German word *Sache* means "thing," "subject matter," "content," "real issue at stake" (in Latin, *res* or *causa*). The word also was used in the motto of the rebellion started by Edmund Husserl and the phenomenological movement against a variety of neo-Kantianisms then dominating conventional academic philosophy: *"Zu den Sachen selbst!"* "Back to the things themselves!" (Gadamer, 1963/1976). Gadamer relates that "Thomas Sheehan once told me that Heidegger once showed him an off-print of Husserl's Logos Essay of 1910, *Philosophy as a Rigorous Science.* There is a passage there where

Husserl says our method and our principle must be '*Zu den Sachen selbst*'—and there the young Heidegger had written in the margin: 'We desire to take Husserl at his word' " (Gadamer, 1986-1987, p. 15).

In theological hermeneutics, the burden of *Sachkritik* was that the chief presupposition for gaining adequate passage from the past of the text to the present situation of preaching is genuine contact with the very reality about which the text is speaking. In philosophy, Husserl's statement, "the neo-Kantians begin with the roof, I begin with the foundations," meant that he would no longer trade in vague and unverifiable abstractions, but go back instead to what could be shown experientially. Hence, Husserl became preoccupied with the phenomenology of perception, which he eventually unfolded in a Fichtean, transcendental direction. Heidegger, his great student and research assistant, in his wonderment about the ontological status of Husserl's transcendental ego, radicalized the movement. Heidegger read the meaning of *Sache* in the light of the Greek *pragmata*, which denotes not just isolated objects of sense perception, but objects of deep practical concern (Strauss, 1970). Here the *Sache* of theological *Sachkritik* meets the *Sache* of phenomenology. Enter Gadamer.

Gadamer and the Hermeneutics of Facticity

Barth and Heidegger revolutionized the reading of the originative classics of western culture by showing us that the interpretation of any classic text is dependent upon our concrete solution to the problem of living, that is, of our asking and answering the question about the right way to live, and thereby personally settling the issue of what is of concern to us. It fell to Gadamer's *Truth and Method* to explain the philosophical basis and implications of this revolution.

This explanation embraces: (1) a critique of aesthetic consciousness in the light of an ontology of the work of art (Gadamer, 1960, pp. 1-161/1991, pp. 1-169); (2) a critique of historical consciousness in the light of an ontology of *Verstehen* and of effective-historical consciousness (pp. 162-360/ pp. 171-379); and (3) an ontology of language (pp. 361-465/pp. 381-491). The difficulty in understanding *Truth and Method* is increased by Gadamer's usage of the terms "ontology" and "consciousness."

First, regarding ontology. After both Kant and Heidegger, it has been widely held in most philosophical circles that we just don't "do" ontology. And this is quite right, if we understand by "ontology" the transformation of premodern metaphysics or philosophy of being as being initiated by Scotus and resumed in early modern times by Francisco Suarez (Courtine, 1990) and carried on after Leibniz in what came to be called the *Schulmetaphysik* taught by Kant's predecessors, Alexander Baumgarten and Christian Wolff. Kant had demolished both the premodern and modern senses of the term "ontology" as the precritical science of being that had not first satisfactorily taken care of the question about knowing ("How do we know we know?"); Heidegger had undermined the asking of the question about being when such asking took place in a way that is thereby forgetful of Being and of the ontological difference between Being and beings. So what is meant by Gadamer's use of the term "ontology"?

Gadamer's ontology is post-critical in that it makes no claims that cannot be "cashed out" phenomenologically, which I take to mean verified in experience (Gadamer, 1965). Secondly, it is post-Heideggerian in that it takes seriously Heidegger's dismantling of premodern and modern philosophy inasmuch as it is caught in the "horizon of *Vorhandenheit*." This second point needs clarification because its critical role in the *Destruktion* being carried out by Heidegger is also important for Gadamer's use of the term "consciousness."

What is meant by the horizon of *Vorhandenheit*? In the first place, this horizon is clearly manifest in modern philosophy's "turn to the subject" (Gadamer, 1962). This turn, which involved the privileging of the question about knowing over the question about being, took the shape of epistemology, or what in German is called *Erkenntnistheorie*. This means then that philosophy's first question is, "How do we know we know the really real?"

The following assumptions, made explicit by Descartes and prevailing afterwards, motivate this epistemological question: (1) the subject/object split, as in Descartes' division between *res cogitans* and *res extensa*; (2) the "problem of the bridge" in which the consciousness of the knower is imagined to be a container, and objects to be known are imagined to be "already-out-there-now," so that the issue is either "How does knowing 'get out there' validly" or "How does it 'get the objects in here' for sure." Hence, one connotation of *Vorhandenheit* is the image or picture of presence as "already-out-there-now" or "already-in-here-now," where consciousness has the status of the "already-in-here-now."

In the second place, the horizon of *Vorhandenheit* is connected with one of the most important achievements of premodern philosophy, the logical ideal of science first explicated in Aristotle's *Posterior Analytics*. An overweening emphasis upon the abstract universality and necessity proper to precisely and explicitly defined terms, and upon the rigor and consistency of inference via correctly formed syllogisms can exercise such an imaginative power over philosophical endeavor that conceptualism and abstract deductivism become the defining marks of true knowledge (Gadamer, 1979, pp. 27-32). This means that in the concern for apodictic knowledge, the focus is on the products of the mind's operation at the expense of all the preconceptual, prepredicative, informal, and tacit factors that go into the performance of understanding and judging correctly. The modern stress on "system" is a residue of this imbalance. The logical control of meaning can only do justice to the domain of the static and closed.

If, therefore, we combine the "already-out-there-now" image of objectivity, and the "already-in-here-now" image of consciousness, with the static
and closed character of the exclusively logical control of meaning, we
closely approximate the web of presuppositions making up the horizon of
Vorhandenheit (Lawrence, 1976). That horizon represents for Heidegger an
antecedent willingness to gain technical control over the entire range of human aspiration and questing. Thus the goal of human living is to subject all
living and being to *Verfügbarkeit,* which connotes both manipulative control
and an orientation toward massive possessiveness. It is also to erect an unverifiable image of the human subject as the isolated lord and master of the
real.

Consequently, according to Heidegger, both premodern and modern
philosophers (insofar as they were under the sway of the horizon of *Vorhandenheit*) installed either a mistaken notion of object (in the case of the an-
cients) or an equally mistaken notion of subject (modern philosophy after
Descartes) at the center of their undertakings. They were thus doomed to
forget the question about being because its scope is radically disproportion-
ate to that horizon.

Heidegger's initial way out of the horizon of *Vorhandenheit* that even
Husserl failed to transcend was an utterly unconventional one: the "hermeneutics of facticity" (Lawrence, 1990; Kisiel, 1993, 1986-1987, 1988, 1989).
We have first to understand correctly what is meant by this novel expression
in order to grasp what Gadamer means by ontology.

Heidegger became convinced that the "primordial motive of philosophy...emerges out of the 'restlessness' *(Beunruhigung)* of one's own *Dasein"*
(Heidegger, n.d.). In the period before the publication of *Being and Time,* he
focused upon facticity—or human being in its contingency as concretely
available to us with a view to elaborating the structures of *Sorge,* "concrete
caring." He departed from the concreteness of our experience of the world
mediated by meaning in order to discover the proper mode of human facticity's givenness, how it is accessible, and how it may be adequately expressed. Heidegger was determined to find terms and relations adequate to
that original complex of concrete experience in its matrix of motives and
tendencies.

Under the influence of Wilhelm Dilthey, the great philosopher who hit
upon hermeneutics as a key to the critique of historical consciousness,
Heidegger realized that *Dasein* is not a Cartesian subject but a being-pre-
sent-to a world that is constituted by meaning. Indeed the odd term "facticity" highlights how *Dasein* exists as a compact interplay between *Rück-griff*
"motivation" and *Vor-griff* "anticipation" or "spontaneous tending-towards."
Its meaning therefore is performative, an "enactment" *(Vollzug)* that relates
(Bezug) motives to tendencies. "Concepts or definitions" *(Be-griffe)* and
sense perception are relatively minor parts of human life as inherently meaningful and concretely expressing itself. As meaningful, life speaks its own

language and expresses itself in concrete situations. Life experiences itself and understands itself concomitantly with and through its anticipatorily structured flow, in an implicit or tacit or non-thematic reflexiveness. This combination of performance and relating constitutes history as meaningful.

Dilthey drew Heidegger's attention to religious thinkers such as Graf Yorck von Wartenburg who pointed him to the young Luther's example of evangelical *fides ex auditu*. This became for Heidegger a model for philosophy as enacted in cooperating with and accompanying one's personal life-experience in heightened vividness and interiority. He understood primitive Christianity's contribution to be the insight into the primordiality of self-experience and into the fact that "life has the character of a coming to a head in the *Selbstwelt*" (Kisiel, 1986-1987, p. 104, see also pp. 104-105, 117-118).

What typifies the self as the *Grund-situation* and *Grund-erfahrung* of philosophy is the restlessness of human presence-to-self-in-the-world: Augustine's *inquietum cor*. Heidegger parallels gaining access to performative meaning or missing it (through the misguided attempt to objectify it) to the two modes of concern for life discussed in the 10th book of the *Confessions*: a detached, noble appreciation of beauty and goodness (*frui*); or utilitarian exploitation (*uti*). Heidegger's analysis of facticity begins also to integrate further Augustinian motifs: becoming a question to oneself (*quaestio mihi factus sum*); becoming a burden to oneself (*oneri mihi sum*) on account of temptation; and being *defluxus in multum* or distracted by the multiplicity of various possibilities and meanings. From Augustine's theme of chaste fear Heidegger was also led to the theme of the this-worldly experience of death, which in turn became a device by which Heidegger could take the Christian focus of unrest about one's own life and handle it outside the context of revelation, grace, and the forgiveness of sins.

When Heidegger turns to Aristotle (Sheehan, 1976), the language of restlessness and concern becomes that of care. And the relationships of temptation surrounding the burden weighing upon Augustine's self as a question to itself is displaced by existential categories of life. Concrete human living bears within itself an inevitable inclination toward ruin so that philosophical interpretation has to take the shape of resistance to the drift towards ruin, and this countermovement is enacted in making the questionable one's own. This presages the roles of authenticity and inauthenticity in *Being and Time*. Even though the religious context of sin and grace and repentance disclosed by faith vanishes altogether, Heidegger integrates into his approach Rilke's statement that "one lives so badly because one always arrives in the present unfinished, incapable, distracted." In the end, says Gadamer,

> To what extent the word, *"Faktizität,"* still possessed religious connotations even for Heidegger may be questionable. But that the limits of apriorist thought were co-present precisely in the area of religion is certain. Above all *"Hermeneutik der Faktizität"* surely means that it is the

self-interpretation of factually concrete life that constitutes *Dasein* as human, and it is what any philosophizing must attach itself to. (Gadamer, 1986-1987, p. 16; author's translation here and for all citations of Gadamer)

Departing from Heidegger's hermeneutics of facticity (Gadamer, 1960, pp. 250-261/1991, pp. 265-271) to overcome aesthetic, Romantic, and historical consciousness places Gadamer in an odd relationship to Heidegger. In *Unterwegs zur Sprache* (1959) Heidegger explained that after *die Kehre* "the turning," the entire vocabulary in *Being and Time*'s analysis of facticity had had to be abandoned, because the whole enterprise of the hermeneutics of facticity was still too embued with the Husserlian and Idealist starting point of transcendental subjectivity, explicit self-consciousness (reflective self-awareness), and self-possession. After "the turning" (in the early 1930s) Heidegger reached the conclusion that all conventional philosophical conceptuality had been tainted by the biases of one or another "language of metaphysics," which he was striving to overcome (Pöggeler, 1963, 1983). He was in what Gadamer calls a *Sprachnot* "linguistic emergency" (Gadamer, 1986a).

Here Gadamer disagreed with him. There is no "language of metaphysics" whose vocabulary is automatically "used up" or necessarily caught in the strictures of its past usages, because at root any language is dialogical. This means that even the so-called "language of metaphysics" only makes sense in light of the questions that were being asked and answered in it. Recovering the questions liberates language by de-rigidifying and de-scholasticizing it. Re-asking the questions to which linguistic statements are intended to be answers helps us realize that language is a horizon framing our asking and answering of questions. And in philosophy, such inquiry cannot dry up or freeze. Language's true point of access is the interplay of questions and answers (Gadamer, 1986b, pp. 10-12).

This is the Gadamer who could take up Heidegger's hermeneutics of facticity and, in the context of his own motivating questions about art and the historical and humane sciences (the *Geisteswissenschaften*, *lettres*, humanities), use it even to convey the chief point of the "turning" in a way that would be accessible to phenomenological verification. In generalizing Heidegger's hermeneutical breakthrough, Gadamer emphasized that:

> Man is what he is in constantly affecting the world and in constantly experiencing the effect of the world upon himself. Not in the isolated freedom of being-over-against, but in daily relation-to-world, in letting oneself in for the conditionings of the world does man win his own self. So, too, does he gain the right position of knowing. (Gadamer, 1967b, p. 94)

Clearly, after the "turning" Heidegger hinted at this by talking about *Ereignis* and *Lichtung*, of *Es gibt...*, of language as the house of Being and humans as the shepherds of Being.

Like Heidegger, Gadamer was determined to avoid the hermeneutically unjustified claims of Husserl about apodicticity and "philosophy as a rigorous science." Unlike Heidegger, he also wished to avoid the language and attitude of fateful dispensation and empty eschatology.

Gadamer was convinced that people are human in existing conversationally in relation to everything that is (1960, pp. 340-360/1991, pp. 358-379). The hermeneutics of facticity was basically correct to situate interpretation within a horizon of caring. Heidegger's insight regarding the ubiquity of language, namely, that human beings live within language as the air they breathe rather than as an instrument they deploy at will, was also absolutely right. In wanting to get to the bottom of the relationship between truth as "dependent upon the temporal-historical movement proper to *Dasein*" and reason as "the self-empowered capacity to perceive truth and make it binding," Gadamer was altogether ready to affirm that reason is "made possible by what it is not" (Gadamer, 1967c, pp. 17, 19). But he does not want us to draw the implication from the experience of dependency or conditionedness of both reason and truth that these are mere "tools in the service of a higher, unconscious, and irresponsible power" (p. 18). For Gadamer "it is the essence of our reason and our spirit to be capable of thinking against what is to our own advantage, to be able to detach ourselves from our needs and interests and to bind ourselves to the law of reality" (p. 20). By reason we have the capacity to acknowledge reality even against our own self-interest: "To be taught, even against our own subjectively certain convictions—that is the way of mediation of authentically historical truth" (p. 21).

Game-Play as the Structure of Human Being-in-the-World

Gadamer's concern with the mediation of truth in history was realized most acutely in his life-long wonder about the experience of the work of art. For Gadamer it epitomizes the reorientation of our human existence in accord with what is highest and best in us, namely, the pure and unrestricted desire to know and be one with the truth. The authentic human experience of the work of art discloses two features traditionally associated with the Christian experience of grace and conversion: (1) *supervening occurrence* in the advent of meaning and value moving in and through the activity of human subjects as creating, performing, or appreciating works of art; (2) *discerning appropriation* in the human being's active involvement or attunement through attentive, intelligent, reasonable, responsible, and loving consent. In fact, for Gadamer, these features are characteristic of authentic human living across the board, and they are engaged and negotiated within a structure explicated in Gadamer's phenomenology of *Spiel*—a word that we translate as "game-play" in order to suggest the game aspect of language-games, of things like sports, but also of what our expression "the game of life" implies; then, too, play, besides denoting the activity of playing in games and acting, also indicates drama, whether as artwork or as the drama of human existence (1960, pp. 97-127/1991, pp. 101-134). Although this game-play structure is perhaps most adequately instantiated in the experience of art, it is valid for all genuine human experience as a mediation of meaning and value. Let us now examine Gadamer's analysis of that structure as shown forth in the experience of art.

Game-play is a "dynamic whole *sui generis* that on its part implicates the subjectivity of the one who is playing" (Gadamer, 1961, p. 128/1976, p. 53). For Gadamer, any truly realized experience is a mediation of internal and external immediacies. This mediation of immediacy has a medial aspect, combining active and passive voices. This can be seen incomparably in game-play.

Once we realize how the structure of game-play works, we will realize that human self-understanding is always actuated with respect to something other, namely the other of intentional awareness, in an event by which both that other and the self-understanding undergo a transformation or sublimation. This realization deconstructs our spontaneous tendency to picture self-transcendence in images of exteriority: getting out to what's already-out-there-now; and to imagine consciousness as being like an insurpassable container. The Enlightenment tradition from Descartes and Locke to Kant pictured objective knowledge and autonomous reason in terms of exteriority and container. But the structure of game-play subverts these mistaken imaginative assumptions about the human subject. According to Gadamer:

> The work of art has...its proper being precisely in that it becomes an experience which transforms the one undergoing the experience. The "subject" of the experience of art, that which remains and lasts, is not the subjectivity of the one who experiences it, but the artwork itself. And that is exactly the point at which the mode of being of game-play becomes significant. For game-play has its own essence independently of the consciousness of those who play. Game-play is also there, indeed is even most properly present, where no independent self-consciousness (*Fürsichsein*) of subjectivity delimits the thematic horizon, and where there are no subjects who expressly behave in the playing mode. The subject of game-play is not the players, but the game-play merely comes to presentation through those players. (1960, p. 98/1991, p. 102)

Primary in the experience of art (and for Gadamer in all experience) *is what is moving in and through* the interaction of subjective and objective elements in the experience. The medium is the message:

> Game-play obviously makes present an order in which the to and fro of the movement of play are as it were self-actuating. It pertains to play that the movement is not only without end or purpose, but also without exertion. It goes as if by itself.... The ordered framework of the game-play lets the players as it were merge with it, thereby removing from them the task of exercising initiative that constitutes the real effort of human existence. This is seen, too, in the spontaneous pressure toward

repetition that arises in the player, and in the constant self-renewal of the game that fixes its form (e.g. the refrain). (1960, p. 100/1991, pp. 104-105)

The rules and regulations that prescribe the contours of the playing field constitute the essence of a game-play.... The playing field in which the game is played out is, so to speak, measured out from within by the game-play itself and is delimited far more by the order that determines the movement of play than by that which it comes up against, i.e., the boundaries of free space that restrict the movement from the outside. (1960, p. 102/1991, p. 107)

Experiencing game-play requires that an order or pattern come into dominance in accord with its own lawfulness (1960, pp. 100-102/1991, pp. 105-107; 1961, pp. 128-129/1976, pp. 53-54). When this dominance is established, the ordered context registers on the player's awareness in a feeling of ease and release and freedom. Such expressions as "getting into the groove," "finding one's momentum," "getting one's timing," obviously intend not harsh constraints but the felt sense of coming into our own in the action of playing. Gadamer calls the ordered context that makes this experience possible "a mutual orientation of absolute contemporaneity" in which what is determinative is not a person's arbitrary decision to act this way or that way, but "the unified pattern of movement as a whole, which conforms the orientation of movement of individual participants into itself" (1961, pp. 128-129/1976, pp. 53-54).

In game-play our trying is a being-tested, our playing a being-played, the risk of not matching up to the demands of the game as beyond one's arbitrary whim increases the fascination of the higher determination flowing out of the game-play. "One cannot...be released into the freedom of playing-oneself-out except by transforming the purposes of one's conduct into the sheer tasks and challenges of the game-play" (1960, p. 103/1991, p. 107). And yet "the real goal of the game-play is not at all the completion of these tasks, but the ordering and patterning of the movement of play itself" (p. 103/p. 107). The entire purpose of the game-play is "self-presentation and self-expression." However, surrendering oneself to the task of the game, according to Gadamer, is actually to play oneself out:

The self-presentation or -expression of the game-play has the effect that the players...achieve their own self-presentation/expression precisely insofar as they play something, i.e., present, make present, express. Only because game-playing is always already a presentation-expression can human game-play discover in presentation-expression itself the task of game-play. (p. 103/p. 108)

Being caught up in what-is-moving-in-and-through the game-play as patterning and ordering allows "the selves of the individuals, their conduct as well as their understanding of themselves, to merge with a higher determination, which is the properly determinative moment" (Gadamer, 1961, pp.

128-129/1976, pp. 53-54). This playful sublimation of ourselves into what is moving in and through our orientation to the world becomes constitutively relevant for art whenever it occurs as communication for someone else (1960, pp. 103-105/1991, pp. 108-110). It is not that "the closed space of the world of game-play...lets a wall fall away." Rather, in presenting a meaningful whole for the spectator, "openness toward the spectator makes up the very closedness of the game-play." The spectator(s) become the "fourth wall" that closes off the play-world of the work of art: "The players experience the game-play as a reality that surpasses them. That holds true especially where it is 'intended' as such a reality—and that is the case where the game-play appears as a presentation for the spectators" (p. 104/p. 109). So game-play is epitomized in the sharing of meaning by players and audience or what Allen Tate has taken pains to call not communication but communion.

What is the reality of this participation in a meaningful whole moving in and through the activity of the constituting components (for example, artist, "material," performers, and audience)? Gadamer calls it "transformation into structure" (1960, pp. 105-115/1991, pp. 110-121). By transformation into structure, he tells us, game-play achieves its proper perfection precisely because it achieves a refinement of form or idealization such that over time "it can be intended and understood as *dasselbe* 'one and the same' " (p. 105/p. 110).

In Gadamer's words, transformation "has the character of a work, of *ergon* and not only of *energeia*." The term "structure" in the phrase "transformation into structure" refers to this poiematic aspect of game-play as art. In addition, a certain kind of change takes place in the act of art. What Nadezhda Mandelstam said of the poet is true of every type of artist: "Every poet is a 'disturber of sense'—that is...he extracts new sense from his understanding of the world" (Mandelstam, 1970/1980, p. 225).

This displacement of form or essence indicated by the word "transformation" is not an accidental, qualitative change but:

> That something all at once and as a whole is another, that this other, which it is as transformed, is its true being over against which its earlier being is as nothing.... So transformation into structure means that what is before, is no longer. But also that that which is now, what is made present in the game-play of art, is what is lastingly true." (Gadamer, 1960, p. 106/1991, p. 111)

This means that the elements that go into the making of a work of art—for example, the "material," the performer, and the audience—are taken up into a meaningful whole that they express, display, or make present in their interplay:

> Transformation into structure is not simply transposition into another world. It is of course another self-enclosed world in which the game-play plays. But inasmuch as it is structure, it has as it were found its

> measure in itself and measures itself against nothing that is outside it-self.... It allows no comparison with reality as the secret standard for every similarity proper to copies. It is elevated above every such comparison—and hence above the question whether it is real—because out of it speaks a superior truth.... The transformation is a transformation into what is true. It is not enchantment in the sense of a bewitchment that looks for a resolving word of change—back into true being. What-is emerges from the presentation of the game-play. In it what is ordinar-ily always concealed and remote is seized upon and brought out into the light. (1960, p. 107/1991, p. 112)

The concept of transformation should characterize the independent and higher mode of being of what we have called structure. In its light, so-called reality is set off as the untransformed, while art is seen as the sublation of this reality into its truth (1960, p. 108/1991, p. 113).

The raw material of reality is not reported on but elaborated, height-ened, developed, and perfected through artistry. The artwork is meaning: in René Wellek's words, "a meaningful system of norms to be fulfilled when experienced" (Wellek, 1942, p. 745).

This heightened clarification of reality by art begets a pleasure and a joy that Gadamer insists is born of knowledge (1960, pp. 107-115/1991, pp. 110-121): "In (art) each person knows: This is the way it is" (p. 108/p. 113). Invoking Aristotle's doctrine of *mimesis* and Plato's teaching on *anamnesis*, Gadamer shows that what is made present in the communion wrought by the mimetic act of making together with the appreciative act of recognition is not something already known and rendered merely "there again." It is more genuinely, more intensely there, in what is not just an imitative repetition, but a real apprehension of and assent to what is essential (pp. 109-110/p. 115).

Gadamer tells us that "despite its orientation toward being actually played, it is a significant totality that as such can be repeatedly presented and understood in its meaning. The structure, however, is also game-play because—despite its ideal unity—it attains its full being only in the act of being played" (1960, p. 111/1991, p. 117). Thus, significant form (Wellek's meaningful system of norms to be followed when experienced) is not enough to constitute the work of art; the enactment of the form in the con-templation of the painting or sculpture, in the reading of the poem, in the theatrical rendition, and so on, is also necessary. The analogy of the sacra-ment is apropos: There the giving and taking of meaning by the author/maker, the players, and the spectator coincide, so that the communication taking place involves both *ex opere operato* and *ex opere operantis*.

As we see, two aspects come together here: "Mediation" of structure occurs only in virtue of the actual making/performing/appreciating; and at the same time the "structure" provides the normative medium of the mak-ing/performing/appreciating (pp. 113-115/pp. 118-121). When these aspects are conjoined there occurs what Gadamer calls "total mediation." This means that each of the mediating factors is completely sublated so that it stays utterly non-thematic, or tacit (p. 112/p. 117). In total mediation, distinctions between the work, the work's material, and the performance of the work become irrelevant and beside the point. On account of the total nature of the mediation, the normative moment of the work and the experience of it are not reached by checking the significant form against something outside itself. Nor may the interpretation of the author/maker or of the original audience supply a standard of judgment. The normative moment is given precisely in the fulfillment or enactment of the total mediation itself (p. 116/p. 122): "That each presentation intends to be correct only furnishes a confirmation of the fact that the non-distinction of the mediation from the work itself is itself the authentic experience of the work" (p. 114/p. 119). Gadamer's idea of total mediation is a complete generalization of this, extending it from poets to every performance, interpretation, and reception of an art work. The enactment or retrieval of meaning involved in mimetic presentation and recognition "does not mean that something is repeated in the proper sense, i.e. is referred back to an original. Rather the retrieval is equiprimordial with the work itself" (1960, p.116/1991, p. 122).

If the work of art were merely contemporary it would present a novelty whose meaning would be exhausted by no more than the discontinuous caprice of the relative moment. A genuine work of art cannot be just contemporary. But it also does not exist in a realm of timelessness to which human beings as conditioned extrinsically by space and time have no access in this life. The zone of punctual simultaneity supposedly proper to "aesthetic consciousness" is a fiction as well. For Gadamer, the transformation into structure as the total mediation of art is *gleichzeitig* "contemporaneous." "A being," he tells us, "that is only inasmuch as it is constantly an other is temporal in a more radical sense than anything belonging to history. It has its being only in becoming and returning" (1960, p. 117/1991, p. 123). Take, for instance, a religious feast like Easter. As a celebration its recurrence is not strictly other than its original occasion. Nor does it simply provide an opportunity for recalling its origin. Instead it transcends such distinctions by re-presenting the original in a regularly recurrent fashion. This happens only in the actual celebration, which depends on the participative presence of those celebrating, in the sense that a "true participation" is "not something we do, but something we suffer (*pathos*), namely, our enraptured encompassment" (p. 118/pp. 124-125). In other words, the key issue is not our subjective conduct, but the ecstatic dimension of what happens to us: our being caught up, out of ourselves, our self-transcendence and self-forgetfulness as correlative to the contemporaneity of the work of art. As contemporaneous, and neither contemporary nor formally simultaneous, the work of art invites us to abide in a meaning. Indeed, "contemporaneity" is a term coined by Kierkegaard to convey a surpassing of the spatialized image of past and present times to indicate "the task imposed on the believer to take what is not simultaneous—one's own present and the saving deed of Christ—and mediate them so totally with one another that the latter is experienced and taken seriously as something present, rather than in the distance of the past" (p. 121/pp. 127-128).

More abstractly, according to Gadamer, contemporaneity expresses the structure by which a long-lasting claim is concretized in a demand that one become engaged through authentic participation in the settling of the validity of the claim (pp. 120-121/pp. 126-127). Contemporaneity is "not a mode of givenness within consciousness but a challenge for consciousness and an achievement exacted of it. It consists in so adhering to the subject matter that it becomes 'contemporaneous,' i.e., that all mediation is sublated into total presence" (p. 121/p. 127).

For Gadamer, in the artistic transformation of something meaningful the structured view or sense of direction exceeds the limits of the particular context being transformed. Thus it calls for a taking or mistaking of oneself on its own terms, in its proper "aesthetic distance" (1960, p. 122/1991, p. 128; 1967a, p. 6/1976, pp. 100-102). This means that to take rather than mistake a work of art we have to undergo a certain "ecstatic self-forgetfulness": "Precisely in virtue of that in which one loses oneself as a spectator is the continuity of meaning demanded of one. It is the truth of one's own world, of the religious and ethical world in which one lives, which is made present before one and in which one knows oneself" (1960, p. 122/1991, p. 128). What T.S. Eliot says of the artist is thus apposite for every aspect of subjective involvement with art work: "The second-rate artist, of course, cannot afford to surrender himself to any common action; for his chief task is the assertion of all the trifling differences which are his distinction; only the man who has so much to give that he can forget himself in his work can afford to collaborate, to exchange, to contribute" (Eliot, 1975, p. 69).

In a unique interpenetration of self-forgetfulness and self-integration, we are wrenched out of our self-entrenched personalities, and have the realization bestowed upon us of what it is to be human: "What tears one away from everything, at the same time gives one back to the totality of his being" (Gadamer, 1960, p. 122/1991, p. 128). Afterwards we are never the same. To understand what is happening to us in life is to undergo change in our lives. Art is always an invitation to wider human activity than one has already been accustomed to: "In an enigmatic way, the familiarity the art work besets us with is at once a shaking up and turning-over of the world as usual. It is not only the 'That is you', which it discloses in a pleasurable and frightening cry—it also tells us, 'You must change your life'" (1967a, p. 8/1976, p. 104). So far from being propaganda for something one is already interested in, it is "never just a strange world of enchantment, of spells, of dreams to which the player, the sculptor, or onlooker is swept away" but it is instead "always still one's own world, which supervenes on one more authentically to the degree that one knows oneself more deeply in it." Recognition heightens awareness and makes us explicitly conscious of something that had already borne us along. "There remains a continuity of meaning which encloses the work of art with the world of human existence from which even the estranged consciousness of cultured society can never completely release itself" (1960, p. 127/1991, p. 134).

To summarize, the transformation into structure occurring in the work of art comprises a medium in which human experience, human belief, human ideals, or human values are all made available for heightened and intensified insight; the work of art, according to Gadamer, reveals the permanent and universal features of human life, and the opportunity to structure life-orientations according to the deeper, permanent values which human beings consider significant. Because the work of art "insists" on its own reality as an autonomous world of mediated meaning, because it confronts us, the experience of the work of art may deny our inauthentic manner of existence and accuse us of our own lack of reality even as it challenges us to feel what a more enhancing and ennobling life might be.

Game-Play: Language-Games, Conversation, Understanding, Interpretation, and Translation

In describing his strategy in *Truth and Method* Gadamer has written: "It made sense to bring the game-play of language into closer connection with the game-play of art in which I had contemplated the parade example of the hermeneutical. Now to consider the universal linguistic constitution of our experience of the world in terms of the model of game-play certainly does suggest itself" (Gadamer, 1986b, p. 5). Indeed, when people first learn to speak it is not so much a learning process as a "game of imitation and exchange." As Gadamer tells us, "In the receptive child's drive to imitate the forming of sounds, the enjoyment in such forming of sounds is paired with the illumination of meaning. No one can really answer in a reasonable manner the question when their first understanding of meaning occurred" (p. 5). Theologian Austin Farrer put this beautifully:

> Our humanity is itself a cultural heritage; the talking animal is talked into talk by those who talk at him.... His mind is not at first his own, but the echo of his elders. The echo turns into a voice, the painted portrait steps down from the frame, and each of us becomes himself. Yet by the time we are aware of our independence, we are what others have made us. We can never unweave the web to the very bottom.... Nor is it only parental impresses of which we are the helpless victims. How many persons, how many conditions have made us what we are; and, in making us so, may have undone us. (Farrer, 1967, p. 114)

When Gadamer claims that we learn everything in language-games, this has nothing to do with the subjective attitude of "just playing" and not being serious. In fact, game-play in general really begins when players become serious, in the sense of not holding themselves back as "just playing" (Gadamer, 1966, p. 152/1976, p. 66). Language for Gadamer is not a set of tools such as vocabulary, grammar, syntax, and so on, but language-in-use. Language gets used in conversation. Because conversation has the structure of game-play, language exists concretely as language-games. Here Gadamer finds himself in agreement with Ludwig Wittgenstein, who hit upon the same insight completely independently (1963, pp. 185-189/1976, pp. 173-177). As Gadamer tells us: "The life of language consists...in the constant further playing out of the game we started when we learned to speak.... It is this continuously played game in which the mutual life together of people is played out" (1966, p. 152/1976, p. 66).

Conversation is structured as game-play, and so has the spirit of game-play with its characteristic "lightness, freedom, and the luck of success—of being fulfilling, and of fulfilling those who are playing" (p. 152/p. 66). This is evident when we achieve mutual understanding or agreement:

> Mutual understanding happens by the fact that talk stands up against talk, but does not remain static. Instead, in talking to each other we pass over into the imaginative world of the other; we as it were open ourselves up to them, and they do so to us. So we play into each other until the game of giving and taking, the conversation proper, begins. No one can deny that in such real conversation there is something of chance, the favor of surprise, finally also of lightness, yes, even of elevation, which pertains to the nature of game-play. And truly the elevation of conversation is experienced not as a loss of self-possession, but, even without ourselves actually attending to it, as an enrichment of ourselves. (1961, p. 131/1976, pp. 56-57)

> As we come together in conversation, and are now...led on further by the conversation, then what is determinative is no longer people as holding themselves in reserve or as willing to be open, but the law of the subject matter about which the conversation is going on, which releases speech and response and finally plays everyone into itself. So wherever a conversation has been successful, afterwards everyone is, as we say, filled with it. The play of speech and response is played out further in the inner conversation of the soul with itself, as Plato so beautifully named thinking. (1966, p. 152/1976, p. 66)

A genial aspect of focusing on the role of conversation in human life and thought is that instead of philosophy being narrowed down to either the phenomenology of perception or logical preoccupations with concepts, propositions, and inferences, this point of departure takes us back to the roots of all answers in questions. Gadamer celebrates the great British historian and philosopher R.G. Collingwood for having first articulated "the logic of question and answer" (1960, pp. 351-360/1991, pp. 369-379). Gadamer went beyond Collingwood to show how when that "logic" is retrieved concretely in dialectic or friendly conversation, it is structured as a game, not just because understanding itself occurs and grows in the to and fro of question and answer; but, as he rather unconventionally observes, this "happens from the side of the things themselves. The subject matter 'yields' questions" (1986b, p. 6).

What we are doing when we are truly conversing is understanding and interpreting. Both words in English can be used to correctly translate Gadamer's key term *Verstehen*, which in German covers not just the act of insight but also the act of articulation or *Auslegung* by which we talk to ourselves, laying out in language what we are actually understanding. "Interpretation belongs to the essential unity of understanding. Whatever is said to us must be so received by us that it speaks and finds a response in our own words and in our own language" (1961, p. 131/1976, p. 57).

That understanding for Gadamer always involves interpretation, is preeminently true in understanding texts:

> Whoever wants to understand a text always performs a projection. We project a meaning of the whole, as soon as a first meaning is manifest in the text. Such a meaning in turn only becomes manifest because one is already reading the text with certain expectations of a determinate meaning. Understanding what is there to be understood consists in working out such a projection, which of course is constantly revised by what emerges in penetrating its meaning further.... [A]ny revision of the projection exists in virtue of the possibility of casting up a new projection;...rival projections towards the elaboration can be generated one after the other, until the unity of sense is fixed unequivocally;...the interpretation is initiated with anticipatory notions that are replaced by more adequate ones: Precisely this ongoing newly-projecting that constitutes the movement of meaning proper to understanding and interpreting is the process that Heidegger describes. (1959, pp. 59-60)

Whenever we read a text "there is no author present at the discussion as an answering partner, and no subject matter present which can be so or otherwise. The text as a work stands on its own" (1986b, p. 9). Does this mean that there is no dialogue? Not at all.

> It seems that here the dialectic of question and answer, insofar as it has any place at all, is only available in one direction, which means from the side of the one seeking to understand the work of art, who questions it and who is called into question by it, and who tries to listen for the answer of the work. As the person one is, one may, just like anyone thinking, be the inquirer and responder at once, in the same manner as happens in a real conversation between two people. But this dialogue of the understanding reader with oneself surely does not seem to be a dialogue with the text, which is fixed and to that extent is finished. Or is this really how it is? Or is there an already finished text given at all?

> In this case the dialectic of question and answer does not come to a standstill.... The reception of a poetic work, whether it be by our outer ear or by that inner ear that listens attentively when we are reading, presents itself as a circular movement in which answers rebound into

further questions and provoke new answers. This motivates our abiding with the work of art, of whatever kind it may be. Abiding is obviously the authentic characteristic in the experience of art. A work of art is never exhausted. (1986b, p. 9)

This is where Gadamer locates the processes of translation in the sense of construing the meaning of something in one language into the terms presented by a second language. We might say that translation is just an exaggerated case of what happens as we make our way through life in general. That human living is conversational means that we are constantly making sense of what presents itself in the foreground of our experience in terms of our linguistic horizon. We do this by trying to find the right word with which to articulate and communicate our experience (both to ourselves and to others), by a process of trial and error, and we rarely if ever achieve a stage of definitiveness beyond all provisionality. As Gadamer tells us:

> If any model can really illustrate the tensions residing in understanding and interpretation, it is that of translation. In it the strange or alien is made our own as strange or alien, and that means neither that it is just permitted to stay alien, nor that it is constructed in one's language by a sheer imitation of its very strangeness; but in [translation] the horizons of past and present are merged in an ongoing movement as it constitutes the very nature of understanding and interpretation (*Verstehen*). (1969, p. 436)

Game-Play: Application to Christian Mission

Theologian Rowan Williams suggests that both Wittgenstein and Dietrich Bonhoeffer were in differing ways converging on what we can now see is a very Gadamerian view of human living:

> Wittgenstein and Bonhoeffer more clearly presuppose that to interpret the symbolic, linguistic, and behavioral complex that "addresses" us in the human world is to have one's own pattern of speech and action conditioned (not determined) by it, to be provoked (called forward) by the ways in which it touches, confirms, resonates, or questions what we have done and said. To interpret means interweaving a text (words and actions, words *and* actions) with our human project, acquiring a partner, a pole of difference that refuses to allow our "project" to return endlessly on itself, as if it were indeed generated from a well of unsullied interiority, "self-consciousness." (Williams, 1988, p. 48)

Gadamer, who was a friend of Bultmann from his days as a young student in Marburg, was interested in Greek philology and recognizes like Williams that life proceeds by interpretation in a process in which the subject is displaced from the center, so that human beings become themselves by playing into a direction of meaning and value that is moving in and through the interplay of subjects with the world. The game-play structure of

life comes into its own perhaps even more strikingly in the Christian experience of grace and faith than in the experience of art (though there is no need
necessarily to separate the two kinds of experience). As Williams phrases the
issue of achieving human wholeness "in...belonging to God, a wholeness
achieved in trust or hope rather than analysis":

> My own identity's "ungraspable" quality thus becomes not an elusive
> level of interiority, but the unknowable presence of the creator's abso-
> lute affirmation, the mysteriousness of grace, past, present, and future,
> not of the "true self" as a hidden thing. My unity as a person is always
> out of my field of vision (I can't see my own face), just as the divine
> condition for there being fields of vision at all, for there being a world
> or worlds, is out of my field of vision (I can't see my own origin).
> (1988, p. 43)

In parallel fashion Gadamer states:

> All understanding in the end is self-understanding, but not in the mode
> of a prior or finally achieved self-possession. For this self-under-
> standing is always realized only in the understanding of a subject mat-
> ter, and does not have the character of a free self-realization. The self
> that we are does not possess itself. One could better put it that instead it
> happens. And that is what theology really says, that faith is just such an
> event, in which a new man is founded. And it says further that it is the
> Word that needs to be believed and understood and by which we over-
> come the abysmal lack of self-knowledge in which we live. (1961, p.
> 130/1976, p. 55)

Gadamer has transposed Bultmann's ideas about self-understanding as
possibly still too tainted by an idealistic subjectivism and existentialism into
the framework of the game-play structure of human life. From this perspective he considers the relationship of Christian faith to understanding and
interpretation in human life.

> Whatever is said to us we must receive into ourselves so that it speaks
> to us and finds a response in our own words in our own language. This
> holds utterly true for the text of proclamation which cannot really be
> understood if it does not appear as being said to our very own selves.
> Here it is the sermon in which the understanding and interpretation of
> the text attains its full reality. Neither the explicating commentary nor
> the exegetical labors of the theologians, but the sermon stands in the
> immediate service of the proclamation inasmuch as it not only mediates
> the understanding of what the Holy Scripture tells us, but witnesses to it
> at the same time. However, the proper fullness of understanding lies not
> in the sermon as such, but in the manner in which it is accepted as a
> call that impinges on each one of us. (pp. 130-131/pp. 57-58)

Gadamer also criticized Bultmann's overemphasis upon the historical-
critical mediation of New Testament texts. Once he half-jokingly told me,
"Bultmann forgets that the books of the New Testament are not 'books' in

the ordinary sense of the term." He was agreeing with Franz Overbeck and his own friend Helmut Kuhn that these texts belong to the genre of *Urliteratur*. This implies that:

> If we understand under the meaning of the text the *mens auctoris*, i.e., the "verifiable" horizon of understanding of any given Christian writer, then we accord the authors of the New Testament a false honor. Their proper honor ought to lie in the fact that they announce the tidings about something that surpasses the horizon of their own under-standing—even if they happen to be named John or Paul. (1964, p. 207/1976, p. 210)

I would like to point out three aspects of what Gadamer has written about the Christian message in the New Testament as an instance of *Urliteratur*. The first is that the authors of the Holy Scriptures are faithful witnesses to a tradition that goes back to the first community and its witnesses. As such they are less authors, strictly speaking, than intermediate witnesses. For Gadamer, not every religious message counts as witness, but witness is the distinguishing mark of the Christian message or Gospel. It witnesses to the passion of Jesus and the resurrection promise of salvation.

> It is an authentic witness because it refers to a particular event: the death of Jesus on the cross. It is a human being who suffers the death of a criminal and who in full awareness of being the Son of God and of being God, insists on the title "Son of Man" and accepts the fate of creatures. (Gadamer, n.d., p. 164)

A second aspect is that the New Testament has the special status of "eminent text." There are three categories of such texts: (1) announcements of the kind common in law, such as promulgated verdicts or statutes; (2) affirmations as are made in poetry (works of art "made out of" language) and in philosophy; (3) addresses as in religious texts, and especially the Scriptures and the preaching/hearing by which they are applied down the ages. For Gadamer an "eminent text" is one which "capture[s] a purely linguistic action and so possesses an eminent relationship to writing and writtenness. In it language is present in such a way that its cognitive relationship to the merely given outside the text disappears just as much as is its communicative relation in the sense of the one being addressed" (Gadamer, 1972, p. 475). According to Gadamer, as an eminent text the Christian Scripture has a normativity that is virtually equivalent to that justified by the idea of inspiration:

> The primordial question to which the text has to be understood as an answer has here...by reason of its origin an inherent supremacy and freedom.... [T]he classical text is "telling" only when it speaks "primordially," i.e., "as if it were spoken just to me alone." That does not at all imply that what speaks in this way is measured against an extra-histori-cal concept of norm. Just the contrary: What speaks in this way thereby posits a standard. Herein lies the problem. The primordial question to

which the text is to be understood as an answer in such a case *lays claim to an identity of meaning which always has already mediated the distance between presence and past.* (p. 476)

An "eminent text" therefore entails "an exceptional mode of historical being, the historical enactment of preservation which—in ever-renewed corroboration—allows something to be true" (1960, p. 271/1991, p. 287). It is proper to such a work to have "an identifiability, a repeatability, and a worthiness to be repeated" that only can be predicated of something that once functioned in the past and continues to function in any succeeding temporal context in an originative way. This means that it is normative, but also constantly becomes constitutive of ourselves. Luther saw this when he said that the Gospel has a *pro me* character. So when we come into contact with the Gospel as an eminent text we realize our "immediate and binding affinity" to a reality which "as past is at once unattainable and presently relevant" (p. 273/p. 289). The Gospel, "far from being evidence documenting something bygone that we may not care to interpret and make our own, is already speaking to us and every person in history in a way that is uniquely appropriate to that particular place and time" (p. 274/p. 289). This means that as an eminent text the Gospel has an autonomous meaning that is self-interpreting and self-authenticating. As Gadamer says so effectively, "The classical...is as Hegel says, 'that which signifies itself and so also interprets itself.' Ultimately this means: The classical is what preserves itself, *because* it signifies itself and interprets itself." (pp. 273-274/p. 289).

A third aspect Gadamer highlights about the Christian message is that the proclamation of the good news and the messianic promise does not have the status of a symbolic form of recognition, which is common to all other religious traditions. Instead, the meaning of the Christian message's "This is you" in the context of the incarnation and Easter message has the status of "sign." "A sign is something only given to one who is ready to accept it as such" (1986a, p. 152). According to Gadamer, "the uniqueness of the Gospel message lies in the fact that it must be accepted against all expectation and hope," because "the claim of the Christian message—and this is what gives it its exclusivity—is that it alone has really overcome death through the proclamation of the representative suffering and death of Jesus as a redemptive act" (pp. 153, 151). As Gadamer put it so radically:

> It is not the infinite wealth of life possibilities that is encountered in [the Christian] "this is you," but rather the extreme poverty of the *Ecce homo.* The expression must be given a quite different emphasis here: "This is you"—a man helplessly exposed to suffering and death. It is precisely in the face of this infinite withholding of happiness that the Easter message is to become Good News. (p. 151)

As a sign, Gadamer tells us, this "is not something that takes the place of seeing, for what distinguishes it precisely from all reports or from its opposite, silence, is the fact that what is shown is only accessible to the one who looks for himself and actually sees something there" (p. 152).

 **Fred Lawrence** is associate professor of Theology at Boston College. He is a graduate of the University of Basel (Switzerland), where he wrote a dissertation, "Believing to Understand: The Hermeneutic Circle in Gadamer and Lonergan." He has served as a consultor to the American Academy of Religion, a trustee of the Lonergan Trust Fund, and a panelist for the Washington DC-based State Justice Institute. Presently he belongs to the Planning Committee for the Michigan Judicial Institute. His publications span the fields of hermeneutics, aesthetics, and judicial education.

From One Medium to Another

———————— ◍ ————————

Part II

Case Studies:

Accepting the Challenge

Case Studies:
Accepting the Challenge

This second section of the book presents a series of case studies of translating from one medium to another. For the most part these studies describe what artists, choreographers, filmmakers, and musicians do when they adapt existing works. Some of the reflections come from current practitioners and some from the ABS Multimedia Translations Project team. What factors influence people as they try to move from one medium to another?

These case studies begin with the description of American evangelist Aimee Semple McPherson's attempt to translate revivalist rhetoric to radio. Given the similarities of form, her move to a new medium seems natural. In the larger picture, though, it provides a context for our century's engagement with new media and offers a test case for moving religious discourse from one medium to another.

The next four chapters examine how artists have traditionally translated from one medium to another. Elizabeth Keen describes the work of choreographers who have taken stories, plays, and Greek legends as the basis for dance. Jennifer González introduces the work of installation artists as expressions of popular culture while Jayne Loader and Alice Bach look at film and video, respectively. Common themes emerge in their descriptions of practical—or applied—translation. Each artist begins with a text base: Keen sketches how choreographers worked from a novel, a drama, or a play; González, how installation artists begin with a cultural expression (from biblical texts to fan magazines); Loader, how screenwriters pick biblical stories; and Bach, how she as a multimedia artist, assembles biblical materials. Then the artist expands the semiotic "content" of the texts through attention to gesture, movement, camera angle, decoration, and interpretation. At the same time, many artists either add to the original—an act Loader and Bach illustrate by noting script additions—or take away from it—an editorial function Keen highlights.

The last three chapters come from people involved in the ABS Multimedia Translations Project. Based on their work in translating the Gospel passages in Mark 5.1-20, Luke 11.15-32, and Luke 1.39-56, their reflections give a kind of three-dimensional view of the project—from the perspectives of music, art, and computing. Their procedures, while resembling those of the artists introduced by the other authors, differ in at least one significant way—their care not to go beyond the biblical text. J. Ritter Werner and Gregor Goethals suggest a theoretical rationale for their parts of the translations: Werner provides a look at the musical mimesis of the translation while Goethals discusses both the background and the practical work on the art that informs the project. Reg Pettus describes the computer programming aspects.

In this work on the Multimedia Translations Project, we see a kind of practical theology, a reflection on revelation much like what the early Church did as it moved from the Scriptures to theology—a more theoretical and abstract expression of the mystery of faith. In the ABS project we see a contemporary attempt at such practical theology—one that wrestles with questions of cultural expression.

6

Tuning In:
A Historical Look At Evangelicals,
Pentecostals and Electronic Media

Edith L. Blumhofer

Historically, evangelicals and pentecostals deployed the electronic media for purposes of personal growth and public evangelism. This connection between Pentecostal faith and electronic media appears clearly in the life and ministry of Aimee Semple McPherson, the best-known North American female evangelist, whose attention was drawn to the power of electronic media by, among other factors, the proximity of her congregation to the then newly-founded Walt Disney studios.

"Draw up your fire-side chair, adjust your ear phones and tune in, for the great...revival is now on the air! May God grant that the radio prove a mighty blessing to old and young, rich and poor, to sick and well, to one and all." — Aimee Semple McPherson, 1924

In the 1920s, Americans expressed unbounded enthusiasm for electronic media. Advances in communication technology proceeded at a dizzying pace, and North American evangelicals quickly jumped on the bandwagon. For them, new technologies—especially radio—seemed more than human achievements. Radio had a miraculous quality, a supernatural dimension making it a gift from God. "Convert the sinner by radio," evangelist Aimee Semple McPherson challenged her supporters in 1923. "[Radio is] the most modern way of preaching the gospel" (1923b, p. 15). McPherson preserves the sense of amazement, novelty, and possibility with which evangelicals and pentecostals marveled at the arrival of commercial radio:

Like some fantastic dream! Like a visionary tale from the Arabian Nights! Like an imaginary fairy tale is the Story of The Radio.... Miraculous in so much as to be almost beyond comprehension; a beautiful, priceless gift from the loving Hand of our Father God; a most unheard of opportunity for converting the world, and reaching the largest possible number of people in the shortest possible time—THE RADIO IN ACTION! (p. 15)

Gospel songs of the 1920s also rallied the faithful to support the cause:

> A radio station for Jesus,
> Let this be our aim and our prayer;
> To send forth the Heavenly message
> As Jesus reveals it "up there."
> A radio station for Jesus,
> We'll broadcast His power to save,
> And tell how to keep us from evil
> His life upon Calvary He gave. (Buffum, 1926)

Other Americans shared the excitement, of course. Evangelicals simply mirrored the general cultural enthusiasm for the newest communications medium. Some tempered their enthusiasm with the recognition that radio had negative as well as positive possibilities. Country clubs that broadcast Sunday services so that golfers could spend more time on the course, or programming that kept people sitting beside their crystal sets instead of attending Sunday evening services threatened congregational life. Radio in the context of other proliferating and socially transforming commodities like the automobile could undermine as well as affirm the faith. But most evangelicals concluded that the benefits outweighed the liabilities and embraced radio as a gift from God.

If the first radio preachers had any misgivings, these disappeared minutes after their first broadcasts, usually overridden by a flood of enthusiastic responses. Most of these came by telephone, often long distance, but occasionally someone ran to the station and accosted a startled preacher to say that the broadcast message had saved their soul (Ward, 1994, p. 31). To the millions of American Protestants who believed evangelism stood at the core of their faith, radio appeared to have unlimited promise for proclaiming the gospel. Suddenly, technology offered access to America at home, day or night. Radio revolutionized American culture; it also transformed popular Protestantism. Religious broadcasting began in earnest in the spring of 1922, a mere 18 months after commercial broadcasting made its debut. The industry mushroomed so rapidly that people still argue vigorously about radio "firsts." Pittsburgh station KDKA has a strong claim that its broadcast of the Harding-Cox election returns to the handful of Americans with radio sets on November 2, 1920 launched the era of commercial broadcast. After a slow start, radio set in motion a cultural revolution. At first, Americans jammed large arenas to listen with awe to speeches and ceremonies from afar— crowding Madison Square Garden in 1920, for example, to listen to the burial of the unknown soldier at Arlington Cemetery.

Then, in the winter of 1921, a radio craze gripped the nation. President Harding set the example by installing a set in the White House study; the Lackawanna railroad delighted passengers with a radio concert; an enterprising military man broadcast an Easter sermon from an airplane. Broadcasts carried easily from coast to coast: *The New York Times* printed schedules for stations as distant as Havana and Los Angeles.

Economists charted the astonishing growth of a new industry. In 1922, Americans invested $60 million in radio sets, parts, and accessories. In 1929, that figure reached $842.5 million, an increase of more than 1,400% (Allen, 1931, p. 166). Sales climbed even during the economic downturn of 1924, thanks, in part, to the broadcasting from Madison Square Garden of the raucous Democratic Convention. On March 4, 1925, Americans gathered in homes and large auditoriums to hear Calvin Coolidge's inaugural address. "They heard it," evangelist Paul Rader enthused, "even better than the crowd about the Capitol in Washington" (Rader, 1925, p. 3). Equally amazing to Rader was the fact that an enterprising New Yorker recorded the address and marketed it on a phonograph record. "This is a new day," Rader assured his immense following, a harbinger of the ultimate new day still to come. "President Coolidge became the First Announcer of a universal message to the whole nation. There will be another ANNOUNCER on the air before long. He will announce His message to the whole world" (p. 3). Looking backward at the end of the decade, journalist and commentator Frederick Lewis Allen quipped perceptively: "At the age of three and a half years, radio broadcasting...attained its majority" (1931, p. 166). In 1927, the government belatedly began assigning wave lengths and curtailing the radio explosion.

Hundreds of American preachers jumped on the radio bandwagon in the 1920s, but a few were the acknowledged pioneers and pacesetters for aspiring religious broadcasters. Among these, none achieved wider fame nor put the radio to more innovative use than Los Angeles evangelist Aimee Semple McPherson. Her story reveals how (and to what ends) evangelicals used electronic media, the sources of their fascination for modern technology, and the transformations media worked on American evangelical self-understanding and practice.

A Descriptive Aside

This chapter explores the history of evangelical and pentecostal use of electronic media. "Evangelical" and "pentecostal" are words that are often used but seldom defined, and so some clarifications at the outset may be useful.

Scottish historian David Bebbington identifies four characteristic features of Evangelicalism: (1) conversionism, (2) biblicism, (3) crucicentrism, and (4) activism (1989, pp. 2-19). Implicit in both "conversionism" and "activism" is the evangelical compulsion to spread the faith and convert the world. In the United States, Evangelicalism is inseparable from the revival tradition, and it has spawned hundreds of mission societies and voluntary associations dedicated to spreading the gospel.

Historically, American Pentecostalism is firmly rooted in the evangelical subculture (Blumhofer, 1993b, pp. 1-112). Classical pentecostals date the beginnings of their movement to scattered turn-of-the-century revivals among radical evangelicals in which speaking in tongues and other "utterance gifts" mentioned in the New Testament were practiced. The best-known of these revivals ran from 1906-1908 at a mission on Azusa Street in Los Angeles. The denominations that acknowledge the direct contributions of this awakening to their history are known as "classical pentecostals" and include the Church of God in Christ, the Assemblies of God, various Churches of God, and the United Pentecostal Church.

Pentecostals have historically been eager to spread their message. At first they understood tongues speech as miraculous ability to speak known languages—in other words, as a tool for the rapid evangelization of the world. Although anticipation of miraculous facility in foreign languages soon faded, classical pentecostals always understood the defining moment in their religious experience—the believer's baptism with the Holy Spirit—as "enduement with power for service." In their vocabulary, "service" generally meant evangelism. Driven by the conviction that Christ was about to burst through the clouds, they saw Pentecostalism as God "thundering forth His last appeal" before the final judgment (Tatman, 1925, p. 3). Thus motivated, they restlessly and tirelessly carried their message of restoration of New Testament experience and the imminence of judgment around the world.

Distinctions between evangelicals and pentecostals are generally clearer to insiders than to outsiders. Their advocacy of spiritual gifts, physical healing, and expressive worship separates pentecostals from other evangelicals (although, since the advent of the charismatic movement in the 1960s, distinctions are further blurred). It may be helpful to think of pentecostals as radical evangelicals.

Historically, both evangelicals and pentecostals have been activists and entrepreneurs. These religious movements are popular (often even populist) movements, sensitive to the popular culture and in touch with the needs and aspirations of ordinary women and men (Hatch, 1989, p. 19). Led by talented communicators with a simple message and a compelling mission directed to average people in their everyday idiom, these movements were made-to-order for electronic media, and the media seemed made-to-order for them.

Both Evangelicalism and Pentecostalism have often been associated with anti-modernism. At one time or another, they tackled the evils of modern science and historical-critical methodology; forbade attendance at theaters, movies, dances, sporting events; rejected fashion fads and makeup; and decried the decadence of American life. Evangelical movements are fraught with tension, however, for even as they critique aspects of modernity, they have consistently embraced and adapted the most modern forms of technology for their own ends. Recognizing this paradox is essential for understanding the history of popular Evangelicalism. They have historically employed modern means for anti-modern ends.

Evangelical movements are also the most adaptive forms of Protestantism. From George Whitefield's dramatic sermons to Charles G. Finney's new measures, from Ira Sankey's gospel hymnody to radio and televangelism, evangelicals have embraced modern media and communication forms. Further, Evangelicalism has often prompted an explosion of print and put text into as many hands as possible. It cultivates testimony and makes use of narrative and story. The centrality of the telling of the gospel story—and one's own story as a continuation—flowed easily into focusing on packaging the essence of the story. For evangelicals, the gospel is the supreme story—the story that changes lives and takes infinite and unique expression in every Christian's experience—and it is always being translated or interpreted. Pentecostals remind other Christians that God is not limited by human speech and that religious experience is itself a form of translation of the gospel message. Indeed, pentecostals believe the Holy Spirit manifests God through dance, drama, song, art, as well as speech and text: Pentecostalism can be seen as a kind of divine authentication or translation packaged in varied ways and using different media.

Aimee Semple McPherson and her contemporary (and occasional associate) Paul Rader had enormous followings among pentecostals, evangelicals, and Protestants in the historic denominations (Blumhofer, 1993a). Their media efforts transcended the boundaries and conflicts that often fracture popular Protestant movements. In the years immediately following World War I, McPherson's stunning rise from oblivion to stardom revealed the penchant of American revivalistic Protestants to embrace as their heroes media stars and entrepreneurs. McPherson was both. She learned to excel in both arenas in a setting that historians of American religious history often overlook—the Salvation Army.

Aimee Semple McPherson: Beginnings

Aimee Semple McPherson made her first broadcast in the spring of 1922 when radio was fast becoming a national obsession. Her fascination for radio revealed much more than a natural curiosity about the new and the novel. Rather, it was the next logical expression of an orientation that characterized millions of her evangelical contemporaries. To understand McPherson's excitement about adapting modern technology for evangelism, one must explore her formative years and the evangelical and pentecostal assumptions that molded her understanding of the gospel. Despite her

photo courtesy of Assemblies of God Archives

Aimee Semple McPherson

extraordinary accomplishments, McPherson is best understood as an ordinary woman with an ordinary message whose extraordinary determination and flair in a particular cultural moment propelled her to fame. In many ways, her assumptions mirrored the deepest convictions and fondest hopes of North American popular Protestantism.

On the one hand, McPherson tried radio, as she did everything else that was new. In 1918 she became the first woman to drive coast to coast on the nation's new road system without the aid of a man. In 1919, when commercial aviation was still a dream, she preached at San Diego's Aviation Field and then, with thousands watching, she took her first flight in a two-seat biplane. She brought the controversial and decidedly unchurchly dramatic style of the Salvation Army into tents, auditoriums, and churches around the country and millions acknowledged its powerful influence. McPherson was daring and creative, and those qualities sharpened her appeal.

On the other hand, however, McPherson used modern media for the same reasons other evangelicals and pentecostals would. First, she was a woman with a compelling message. Second, her message was a simple "either or" proposition suited to broadcast media and the stage. In the same years that the country responded with wonder to Hollywood's amazing new feats, reporters respectfully acknowledged Aimee Semple McPherson as the best performer of all. Third, ordinary evangelicals respond especially well to able communicators whose religion has a compelling emotive component. Broadcast technology vastly extended the audience and influence of gifted evangelical media stars whose able, persuasive rhetoric swayed the masses. American evangelicals tend to be impressed by numbers, and radio brought them a potential audience that exceeded their wildest dreams.

Although many of her cohorts quickly joined the rush to use electronic media in the 1920s, Aimee Semple McPherson stood apart from them as an American sensation, an evangelist who had spoken to more people than any evangelist before her. Whatever she did seemed newsworthy. On average, she made the front page of America's biggest newspapers three times a week through the 1920s. Yet, as she often reminded her immense following, she was one of them.

Every year on her October birthday she retold the story of her childhood on the Canadian farm near Ingersoll, Ontario, where she was born Aimee Elizabeth Kennedy in 1890. Deeply influenced by her Salvationist mother, Minnie Pearce Kennedy, Aimee's understanding of Christianity was molded by the early Ontario Salvation Army. In 1907 her faith was awakened in a pentecostal mission in Ingersoll, and the next year she married Robert Semple, the evangelist who had converted her. They went to Hong Kong as missionaries in 1910. Two months after their arrival, Robert died. Their daughter was born a month later, and then Aimee sailed for home, a bewildered 19-year-old widow. She settled first in New York (where she and her mother worked for the Salvation Army) and then, in 1912, in Rhode Island with her new husband, Harold McPherson.

Focused and determined to get what she wanted, Aimee proved restive under the conventional constraints of her second marriage. Gifted with unerring theatrical instincts, a flair for publicity, and a fertile imagination (all of which had been honed among her Salvationist friends), she abandoned the daily routine for the unpredictable life of an itinerant evangelist. From 1916 through 1918, she traveled up and down the east coast in a car plastered with bible verses and evangelistic slogans, putting in long hours of work, shipping her tent from place to place, and managing most of the operation herself. For a few months Harold McPherson traveled with her, but he faded from the limelight as her popularity grew. Late in 1918, along with a vast stream of other Americans, McPherson headed west. By 1919, the largest auditoriums in the country could not hold the crowds that thronged her meetings.

She made Los Angeles her home base, and there, on New Year's Day in 1923, she opened Angelus Temple as a hub for her burgeoning evangelistic efforts. Crowds milled about whenever the doors were open, and Angelus Temple came to be a southern California tourist attraction. When McPherson announced an illustrated sermon, Los Angeles officials adapted city trolley schedules. Some of America's best-loved evangelical preachers visited Angelus Temple—William Jennings Bryan, Billy Sunday, Paul Rader. The audience often included curious sophisticates like H. L. Mencken, or famous visitors from nearby Hollywood who wondered about McPherson's immense popular appeal. McPherson was as much a star in her world as her Hollywood neighbors were in theirs.

In 1922 Aimee Semple McPherson was approaching the height of her fame when the Rockridge Radio Station in Oakland invited her to broadcast a Sunday morning message. The time seemed propitious. In nearby Saratoga, some 50,000 people were gathered for the annual blossom festival. On Saturday night, they danced outdoors to music broadcast from the Rockridge Station; on Sunday the station manager thought it appropriate to broadcast a sermon. Everyone knew of McPherson, who was in San Francisco conducting meetings at the coliseum: Her fame made her the logical choice for the Rockridge manager. When she took the ferry to Oakland that April Sunday morning, she added another feat to her growing list of "firsts": She became the first woman in the world to preach a sermon over the wireless telephone (McPherson, 1923c, p. 423). Two years later, she became the first American woman to own a radio station. Her KFSG was also the first church-owned station in the United States.

At first, McPherson found broadcasting at once thrilling and intimidating:

> All the way across the ferry, our hearts beat nervously as mother and I talked of the great possibilities and prayed for the words to speak. When facing the machinery and electrical apparatus of the sending station, our nervousness was increased, especially when we found a newspaper camera man there for a picture and story, also neighbors assembled to hear the sermon. But after putting them all out...I felt more at ease—that is, as much at ease as it is possible for one to feel facing that great horn and having only its dark, mysterious looking depths for a visible audience....
>
> In a moment I found myself talking into that great receiver—talking somehow as I had seldom talked before...all I could think of was the thousands at the Blossom Festival, the sailor boys, mothers' boys on the ships at sea, the sick in the homes where receivers had been installed, and I prayed and preached and prayed again and did most everything but take up the collection. (p. 423)

The response was immediate and gratifying. Her sermon reached thousands of miles and hundreds of thousands of people, some of whom immediately called long distance to report clear reception and spiritual blessings. When McPherson boarded the ferry for the return trip to the thousands who would throng her afternoon service, she had begun to dream in earnest about the possibilities of radio.

Radio and the Popular Evangelical Ethos

McPherson found it easy to embrace modern technology because she had seen it used effectively all of her life. McPherson was a child of the Salvation Army in its formative years in Canada. She thrilled to the Army's illustrated sermons, to the popular music Salvationists favored, to the flare with which they did everything. She liked the simplicity of its colorful idiom, punctuated with colloquialisms and delivered with feeling bent on eliciting response. Upbeat, toe-tapping music; silver bands; forthright, down-to-earth injunctions to renounce sin and know the Savior; banners, parades, and entertainments—all of these combined to give outlet to the deepest human emotions and to challenge the world to change.

In North America, the Salvation Army is a neglected but central part of the story of the evangelical appropriation of modern technology for anti-modern ends. From the time of Whitefield, of course, the faithful had realized just how readily the line between stage and revival platform, between actor and revival preacher could be blurred (Stout, 1991). Under the capable leadership of people like Evangeline Booth, first Canadian and then American Salvationists often introduced modern technology into popular Protestantism. In the 1890s, the population of Ingersoll, Ontario stood at 4,500. Salvationists arrived with fanfare and fervor, and in six months erected a barracks with a seating capacity of 700. Crowds jammed the facility for programs that featured the first gramophones and stereopticons to appear in Ingersoll. In Salvationist hands, the possibilities of such modern inventions for evangelism seemed limitless. The staid members of Ingersoll's respectable churches mingled with the unlettered and dispossessed at Army entertainments, willingly paying the fee Salvationists always charged to hear the time-honored gospel message expressed through new media.

New technology was not the only weapon in the Army arsenal, of course. Music figured largely among its munitions. Salvationist music drew on popular sources. Song was a form of testimony, and anyone might choose to express a religious experience in verse and set it to a popular tune. Army songs often lacked sophistication, but they were catchy, irresistible, and a sure way of popularizing the message. They were part of a musical revolution with broad and enduring implications for Anglo-American Protestantism. Army music was emphatically the people's music, telling the people's stories and the biblical narrative in a popular idiom, and the people accompanied it with whatever portable instruments they had. Army services featured pianos more than organs, and the faithful brought trumpets, tambourines, and drums. The music was participatory and joyous.

In addition to uniforms and banners, the Army offered an array of trinkets to remind the faithful of their allegiance. For example, by the 1890s North American Salvationists could show their loyalty by eating from official Army china featuring a picture of Army founders William and Catherine Booth, or by displaying a changing variety of other items emblazoned with the Army's "Blood and Fire" logo. The Army fired imaginations by defying the wisdom that dictated the separation of the church from the forms of popular culture. In so doing, it helped pave the way for religious broadcasting.

Shaped by this fluid and intrepid Army ethos, Aimee Semple McPherson found in Pentecostalism a less structured arena in which to develop her religious instincts. During her heyday, however, she belonged to no group in particular: She was "everybody's sister." And as "everybody's sister" she modeled inclinations that permeated popular Evangelicalism in both its denomination and independent forms.

McPherson had an established reputation as a master communicator before she built her radio station. The station was only the third in Los Angeles when she began broadcasting early in 1924. It extended her audience, but it also held together her far-flung network and gave her instant access into the homes of her millions of followers. People everywhere came to know her voice although they had never seen her—an astonishing reality that defied imagination. Radio allowed McPherson and her associates to cater to vastly different audiences by designing special programming. She could mobilize her following to respond to disasters like the devastating Santa Barbara earthquake of 1925, or when she felt misunderstood and abused, she could take the microphone and explain her views before the city's newscasters had prepared their text.

In 1924, the possibilities of religious broadcasting had only begun to dawn on American religious leaders. Always intrigued by modern devices, McPherson had owned a receiver for some time, and she took her turn in the slot that a station reserved for Protestant preachers on Sunday mornings. In 1923, she consulted the operators of Los Angeles's two stations, who advised her that she could install a station at her Temple for under $25,000. Within 100 miles of the city, they told her, there were 200,000 receiving sets, and more were being purchased every day. McPherson challenged her congregation and the far-flung readers of her monthly magazine, *The Bridal Call* with "Help convert the world by radio!" and they rose to the occasion. With a handful of others, most notably her occasional associate, evangelist Paul Rader, and John Roach Straton, a prominent New York City fundamentalist, McPherson became a pioneer in the new, soon-to-explode field of religious broadcasting. Her style proved enormously successful. Her religion lacked mystery and lent itself to clear, pithy expression. The Salvationist music she favored was upbeat, featuring catchy choruses and lively accompaniment. She already knew how to build a network and hold a constituency. Radio was simply the next step in an ongoing process of adapting both media and personal style to accomplish a goal. Illustrated sermons were another step. Controversial in some circles, they nonetheless assured overflow crowds at Angelus Temple where the press called McPherson the best star of all in star-crazed Los Angeles. KFSG (Kall Four-Square Gospel) went on the air on February 6, 1924 in the midst of Los Angeles's second annual Radio and Electrical Exposition at the Biltmore Hotel. It is difficult to recall just how innovative and exciting simple radio technology was in the 1920s. An overflow crowd at Angelus Temple participated in a radio dedicatory service featuring the president of the Los Angeles city council, a judge of the superior court, *Los Angeles Times*' publisher Harry Chandler, and prominent area pastors. McPherson exuded enthusiasm: "What an opportunity to preach the gospel over the air! They who are sick; they who are invalids; they who are shut-ins, some of whom have lain for thirty years upon their couches of pain, are longing for the Message!" "Here is the chance to do missionary work!" she mused elsewhere. "This is the opportunity to win hundreds of thousands of souls to Jesus Christ! 'Give the winds a mighty voice, Jesus saves, Jesus saves' " (1923b, pp. 15, 18).

Newspapers around the country added KFSG to the program schedules they carried. Every morning, McPherson walked the short distance from the parsonage to the radio studio to do a live broadcast at 7:00 that she called "The Sunshine Hour." All of her sermons were broadcast live, a situation that considerably cramped her preaching style by forcing her to stand at the microphone. The technology soon made her voice one of the most familiar in the United States.

McPherson never lacked would-be radio personalities eager to fill KFSG time slots. The station broadcast midnight organ recitals, classes in subjects of general interest, readings from classic books, and children's programming featuring McPherson's daughter, Roberta, as "Aunt Bertie." Converts gave thrilling testimonies, too, sometimes broadcasting addresses of speakeasies and gambling halls and naming people engaged in white slave traffic. People frequently sent postcards from distant cities describing a song or sermon someone had heard at a particular time and asking for verification that they had picked up the Angelus Temple signal.

Early on the morning of June 29, 1925, the radio underscored the impulsive qualities that made McPherson a star. One of the Temple faithful who had moved to Santa Barbara called the parsonage before dawn to tell McPherson that an earthquake was devastating the city. McPherson heard a loud crash before the line went dead. She hurried to the radio station next door. Running in on a broadcast, she pushed a startled singer aside and told the world that there had been a terrible earthquake in Santa Barbara. On the spur of the moment, she asked her people to collect food and clothing and bring it to the Temple. She instructed those who owned trucks to fill them with gas and be prepared to drive emergency supplies to Santa Barbara. Before the *Los Angeles Times* special earthquake reporting hit the streets, the first of two convoys from Angelus Temple was rumbling toward Santa Barbara, a hundred miles to the north. By the time the Red Cross convened a meeting to organize aid, a second convoy had arrived with blankets and food for the homeless. McPherson's followers, ever ready to heed her slightest suggestion, responded with commendable spirit in the crisis, verifying McPherson's instincts about the creative potential of modern media for fulfilling the church's task (Blumhofer, 1993a, p. 269).

Radio was not the only new medium McPherson employed. In July of 1923, her monthly magazine, *The Bridal Call*, reported that she had "made the first eight-minute record ever known" and that "by special machinery now specially constructed and perfected, it is expected that she will make 14-minute records, containing a complete sermon by turning the record and taking practically a half hour" (McPherson, 1923a, p. 31).

Early in 1926, exhausted by years of incessant public demands, McPherson sailed for Europe and the Holy Land. Rader, the man she chose to fill her pulpit shared her style and message as well as her fascination for modern technology. Rader was a Chicago-based nationally known evangelist. One-time pastor of Chicago's Moody Memorial Church and former head of the Christian and Missionary Alliance, Rader had moved his ministry into a commodious tabernacle in the heart of Chicago. Like McPherson, he regarded radio as an invaluable tool that would facilitate his task of gospel proclamation. Also like McPherson, Rader began gradually, accepting opportunities as they came. When a Chicago station offered him all day Sunday, he seized the chance as "a new venture for God." His staff worried about programming and funding, but Rader felt vindicated in this venture of faith by a letter after the first Sunday from a dying man in Michigan who wrote of the heavenly blessing that touched his soul during the broadcast.

Radio enabled Rader to offer something for everyone. In addition to tabernacle services, he broadcast a sacred dinner concert, followed by the Sunshine Hour, the Aerial Girls, the Radio Rangers, a missionary hour, the Young Women's Council, an orchestra concert, and a request program. He ended the day near midnight with the Back Home Hour. Each unit attracted different listeners, of course, and evangelicals like Rader proved quick to find ways to build networks. In December 1925 he began publishing a slick monthly magazine, the *National Radio Chapel Announcer*. He designed the Aerial Girls and the Radio Rangers as girls and boys clubs that in some ways resembled Girl and Boy Scouts. As McPherson's radio efforts radiated from Angelus Temple, Rader's broadcasts were conceived as part of the work of his Chicago Tabernacle. Those in radio land who did not live near enough to attend dreamed of visiting their media stars: Treks to Chicago Tabernacle or Angelus Temple became vacation highlights.

The evangelicals and pentecostals who pioneered in religious broadcasting generally stood somewhat apart from the crowd, even in the fluid world of revivalistic religion. They were women and men who had the resources and daring to test the market, adapt their style, and experiment. For them, radio was generally a next logical step, part of a progression of steps that popularized Christian style and idiom and that was well underway before radio became available. Most were less churchly than traditional Protestants, more prone to tabernacle evangelism and the expressive dramatic style of the early Salvation Army. They experimented with music; preached pithy, straightforward sermons; geared their programming to all sectors of society; followed up on prospects. They were energetic, restless, and motivated. In the process of adapting what the world had to offer, they tapped deep cultural memories that, ironically, bound these exploiters of the most modern media to people who shared their distrust of modernity.

By the late 1920s, the airwaves were full of religious broadcasters. Few had national followings, but some bought radio stations that would evolve as molders and mirrors of the popular Protestant ethos. In the next decade, evangelical religious broadcasters would begin to feel threatened, both by regulation of the industry and by mainstream Protestants in positions of cultural authority. But that is a later chapter in a slightly different story (Voskuil, 1990).

McPherson and Rader are case studies in how evangelicals have used media—in their rationale and its implementation. One can trace their debt to the Salvation Army and the vast popularization that Army style ultimately worked on American popular Protestantism. But behind the narrative lie several fundamental features of Evangelicalism and Pentecostalism. Most basically, these are essentially adaptive and audience-conscious popular expressions of Christianity. They appeal to the masses rather than to an elite. The priority they place on communicating the gospel elevates media stars and entrepreneurs who in turn gain a wide hearing. These movements offer an upbeat gospel promising joy, peace, and wholeness. Nathan Hatch has noted that the strength of evangelical movements has been their identification with the people and their passion about communicating their message (1989, pp. 214-219).

While this emphasis on communication, supported by the democratic structure and spirit of these movements, has won a vast audience, receptivity toward American popular culture quickly became a weakness as well as a strength as popular culture tended to move beyond influencing what people thought and felt to shaping how they thought and felt. Electronic media gradually influenced the form and the content of the evangelical message. A few years ago, an influential evangelical editor noted that popular Evangelicalism seemed to have lost any hope to forge an alternative to the methods and message of the secular popular culture and seemed content with a Christian popular culture that followed the lead of the secular. He proposed that this may pose "as serious a [challenge] for modern Christians as persecution and plagues were for the saints of earlier centuries" (Myers, 1989, p. xii).

Such concerns may flow from decisions made in the 1920s, but they certainly did not agitate McPherson's generation of revivalistic evangelicals. In embracing electronic media, they intended only to enhance their communications ability and to preempt the abandoning of technology to "the world." They acted without deliberation and in accordance with impulses deeply rooted in their tradition. And in so doing, they influenced the future course of Evangelicalism more profoundly than they realized or intended.

Deep within the evangelical tradition that runs through much of American Protestantism is a challenge articulated by people like McPherson and Rader. Use modern technology for redemptive ends: Failure to do so amounts to abandoning the medium to "the world."

"What a congregation! What an unprecedented opportunity!" McPherson once mused as she rallied her supporters to get behind her radio station:

> The moving pictures—the silver sheet which might have done so much good in the spreading of the Gospel, seems to have been captured by the world almost entirely. Shall we let them have the radio too? Or shall we say: "No, this is Father's Air and Earth, and we will send the Message upon its breezes to spread the Gospel in this wholesale and miraculous manner." (McPherson, 1923b, p. 18)

The answer seemed obvious then, and modern evangelicals and pentecostals still concur.

Edith Blumhofer is research project manager at the University of Chicago's Divinity School. She was formerly a religion officer at the Pew Charitable Trusts and the director of the Institute for the Study of American Evangelicals (ISAE) at Wheaton College. A specialist in American religious history, she holds a Ph.D. from Harvard and a B.A. and M.A. from Hunter College, CUNY. Her most recent publications include *Restoring the Faith: the Assemblies of God, Pentecostalism, and American Culture* (University of Illinois Press, 1993) and *Aimee Semple McPherson: Everybody's Sister* (Eerdmans, 1993).

7

Telling the Story in Dance

Elizabeth Keen

The use of narrative in choreography involves the metamorphosis of a story related in words to one conveyed by movement. The guidelines for clarity, intensity, and expressive power differ in the two media and there are further considerations if the presentation is perceived live or on film or video tape. This chapter attempts to present and analyze some of the ways to make the journey from storytelling in words to storytelling in dance by examining George Balanchine's *The Prodigal Son*, José Limón's *The Moor's Pavane,* and Martha Graham's *Night Journey.*

There is nothing like a good story, and if you are a choreographer you have no choice but to tell that story in movement. This chapter investigates how this is accomplished. But first, how to answer the skeptic who asks, why dance at all if you can speak? Even if persuaded that dance is a kind of language that can be as specific in its form as words are in content, an encyclopedia of movement could never equal the wealth of an unabridged dictionary. The dance believer then would hasten to reply that this art is not limited to offering the equivalent of moves for verbiage, but is able to provide a supplementary realm of riches, a virtual reality capable of insight not found in the verbal world. More than that, historically, dance is endemic to the human race.

From primitive tribe to advanced culture, societies have danced their lighter moods, their deepest feelings, rituals, celebrations, myths, and interactions of all kinds. Sometimes this expression is traditional as in folk dance; sometimes it is currently collective, as in ever-evolving popular social dance. At other times, it is the individual who takes over—the choreographer who either extends the limits of past dance forms or who is that very rare thing, an original.

In the primitive world, there were dances for every important occasion of tribal life: birth, coming of age, marriage, death, worship, war, peace, political events, sowing, and reaping. Today's society has changed; not

151

everyone cares or needs to dance. Still, there are those who must dance and for whom joining movements into phrases, and phrases into dances is an activity necessary to make sense out of the chaos that life serves up. For these people there is a kinetic magic in dance that allows for a gamut of expression, encounter, experience, and perception unavailable in other media.

From the point of view of western European-American dance history, it is only in the 20th century that dance storytelling on a major scale has achieved true independence. In medieval times, storytelling using movement could be found in miracle and mystery plays, but, as in the later tradition of *commedia dell'arte,* it was subordinate to text. During the Renaissance, people danced in court entertainments and masques, but character was conveyed more by costume than by the differentiation of steps. Dance was often called on by Shakespeare and subsequent playwrights, particularly in comedies, but it was used to highlight celebrations; for example, the sheepshearing festival in *The Winter's Tale;* wedding engagements at the end of *As You Like It;* and that all's-finally-well-that-ends-well feeling at the conclusion of Farquhar's *The Beaux' Stratagem.* These dances, though, seldom advanced the plot. Even in *Romeo and Juliet,* where the young lovers meet during a dance, it is conversation that expresses their budding love; their dancing is a secondary activity.

The 17th century found dance joined up with theater in Molière, but it occurred between acts and was rarely related to the play. French Baroque court dance of the late 17th and first half of the 18th century was a highly advanced form, but its chief interest lay in the successful execution of its very difficult step vocabulary with a restrained, harmonious, and seemingly natural flair. Theatrics played little part in this noble style. Noverre (1727-1810) was interested in dramatic reform and left a treatise on emotional expression, but, unfortunately, no one knows exactly what he meant in practice. It was the 19th century that saw the development of the three-, four-, and even five-act story ballet. As a rule, however, mime was the medium that informed audiences what was going on. Acting by those wearing costumes was also useful, as in Act I of *La Bayadere.* The stories of the ballets were often excuses for divertissements: solos, duets, trios, and larger groupings. While there were also notable achievements as in the duets, white and black of *Swan Lake* and Act II of *Giselle,* these were exceptions. It remained for Fokine *(Petrouchka),* Nijinska *(Les Noces),* and Balanchine *(Prodigal Son),* all working under the patronage of Diaghilev in the Ballets Russes years (1909-1929), to take major steps in creating a cohesion of story and dance.

The 20th century's love of speed, streamlining, and compression was to have an important influence on the merging of dance and drama. One effect would lead to abstraction; a counter-effect would lead to expressionism.

As do all arts, dance exists on a scale ranging from the representational to the nearly totally abstract. At either end of this spectrum, however, lie certain dangers. Representational dance, if pushed too far, can easily turn into mime or one of its near relatives such as employing gesture to signify the alphabet as in sign language for the deaf; gesture as a word equivalent as in Nritya, the East Indian tradition of dramatic dance; or gesture as a particular idea, as in the use of stock gestures with agreed-upon and readily understood meanings in 19th century ballet classics. Although the latter use of gesture did serve to advance the plot, it also served to bring the dancing to a standstill.

The other end of the spectrum, that of abstract dance, presents another problem. Is pure abstraction in dance even a realistic possibility? Since the very medium of communication in dance is the human body and since even extremely technical and virtuosic dance movement bears at least some relationship to the natural movement of every member of the audience, can a dance ever be devoid of emotive or narrative content? The paint with which Mondrian outlines his squares and rectangles does not come from a tube with arms, legs, torso, or head. One perceives it only as color applied to the canvas in a particular way. This color has no human shape. It engages the mind only and is not felt vicariously in the body, as dance is to even the most sedentary audience member. Even when the body is encased and obscured by form-obliterating costume, some human reference is discernible.

Despite this limitation, there are many dance makers—some of the highest quality—who prefer to create in comparatively abstract terms, using line, shape, force, and the myriad dynamic qualities of motion in and of themselves to engender continuity, relationship, or its absence. From the ballet world, for example, there is George Balanchine, whose plotless works continue to exasperate those steeped in the comfort of swan lakes and sleeping beauties. In the modern dance field there is Merce Cunningham, for whom drama lies in the contrast of movement values, not in narrative. Cunningham departs even further from causality in that his work contains no obvious structure other than similarity of movements or their treatment. Nor does the dancing relate to the accompanying music or sound score with which it is meant simply to co-exist, not to mesh.

While many choreographers will always wish to maximize abstraction in their work, enough of them are attracted to the use of narrative in dance to make an investigation into how they accomplish this worthwhile. There are many decisions to be made. Given the facts of the narrative in question, in what order will the story unfold? Will any parts of the story be eliminated? Which parts need to be fleshed out? What general dance style will be used: historical, ethnic, classical ballet or classical modern, contemporary ballet or contemporary modern? Will known movement vocabulary be infused with the appropriate emotive intention or will movement be invented particular to the needs of the immediate work? What qualities of movement are special to the work as a whole, and which to individual characters within the work? How much of a role is intrinsic to the form of the choreography; how much is open to the timing and dynamic choices of the individual performer? Is the dancer enacting a living being as he or she dances, or is the face a mask devoid of the feeling revealed by the body?

In focusing on how a verbal account transforms into dance, one could do no better than to study the works of three outstanding choreographers of this century: specifically, George Balanchine's *The Prodigal Son* (1929), based, via Pushkin, on the New Testament parable; José Limón's *The Moor's Pavane* (1949), a distillation of the Othello legend; and Martha Graham's *Night Journey* (1947), a re-working of the Oedipus myth. In each case I will examine the source of the narrative to be adapted, how the initial story is altered in terms of content, plotting, i.e., the order in which the events take place, and overall form. Next, I will look into the general style of the dance, individuals' stylistic variations, and finally provide a verbal description of the dance and refer to some of its outstanding features.

The Prodigal Son

Balanchine's *Prodigal Son* was produced by Diaghilev for the Ballets Russes and was first performed in Paris in 1929. Scenery and costumes were designed by the French painter Georges Rouault. Sergei Prokofiev composed the commissioned score. The role of the Prodigal Son was played by Serge Lifar, and that of the Siren by Felia Doubrovska (Balanchine, 1954, p. 239).

Source

The scenario for the ballet was suggested by Boris Kochno, Diaghilev's secretary and production assistant. The original source of the story is Luke 15.11-32, but the libretto also has close links to Pushkin's short story, *The Postmaster*, in which a traveler awaiting the fresh horses that will speed him on his journey, passes the time viewing some pictures on the wall of the postmaster's home (Taper, 1960, pp. 116-119). To quote Pushkin:

> They illustrated the parable of the Prodigal Son. In the first one, a venerable old man, in nightcap and dressing gown, was bidding farewell to a restless youth who was hastily accepting his blessing and a bag of money. The second one depicted the young man's lewd behavior in vivid colors: He was seated at a table, surrounded by false friends and shameless women. Farther on, the ruined youth, in rags and with a three-cornered hat on his head, was tending swine and sharing their meal; deep sorrow and repentance were reflected in his features. The last picture showed his return to his father: The warm-hearted old man, in the same nightcap and dressing gown, was running forward to meet him; the Prodigal Son was on his knees; in the background the cook

was killing the fatted calf, and the elder brother was asking the servants about the cause of all the rejoicing. (1983, p. 95)

Balanchine was familiar with this story as well as Luke's account, so it is interesting to look at what he deleted and what he emphasized or enhanced. Firstly, he makes nothing of how the Prodigal Son manages to stay alive as a swineherd. This takes up six verses in Luke and is described in Pushkin's second picture. Similarly, he omits any reference to the killing of the fatted calf and the older brother's anger at his father's joy that his other son has come home. Balanchine could have easily dragged in swine, the older brother and a calf on a spit. He even had some reason and opportunity to do so since he had more music than he felt he needed. Balanchine has been quoted as saying, "Prokofiev was a bastard. He would not change anything. So I had to invent to fill the music" (Brockway, 1995, p. 8). Balanchine, however, considered none of these incidents dance-worthy, writing of the killing of the calf and the brother's anger: "It couldn't fail to take up a great deal of time with no dramatic interest, (therefore) we wisely omitted it from the idea of the ballet" (Balanchine, 1954, p. 322).

Throughout his long career, economy would always be Balanchine's preference. In keeping with this, in this ballet, he chose to focus on the father-Prodigal Son relationship and the son's follies, making for a relatively simple chronological scheme of home-adventure-home. For, like the three prints on the postmaster's wall, the ballet is in three scenes. Of these the second scene is the longest and most complicated, the ruination of the young man absorbing most of Balanchine's attention. The reason is not hard to discern: It offers the most danceable material, although Luke devotes less than one line to it ("where he wasted his money in reckless living," Luke 15.13 Today's English Version) and Pushkin not many more.

Style

With the exception of the Prodigal Son's very first solo, the opening and closing scenes might have been staged by a director rather than a choreographer. Here, Balanchine has selected a very realistic movement style. Although this dance was created for a ballet company and continues to be performed in that venue, actual ballet technique is only required by the Prodigal Son and the Siren. In Scene 1, father, son, and daughters interact via simple naturalistic gestures as does the son with his servant-companions. These are close to the gestures actors would use if working in a spoken scene. By contrast, in Scene 2, the entourage of cloddish dolts whom the son and his companions meet, move in a stiff and clownish way, like performers trained more as acrobats than dancers. For example, the dolts go through a series of gamelike activities: follow the leader and exaggerated patty-cake; they form a human merry-go-round and make a pyramid. For this, Balanchine drew on earlier experience. In 1923, before he left Russia, he had worked with an experimental theater group called FEKS of the Eccentric

Actor Factory. At that time he was employing circus movement such as splits, back-bends, and high lifts in his work (Cohen, 1992, p. 54).

Balanchine may also have been influenced by Nijinska's use of group formations in *Les Noces* (Ballet Russes, 1923), a practice that revealed an awareness of the simplification of forms favored by constructivist painters (Garafola, 1989, p. 139). Her use of repetition of line was appropriate for the wedding rituals of *Les Noces*, where individual personality is subordinate to the peasant society as a whole. Balanchine temperamentally preferred this kind of depersonalized approach rather than the excesses that were popular in ballets of the time.

His approach was not appreciated by some of the public who had grown accustomed to the exoticism of dances like Fokine's *Firebird* and the oriental opulence of his *Scheherazade* (1911). Prokofiev, when he arrived for orchestra rehearsals shortly before the premiere, was especially angered and upset by the sparseness of *Prodigal Son*. He compared it unfavorably to the realism of *Scheherazade* with its plethora of cushions strewn about the stage, its opium pipes and goblets (Taper, 1960, p. 119). Balanchine reported that "when wine was served he wanted real wine" (1954, p. 322).

Balanchine's own propensity for streamlining kept props and furnishings to a minimum in this ballet. The only props are long trumpets and amphorae (wine jugs) along with the gifts and provisions with which the Prodigal Son and his two servant-companions set out on their journey. There are no goblets; the act of drinking is simulated with gesture. For scenery, there are Rouault's back-drops. The backdrop used in the first and third scene represents the father's estate and shows land surrounding a tent; entrances are possible through a flap in the tent. The other drop, used in the second scene, shows sky surrounding the inside of a different tent, perhaps the Siren's dwelling or a taverna-like place. A long outsized table with some plates and vases with flowers, rather crudely rendered, has been painted in. The only additional item on the stage is a long fence, about 14 feet long by two feet high, that has a central gate. It sets the boundaries of the father's property in Scenes 1 and 3 and, turned upside down, becomes a table and later a boat in the middle scene. No chairs were considered necessary. Prokofiev, by far the better established of the two artists, argued fiercely for the use of real objects in a realistic setting. The young Balanchine in his mid-20s, 15 years Prokofiev's junior, had little clout at the time, but in this case, Diaghilev backed Balanchine's stylistic choices (Taper, 1960, p. 119).

The dance style of the Prodigal Son himself varies throughout the piece. In Scene 1 his movement shows the two sides of his character: the well-brought-up youth and the rebel. These two aspects are reflected by either naturalistic acting or by bold, energetic running and leaping phrases that require both power and trained balletic skill. When he and his two companions meet the group of doltish villagers, he shifts consciously into an imitation of their cruder movements and mannerisms. When he encounters

Photograph © by Paul Kolnik

**Figure 1: The drinking scene from Prodigal Son. The Siren domi-
nates with arms held in stylized oriental gesture. Helène
Alexopoulos is the Siren; Peter Boal is the Prodigal Son.**

the Siren he takes on some of the stylization of her movements, particularly
the arms. Balanchine is here showing how the naive young man allows himself to be influenced by those he meets. Later, when fleeced and beaten, he
returns to more naturalistic movement, weighted by exhaustion, despair, and
the struggle for survival. His movements are very lifelike, though energized
and somewhat exaggerated for the stage.

The movement style of the Siren, a seductress, is the opposite of what
might be anticipated. It is erotic, but remote, as if filtered through ice. "The
Siren, for example, I did not think of as a French courtesan, which some
people apparently would have preferred; I conceived her to be cool, strict,
and calculating" (Balanchine, 1954, p. 322).

In her first entrance the Siren strikes a stylized pose that she returns to
again and again. She stands on one leg, the other pointed forward but with
the knee a little bent so that the tip of her point is somewhat dug into the
floor. One arm is up, the other arm down, both elbows are a little bent and
each hand is bent backward as far as possible at the wrist. The palm of the
raised arm faces up while that of the opposite arm faces down, a pose remi-
niscent of East Indian dance. (See Figure 1) This position is based on one
used by Fokine in *Scheherazade,* and was probably used by other choreogra-

phers of the time. By 1929 this shape had become stale and overused to signify exotic Eastern sensuality. In Fokine's ballet, the women of the harem continually run back and forth holding both of their arms aloft in this manner. Balanchine, deftly exploiting an inherited convention, adapted this gesture by raising one arm and lowering the other, and employed it particularly to demarcate each successive phase of the Siren's conquest. When the Prodigal Son joins her in their duet of consummation, he assumes the position of her arms. A further borrowing of the Siren's arm motif can be found in *The Cage*, choreographed in 1951 by Jerome Robbins, who danced the title role in the 1950 revival of *Prodigal Son*. In *The Cage*, women are portrayed as devouring insects; the female chorus often hovers on point with the opposite leg extended in high attitude to the side and both arms high to the side with elbows slightly bent, and wrists pressed back to the extreme with the palms down.

The Siren is characteristically unhurried. She proceeds with slow steady detachment to effect the Prodigal Son's subjugation. She moves speedily only at the very end of their encounter, when he is barely conscious. Only then does she betray her greed, rushing in to hastily snatch the gold medallion he wears from his neck. Otherwise, her progress is slow and inexorable.

Description of the Dance

There are three time frames for the unfolding of the ballet's action. Each is represented by a change of scenery. In Scene 1, the Prodigal Son's servant-companions arrive bearing long trumpets and amphorae which they set down. The Prodigal Son enters from the tent, examines the provisions, and then greets his sisters who also appear through the tent entrance. He joins them in a playful hand wrestle, but then throws them off rudely. The music changes from a slow introductory passage to a brisk 6/8 time. He then bursts into a brash solo, pounding one thigh with his fists. He dashes in different directions as if pushing at the limits of his space. Each change of direction culminates in a distinctive leap or skip, signaling his impatience to be gone. He mimes a shout in four directions and pirouettes fiercely, curving back toward his sisters, then pirouettes and runs in a curve again which brings him close to the entrance of the tent. He seems to whistle or call out again, perhaps cursing. Unexpectedly, his father enters and all action stops. The father and son square off; their antagonism is apparent. This is the first of a sequence of freeze-frames that are emphasized by the music and by which the viewer can track the course of the ballet's dramatic action. As the father moves into the scene, his son retreats somewhat. When the father gestures to his children to join him, the sisters respond immediately by offering their hands. The Prodigal Son only reluctantly comes into the family circle, staying immobile until his father takes the boy's hand in his own. When the father raises his hand in blessing over his children, his son barely manages to bow his head. As the father puts his own hands over his face in prayer, his son sneaks out of the grouping, being observed only by the sisters.

Immediately the music returns to the 6/8 theme and the Prodigal Son dances a close variation of his first solo. Pointing to his servants, he orders them to leave through the gate of the fence. With a harsh gesture to his father he defiantly leaps over the gate and, after a repeat of his fierce pirouettes, calls out to his servants, freezes momentarily, and quickly exits without looking back. The father, visibly saddened, looks in the direction of his departing son for the third still moment and then turns to slowly usher his daughters back into the tent. The stage goes black.

Lights come up on a new backdrop, a sky surrounding the inside of a taverna-like setting. Nine bald-headed men enter, forming a strutting boorish unit. Their crassness contrasts sharply with the father's civility. They are grotesquely earthbound, as opposed to the soaring leaps of the Prodigal Son. They pick up the fence unit, move it to upstage center, and turn it over to create a table. They play their games and gather to the right of center in a pyramid formation as the Prodigal Son and his two friends enter. The dolts reach out in response to the Prodigal Son's efforts to shake their hands but retract them without making contact. This bewilders the Prodigal Son. He retreats farther as they try to touch him and finger his clothing. He mollifies the goons by offering them the trumpets and wine containers. This move is successful and all the men play at becoming "hail-fellows-well-met." Trios are formed by two men who lift a third; the Prodigal Son is carried by his servants. Hands are shaken by the men held on high. The dolts gather around and pull at him to the right and left, all in good fun. They then sprawl around the table and watch half-heartedly while the Prodigal Son and his two friends entertain them with a dance. This section concludes with a communal hand-pumping gesture similar to that used by present day athletes before a game. The Prodigal Son then leaps over the table as he earlier had leapt his father's gate. This jump startles the goons who fall away sharply, leaving the Prodigal Son outlined behind the table, his hand to his mouth in a trumpet-like call, recalling his brash shouts in Scene 1. His pose is filled with power and certitude; the other men have been thrown away from center by the very force of his jump. This becomes freeze frame Number 4 and it makes the Prodigal Son the most powerful figure on stage.

The Siren enters, stylishly posing for the first time with her oriental bent-arm design. She is dressed in a short tunic and a very long crimson velvet cape which trails from her shoulders. As she traverses the stage she wraps the fabric around her arms and then between her legs. All eyes are upon her suggestive actions. The Prodigal Son has settled onto the table, clearly attracted. She lowers herself to the floor in front of him and walks on all fours using two hands and her points. Forming a bridge, her chest open to the sky and the Prodigal Son's gaze, she parades past him and stops, concealing herself under her cape. This sequence lures the Prodigal Son off the table to her. He draws off her cape which she has secretly detached, having predicted his move. She has after all practiced this enticement before. The Siren rises and dances. Her high extensions show off her long legs. The Prodigal Son backs off a bit as she turns languorously several times with one leg in second position attitude. She faces him and takes a slow mincing walk on point, twisting her hips from side to side. He ventures towards her, putting his hands on her waist. She backs him towards the table and pauses; he retreats. She caresses his arm and returns his hands to her waist, and with the same walk forces him back, pushing him down onto the table. She is then thrown by the men in front of the table to those behind the table, passing over the Prodigal Son. She attains a final position held aloft, arms à l'orientale, dominating the innocent man below. This all happens with startling quickness, becoming freeze frame Number 5—an omen of what will ensue. The viewer senses this; the hero is unaware.

In the transition that follows, the Siren is lowered to the floor as her "victim-to-be" slips off the table. They confront each other briefly before moving to opposite sides of the stage. The Siren assumes her characteristic pose which is mirrored by the Prodigal Son. They then engage in a duet, the actions of which are erotic, the tone cool—a striking combination. The main images of this duet are:

(1) The two stand facing front, mirroring one another, each with one arm high, the other low.

(2) Then slowly walking sideways until they meet and stop, the man behind the woman, their arms blending into a four-armed Shiva (the Hindu God of Dance, Love, and Destruction).

(3) Facing each other, the woman wraps one leg around the man's, they revolve slowly in one spot. His face is on a level with her breasts, his arms are thrown wide in vulnerable acceptance.

(4) She sits on his shoulders, facing away from him and slides down his back.

(5) She coils herself around his torso and slides down the length of his body.

(6) He sits with his knees drawn up in front; she sits on his head with her feet on his knees. She then stands and slides down his shins as he holds her ankles.

(7) He makes a back-bend bridge imitating the move in her initial solo. She lays across him at an angle.

(8) They finish in a double swastika, their limbs entangled on the floor. Their arms reach upward in oriental angles. The action freezes for the sixth time as they achieve a brief union of sorts.

After a slight pause the dolts unceremoniously disrupt this union by pulling the two apart. They spin the Prodigal Son to disorient him, passing him roughly from man to man. Now initiated, he stumbles to the table upon which the Siren stands dominating him in her usual pose. The discarded lover is still deluded that he is in favor as they all drink together. They toast four times and toss down the imaginary wine. He mounts the table in pursuit of the Siren who moves to stage right. There follows a series of phrases all signaling the Siren's ascendancy and the son's corresponding diminution of power. In the first of two moves he backs along the table from right to left as she, lifted above him, follows pouring wine from one of the vases down his throat. As he is dragged by his feet back along the table, she is suspended face down above him, her mouth a few inches above his.

Next, they are both held aloft and passed one over the other, their legs splayed. Their bodies don't touch, but the idea is bald, the image bold. Then, suspended vertically upside down, they hold each other by the shoulders and sway back and forth. Standing once again, the Siren shakes the Prodigal Son from side to side. Then the goons take over; throwing him from one end of the stage to the other, and then stomping him in the center.

The Prodigal Son goes to the Siren for support. When she ignores him he runs away across the length of the table, perhaps hoping to make his escape with one more leap to freedom; however, the goons have raced to meet him and tilt the table up on its end turning it into a slide before he can jump off. He slithers down its length, landing at the feet of the Siren who wastes no time in planting the point of her toe shoe on his chest, with one arm held high in her usual commanding position. This becomes freeze frame Number 7. Then the Prodigal Son's servant-companions turn on him, slinging him this way and that before hurling him upstage where he is stopped abruptly by the now up-ended table, as if pinned there. All the men gather on either side, placing their hands in two vertical columns over the length of the victim's body. They then vibrate their fingers like the wings of flies against a flayed corpse. In keeping with Balanchine's choice of a cool approach to a hot situation, this image is understated and chilling. The victim is then turned upside down. Imaginary coins are shaken from his body and grabbed up by the men. He is returned to his "cross" and stripped of most of his clothing. For a final insult the Siren, who has been standing to one side, impassively sanctioning this activity, darts in and rips off his gold medallion. She exits with satisfaction. He is alone briefly, and then two of the men, joined back to back, scuttle across the stage with crab-like movements and are gone. He is alone, again. This becomes freeze frame Number 8. From here the Prodigal Son, truly spent, slowly awakens to what has transpired. He faces his losses and, barely able to move, travels to the side of the stage where he mimes splashing water on his face, an act of attempted purification. He then exits.

This scene is followed by a reappearance of the Siren's entourage; the men cavort a bit with the trumpets and amphorae, and drag the table to its original fence position. The Siren makes a perfunctory reappearance. All of this is repetitive of earlier action and not very interesting. Probably it was included to cover a costume change for the Prodigal Son, as well as to give the illusion of the passage of time. Nonetheless, this interlude concludes with an ingenious image as the men get onto the fence structure as if embarking on a boat. Some blow their horns, others use their arms as oars, and the Siren becomes a figure on the bowsprit with her cape billowing behind as the sail. Balanchine writes that he invented this "desperately" a few hours before the premiere because there remained some unfilled music. He intended to change it later but it was so well received that he let it stay (Balanchine, 1954, p. 322).

In the final scene of the ballet, we see the Prodigal Son struggling along on his knees, an idea Balanchine says he took from Pushkin's description. With the help of a staff he drags himself along, rises to his feet, looks for his home, collapses, and walking on his knees again, makes his way with great difficulty to the gate where he falls flat, face down. His sisters, finding him there, drag him inside. Then quietly his father appears and slowly approaches, with arms outstretched. The young man rises to discover his father, they lock gazes, and he turns away in shame, leaning on the fence for support. His father then turns away, walks a few steps back to his tent, only to turn to face his son, and once again to open his arms toward him. His son then walks on his knees very slowly with his arms gripped behind him. About three feet from his father, he reaches out his arms—the father's arms have by now dropped to his sides—to fall forward at his father's feet. Arduously climbing up the patriarch's body, he pulls his way onto his father's breast. In a tremendously touching moment the father then wraps his arms around his returned child, enfolding him in his cape. This is the final moment of the ballet: hard-won reconciliation without any moralizing.

The Moor's Pavane

The Moor's Pavane received its first performance at the Connecticut College American Dance Festival in New London in August of 1949. This dance involves the interactions of four characters. They are listed in the program as the Moor, His Friend, The Friend's Wife, and The Moor's Wife. One thinks inevitably of the theater's most famous Moor, Othello. Limón was adamant, however, that his ballet was not meant as a representation of Shakespeare's play, even though the same program notes list the Pavane's sub-title as, "Variations on the theme of Othello," and the original costume sketches by Pauline Lawrence, Limón's wife, are labeled Othello, Iago, Emilia, and Desdemona. In the original cast these roles were performed by Limón, Lucas Hoving, Pauline Koner and Betty Jones, respectively. This cast was to stay together for many years. On the 10th anniversary of the dance's premiere, Limón wrote a letter to his fellow artists. "I know how hard I tried not to make a 'dance version' of Shakespeare's *Othello,"* he said.

> I had worked with all will and conscience to find a form that might prove valid and pertinent in terms of dance. I did not wish to infringe, nor paraphrase.... I had sought not a "retelling" of [the play], but a dance based on the old Italian legend. (Limón, 1959, p. 1)

Source

The legend to which Limón refers was recounted by Giovanni Battista Giraldi in *Ecatomiti* (1565), and was the main source from which Shakespeare fashioned his play in 1604. Besides the addition of his superb language and insight, the Bard made many modifications of plot and character. Giraldi's account is in labored prose with heavy-handed complications of plot and unsubtle personalities. It reads like a grade B movie treatment. In it, Iago is a handsome ensign who falls in love with "Disdemona," as she is there named. She rejects him, and therefore he hates her, wants no one else to have her, and in revenge he convinces her husband, the Moor, that she has cuckolded him. For a denouement the Ensign and the Moor beat her to death with a sand-filled stocking. The Moor is killed by Disdemona's relatives, and the Ensign is arrested.

By comparison, in Shakespeare's play, Iago's machinations are focused on Othello, not Desdemona. His scheming stems not simply from being passed over for promotion by his commander, Othello, for Cassio, a fellow officer. Iago's desire to get even joins with his compulsion to undermine, disconcert, and cause disarray, even to the point of eventual destruction. The closing of Shakespeare's *Othello* (1968) finds the Moor kissing Desdemona, then smothering her. When he realizes her innocence he kills himself, though not before revealing the nobility of his character, complete with its tragic flaw, in some memorable verse:

> When you shall these unlucky deeds relate
> Speak of me as I am: nothing extenuate,
> Nor set down aught in malice. Then must you speak
> Of one that loved not wisely, but too well;
> Of one, not easily jealous but, being wrought,
> Perplexed in the extreme; of one whose hand
> Like the base Indian threw a pearl away
> Richer than all his tribe....
>
> (Act 5, scene 2, lines 337-344)

> I kiss'd thee, ere I killed thee: no way but this,
> Killing myself, to die upon a kiss.

(He falls on the bed where Desdemona lies, and he dies.)

(Act 5, scene 2, lines 355-356)

Ironically, Iago's fate is left to Cassio, the new governor of Cyprus, to decide.

Shakespeare has complicated Iago's character, presenting him not as a simple trickster, but as one with hate in his heart who dissembles his true intentions. According to Charles Lamb:

> It was not a man setting his wits at a child, and winking all the while at other children who are mightily pleased at being let into the secret; but a consummate villain entrapping a noble nature...where the manner was as fathomless as the purpose seemed dark. (1968, p. 14)

By the end of Limón's work, Othello has murdered Desdemona and is seen in despair and deep regret next to her corpse with his arm embracing her inert body. Iago's fate is unknown, nor are his precise motivations even made clear. For one thing *Pavane* begins at the very moment Iago is arousing the Moor's suspicions; for another, while this aspect of Iago's make-up could be partially sketched in a scene, Cassio has been eliminated from the cast. Iago's dark intentions are known, and are seen at work, but their exact nature is better described in words than movement. Dance can reveal an action and it can convey a mood, but not with this kind of detail.

Shakespeare had ennobled Cinthio's Moor. The idea of human beings elevated by their struggle against life's "sea of troubles," resonated within Limón. In relating his reaction to Doris Humphrey's final performance in 1945, he writes, "I saw that life and art are in their very essence tragic, and for that reason noble and beautiful and exalted. I saw a confirmation of my goal.... She gave me a vision of the beauty and majesty of tragedy" (1959, p. 2).

Nobility of spirit brought low by jealousy may have been the key attraction of Cinthio's tale for Shakespeare. It was not a new theme for the Bard. He had treated it farcically in *The Merry Wives of Windsor* (1600) where Falstaff is ludicrously exposed for his delusory power to seduce and cause jealousy; seriously in *The Winter's Tale* (1610) where Leontes' suspicions are entirely of his own making; and later in *Cymbelene* (1611) where Posthumus, like Othello, is tricked into believing that his wife has been adulterous.

The destructive power of jealousy held a fascination for Limón as well. He writes that *"Othello* had always had a profound and powerful attraction for [him]" (Limón, 1959, p. 1). It is tempting to speculate on the exact nature of this fascination. All who knew him speak of Limón's utmost courtesy towards others but Pauline Koner has remarked on the "dark" side of Limón's character and Lucas Hoving mentions the complexity of his personality. Be that as it may, the idea to make *Othello* the basis of a ballet actually came from a friend, Betty Dooley. It was she who suggested that

Limón should reduce the cast to four dominant characters and utilize dances of the High Renaissance. Limón brooded on what form this dance might take for three years before starting to choreograph (Limón, 1959, p. 1). Ultimately he chose to alternate scenes of personal emotional involvement that advance the plot with formal dance sections that make use of the floor patterns and figures (meaning how the dancers exchange places across the space) seen in English country dancing, a tradition developed in the 16th and 17th centuries.

The actual steps that Limón uses in these sections have little to do with those described in Arbeau's *Orchesography* (first published in 1589) and other contemporary sources. They are an imaginative invention that goes far beyond the footwork and limited torso and leg gestures of the authentic pavane and other pre-classic dances. Louis Horst writes that the origin of the pavane "can be traced to the formal and austere court life of inquisitional Spain" and later, "was developed into a processional pageant of great dignity and an imposing spectacle" in the European courts (Horst, 1987, pp. 7-8). As innovatively used by Limón in his ballet, the formal pavane-like sections grow wilder as his characters are pulled by the tides of emotional accusation and protestation, and by the tension between trust and disbelief.

Style

The movement style of Limón's dance blends the formality mentioned above with movement allied to the essential qualities of each character. Character trait and movement quality are so fused that it is difficult to describe one without defining the other.

The Moor:	Forceful and controlled, his anger is contained only with tremendous effort. When it is released the resulting movements are strongly directed. When turned inward, his whole body smolders with the constraint.
Iago:	He is also controlled, but his movement quality is lighter. He is firm when attempting to exert his will over another, but can be evasive and quick to retreat when confronted by the Moor.
Emilia:	Self-assured and coquettish, she is sprightly and energetic. Somewhat ingratiating, she knows her own mind with Iago despite the sensual bond between them.
Desdemona:	She is soft, yielding, and pliant. She responds to others rather than initiating action herself.

All of these individual qualities are subsumed by a general movement style that reflects the Doris Humphrey/Charles Weidman technique that Limón, who trained with these two modern dance pioneers, absorbed. He also danced in their jointly directed company before forming his own. Elements of this technique and compositional approach include a strong sense of the body's weight in response to gravity, and the use of this sense in swinging motions. There is an emphasis on fall and rebound, or recovery from the drop of weight, and the use of stylized gesture.

Form and Description of the Dance

The Moor's Pavane consists of 10 sections, some of which are extremely complex choreographically, while others are more simple. Its music, selections from *The Gordian Knot Untied* and *Abdelzar Suite* by Henry Purcell (1658-1695), was suggested to Limón by Doris Humphrey, who was at that time and until her death in 1958 artistic director to Limón's company. Limón had had a difficult time finding appropriate music, and most of his ballet had been choreographed before the choice of Purcell's music. He notes that since the music originally had been written to enhance theatrical situations, "it was a relatively simple matter to select sections which fitted our dance, and in turn, to adjust that dance to the music" (Limón, 1959, p. 6).

The fact that the dance could stand on its own, without music, is testimony to its choreographic strength and clarity. Many dances have little value without the fill of music, though once a dance and its music are yoked together they must be deemed one artistic entity.

Limón's ballet opens on an elegant and gracious note with a series of formal bows between the four protagonists who face each other in the center of the stage. Symmetrically, Iago opposes Othello while Desdemona opposes Emilia. They exchange places, and there is a brief antagonism between the two men as they pass each other. At the end of the first musical section, the Moor presents his wife with a handkerchief, an event pointedly witnessed by the other couple. The viewer senses that there is some significance in this action, but the moment passes quickly as it is interrupted by a return to the first musical section, causing the four to repeat their opening movement patterns. Desdemona continues to hold the handkerchief as she dances. Sarah Stackhouse, a former Limón principal dancer, cautions that, "the handkerchief must always be visible to the audience. When any dancer tucks it in dress or belt or has it in hand, a part of it is always left exposed" (Stackhouse, 1994, p. 3).

Limón's aim was to represent a universal human situation in his dance, and therefore to stand independent of legend or play. It greatly helps, however, in comprehending *Pavane* with any depth to know that the handkerchief is a symbol of Desdemona's infidelity. Shakespeare (1968) took great pains to outline the significance of the handkerchief:

Figure 2: Lucas Hoving as Iago taunts the Moor, danced by José Limón. Iago flaunts the handkerchief he offers as proof of Desdemona's infidelity.

> That handkerchief
> Did an Egyptian to my mother give:
> She was a charmer and could almost read
> The thoughts of people. She told her, while she kept it,
> 'Twould make her amiable and subdue my father
> Entirely to her love; but if she lost it
> Or made a gift of it, my father's eye
> Should hold her loathèd, and his spirits should hunt
> After new fancies. She dying, gave it me,
> And bid me, when my fate would have me wive,
> To give it her. I did so; and take heed on't:
> Make it a darling, like your precious eye.
> To lose or give't away, were such perdition
> As nothing else could match.
>
> (Act III, scene 4, lines 55-68)

In the ballet, the precious value of the handkerchief can be conveyed by the manner with which it is handled by Desdemona, but words are needed to convey its history. Fortunately, *Othello* the play is widely read.

The second section of *Pavane* is an allegro which is also formal but more free-flowing. The tempo is faster with a triple meter, contrasted with the opening's measured duple meter. At the cadence of this refrain, Iago calls the Moor to him with an oddly loathsome gesture; his arm is out-stretched, the palm down and the fingers slimily raking the air. With the third section, Limón introduces the plot. Iago, standing behind the Moor, hooks a leg around him and whispers insinuatingly in his left ear and then insistently in his right. The Moor rejects Iago's information and chases his "friend" off. Iago retreats obsequiously.

Complex and tightly packed, section four advances the plot further. Within the first six counts of the music, Othello, seething with doubt, makes six strong moves which represent the motif of his jealousy. Desdemona responds with concern and extraordinary sweetness. Beyond the couple one sees Iago still on the floor where the Moor has driven him. Iago's body language dissembles that he was only trying to help. (See Figure 2) The Moor repeats the jealousy motif and he and his wife dance together. He displays tenderness toward her as if she has allayed his suspicions, but this is short-lived. Iago, like the proverbial snake-in-the grass, creeps towards the couple. He uses the music of the Moor's jealousy theme to take over the space. The three dance together, Iago insinuating himself between the other two, as if to steal the handkerchief himself. The Moor repeats the jealously motif for the third time, using the same moves, but increasing their size and covering more space. All four dancers come together. The scene ends with Desdemona taking the Moor's hand and resting her head on his shoulder.

At this point it is important to mention that nowhere in the dance do any of the characters leave the stage. Thus, Limón respects the unities of time, place, and action that Aristotle required of classical tragedy. The result is a hot focus, a forcing of the issues with barely any release of tension. When the attention is on one duo or another, the other two dancers either frame the action, witness it from the side, or convey their own state of mind in a unobtrusive manner, so that when they re-enter the movement arena they have never left its emotive course.

The fifth section of the ballet is a duet for Iago and Emilia. In it, Iago attempts to persuade his wife to carry out his scheme to steal the handker-chief. Emilia resists; it is her nature not to give in too easily, but Iago cajoles and threatens. There is clearly a sensuous connection between the two that Iago exploits. They dance passionately together. Three times Emilia does a splendid back turn, is caught by Iago, and forced to concentrate on the handkerchief which is held in Desdemona's nearest hand as she poses with Othello at the front of the stage to one side. The third time that this movement sequence occurs, Emilia and Iago are very close to the handker-chief. The intent is unmistakable.

It would be misleading at this point to think that the dance was sput-tering along from one incident to the next. It was Limón's choreographic brilliance to make each episode move rapidly on to the next, yet be com-pletely clear and separate in itself. In this, he was helped at times by the superb talents of his original cast. Lucas Hoving has mentioned how much movement Limón worked out with his dancers. Ms. Koner, who had to be away from one rehearsal period, reports that on her return she watched her stand-in, Ruth Currier, go through the dance as it then existed. She told Limón that the meaning of the handkerchief did not track clearly enough for her to follow and portray properly. She and Lucas Hoving both remarked on the long discussions they had between themselves concerning charac-terization. It is evident that Koner helped Limón to restructure aspects of his choreography in order to clarify Emilia's scenes with Iago (Koner, 1989, p. 202).

Section six alternates two kinds of action: Either Emilia tends Desde-mona's hair, pointedly admiring and handling the handkerchief, and the men are off to the side, or all four dancers pavane together. This sequence occurs twice. At the start of the second pavane, Desdemona, in her haste to join the Moor, drops the handkerchief. Emilia spies it, swoops down, and plucks it from the floor. Unobserved, she tucks it in her bodice, and then rejoins the ongoing pavane.

In section seven the men fight for a second time. This dance is of great intensity. Iago goes after the Moor, again pressing his point by wrapping his leg around the Moor from behind. The Moor struggles, pushing away both Iago and Iago's insinuations which have penetrated more deeply, to judge from Othello's increased fury. He pushes Iago to the floor, "stomping" him with his shin. Iago counters by leeching his body onto the Moor's back. Iago (and the burden of his ideas) is then dragged the length of the stage, only to be driven diagonally back once more by the enraged Moor. Iago again re-treats with obsequious cunning. These last moves have taken place in vivid silence with the tension rising considerably.

The eighth section begins as a trio. The Moor, Desdemona, and Emilia move slowly to a largo that stresses the minor key in which it is composed and contrasts with the musical and physical activity of the previous scene. The trio faces front, moving in unison with a slow side extension of the left leg, which is then carried to the front. They continue together briefly and then isolate Emilia to the left side. The others are placed in a diagonal line that leads the eye toward her. Othello is farthest away, with his back to the action; Iago is next, seated on the floor where the Moor left him, and Desde-mona is closest to her "lady-in-waiting" but also facing away, looking to her husband who will not look at her. During the repeat of this scene's opening music, Emilia dances a solo and reveals the handkerchief. She plays with it, clearly pleased with herself. Iago, observing this, rises to join her. Emilia teases and taunts her husband with the handkerchief that she refuses to relinquish, constantly eluding his grasp and resisting his blandishments. In the end, feigning indifference, she makes the handkerchief available to him with a casual flick of her wrist. Iago wastes no time in snatching it up. During the latter duet, Othello and Desdemona are off to the side, upstage. Desdemona seems to be pleading with the Moor to believe her.

In the ninth section, the complexity continues. Desdemona and the Moor come downstage and begin a tender duet. Desdemona is ever the beseeching, pliant supplicant; the Moor is overcome with his deep love for her, alternately caressing and hurting her. Pressed down by his distress, his body is bent for the first time. All four perform the pavane, making the revolving formation with left hands joined in the center, known as a star. At the end, the women, perplexed by the Moor's behavior, withdraw upstage. The viewer's attention is now drawn to the men. In another interaction danced in powerful silence, Iago hooks Othello with his leg and forces him to look at the handkerchief now in Iago's possession. This is proof in Othello's mind of all Iago has implied. The force of their danced confrontation matches Shakespeare's (1968) words:

> Villain, be sure thou prove my love a whore;
> Be sure of it: give me the ocular proof,
> Or by the worth of mine eternal soul,
> Thou hadst been better been born a dog
> Than answer my waked wrath!
>
> (Act III, scene 3, lines 356-360)

As the music resumes, the men are caught up in swirling close contact. One or the other is forced to the ground as each vies for the upper hand. Iago taunts Othello with the handkerchief; Othello chases him down. Then, suddenly, all are dancing together, each of the women entering to encircle a man as if to separate the warring pair. Now the quartet is more energized with the couples sweeping past one another to reform the star. They all dance with an awareness of impending calamity, though as yet, the women do not know the exact cause of the Moor's disturbed temper. Stackhouse writes of the space being "stirred" and entitles this part, "Passion Crosses" (1994, p. 13). At the close, Iago has thrown Desdemona center stage into Othello's arms.

The conclusion of the dance begins with the repeat of the tender music that opened the previous section. Ever-trusting Desdemona puts herself into Othello's hands. Her throat and her whole being are open to him. She is totally vulnerable and still unwilling to think her husband won't believe her innocent. He embraces her and rocks her in a curious pièta, then turning on her, accuses her once more. Desdemona finally realizes she cannot shift or penetrate the wave of his irrational jealousy. She flees; Othello runs her down. She attempts to escape again and is pursued a second and third time. He captures her but unexpectedly only kisses her. Iago and Emilia, flanking the central couple on either side, walk gravely towards the audience, and they then come center, pausing in front of the other pair. Their function now is to be an objective chorus for Othello and Desdemona. Emilia spreads her skirts wide. All that the audience can see are the swinging arms of the Moor as he beats his wife to death. Iago and Emilia step aside to frame a ghastly tableau.

Desdemona lies dead, her head towards the audience. Othello kneels at her feet, facing away from the audience, and on either side Emilia and Iago take in what has occurred. Emilia runs to the Moor, seizing his shoulder in accusation. The Moor shows her the handkerchief. She immediately grasps what Iago has done and understands her unwitting complicity. She thrusts the handkerchief accusingly at Iago, who attempts to throttle her. They are held apart by the Moor, who pulls each separately to himself and casts them away. He then falls in despair on the body of his beloved and finally-believed wife. The last gestures belong to Iago and Emilia. Together in formal bow-like closure, they indicate Desdemona and Othello with a sweeping move of the arms. Emilia is distraught, Iago impassive. The curtain falls.

Night Journey

Martha Graham's *Night Journey* was first presented in 1947 at the Cambridge High and Latin School in Cambridge, MA. The superb score by William Schuman had been commissioned by the Coolidge Foundation. Graham danced the role of Jocasta, while Oedipus was performed by Erik Hawkins, then her husband. It was he, a former classics major at Harvard, who had directed Graham's attention to Greek literature. In the previous year, she had created *Cave of the Heart* and *Errand into the Maze*, her first works using Greek mythology as a source. This was the inauguration of a series of masterpieces of this variety that culminated in 1958 with *Clytemnestra*, a full evening-length ballet.

From the late 1920s to 1946 the themes of her best work had often been drawn from American sources; for example *Frontier* (1935) and *Appalachian Spring* (1944) refer to the pioneer experience, and *Primitive Mysteries* (1931) and *El Penitente* (1940) reflect an interest in the southwest Indian ethos. Other work sprang from her reactions to contemporary events, as in *Deep Song* (1937) or from personal experiences, as in *Heretic* (1929).

Source

For her new work, Graham decided to investigate the Oedipus legend, particularly as restated by Sophocles in *King Oedipus,* written in the fifth century B.C. This widely known legend tells the story of a man who was destined from birth to murder his father and marry his mother. The play does not follow the chronological order of his hapless life. Instead, Sophocles (1947) begins with an announcement of the disasters that have befallen the city of Thebes. Crops have failed, children are still-born, and disease is rife. The King of Thebes, a certain Oedipus, steps forward to assure citizenry and priest alike that he will do anything to root out these problems at their source. When advised by Creon, his brother-in-law, of the oracle of Apollo's pronouncement, that:

> There is an unclean thing
> Born and nursed on our soil, polluting our soil
> Which must be driven away, not kept to destroy us.
>
> (Sophocles, 1947, p. 28)

and that the unknown killer of Laius, the previous Theban king, must be brought to justice, Oedipus replies:

> I will start afresh, and bring everything into the light.
>
> (p. 29)

After tracking down clue after clue, Oedipus torturously discovers that he, himself, is the cause of his country's devastation. We follow Oedipus on his journey of self-discovery, learning, as he does, that despite the preventive steps taken by his birth parents to have him killed in infancy; despite his own precautions to flee from those he believed to be his parents; despite all possible measures taken, he ultimately fulfills the prophecy given at his birth. However unwittingly, he has murdered his father and married and lain with his mother. Thus he proves, as the ancient Greeks believed, that no man can escape his fate.

Form of this Ballet

Martha Graham, not one to loll about with surface issues, took on the theme of incest. She chose to make Jocasta, not Oedipus, the focus of her ballet by presenting the ballet from Jocasta's point of view and changed the order of the story's events. Additionally, and like Limón, she reduced her cast to its primary protagonists: Queen Jocasta, King Oedipus, and Tiresias, the blind seer, the only one to see the truth and the one who, in fact, represents truth itself (Stodelle, 1984, p. 149). Graham retained the Chorus, which she called Daughters of the Night, and created a Chorus Leader. The Chorus is a powerful presence and serves many functions. They witness the truth, express community outrage, formally usher in Oedipus to meet his mother whom he will marry, and dance with a demonic possession expressive of their deep horror when faced with mankind's strongest taboos. Completely eliminated by Graham are Creon, a priest, a messenger, a shepherd, and attendants of the King and Queen. They are inessential to Graham's purpose, and would only clutter the stage. She substituted her female chorus for the play's chorus of elders and Theban citizens. For Graham, the Daughters of the Night represent "the terrors we all have. They are memories of things we dread to remember.... They must be recognized and lived through until they leave your mind" (Graham, 1991, p. 213).

Graham's version of the Oedipus myth was influenced by psychoanalysis, with its probing of the past. Psychoanalysis, in turn, strongly influenced film, via the technique of the flashback. Sensitive to these contemporary developments, Graham began her ballet with Jocasta on stage, alone, in the act of committing suicide, her hands reaching upward, holding a rope. (See Figure 3) She is interrupted by the entrance of Tiresias and the repeated percussive sounding of his staff as he makes his relentless way towards her. He slips his staff under the rope and hurls it to the marriage bed. The Chorus races onto the stage like harbingers of doom. Then, utilizing the convention of flashback, Jocasta re-experiences the enormity of her misdeeds by reliving the events of her life, from the arrival of Oedipus as an adult, through their courtship, sexual consummation and marriage, and the horrific realization that they are mother and son as well as man and wife. Tiresias demands this "before [Jocasta] can be permitted the peace and forgetfulness of death" (Graham, 1991, p. 213).

Style

Graham's early work was stark and uncompromising. Like her peers, Doris Humphrey and Charles Weidman, she struggled with herself and her dancers to find new and expressive forms. In addition to teaching in her own studio, she worked to train actors in movement at the Neighborhood Playhouse in New York City. The year before she choreographed *Night Journey*, she worked intensively on a production based on the *Eumenides* with Sanford Meisner, the head of the school and a director, and with Louis Horst, her mentor and musical director. She also worked with the acting students on studies in archaic style related to *Agamemnon* (Soares, 1992, p. 47). This was important preparation for her new dance style.

Ethel Winter, a leading dancer in the Martha Graham Company from 1944 to 1969, who danced in the premiere of *Night Journey* as a member of the Chorus, says that Graham used a modified archaism in the dancers' movement. This kind of movement, which forces the body to appear two-dimensional, like the figures in a Greek frieze, was the basis of the ballet's style. Archaism is also evident in the movements of Jocasta and Oedipus, though less so with Tiresias; however, Graham didn't limit herself to this stylistic flattening when she needed depth for force and invention of movement.

***Figure 3*: Martha Graham as Jocasta in the denouement of *Night Journey*. The rope, previously a symbol of the ties that bind Oedipus and Jocasta, is used here as the instrument of her self-inflicted death.**

Additionally, some of Jocasta's phrases are close to actual gesture, as when she crosses each hand to the opposite breast, quickly lowers these crossed hands to her loins, and then abruptly turns with hands raised to her temples. In another move Graham plunges from a deep pitch turn, with a very high leg extension, to a swift fall accomplished by sliding the foot of the extended leg immediately sideways along the floor and catching the weight of the body on one out-stretched hand. Graham writes, "I felt that when Jocasta became aware of the enormity of her crime, a cry from the lips would not be enough. It had to be a cry from the loins themselves, the loins that had committed sin" (Terry, 1975, p. 107). The viewer may or may not

make the specific connection that Graham describes, but somehow the extreme shape and timing of the movement signals its meaning without being
directly representational.

The sense of Graham's dance-drama is further enhanced by the contribution of her collaborator, Isamu Noguchi, the sculptor and set designer. For
example, Graham had requested a bed for the set. According to Agnes De
Mille, "Noguchi did not want to give her a bed. He provided instead the
abstract figures of a man and a woman lying facing each other" (De Mille,
1991, p. 281). This set piece is raised about two feet off the floor by four
slim stanchions and is raked at such an angle that the upstage end is higher
than the downstage end, making it possible to see clearly all aspects of
movement happening on it. Noguchi also provided a series of low structures,
many in the shape of an hourglass or Mediterranean drum, that create a
lateral path to the bed from stage-right. There is another stool, placed at the
front of the stage, that is used to isolate Jocasta either alone or with Oedipus.

Props also figure prominently in *Night Journey*; for instance, there is
the cord that Jocasta holds, seen when the curtain rises. Throughout the ballet this, the rope that Jocasta will use in her suicide, is always on stage and
is used in a variety of symbolic ways. At times it stands for the umbilical
cord that links the ill-fated pair and also the entangled mesh of their incestuous relationship. Late in the ballet, as first the Chorus and then Tiresias
dance their reactions, Jocasta and Oedipus make a series of interconnected
erotic shapes, wrapping themselves in the rope which they use for support.
Ernestine Stodelle refers to this as "a cat's cradle of self-deception"
(Stodelle, 1984, p. 149).

Description of the Dance

The action of *Night Journey* advances in four phases. In the first, Jocasta, on the brink of taking her life, is confronted by Tiresias and the Chorus. She is in emotional turmoil brought on by the recognition that she has
been living in an incestuous relationship with her own son. In the second
phase, Jocasta relives her experiences with the mature Oedipus—his arrival,
their courtship and intimacy. In the third phase, the Chorus and Tiresias
make additional dance statements expressing the severity of the couple's
situation. Tiresias destroys the illusion of the soundness of their marriage. In
the denouement Oedipus, in recognition of his guilt, gouges out his eyes. In
the final moments of the dance, Jocasta hangs herself, thus bringing the ballet full circle to its beginning.

Phase One. The curtain rises to reveal Jocasta, her back to the audience, gazing upward at the rope stretched between her hands. Tiresias, the
blind seer, enters. We hear him before we see him as he thrusts his staff onto
the floor, his progress being accompanied by a series of percussive
thuds—the sound of fate. Using his staff as a hook, he flicks the rope out of

Jocasta's hands and in one move flings it upstage to the bed. As Jocasta runs forward, the Chorus races in from the side. With these powerful choreographic strokes, Jocasta's journey into the night begins.

Having run forward, Jocasta falls to the floor and then rises quickly. She skirts the Chorus as if avoiding their gaze and returns to the bed, settling on the floor in front of it, her legs stretched to the side, at once decorative and unbalanced. In the foreground, the Chorus crosses the stage. At one point they pause to stamp the floor several times, bringing a cupped hand in front of their mouths as if to hold back what they might say and aghast at what they have learned. Jocasta rises to pace, countering the lateral movement of the Leader of the Chorus who is downstage of her in a parallel lane. When Tiresias strikes the bed with his staff, Jocasta first recoils and then grabs for the staff. Connected by the staff, Tiresias drags her briefly along the floor. As the Chorus exits, Jocasta, in a state of anguish, begins her solo.

She refers to the bed, is repelled by it, and moves as far from it as the stage permits. She gestures alternately to breasts and loins and turns in revulsion. This motif is repeated, wedding explicit reference with elegant design. Jocasta returns to the area of the bed to confront Tiresias. She throws herself at him, struggles with him and is rebuffed, and falls backward. This motif is repeated. As Tiresias exits, Jocasta leans on the bed, supporting her weight on her hands with difficulty. Her torso is upright and her head is thrown back. Exhausted, Jocasta lowers herself slowly and rolls across the bed to its far side. For the moment, she will rest. Phase 1 is over.

Phase Two. The second phase begins with a processional as Oedipus is led in by the Women of the Chorus. He has just come from solving the Riddle of the Sphinx and his reward is the Queen. The women hold green branches, a decorative element derived from Graham's tenure with the Denishawn Company, but which may also be a reference to Sophocles. Early in Sophocles' play, when the facts revealed to the protagonists could still be interpreted as reassuring, Jocasta appears "carrying a garlanded branch and incense." Her words are:

> My lords, I am mindful to visit the holy temples
> Bringing in my hands these tokens of supplication.
> The king is over-wrought
> Listening to every word
> That feeds his apprehension. I can do nothing to
> Comfort him.
>
> (Sophocles, 1947, p. 50)

These lines are interesting, not just for their reference to garlands, but because they highlight the reversal of importance of the King and Queen from Sophocles to Graham. In *King Oedipus*, Jocasta exits many pages before the play is over; news of her death is brought to Oedipus. It is his self-inflicted blindness that is the most important action. In *Night Journey*, the order of these events is changed; Jocasta's death follows the blinding of Oedipus. Though both events are important, Jocasta's demise occurs center stage moments before the curtain descends.

Returning to the second part of *Night Journey*, the Chorus is now gathered to either side of the stools that will serve as stepping stones for Oedipus to enter Jocasta's chamber. Oedipus continues in his circular path along the periphery of the stage, headed for the entry way to the palace. He moves stiffly and somewhat pompously. He is followed by the Leader of the Chorus. Three times she runs to encircle him, trying to deflect him from his doomed course. The third time Oedipus, unstoppable, throws her to the ground. The Chorus smacks their fronds down on each stepping stone prior to each forceful step Oedipus takes across them. He then arrives at the far end of Jocasta's bed.

Pulling Jocasta to her feet, Oedipus carries her forward until he places her on the down-stage stool. He moves a short distance away and presents himself rather arrogantly, thrusting his arm repeatedly through an opening in his cape in a phallic gesture. Curiously, this cape also conceals his face, a reference to his virtual blindness in view of the actual circumstances. Oedipus next moves to Jocasta, stepping up on the back of her stool to stand behind her. He lifts his knee and swings his leg around her shoulder to place his foot on her thigh. Jocasta, seated below him, carries two fronds which she holds to her left at shoulder level. The pair form a strikingly designed tableau signifying male domination. However, this has yet to be proved. After all, Jocasta is Queen. Oedipus steps aside; Jocasta waits coolly, as Oedipus, approaching, bows by tilting forward on one leg with the other leg raised high to the back. His head is very near her lap—a fleeting allusion both to sex and to a child burying his head in his mother's lap. This dance motif is the first of several times where the mother-child image is evoked. Oedipus again withdraws to one side while Jocasta maintains a certain remoteness.

What follows is a dance by Jocasta of subtle seduction in which she signals her eventual submission by bowing deeply at Oedipus' feet with her face to the floor. In the dance she is both dignified, as befits a queen, and suggestive. Of this moment, Graham has written, "She is inviting him into the intimacy of her body" (Graham, 1991, p. 214). Oedipus indicates possession by coming to her and draping his cloak around her body. In agreement for the first time, they then dance a few phrases in complete unison. They are of one mind and are about to become of one body. As they approach the bed, the Leader of the Chorus who has been crouching, all but forgotten in the background, stamps her foot in dread and in protest and runs from the stage. She can watch no longer.

The action that follows contains two love-making passages. In the first, there is a sense of sexual violence when Oedipus reaches across Jocasta's body from behind to place a hand over each breast. His movements are strong, not tender. When he lifts Jocasta into the air and spins them both around, her legs are splayed. In the next moment she is cradling him, fleetingly recalling Oedipus as her son. "She hears in her imagination a baby cry," writes Graham. "It is the cry of her lover as he subjects her to his wishes. It is the cry of a baby for its mother" (p. 215). The lovers now rest for a short time, lying next to each other on the floor. When they stand again they dance intimately. Jocasta seems both mother and mistress. There is a memorable lift and another revolving one, where Oedipus holds Jocasta vertically upside-down by the wrists with her legs folded in the lotus position and her pelvis held against his by centripetal force. The suggestiveness of the position is almost lost in the design of the pose.

Phase Three. Phase 2 becomes Phase 3 with the swift re-entry of the Chorus. The music has changed to a harsh, repetitive bowing from the strings. The atmosphere becomes anxious. As the Chorus dances in the foreground, moving very persuasively in effective unison, Jocasta and Oedipus, either on the bed or close to it, form a series of erotic shapes. They are linked by Jocasta's rope. Bound all too closely together they form shifting designs. The Chorus continues its hair-raising dance of daring shifts of weight and falls. They are the Furies. They cleave to either side of the stage as Tiresias enters at a mad pace, using his staff as a pogo stick. The sound of its rhythm, and the pace of fate itself, have accelerated. Revelation is imminent. In the background, the couple stands, caught in a freeze frame, leaning away from each other against the rope that twists around their bodies. The Seer heads towards them and mounts the bed behind them. He uses his staff almost gently to touch the rope. The pair crumples; they have realized their sin instantly. The edifice of their illicit relationship has collapsed.

Jocasta reacts first and zig-zags across the stage in a run. Each change of direction is punctuated by a pelvic contraction that lifts one leg and throws the head back, which is both a cry from the loins and a scream from the mouth. She ends in a state of collapse at the bed. Next, Oedipus, disentangling himself from the rope, throws it far forward, as if it were a poisonous snake. He steps up on the foot of the bed, only to fall straight forward. He is caught by the Women of the Chorus, who lower him to the floor. Their furious energy spent, the Daughters of the Night exit. Their Leader follows, but not before she uses the branches to beat the path of stools along which Oedipus traveled on his re-entry into his mother's life.

Denouement. Now in agony, Oedipus rises to dance a few phrases before approaching Jocasta. With great restraint he removes the brooch she has worn on her dress. Raising it as if to the gods he unknowingly has defied, he plunges it into his eyes. At last he has seen the light; blinded, he leaves the stage.

Jocasta slowly rises, feeling the air above the bed as if to remember all that took place there. Even more inexorably she moves towards the front of the stage, picking up the rope from where Oedipus has thrown it. She wraps the rope around her neck, holding the ends high. Falling backward, she strangles herself as she descends to the floor. In the final moments of the dance we see Tiresias with his staff, pounding his way across the stage past the body of the fallen queen. The sounds diminish. The curtain falls.

Conclusion

The preceding examination of *The Prodigal Son, The Moor's Pavane,* and *Night Journey* has shown that in order to adapt a story to dance the choreographer must be able to understand the narrative in its most basic form and find its essential drama. Those extra elements that might distract from the narrative line, as well as any aspect of the story that might resist dance expression, must be eliminated. In addition to utilizing known movement vocabulary, the choreographer must often develop new movement specific to each work so that characterization and interaction emerge. The choreographer must identify in some way with the basic emotional journey and/or conflict of the story and choose those performers who have the empathy, technique, and power of expression to bring the role into dancing existence. Appropriate music must be found or sometimes written and, if needed, props, scenery, and costumes must be made. Often this requires collaboration with other like-minded but independent artists.

All these elements must be closely considered and worked out. This process in itself, though, does not guarantee the strength of the dance. There is no formula for a great dance, however much one may analyze the elements of a successful work after its creation. Ultimately, choreographic merit is dependent on the level of insight, craft, and artistry of its creator.

In order for choreography to rise above the ordinary, there needs to be a compelling connection between the artist and the story and a necessity to employ craft and imagination to reveal what lies beyond the bare outline of events. As interesting as it may be to uncover these deeper, underlying motivations, this is not the kind of information choreographers generally care to divulge. Even if the artist's deepest motivation were known, it would not explain the resulting artistic achievement. Motivation and drive are not substitutes for craft and insight.

The work of great choreographers, moreover, has a way of resisting categorization. One can view the work of Cunningham, the great master of abstraction, as a broad metaphor for certain aspects of human experience. How can a viewer interpret Cunningham's *Summerspace* or *Winterbranch*? The former certainly seems to reflect some of the timing and fullness of summertime, while the latter reflects the harsh quality of winter. Is this intended or is everything in the viewer's mind? To further complicate the matter, Cunningham is fully capable of lifting whole sections of a variety of different choreographies and assembling them in an "Events" performance, where the sections are seen removed from their original context with different sound scores. Balanchine, too, eludes easy generalization. Besides the plotless ballets that reflect his interpretation of the accompanying musical score, he has created evening length story ballets such as *A Midsummer's Night Dream, Don Quixote,* and *Coppélia.* He has choreographed dances for Broadway musicals, *Girl Crazy* and *On Your Toes* to name just two, not to mention an enormous number of male and female duets open to many interpretations. José Limón is known for his commitment to humanistic values in art; yet, in *Missa Brevis* and *A Choreographic Offering,* two of his greatest works, it is the abstract elements that dominate.

A last cautionary note: It is important to remember that dance is a physical, temporal, and kinetic art form. Its efficacy lies in its immediacy. It is possible to choreograph a well-performed but boring piece, lacking in poignancy and excitement. Conversely, a dance, no matter how well choreographed, can wilt and die without dancers trained to its style. Only they can bring meaning to the continuity of its steps.

Finally, words are extremely limited in their ability to describe the particularity of movement. Words may seem to describe a dance, especially if the dance in question has been seen by the reader, but at best they can only approximate what happens in the dance. Therefore, I wholeheartedly encourage any reader of this chapter to see live performances of the dances discussed, or if that is not possible, to take advantage of video and film collections in school and performing arts libraries.

Elizabeth Keen, choreographer and teacher, stages dances primarily for opera and theater. Credits include "The Winter's Tale," "Animal Farm," "The Tempest," and "Yonadab," all directed by Sir Peter Hall (Royal National Theater, London). Additional credits include "L'ange de Feu" directed by Andrei Serban (Los Angeles Opera and L'Opera Bastille); "Salome" with Maria Ewing (The Kennedy Center and Royal Opera at Covent Garden); "La Traviata" and "Falstaff" (Glyndebourne Opera Festival); "Carmen" (The Metropolitan Opera, NYC); "A Comedy of Errors" (New York Shakespeare Festival); "Guys and Dolls" (Goodman Theater, Chicago); and "Kiss Me Kate" (ArtPark, NY). A graduate of Barnard College and Sarah Lawrence College, she is currently on the faculty of the Dance Division of The Juilliard School.

8

Installation Art:
Sacred Places in Secular Spaces

Jennifer A. González

Installation art creates an environment to encompass the viewer/partici-
pant. This chapter provides a brief overview of contemporary installation art, followed by a close analysis of the works of Amalia Mesa-
Bains, Renée Stout, and Jenni Lukač. Each of these artists has used the
form of the altar or shrine to create sacred places within the secular
space of the public museum or gallery. Through an analysis of the material signs and visual rhetoric used in these structures, their potential to
reveal historical narratives, as well as to act as sites for the contemplation of cultural memory is explored.

What Is Installation Art?

The term "installation art" generally describes a broad range of artistic
practices, from large-scale formal reinterpretations of the architectural space
of the gallery to the creation of artificial or imaginary environments using
various objects, words, or images. Installation art is distinguishable from
other forms of sculpture and "environment" art by two characteristics: its
temporary nature and its collaborative play with the composition space of
the interior it inhabits. Found almost exclusively in cultural centers, galler-
ies, and museums, an installation uses these sites as its material or conceptual palette. In other words, the work of art may take up the question of the
historical, political, and ideological "site" of the exhibition, as in the work
of such artists as Barbara Bloom and Fred Wilson; or it may use the formal
constraints of the site (placement, size, architectural details, material properties) to create a metaphysical commentary, as in the work of Gordon Matta-
Clark and Kazuo Katase; or it may provide its own technical apparatus, as in
the works of Nam June Paik or Jenny Holzer.

The temporary nature of the installation provides it with an important
performative function. In some cases the installation will be constructed to

change over time, as was the case of Anya Gallaccio's room of roses at the London ICA in 1992. Entitled *Red on Green*, the work consisted of a thick carpet of red roses left to slowly decay on the floor of the gallery space, revealing the thorns and leaves underneath. In other cases, the installation creates a momentary atmosphere or a new definition for the exhibition space such that the site itself performs differently. Per Barclay's 1990 installation at the Palazzo Barolo in Turin transformed the baroque interior of *The Chinese Room* into a toxic reflecting pool by filling the floor with an inch or so of motor oil. In other cases, the viewer may be asked to participate in the performance of the work by interacting with the piece. Betye Saar's installed *Mti* became a communal offering as viewers were inspired to leave material tokens of remembrance on the site of the work. In each instance, the link between the work and the site was redefined. Indeed, the differentiation between site and work can become blurred to such a degree that it becomes difficult to say whether it is the site which creates the interpretive context for the work or the work which redefines the site.

As well as producing a performative effect, the temporary nature of the installation work changes its relation to institutions and to traditional forms of artistic practice. As the artist Joseph Kosuth comments:

> [Installations] practice a commitment to a particular location and are largely formed by that context, be it architectural, social, psychological, institutional.... Such work constructs its own "event context" for the experience of the viewer and in so doing establishes the subjective role of the viewer within the signifying activity as part of the viewer's experience.... In an important way, installations return the language of art to something more akin to "speech acts" (non-pragmatised, of course) and a change of direction away from gilded illuminations. (Kosuth, 1993, p. 95)

Not being transportable, an installation does not function in the same way as most other art forms within the constraints of the market and the museum. Being ephemeral, an installation sets up a temporary experience that will survive only in the corporal and conceptual registers of the viewers, and occasionally in textual and photographic documentation. It is in this sense that an installation constructs its own "event context" which is fixed in a particular space for a limited period of time.

Kosuth (1993) argues that this temporary "fixed-ness" of installation art allows it to escape the "commodity aura" that attaches to other individual and mobile works such as traditional painting and sculpture. Indeed, some installation artists, influenced by the Anti-object Conceptual Art of the 1970s, claim to be participating in a similar rejection of economic determination through the production of non-salable work. Nevertheless, installation art does not differ from the other arts in its relation to a system of art patronage. Installation artists can only produce a work if they have the financial support provided by a cultural center, museum, gallery, or individual donor.

Thus, installation art must always be thought of as a negotiated creation, not unlike those collaborations produced in previous eras for institutions such as the church and state. Often the work of installation art is done by a team of apprentices under the guidance of the artist. This collaboration, coupled with the use of esoteric and expensive materials, can often end up costing much more than individual salable works of art. (The labor intensive installations of Anne Hamilton are such an example.) Installations may also be produced for community events by members of that community. An excellent example of this kind of art production can be found in the altar-installations at the Mission Cultural Center, San Francisco, during the Mexican-American celebration for *Dia de los Muertos* (Day of the Dead). Artists join with community activists to produce remembrances of the dead that take the form of altar-installations.

This brief overview gives some indication of the range of installation art being produced today. My discussion here has been excerpted from González (in press) and focuses on three installation artists who are working with the visual idioms of sacred spaces.

Amalia Mesa-Bains

The artwork of the San Francisco-based Chicana artist and activist Amalia Mesa-Bains plays with the distinction between history and myth, public and private life, and intimate and communal memory. She makes use of her audience's impulse to read objects as archaeological artifacts, and thus creates a feeling of historical "authenticity" in her installations, designed to persuade the viewer to confront notions of cultural and personal identity. Most of Mesa-Bains' installations take on the formal aspects of an altar, shrine, or museum display. It is, in fact, the "mixing" of these formal domains that best characterizes her work.

Starting in 1975, Amalia Mesa-Bains began building community altars in local gallery spaces as part of a Chicano cultural reclamation project (Ybarra-Frausto, 1987). Scholar Tomás Ybarra-Frausto notes, "Creating *altares* as gallery installations was one example among innumerable efforts to validate and reinterpret Chicano vernacular traditions adapting them to vital new social contexts" (1987, p. 4). Out of this experience Mesa-Bains developed new uses for local cultural artifacts and moved from the formality of traditional home altars into a more experimental mode. I will discuss one work by the artist, which emphasizes her use of a material rhetoric that produces topographical mappings of cultural and institutional affiliations.

In the *Ofrenda for Dolores Del Rio* (1991), Mesa-Bains pays homage to a secular icon of Hollywood cinema, Dolores Del Rio, through a pseudo-canonization that unfolds in the space of the gallery. The altar-installation as

Collection of the artist

Figure 1

a whole, in its symmetry and abundance, demands frontal attention. The flounces of pink cascading satins and lace, crushed rose petals and bright glitter strewn about the floor that frame the space of the altar, celebrate and glorify the figure depicted within. The "offerings" of gold and silver-painted fruit placed upon the lower tier, and the jewel encrusted shrine housing the madonna-like image of Del Rio are testimony to the regal and saintly quality of this movie star. (See Figure 1) Certainly a structure of praise and display, the altar-installation could be said to present an epideictic argument for the canonization of a cultural heroine. But there is more involved in the concatenation of objects that constitutes this visual pronouncement. Not only are there many signs to be read within an overall hierarchy of meaning, with each one functioning in proximity to the others, but the method of construction and the cultural references that are made in this installation reveal a revisionist visual ethnography. How, then, does the composition form a rhetoric of objects?

To answer this question it might be useful to perform a close reading or decomposition of the tropes and formal qualities of the piece that are evocative of classical rhetoric. Accumulation, opposition, metonymy, metaphor, synecdoche, and ornament are all present. There is an accumulation of information, or "heaping up" of evidence that praises Dolores Del Rio as both human and divine. The installation is literally overflowing with intimate objects such as lipsticks, perfume, tea cups, dolls, and photographs, as well as decorative elements such as netting, lace, satin, glitter, flower petals, candles, and religious icons; the former objects reflect a personal life, the latter reflect the life of a glamorous star or a saint. This opposition between private and public life is presented as the material difference between a Mexican childhood (signified in the juxtaposition of a doll, Mexican flag, tea cup, etc.) and Hollywood stardom (signified in the grouping of an elegant fan, cosmetics, a bottle of liquor, etc.). These two collections of objects placed on opposite sides of the altar-installation, revealing a conflict of dual identity, are symbolically condensed by the central placement of a photograph of Del Rio herself. It is the metonymical placement of these objects that determines the possible readings they will provoke. Each object also functions metaphorically, standing in for a larger group of symbolic associations. For example, the fabrics and lace are not only decorative, they are also a metaphor for femininity; the white toy skulls are not only a memento of the Mexican *Día de los Muertos* festival, they are also a metaphor for death itself. Other objects function synecdochally: The film canisters at the base of the altar stand in for Del Rio's film career; the ornate fan is evocative of the elaborate costumes worn by the actress and pictured in the rows of photographs near by. Each of these devices—accumulation, opposition, metonymy, metaphor, synecdoche—contributes, along with others, to the clearly dominant rhetoric of the work: ornamentation.

Historically, ornamentation has held an important part in the over all "system" of rhetoric as that general category or classification of tropes and figures that provided the play and spice of an argument. Here an argument of ornamentation is being made for the reevaluation of the role of *Dolores Del Rio* as cultural heroine and icon for a generation of Mexican-American women. The abundance of found objects, old toys, glitter, and lace in the *Ofrenda* also reveal a more locally defined aesthetic of ornamentation, identified by Ybarra-Frausto as *rasquache:*

> In the realm of taste, to be *rasquache* is to be unfettered and unrestrained, to favor the elaborate over the simple, the flamboyant over the severe. Bright colors (*chillantes*) are preferred to somber, high intensity to low, the shimmering and sparkling over the muted and subdued. The *rasquache* inclination piles pattern on pattern, filling all available space

with bold display. Ornamentation and elaboration prevail and are joined with a delight in texture and sensuous surfaces. (1991, pp. 133-134)

Flamboyant, glittering, full to the margins with an abundance of heterogeneous objects, Mesa-Bains' altar-installation is most certainly informed by a *rasquache* aesthetic. But this aesthetic also corresponds to a more general *rhetorical tactic* of *rasquachismo* which is

> neither an idea nor a style, but more of a pervasive attitude or taste. Very generally *rasquachismo* is an underdog perspective—a view from *los de abajo*. It is a stance rooted in resourcefulness and adaptability, yet ever mindful of aesthetics:

> *Movidas* are whatever coping strategies one uses to gain time, to make options, to retain hope. *Rasquachismo* is a compendium of all the *movidas* deployed in immediate, day-to-day living. Resilience and resourcefulness spring from making do with what is at hand.... This utilization of available resources makes for syncretism, juxtaposition, and integration. *Rasquachismo* is a sensibility attuned to mixtures and confluence. Communion is preferred over purity. (Ybarra-Frausto, 1991, p. 133)

Rasquachismo works from the stance of flexibility and "making do." Rather than being merely *reactive*, however, *rasquachismo* seeks to create new forms using mixture and juxtaposition—focusing on aesthetic expression rather than mere survival.

In clarifying the role of gender in her work, Amalia Mesa-Bains has chosen to use her own neologism "*domesticana*" to describe a specifically *Chicana rasquache* (Mesa-Bains, 1992, p. 5). A practice based on the Chicana form of "making do," *domesticana* is seen by Mesa-Bains as the affirmation of cultural domestic *values* in combination with an emancipation from traditional feminine *roles*. Using "techniques of subversion through play with traditional imagery and cultural material," *domesticana* characterizes the activity of taking the space of "the feminine" and transforming its traditional isolation into a powerful representation of lived experience. *Domesticana* becomes the method by which the private space of the home is brought into the public space of creativity, not merely to reflect but to actively construct new ideologies. I see the work of Amalia Mesa-Bains, in the *Ofrenda for Dolores Del Rio*, as an attempt to both emulate and undermine the authority of traditional institutions—such as the church and the museum by presenting a revisionist canonization of a cultural heroine, complete with photographs, "ethnographic artifacts," and ornamental display. The artist rhetorically articulates a memory which is both personal and social. She writes:

> The installations serve as devices of intimate storytelling through an aesthetic of accumulation; accumulation of experience, reference, memory, and transfiguration. Historical works such as the Dolores Del Rio Altar contextualize a domestic icon of the cinema within the Holly-

wood/Mexicana dual worlds and act as well for my personal narrative of life events. (p. 9)

Renée Stout

Renée Stout's installation entitled *My Altar/My Grandmother's Altar* was produced as part of the *Sites of Recollection: Four Altars and a Rap Opera* exhibition at Williams College in 1992. Set up as a living-room space, this installation piece includes two armchairs that, while sitting side by side face in opposite directions. In front of the two chairs, against opposite walls, stand two constructions evocative of private altars. As a whole, the installation invites the audience to feel "at home" in a domestic space, and at the same time to be aware of an opposition of views, values, and family generations represented in the material signs of each altar installation.

The "grandmother's altar" consists of a large color television set placed on the floor, atop which sit the photographed faces of what appear to be extended family members and friends. (See Figure 2) Also present are flowers, shells, and devotional figurines neatly placed in rows, with balanced symmetry, upon a white lace runner. Drawing upon the familiarity of this

© *1996 Nicholas Whitman*

Figure 2

kind of domestic space, Stout's conventional material and spatial groupings of objects lead her audience to read the photographic images as a family tree. On the screen of the television runs a video-loop of pop-religious figure and televangelist Pat Robertson. His 1-800 telephone number flashes continually on the screen to remind his faithful viewers to continue their donations to his "700 Club" fund. On the wall above the television-altar are placed chromolithograph figures of Christ and the Virgin Mary, a centrally placed photograph of two young boys appearing to date from the 1940s, a wooden crucifix, and other Christian devotional scenes.

Here is a rhetoric of objects that is less narrative, less historical, and less emphatic than that which appears in the work of Amalia Mesa-Bains, but that nevertheless functions to create a microcosmic view of the systems of faith and the systems of social networks that define the implied "inhabitant" of the scene. On the seat of the "grandmother's" chair is a worn, threadbare Bible that has clearly seen much use. Between this and the other armchair is a small table with a lighted, covered lamp—on one side of which there are, again, crocheted lace doilies, and a few more photographs. The "evidence" provided suggests this "inhabitant" can be located in the nexus of several institutional frameworks: the traditional church, the evangelical media community, and the extended family. An eclecticism of social affiliations is thus present, but is clearly structured around a hierarchy of unified belief.

The artist's altar—implied by the possessive use of the word "my" in Stout's title—is more varied. (See Figure 3) Inside a wooden cabinet, only a foot or so taller than the television set that faces it from across the room, can be found a diverse array of religious and cultural "signs" including a reproduction of a Native American doll; a reproduction of a Kongo *n'kisi* figure; maracas; earth from several different countries in Africa, Europe, and Central America in labeled glass jars; bones; postcards and toys. The cabinet has two glass doors, open to allow a closer inspection of the materials placed on the shelves inside. Two drawers at the base of the cabinet are also open, revealing collections of photographs and books. Like the "grandmother's altar," the "artist's altar" is topped with photographs of family, friends, and ancestors. An image of a Black Christian saint hangs on the wall above, flanked on either side by brightly sequined signs of the Vodun religion, creating a formal balance with the sacred images that hang over the "grandmother's altar." Also atop the cabinet are four votive candles, an Aztec calendar, incense holder, and a carved wooden figurine that appears to be of African origin. On the "artist's" armchair rests a *Dictionary of World Religions*.

Despite the seemingly casual placement of objects, the production of this display can be seen as the direct result of historical research. Included are signs of what the artist considers the constituents of her individual subjectivity—signs that have been and continue to be elided by the mainstream

© *1996 Nicholas Whitman*

Figure 3

religious culture to which her grandmother has assimilated. Thus, in Renée
Stout's installation, the diverse display of both religious and secular items in
the artist's altar stands literally in opposition to the "grandmother's" sacred
signs. In reflecting on this piece Stout commented, "Between my altar and
my grandmother's altar there is a clash in the middle of the room: between
televangelism—where you are only allowed to think in one paradigm—and
the other evidence of world religions. The center is a debate between the
two positions" (Personal interview with author. August 1, 1994). The "artist's" altar thus functions as a recuperation of religious and cultural signs
that demarcate a complex ancestry made up of people from African, Mexican, Irish, and Native American cultures. The cabinet with glass doors open,
produces somewhat different connotations than the anthropological and

archaeological museum displays to which it makes a visual reference. As the artist commented:

> The cabinet is open to encourage the viewer to pick up and touch every-thing that is in it. There is no barrier of the glass saying this is a culture that you can't touch.... I wanted the viewer to get the experience of my own search. Digging under the surface and looking at things. (Personal interview with the author. August 1, 1994)

Through the creation of a visual dialogue between the religious life of her Christian grandmother and her own topography of sacred cultural relics, Stout points to the necessarily negotiated space of worship and cultural iden-tity. As critic Philip Brookman has written, "This room offers a kind of sanctuary for reflection and private thoughts about memory, family, and the assimilation of African-American ethnicity and ethos by Christianity and television media" (1992, p. 16). But it also offers alternatives to that assimi-lation and raises questions about the "too easy" assignment of ethnic and racial identity. The cultures represented here are more than African-Ameri-can. Stout's work makes "concrete" the oppositions that exist between a sin-gular (traditional) and a multiple (critical) reading of ethnic and "spiritual" affiliation. Yet, both readings are shown to operate in the context of a single family structure—grandmother, granddaughter—that shares a domestic his-tory.

Jenni Lukač

The work of Jenni Lukač, while less autobiographical than that of Amalia Mesa-Bains and Renée Stout, is nevertheless similarly inflected with religious iconography. As a child, Lukač spent many hours in churches and funeral homes with her mother, who played the organ. In these environments she often had the opportunity to observe the activities of women who tended altars—and the dead. As she comments, "It did not occur to me that my continual early backstage presence in these places was unusual for a child. Only later did I see the influence it had on my personality—particularly being so much in the company of the dead at such a young age" (Personal interview with author. July 29, 1994). But rather than producing morbid symptoms, Lukač's early years of haunting churches and mortuaries devel-oped into a fascination with the ritual of memorial. This fascination later took the form of a curiosity concerning the role material objects play in the context of remembrance.

For this reason, and in part because of her conversion to Judaism, Lukač makes an important distinction in her work between the altar and the shrine—the altar is seen as a site of social sacrifice, whereas the shrine is a site of remembrance. For Lukač these two formal spaces have a strictly metaphorical and symbolic function that can nevertheless lead to affective responses in her audience. As she comments, "Both require the complicity of the visitor to complete the work and [both] elicit involuntary visceral responses learned at an early age through acculturation" (Personal interview with author, July 29, 1994).

In Lukač's installation entitled *Votive Shrine* of 1993, these two formal elements come together. There are several moments of relinquishing: Objects are sacrificed to the installation; artwork is given over to the public; and, in the case of this installation, the sacrifice of life itself is memorialized. At the same time, Lukač sees herself as a scribe of public events. Using news photographs as icons, she maps significant historical and political events and persons onto the landscape of a religious shrine in order to change the viewer's perspective of the past. Individuals are shown to be both metaphorical and literal martyrs of contemporary systems of domination. Thus, the piece works as both shrine and altar.

Taking the shape of nave and transept of a church, the installation is furnished as a domestic space, suggesting that the site of memorial is in this case both sacred and secular. (See Figure 4) Small end tables, lamps, dressers, and chairs are placed along the walls in a more or less symmetrical fashion. At the center of the room, along the back wall stands an altar-like

© 1996 Nicholas Whitman

Figure 4

structure composed of two television sets with a video-looped image of burning candles, and a large marble-topped buffet containing photographs, commemorative plates, and trinkets behind its glass doors. Directly above hangs the "Martyr Shrine"—a wooden light box in the shape of a small house which contains photographs of both contemporary and historical martyrs. Those who have been killed by injustice, racism, war, and prejudice are gathered together and represented as equals in the context of cultural memory. Other shrines—women's, men's, daughters', sons'—adorn the "side-chapels" of the installation space. Lukač claims that her decision to organize _Votive Shrine_ into categories of male and female is based upon the fact that photography has historically figured men and women differently. Thus the question of gender representation lingers in the details of the piece. The Men's shrine contains contemporary and historical images of fathers holding children, Gillette razor blade wrappers, golf balls, and little drawers where "girlie" images can be concealed. The Daughters' shrine houses miniature pink porcelain dolls and dance slippers, along with images of young girls—such as Anne Frank—who have withstood or succumbed to the events of their time. As one critic points out, "Throughout the installation, there is a painful sense of the roles being rehearsed for the way in which they will be remembered" (Finnegan, 1990, p. 76). In each case, photographs of known and unknown figures form a commentary on the act of remembrance. In writing of photography in another context Lukač comments:

> The photographic image serves as a mediator between ourselves and the past; between our personal histories and the great rush of global events; between the living and dead. Our individual human memories, not so long ago filled with images and sensations directly perceived, are now bombarded with an endless succession of surrogate presences. (1992, p. 4)

Votive Shrine overwhelms the viewer with its multitude of unique faces. Seeking an ethnically diverse and global perspective, its extensive accumulation of photographs suggests an almost obsessive concern with the wide variety of cultural differences that are necessarily compressed within any given account of history. Unlike other memorials, this work—like that of Mesa-Bains and Stout—is also a study in multiple temporality. It does not commemorate a particular time or event; it rather commemorates those human relations that are the conditions for events. Critic Daniel Barbiero has suggested, "These relics and structures in their totality make up something we can term an historico-cumulus, i.e., a sedimented collection of worked material and categories of meaning" (1991, p. 64). But the work also raises questions about the ways in which the viewer of photography is interpellated as a witness. The relationship between audience and image is personalized by the "domesticity" of the installation. Viewers are expected to identify with the faces in the photographs, trace a subjective path through the historical cosmology that is presented, and thus admit to a role as witness, past or present, to the events depicted.

In some sense, photography for Lukač is a way of putting the body back into a social network. These installations are not about the absence of bodies, but a re-situating of the body in an historical topography. The dialectic of past and present is made more powerful by their seeming co-existence in a material object. As the artist comments:

> The idea of object and memory and image and memory has been revolutionary, in a sense, because of the holocaust. So what is left over of these people who were alive? Their detritus. Now what do you do with all of those eyeglasses and all those shoes and all those suitcases? (Personal interview with author. July 29, 1994)

For Lukač, modernism, both intellectual and artistic, has been an attempt to transcend or to live outside of history. It finds escape from the past by using all possible means to guard against the "contaminating presence" of antique cultural signs and artifacts. At the same time, modernism overvalues the truth claims of such objects to such a degree that they become highly charged when used as signs of transformative moments or infamous events. Her work, which might be characterized as anti-modernist rather than post-modernist, recognizes that the historical document or trace will always exist in one form or another. As symptoms of social conditions, or as traces of past activity, material objects float on the surface of history. It is the recognition that they can always be "reinterpreted" which makes our relationship to the objects and signs of history flexible and dynamic. And as Lukač suggests, it is only through a dynamic re-interpretation of material culture that certain hidden stories will be revealed.

Questions for Consideration

In conclusion, I would like to address questions that may be raised concerning multimedia translation and the use of material objects in installation art. For example: "How do objects form an argument?"; "How does a collection, assemblage, or installation tell a history or narrative?"; and "How does the context of installation art create an atmosphere for contemplation?"

One of the ways in which cultural artifacts are traditionally used to make arguments is through their placement in a museum dedicated to the fine arts or anthropology. The contextualization of objects within an institutional framework, and their careful placement in proximity to others call upon the viewer to create mental associations. For example, we are often persuaded to hold a particular interpretation of history through a linear or chronological placement of material evidence. In this case, the context of the museum confers authority upon the material signs of history.

In the case of the artists considered above, the use of the sacred space of shrine or sanctuary is a strategic move. Lukač refers to her use of religious objects as "soft hooks" that entice the viewer into an intellectual analysis of human relationships. Each artist relies upon a reinterpretation of commonly recognized objects and images to challenge and reconstruct assumptions about the relation of the sacred to the secular in mainstream American culture. They make reference to conflicting world views through which histories of particular places and peoples are read. In this case the sacred forms a political framework for a choice of visual symbols and metaphors. The iconography of the sacred is used as a rhetorical tactic to envelop the viewer in a space of reverence and contemplation, as well as to provoke the viewer to reconsider his or her own place in a contemporary "archeological" history.

In the installation works I have discussed, objects have been used to form arguments of praise, as in the *Ofrenda for Dolores Del Rio*, or arguments for a social hierarchy, as in the "grandmother's altar," or arguments of political history, as in *Votive Shrine*. The accumulation and placement of these cultural artifacts within pseudo institutional spaces created within the installation itself—such as the museum, the home, and the church—draws upon the audience's experiences in these traditional secular and sacred spaces. As Jenni Lukač observed, the degree to which members of the audience have been shaped by acculturation in these institutions is the degree to which they will be affected by the artist's material argument.

If the placement and mere presence of historical objects and cultural artifacts can make an argument about the role of an individual within institutional frameworks, then this kind of representation can also be used to construct narratives. However, this production of narrative is the responsibility, not of the artists, but of the viewers of the installations themselves. In each of the installations discussed, there are a multitude of familiar objects juxtaposed with more uncommon artifacts in a non-traditional context. The viewer is tacitly "invited" to create meaningful links between the objects in each installation. He or she thus plays the role of the archaeologist in creating a story of some kind from the fragments in the work. A translation from the "material" to the "conceptual" takes place to the degree that the artifacts in the installation function as reference points to a larger social history in which the viewer is implicated.

Lastly, the installation puts the viewer in a contemplative space. By making the entire interior of the art gallery like a shrine, by thinking through the visual devices used in both domestic space and sacred space, the artists I have discussed above are creating a site of reflection for the viewer. Because it is all-encompassing, installation art shares features with virtual reality technology. Installations can effectively remove the viewer from his or her everyday experience—something that traditional art gallery and museum spaces rarely do. And it is perhaps only through changing the physical context of reception that new levels of awareness and participation can be attained.

Jennifer A. González teaches the History of Contemporary Art at the Rhode Island School of Design. She studied both Philosophy and Art at Yale University and recently received her Ph.D. in the History of Consciousness from the University of California, Santa Cruz. Her dissertation is concerned with the use of material culture in the representation of new narrative histories in contemporary installation art.

9

Film Language and Communication: From Cecil B. De Mille to Martin Scorcese

Jayne Loader

This chapter examines three kinds of film language: visual language or *mise en scène* (the language of classic Hollywood cinema), the language of the screenplay (dominant in today's film industry), and the language of commerce. After illustrating the ways in which these languages are spoken in a select group of biblical films, this chapter suggests strategies for communicating biblical texts via the new media.

Three Kinds of Film Language

Cinema is multilingual, like Babel after the tower fell.

Visual language is the province of the director, interpreted by the cinematographer: a language of composition, camera angles, depth of field, and color. There's the language of technology: silence or sound; black and white or color; 35mm, 16mm, or 8mm film; CinemaScope, Cinerama, 3-D, Beta, VHS, or PixelVision.

Film theory often speaks the language of the apparatus: What happens to us, physically and emotionally, when we sit and watch a glowing screen in a darkened room? Ideology speaks the language of race, class, and gender. Screenplay language includes the actual words spoken by the actors. Through the language of acting, words and actions are interpreted: body language and facial language as well as the language of intonation and of creating believable characters and emotions. The language of music underscores all of these, adding layers of intensity. The language of editing unifies the whole and creates pace. The language of commerce—of profits and losses—is, for most films, their *raison d'être*.

Three kinds of film language are of particular interest in cinematic interpretations of biblical texts: visual language or *mise en scène*, which is the language of classic Hollywood cinema; the language of screenplay structure, which dominates the film industry today; and the language of commerce, which in contemporary film has completely subordinated all other languages.

A Personal Interest

I have a personal interest in filmed translations of the Bible, because one such film had a powerful effect on my life: *The Story of Ruth* (1960), unmemorable and undistinguished, derived from the Book of Ruth, a scant three pages, one of the shortest books in the Bible.

In this book, Ruth the Moabitess marries a Judean, Mahlon. He dies, and his mother Naomi plans to return to Judah. Ruth, however, is loyal to Naomi. "I will go where you go, I will live where you live; your people will be my people, your God will be my God" (Ruth 1.16 Contemporary English Version). Keeping the Fifth Commandment—to honor your father and your mother (or, in this case, your mother-in-law)—is the lesson of Ruth's story. But what made the story a natural for Hollywood is Ruth's reward.

Film footage from The Story of Ruth. Courtesy of Twentieth Century Fox Film Corporation.
Figure 1: Hollywood gives Ruth a sordid past to make *The Story of Ruth* more colorful and exotic. Here Ruth appears in her "prequel" days in the temple of Chemosh.

Film footage from The Story of Ruth. Courtesy of Twentieth Century Fox Film Corporation.
Figure 2: **Boaz (Stuart Whitman) assures Ruth (Viveca Lindfors, center) of his protection in the 1960 production of** *The Story of Ruth.*

Returning to Judah, Ruth and Naomi are destitute, so Ruth must glean in the barley fields of Boaz, Naomi's rich kinsman. Boaz sees Ruth, protects her from being molested by field hands, and feeds her a delicious lunch of bread and vinegar. With a little scheming on the part of crafty old Naomi, and with creative use of the Law of Moses by Boaz, one thing leads to another, Boaz marries Ruth, Ruth has a son—an ancestor of David, Solomon, and Jesus—and everybody lives happily ever after. In other words, Ruth is the Old Testament Cinderella.

This should be enough story for a 90-minute movie, right? Not in Hollywood. In order to make *The Story of Ruth* just a tiny bit sexier, to add more color and exoticism and violence—and to utilize the capabilities of CinemaScope—somebody decided to give Ruth a sordid past. (Figures 1 and 2) So there's the story of Ruth, but first, there's the prequel to the story of Ruth. It goes like this:

When Ruth is a little girl in Moab, she's sold by her evil father to the high priest at the temple of the bloody god Chemosh. And because Ruth is beautiful and perfect, she's selected to be a virgin sacrifice. But as Ruth is being led away by the high priest—which is about the same time Ruth realizes that being a virgin sacrifice isn't a particularly smart career move—the priest notices something on Ruth's arm: a blemish! So Ruth is disqualified because she isn't perfect, and the second-best little girl gets sacrificed instead. Later on, Ruth realizes she's been spared for A Reason: Her blemish was a gift from God.

About now, you're probably asking yourself how *The Story of Ruth* relates to me. How many temples to Chemosh are there in Texas, anyway? Part of it was that I, like Ruth, had a greedy, abandoning father. He hadn't exactly sold me, true. But my new stepfather did look suspiciously like the high priest! More to the point, I, like Ruth, had a blemish. In fact, I had a rather large scar. And after seeing *The Story of Ruth*, I became convinced that I, like Ruth, was among God's chosen. God had sent the scar that had marred my perfection as a sign, sparing me for A Purpose. A virgin sacrifice no more, I would go forth from the barley fields of Weatherford, Texas, to meet my destiny: marriage to a rich man, with whom I would live happily ever after.

And thus, all of my troubles began.

I tell *The Story of Jayne* to amuse you, of course, but also to illustrate one of the dangers we face when we try to translate biblical literature to film. The prequel to *The Story of Ruth*—made up by the filmmakers to tell a better story—was far more vivid than the biblical original. But, by adding subplots, new characters, prequels and sequels, structure and conflict, we run the risk of obscuring the story we're ostensibly trying to tell. The additions we create to improve a story for the screen, to explain it to our audience, or motivate our characters, often overshadow the story itself. And because our revisions are phrased in the language of cinema—a visual language first and foremost—-they are often far more vivid than the original, written for the printed page.

Visual Language

Hollywood recreations of the Bible are particularly shameless in their over-embellishments. Bible stories, in and of themselves, are not seen as entertaining enough to hold the interest of the audience. What is entertaining? The orgies of ancient Rome!

Cecil B. De Mille's *Sign of the Cross* (1932) was allegedly motivated by lofty sentiments. De Mille's *King of Kings* (1927) is regarded by some scholars as the best biblical film ever made and is probably the most-seen example of the genre. As De Mille wrote, "*The Ten Commandments* (1923) had been the story of the Giving of the Law, The *King of Kings* was a story of the Interpretation of the Law. *Sign of the Cross*...would tell of the Preservation of the Law" (Forshey, 1992, p. 15). In fact, *Sign of the Cross* features half an hour of arena atrocities: Christians boiling in oil; pygmies skewered on tridents by marauding Amazons; men, women, and children eaten by lions and crushed by elephants; and Charles Laughton completely over-the-top as the mad emperor Nero, observing the action while caressing the buttocks of a half-naked slave-boy. As two British film scholars put it, "Biblical film orgies offer Hollywood semi-respectable opportunities for flesh exposure in scenes justified historically and morally as images of decadence and corruption of civilized law" (Babington & Evans, 1993, p. 65).

This is the Hollywood model for the biblical spectacular as we know and love it. It appeals visually to prurient, even sadistic, impulses while condemning verbally these acts and images with lines delivered by its Christian characters or the ubiquitous voice-of-God narrator. But what do audiences remember from movies like *Sign of the Cross*, *Ben-Hur* (1959), *The Robe* (1953), *David and Bathsheba* (1951), *Samson and Delilah* (1949), and *Demetrius and the Gladiators* (1954)? The images or the words? I know what I remember: the bad old days, lovingly depicted; the chariot races; the dance of the seven veils; the orgies; the golden calf; the sacrifices and slave auctions; the ravished Christian maidens; Salome kissing the severed head of John the Baptist; the barely-repressed homoeroticism; and the shaved chests and oiled, oversized muscles of Steve Reeves and Victor Mature. In the world of the biblical spectacular, evil is glamorous, colorful, sexy, memorable. Goodness and virtue are boring, forgettable, and dull.

In Nicholas Ray's *King of Kings* (1961), for example, the director—a master of *mise en scène*—makes great use of color to tell his story. Red predominates: the red of fires, burning the bodies of Jews, recalling the Holocaust and the crematoriums; the red of lust (Salome's lips) and war (the capes of the Roman soldiers). Even the waters of Jerusalem run red with blood-like rust, when Barabbas forges weapons for his doomed rebellion. Dialogue echoes the color scheme. When Salome taunts John the Baptist, "Is there blood in your veins?" she says, "I want to see!" What she wants to see is red.

Gold ordains the palaces of Herod and Pilate. The floor is inlaid with gold, ebony, and the ever-present red. Salome, her mother Herodias, and Pilate's wife Claudia are drenched in it. Salome's head and hips are girded in golden cobras whose heads protrude phallicly from her groin and brain, emphasizing her sexual and intellectual power over the ineffectual palace men.

By contrast, Jesus' followers are clothed in dull browns and blues. Their hovels are dark and unappealing. This may well be historically accurate, but it has visual meaning as well, which subverts the film's ostensible goal. Lack of color symbolizes simplicity, poverty, and frugality, but is also eminently forgettable. It fails to catch the eye, and thus the attention, of the viewer. And Philip Yiordan's script mirrors the art direction: None of the Jewish characters—not even the rebel Barabbas or the traitor Judas—are as memorable as any one of the Romans. Only Jeffrey Hunter's Jesus—physically beautiful, bathed in light, clothed in white—transcends Ray's vision of Christianity as terminally boring (Hollywood's version of the kiss of death).

Language of the Screenplay

The plots of most biblical films reflect this gut-level feeling on the part of filmmakers that Bible stories are dull, with characters who lack proper motivation. Therefore, they must be reinvented for the screen, gussied up. Actions that, in the Bible, are motivated by concepts like faith or divine intervention have to be given real-world explanations in the movies. Otherwise, how can audiences identify? As James M. Wall wrote, attempting to explain the decline of the biblical spectacular:

> Today's audience will not accept any regular intrusion of a supernatural order into ordinary life unless the story creates an atmosphere of feasibility.... The majority of filmgoers cannot discern pure spirits directing events in the earthly realm. There is just too much emphasis on the structure of physical reality as determining events to picture a non-physical Being or beings as the agents responsible for change." (quoted in Martin, 1981, pp. 68-69)

Perhaps this is untrue today—how easily people accept the concepts of angels and a devil, how drawn they are to the supernatural—but filmmakers of the past shared Wall's viewpoint and felt compelled to provide real-world explanations of biblical events to their presumably skeptical audiences.

Take Judas's betrayal of Jesus. In the lost silent film *Mary Magdalene* (1914), Mary is the lover of Judas, who leaves him to follow Christ. Judas becomes a disciple to be near Mary, believing Mary to be in love with Jesus. He then betrays Jesus out of sexual jealousy (Campbell, 1981, p. 88).

In De Mille's *King of Kings*, Judas is again the lover of Mary Magdalene, who personifies Old Testament exoticism. She is a rich courtesan with jewels, slaves, suitors, and a vast palace, yards of oiled, naked flesh, zebras to pull her chariot, and even a pet leopard (as if we didn't, by then, get the point that her animalistic, primal sexuality should be caged, or at the very least, leashed). Judas leaves Mary Magdalene to follow Christ, and Mary Magdalene follows Judas. Jesus literally casts Lust and Pride from her body. (Her first act, post-exorcism, is to put on more clothes.) Judas's motive for betraying Jesus? Sexual jealousy.

In the 1954 independent production *Day of Triumph*, Judas is a member of a secret revolutionary group in Jerusalem, which wants to use Jesus to spark a revolt against the ruling Romans. Judas has Jesus arrested so Jesus will enlist in the revolutionary cause. His motive for the betrayal is political (p. 129).

In Nicholas Ray's *King of Kings*, Judas is again a political zealot, in league with the rebel leader Barabbas (later to be spared from crucifixion by the mob). Barabbas' new, expanded role is based on a single line in the Bible which describes him this way: "Now Barabbas was in jail because he had started a riot in the city and had murdered someone" (Luke 23.19 Contemporary English Version). Judas and Barabbas are frustrated, because Jesus refuses to use his miracle-working abilities to overthrow Roman rule.

Judas puts Jesus in jeopardy so he will defend himself with violence, rise up and smite the Romans, and free the Jewish people. Judas' motive for the betrayal is again political.

In Martin Scorcese's *The Last Temptation of Christ*, Harvey Keitel's Judas is presented as a dear friend to Willem DaFoe's Jesus. (Even when Judas slaps Jesus, it's with humor and affection: like Moe slapping Curly in *The Three Stooges*.) Scorcese frames Judas and Jesus in two-shots, even when they speak to one another, rather than using conventional shot/reverse shot editing, to emphasize their closeness and subvert the expectations of the audience.

In Scorcese's world, danger comes not from Judas, the loyal male friend who must be persuaded by Jesus to betray him, but from the woman Mary Magdalene and from the possibility that, because of her, Christ will choose not to be crucified. Jesus is not threatened by Judas, but rather by his own procreative sexuality. As in the De Mille *King of Kings*, animals—lizards, snakes, and monkeys—suggest the fecundity of the female world and the base, animalist nature of sex. Jesus must reject temptation three times: in the brothel, when Mary Magdalene asks for his love; in the wilderness, when a serpentine devil speaks in the Magdalene's voice; and in the midst of the crucifixion, when Satan appears as a girl-child and lures him down from the cross with fantasies of sex and procreation with Mary Magdalene and, after her death, with Mary and Martha, too! In the Scorcesean universe, women are biological traps for men. The devil tempts Jesus in the same way that Cathy Moriarty tempted Robert de Niro in *Raging Bull* (1980) before the big fight. Children and domesticity lead to spiritual castration. When men are weak or stupid enough to let themselves fall under the sway of women, they give up their sacred calling. The devil is a woman indeed.

In contrast, George Stevens' *The Greatest Story Ever Told* (1965) —critically reviled and financially disastrous—is the most literal of all the New Testament films. Leisurely paced, even talky as it explores the meanings of the parables, it sticks closely to the Scriptures. Mary Magdalene is unimportant, and Judas sympathetic and completely unmotivated. The reasons for the betrayal are murky, as in the Bible, which presents the betrayal as an element in a divine plan that must take place if Jesus is to be crucified and resurrected.

Point-of-view shots are another element of film language that figure prominently in biblical films. Nicholas Ray—whose use of high angle/low angle shot combinations in *Rebel without a Cause* (1955) to express familial relationships convinced me to study film—makes masterful use of shot combinations and point-of-view in *King of Kings*. When John the Baptist preaches under the balcony of the palace, Ray cuts back and forth from extreme high angles of John to extreme low angles of the Romans on the balcony. This is by-the-book composition and editing, exactly what one would expect when naturalistically shooting such a scene. The camera looks up at the characters on the balcony, down at the man in the street. Then, Ray subverts cinematic convention: when Pilate throws down a coin—gold, of course—dismissing John as a beggar, we cut from a low angle shot of Pilate to an equally low angle shot of John on the street. (To shoot John from this angle, Ray would have needed to dig a hole in the set in which to place the camera, a trick invented by Orson Welles.) Empowered by the camera angle, John picks up the golden coin and throws it back up at the oppressors.

Christopher Vogler, a disciple of Joseph Campbell, describes an old rule of initiation in secret societies: "disorientation leads to suggestibility...getting the audience a little off-base and upsetting their normal perceptions can put them into a receptive mood. They begin to suspend their disbelief and enter more readily into a Special World of fantasy" (1992, p. 101).

Nicholas Ray is a master of using camera angles and editing to disorient the audience and subvert their expectations, as he proves in the scene where Jesus goes to visit John the Baptist in prison and finds the Baptist literally at the bottom of a pit. Weak, wounded, and chained, John climbs up a long incline to touch Jesus' hand through the bars in a screen-filling closeup. But despite their physical locations vis-à-vis one another, the camera never looks down at John or up at Jesus. Both of them are shot dead-on, from the side, emphasizing their brotherhood and spiritual equality.

Ray uses camera angles like this throughout *King of Kings* to represent the power relationships between the characters. Even God gets point-of-view shots in this movie: looking down benevolently, like a proud father, over Jesus' shoulder, as he preaches the Sermon on the Mount, and directly down from Heaven at the top of Jesus' head during the crucifixion.

The invention of CinemaScope in the 1950s and the biblical spectacular are inextricably linked. Indeed, *The Robe* was the first CinemaScope film. Studios—particularly Twentieth Century Fox—needed to make big films to take advantage of this expensive new toy: big films with spectacular visuals to fill the new, over-sized screen (armies clashing, chariots racing, mobs rioting); big films with big budgets that would hopefully be recouped when audiences throughout the world flocked to see them. The Bible, as a commodity presold to millions and the most popular single title in the world, was a perfect choice for CinemaScope.

Nicholas Ray uses the combination of CinemaScope and Jeffrey Hunter's vivid blue eyes to great effect in *King of Kings*. (Figure 3) Hunter's eyes literally bore into the viewer in two extreme closeups that fill the massive screen: first, when Jesus meets John the Baptist; next, when Jesus cures a blind man. Jesus' gaze is so powerful, it melts the cataracts off the blind man's eyes. But when Jesus performs another healing miracle, you see Jesus look into the eyes of an afflicted person in a medium shot, almost as if Jesus' gaze was too powerful to show a third time. The extreme closeup is deliberately withheld from the viewer, forcing the audience to remember it from previous scenes, to be an active rather than passive participant in the

Figure 3: Director Nicholas Ray uses the combination of CinemaScope and Jeffrey Hunter's vivid blue eyes to great effect in *King of Kings.*

viewing process. Again, Ray subverts our expectations to draw us into a deeper, more emotional involvement with his film.

Compare the use of extreme closeups in Ray's *King of Kings* with a scene in De Mille's original, where the blind person is not a man, but a child, a little girl (for added vulnerability). We're 15 minutes into the film—time spent lollygagging in Mary Magdalene's palace—before we see Jesus for the first time, from the child's point of view. We see a black screen and then a dazzling light, which resolves itself into Jesus' face, wise and kind, looking down upon us, father to child, teacher to pupil. Our blindness is cured and Jesus is our first sight. This is one of the most spectacular and effective entrances in film history.

Dialogue reflects this visual symbolism. When Jesus "speaks" (via an intertitle), he says, "I am come as a light into the world, that whosoever believeth in me shall not abide in darkness." Thus De Mille makes faith both visible and literal, effectively translating a miracle to the screen without color, sound, or complicated special effects. Perhaps that's why De Mille's *King of Kings* has been subtitled in two dozen languages, carried up the Ganges and the Congo by missionaries, and seen by over half a billion people (Campbell, 1981, p. 107). Although we never get another child's point-of-view shot in the De Mille *King of Kings*, the need for trusting, childlike faith—established by the original glimpse of Jesus—permeates the movie, as does the theme of Jesus as a light that banishes blindness. This theme is underscored by the Victorian hymn "Lead Kindly Light," played on theater organs during the silent era and appended to prints after the coming of sound.

Compare this masterly use of film language with George Stevens' *The Greatest Story Ever Told*. When Jesus cures a blind man named Aaron, the blind man (actor Ed Wynn) looks up and says, "You've grown very tall." But when the director cuts to Aaron's point of view, there's nobody there at all, just empty blue sky. What is that supposed to mean? This is inept use of film language. The point is murky as point of view.

In Martin Scorcese's *The Last Temptation of Christ* (1988), the director makes Christ the subject, rather than the object, of our gaze. For the first time in film history, we see through Christ's eyes: the tortured point of view, the self-doubt, the self-consciousness. A shaky hand-held camera projects inner torment via a plethora of stationary and traveling point-of-view shots, while Willem DaFoe's tortured interior monologues emphasize uncertainty, incoherence, and the ever-present doubt.

Language of Commerce

How fluent were biblical films in speaking the language of commerce? Spectacularly so, particularly in the 1950s. *David and Bathsheba* was the most successful film of 1951; *Quo Vadis*, the second most popular of 1952; *The Robe*, the biggest of 1953. Stanley Kubrick's *Spartacus* was the top earner in 1960. And *Ben-Hur* was the biggest film of the decade, followed closely by *The Ten Commandments* (Babington & Evans, 1993, p. 55).

Not only were biblical films popular with audiences, but they were showered with Academy Awards. Both *Ben-Hur* and *Spartacus* won Best Picture; Charlton Heston, Hugh Griffith, and Peter Ustinov were honored for their acting; William Wyler won Best Director; and throughout the decade biblical films dominated the craft awards—art direction, set direction, cinematography, and costume design (p. 66).

Given which films we remember from the 1950s, this is astonishing. When film students study genre, they see the film noir, the western, and the musicals of the 1950s. Repertory cinemas and college film societies screen Nicholas Ray's *Johnny Guitar* (1954), *In a Lonely Place* (1950), *Bigger than Life* (1956), and *Rebel without a Cause*, but seldom *King of Kings*, which made more money than any of those. Instead of A-list biblical spectaculars, we study *Kiss Me Deadly* (1955), *High Noon* (1952), *They Live by Night* (1948), *Gilda* (1946), and *Crossfire* (1947)—B movies, which deal metaphorically, via their *mise en scène*, with the Blacklist, the Atomic Age, and Cold War paranoia.

One could argue that this is because the B-films are artistically superior or because film makers working in these then under-appreciated genres were free to develop film language—despite or because of genre conventions—without losing their studios vast amounts of money. But Nicholas Ray didn't cease being himself when he made *King of Kings*. Talent doesn't vanish miraculously, just because one has a budget. The themes Ray explores in his B-films and the techniques he uses to advance them permeate *King of Kings*. So why not study it? Could it be because *King of Kings* is about Jesus?

If one looks at any standard reference work, it's hard not to conclude that biblical films have been deliberately written out of film history. Andrew Dowdy mentions only *Ben-Hur* (in one sentence) and *Spartacus*, written by Dalton Trumbo, as a milestone in the breaking of the Blacklist (Dowdy, 1973, pp. 157, 44). If you search "film, history of," in the Grolier Multimedia Encyclopedia, and click on the 1950s, you'll find references to the Cold War, the Blacklist, Roberto Rosselini's *The Miracle*, censorship, *On The Waterfront*, film noir, and the MGM musical, but not a word about a single one of the biblical films that were once considered the best of the decade.

Why have biblical films been ignored, particularly since so many of them were interesting and highly profitable works? And why are no biblical films being made today? This has something to do with many factors, including the power of Christian fundamentalism, religious broadcasters like Pat Robertson, the boycotts of Donald Wildmon, and the outrage that greeted *The Last Temptation of Christ*.

Screenplay Structure

But perhaps the real answer lies elsewhere: in the language of screenplay structure, which dominates the film industry today. This language demands a certain rigidly codified form for screenplays. Why is this? To ensure the commercial success of the film? As if this were possible! I would argue that these structural rules exist so that story analysts can have a set of standards with which to justify their decisions for rejecting a project, as most are. In other words, the language of screenplay structure is a language with which studio employees communicate with one another, with the screen writers for whom they serve as threshold guardians, and with the bosses they must avoid offending at all costs. Natalie Lemberg explains the process in a 1995 electronic article "Vaulting the Moat" in the *Creative Screenwriting Newsletter*:

> Story analysts, more casually called readers, are like a moat between screen writers and producers, directors and studio executives in the castle.... Most scripts submitted to a studio, producer, or agency are first synopsized and commented upon by a reader in a 2-4 page report called "coverage." Coverage includes the details of the submission, a one or

two sentence summary called a "logline," a graphic scorecard, called a "box score," and a "call": Pass, Consider, or Recommend. Busy buyers use the coverage to decide which scripts to read themselves, and which scripts to pass on without reading. It's very tough to get across this moat because studio readers are expected to pass on 97% of the scripts they read. Readers are frequently chided for saying "yes," that is, for sending an executive home with a bad script to read.... On the other hand, readers are only chided for saying "no" when another company publicly says "yes" on the same script, or, as we will see, in the case of extreme financial or critical success.

Screen writers spend years trying to figure out what the ideal form of the screenplay should be in order to get across the moat Lemberg describes so vividly. In pursuit of success, they take classes in screen writing at film schools and marathon story structure courses from entrepreneurs like Syd Field, Robert McKee, and John Truby. They go to so-called writers' boot camps. And they talk to one another via their computers.

A few of the ideas about screenplay methodology and structure that are being discussed over the Internet today include:

- the three-act structure (the grandddaddy of them all, whose biggest promoter, Syd Fields, was recently depicted as the devil in a parody distributed on the Internet);
- the two-goal structure (plots that have a reversal in the middle of the film and thus that change the protagonist's goal) (Posted on-line by D. Siegel, 1995);
- the three p's (the premise, the people, and the plot);
- the four-act paradigm (the fourth act is carved from the middle of the traditional second act of the three-act structure);
- the nine-act structure (Posted on-line by D. Siegel, 1995);
- the twelve-step program; and
- George Polti's "Thirty-seven Dramatic Situations."

Despite the cutthroat nature of contemporary Hollywood, established screen writers are remarkably generous with their advice to novices. In "Vaulting the Moat," Natalie Lemberg offers these tips:

> Your story should have a strong premise, defined as either a high concept hook, or a well-developed theme. Characters should begin with motivating needs, face escalating obstacles in reaching their goals, and change as a result of their journey. Subplots should be resolved, and bad guys dealt comeuppance. (1995)

In order to sell their scripts, screen writers must learn to speak the language spoken within the offices of Hollywood studio bosses. In fact, they must internalize it. Consider this advice from screen writer Nick Falacci (Posted on-line, 1995):

> Write your story on a single sheet of paper. Not two, not three, not 37. ONE PAGE. What this accomplishes is that it forces you to strip the

narrative down to the bare bones.... You are looking for an airtight page of critical moments that go BOOM - BOOM -BOOM with no room for anyone to think, "But why does that happen *that* way?"... Producers and agents and execs are always reading one-pagers. That's how many, if not most, people will be "reading" your script anyway.

When structure is everything, spontaneity vanishes entirely. Screen writer Lisa Dethridge suggests the following (Posted on Listserv, 1995):

Take your screenplay, turn it into seven sentences. That's right, seven real sentences. One for each plot point/act break, one for the inciting incident, one for the setup and two "extra." When you can successfully do that (success: When your audience gets the "ah ha!" reaction from the seven sentence outline), then feel free to expand it to a page, to allow you to write a bit of the tone and maybe even include the B-line.

Screen writers must not only tailor their scripts according to the language of screenplay structure, but learn to speak the language of commerce as well. As screen writer John Hill (*Quigley Down Under, 1990*) advises (Posted on Listserv, 1995):

Write a high concept genre script with lead role for a bankable, genre-appropriate superstar and make sure your hot, great 25-words-or-less premise, yes, literally, 25 words or less, plus your tone/genre also have recent (five to eight years) profitable precedents at the box office.

In order to be produced, screenplays must be high concept. Justin Wyatt, in his new book, *High Concept* (1994), defines it as:

a striking, easily reducible narrative which also offers a high degree of marketability. High concept films combine several elements: a narrative that could be summarized in a single phrase; an image or song that the potential audience associated with the film; "total look" style of cinematography characteristic of television and magazine advertisements and music videos; pre-sold stars or subject matter; character typing rather than character exposition; and merchandising tie-ins. (Online book review by S. Mintz, 1995)

Wyatt traces the rise of the high-concept movie to industry conglomeration and the growing dominance of the film industry's marketing departments and their reliance on market research to make decisions about which films will get made. High concept is an attempt to quantify the film industry and predict box office success, thereby reducing financial risk for the studios to zero.

In pursuit of the perfect, high concept screenplay, screen writers also read the books of Joseph Campbell, or—much more likely—they read books or articles in which Campbell's ideas are simplified, formularized, and specifically applied to screenplays. These days, in Hollywood, Joseph Campbell is a virtual god. Consider this post on the Internet, describing a Bill Moyers' interview with Campbell:

Bill Moyers treats this as an average interview, coming from his WASP-ish background and trying to grasp the individual straws that Joseph hands him.... Here is this little impish wizard seated in front of him, and Bill wants to think that he is simply a renowned academic. Joseph, for his part, is a faerie, beckoning Moyers out of the land of objective interviews into the magic kingdom. Bill can't go there, because he doesn't have the willingness to let go of terra firma. Joseph is floating, playing, cajoling and teasing, trying to get Bill to see how magical and mystical this moment right here right now is, and Bill says that's a very interesting point of view.... Joseph is saying that the chair Bill is sitting on literally doesn't exist, that there is only one dance and we are part of it, that Bill himself is on a journey of mythic proportions. (Posted on-line by D. Siegel, 1995)

There are even screenplay programs which take the ideas of Joseph Campbell and translate them for you, into the language of the computer, thus taking the work of structuring your script correctly (as demanded by the language of commerce) out of your hands. Such programs include *Writer's Block, Generator, Storyline Pro, Plots Unlimited, Dramatica*, and *Collaborator 3*.

Perhaps the language of screenplay structure, subsumed by the language of commerce, explains why no Hollywood films have been made about the Bible since Scorsese's *Last Temptation*. Try to cram the story of Jesus into a three-act, four-act, or nine-act structure. It's impossible. The New Testament is episodic. There are too many characters and all of them talk too much. This is why biblical epics, studied today, look bloated, over-long, and overpopulated. There's plot, but no sub-plots. Secondary characters lack credible motivation. The main character is difficult for audiences to identify with, and particularly for studio executives, under the influence of Joseph Campbell, to understand. As Christopher Vogler writes in his influential interpretation of Campbell:

Every hero needs both an inner and an outer problem.... Characters without inner challenges seem flat and uninvolving, however heroically they may act. They need an inner problem, a personality flaw or a moral dilemma to work out. They need to learn something in the course of the story: how to get along with others, how to trust themselves, how to see beyond outward appearances. Audiences love to see characters learning, growing, and dealing with the inner and outer challenges of life. (1992, p. 103, 104)

Perhaps the reason Scorsese was so attracted to *The Last Temptation* was because it postulated an inner challenge for Jesus (his sexual attraction to Mary Magdalene) and showed him changing and growing over the film, like a true mythic hero.

One tried and true method of interpreting biblical texts that is curiously very much in vogue in both film and popular literature today is to focus on the minor characters of classic stories, retelling the stories through their eyes, thus providing fresh perspectives on beloved classics (i.e., pre-sold commodities). One such project, which has been recently released, is the filmed version (1996) of Valerie Martin's novel, *Mary Reilly*, which re-tells *Dr. Jekyll and Mr. Hyde* through the eyes of his maid...Julia Roberts.

Many people seem to think this method of story-(re)telling began in the 1960s, with films such as Thomas Berger's *Little Big Man* (1964), about an imaginary survivor of the battle of Little Big Horn; Tom Stoppard's *Rosencrantz and Guildenstern Are Dead* (1966), which retells Hamlet through the eyes of two courtiers; and Jean Rhys' powerful and overlooked *The Wide Sargasso Sea* (1966), a prequel to Charlotte Bronte's *Jane Eyre*, which tells the story of the first Mrs. Rochester, the original madwoman in the attic. In fact, writers interested in translating the Bible to stage and screen audiences made good use of this minor character technique as far back as Oscar Wilde's *Salome* (1893). There have been at least four Salome films as well as films about other minor biblical characters, including Mary Magdalene, Barabbas, and Ruth, not to mention films about fictional charac-ters whose lives are somehow changed by Christ, including *The Robe*, *Ben-Hur*, and *Demetrius and the Gladiators*. But despite the plethora of minor biblical characters whose stories remain untold by Hollywood, there's been no rush to make these kinds of films today.

To the people making decisions in Hollywood, the Bible is dated, old-fashioned, and non-commercial. As screen writer guru Robert McKee teaches, contemporary cinema is motivated by extra-personal conflicts. Inner conflicts are the realm of the novel. Pure cinema is the chase scene. Thus the Bible is not a candidate for translation to the big screen, despite its value as a pre-sold commodity. In fact, I seriously doubt that anyone, even Scor-cese, could get a big-budget biblical project green-lighted in Hollywood to-day. As screen writer Buck Tyson put it, "Who wants to watch an American film full of pauses anyway?" (Posted on-line, 1995)

Given current popular tastes, should one attempt to make biblical films at all? Judith Crist felt it was impossible to represent Jesus on film. In a review of *The Greatest Story Ever Told*, she asked:

> How to personify the mystery and divinity and, once personified, how to make the figure move among men?... The great big screen and the great big names are too much for the survival of matters of the spirit. So many aspects of big movie-making intervene that the Passion cannot predominate. (quoted in Forshey, 1992, p. 85)

The neo-Luddite Jerry Mander—whose comrade, Kirkpatrick Sale, re-cently smashed a computer with a sledgehammer during a speech in New York City, making himself and his cause appear ridiculous—argues that modern media are ill-equipped to communicate the sacred. He believes the language of the apparatus is such that people who wish to make "progres-sive" media cannot speak with it, or overcome its inherently negative quali-ties, without being co-opted. The act of sitting in the dark, watching a flickering light, the rays of which penetrate our eyes and our brains, separates us from nature, and thus the sacred. (Walt Disney's remarkably ecofeminist *Pochohontas* [1995] visualizes this nature/culture dichotomy. The white, male, European, mechanical, rational world is vividly opposed to the world of the Indians: non-white, female, nature-centered, and spiritual.) The result is a nation of people too sped up to attune themselves to slower, natural, primordial rhythms. Mander writes:

> Once we accept life within a technically mediated reality, we become less aware of anything that preceded it. We have a hard time imagining life before television or cars. We do not remember a United States of mainly forests and quiet. The information that nature offers to our minds and to our senses is nearly absent from our lives.... It's little wonder that we find incomprehensible any societies that choose to live within nature.... Living constantly inside an environment of our own invention, reacting solely to things we ourselves have created, we are essentially living inside our own minds. Where evolution was once an interactive process between human beings and a natural, unmediated world, evolution is now an interaction between human beings and our own artifacts.... We become ever more enclosed and ever less aware of that fact. (Mander, 1992, p. 32)

Immersed in our new technologies, we know that seeing is not believing. Our senses are so jaded from special effects, creating hitherto impossible sights, that if Jesus came down from heaven today and performed a miracle—the subject of Herbert Achtenbusch's remarkable, seldom-seen *Das Gespenst* (1982)—most skeptics would look for the holographic apparatus from which his image must have been projected.

Mander's focus is on television, but many of his arguments can be extended to film as well, particularly the contemporary Hollywood film, which owes so much of its style to the relentless pace of television, rock videos, and TV advertising—with its unceasing barrage of technical events—a pace which makes us both stupid and speedy at the same time, hardly a fit state in which to contemplate the spiritual. Film has become TV advertising on the big screen. Product placement and character merchandising only reinforce this merger.

In the middle of a montage film like *Natural Born Killers* (1994), for example, you don't pull out and contemplate the images or the ideas. To do so would cause you to fall behind what Mander calls the "image stream." You either withdraw from the experience entirely, or surrender to its dubious pleasures, allowing the images to enter you at their own speed. Thus, you become a passive receptacle: dumb and dumber. So while you may indeed end up with a conclusion of sorts implanted in your brain—particularly if you've just seen an Oliver Stone film—it's not your conclusion. You haven't reached it.

It's possible that we may have reached the end of the line in using films to communicate complex ideas. The language of the blockbuster admits little possibility of thought. (It isn't called *Johnny Mnemonic* [1995] for nothing.) Corporate ideology, corporate priorities, corporate behavior, corporate value systems, and corporate language are behind the bloated, big-budget extravaganzas of Hollywood today, whose religion is commodity fetishism, worshiped at the mall. As Hollywood attempts to deliver to advertisers the desired target audience—male and adolescent—the population deemed unprofitable is left behind, along with the unquantifiable: taste, complexity, art, and meaning.

All of this goes a long way toward explaining why I'm not actively trying to make movies right now (although I would probably reenter the fray if someone handed me a very large check). Instead, I'm making multimedia, which, given the prevailing values in Hollywood, seems to me like a more appropriate venue for both political art and intellectual discourse. CD-ROMs seem particularly well-suited for telling biblical stories. Not only are they participatory—by their very nature forcing people to actively engage the material, rather than passively receiving it—but they also allow pauses for thought and reflection. Because they are not limited by time, they can offer more complexity and background, both visual and textual. They can deliver whatever it takes to achieve understanding, from an essay to a volume, replete with video, photographs, virtual spaces, music, and sounds. Multimedia allows an unlimited number of stories to be told. One could do a CD-ROM about the life of Christ in which the lives of all of the minor characters were included. Points of intersection—in their lives and their ideas—could be mapped and explored, without the arbitrary imposition of three-act structure. Biblical films could be excerpted and analyzed, and creativity unleashed. Only disk space, and our imaginations, limit us.

Jayne Loader, a writer/director who recently entered the field of multimedia, co-directed the documentary classic *The Atomic Cafe*, which inspired her award-winning CD-ROM, *Public Shelter*. Her novel, *Between Pictures*, and short story collection, *Wild America*, were both published by Grove Press. Ms. Loader has guested on *The Today Show* and *Late Night With David Letterman* and has been profiled in *The New York Times, Rolling Stone*, and *People*. She also writes a popular online column, WWWench. Future projects include *Hoop Dreams*, a CD-ROM and Website based on the acclaimed documentary, and *Flygirls*, an historical novel about women aviators, which will be repurposed as a CD-ROM and Website designed to teach science, acronautics, celestial navigation, history, and technology to girls.

10

Out of the Garden and into the Mall: Eve's Journey from Eden to MTV

Alice Bach

This chapter follows the biblical figure of Eve from her appearance in the Genesis stories of the Old Testament to various modern incarnations in advertising and film. Bringing feminist and audience analysis to bear on this trajectory of Eve, it shows how in popular culture today the archetypal woman—and thereby all women—has been reduced to a single dominant role, namely, woman as companion to man. A film *Out of the Garden* accompanied the original presentation of this essay.

I was a month into creating *Out of the Garden*, my second multimedia exploration, before I realized why the process holds me in its thrall. The title holds a clue: When I am propelled *out of the garden*, I am propelled into a parallel universe of discourse, tangled terrain, the dark continent, the unruly garden of the feminine. The multimedia work that I am producing is not in principle governed by preestablished rules, and thus, cannot be judged by applying familiar categories to the work. The traditional rules of the game so familiar in the Garden do not control the postmodern, postgarden world of multimedia. Working in film montage has allowed me to experience the power of feminine artistic production as an organic process of conquering and reclaiming, appropriating and formulating, as well as forgetting and subverting. Simply put, in the montage you will identify strong traditional images as well as my feminist break with them. Some of the images and film clips will seem banal, some will have the welcome familiarity of a half-remembered song. The resulting work allows unpredictable connections for the audience. Because there are no scholarly or artistic norms for multimedia (yet), I am free to search for new forms of presentation, to enjoy the pleasure of hybridizing familiar creations, and to impart a stronger sense of the unpresentable.

Out of the Garden

What you see in this film seems at first like odds and ends of thought: film clips juxtaposed with familiar songs, collections of advertisements giving an unusual timbre to traditional midrash on Genesis, the stock characters of Adam and Eve interpreted visually from Michelangelo to Michael Jackson. But do not fear: There is someone in charge here. You, the spectator, are the connecting link. In creating this film, I became increasingly aware of the function of the audience as author. The multiple identities of each audience member determine the film's various interpretations. As scholars of religion, you have the foundational text of Genesis 1-3 inscribed upon your hearts. Thus you will hear the biblical echoes whispering underneath the modern voices. The social theorists among you will recognize how the original advertisements or films create desire for sleek bodied women, shiny chromed cars, spic and spanned floors—the American Eden. Cultural theorists will see how thoroughly and profoundly the appropriations of the biblical material have been achieved and encoded within popular media: film, print and electronic ads, music videos. Connecting the fruit offered by the Material Girl with that offered by the woman in the garden may at first seem like too great a cultural leap. But Madonna's *Vogue* world is actually a playful rearrangement of conventional cultural symbols.

There are no naive viewers here, no one who will not provide some glue, some link among images. Thus, there is a panoply of films being shown simultaneously. A compilation film such as *Out of the Garden* shows the interrelatedness of familiar images—and particularly the deep roots of the biblical tree greening into our own symbols of good and evil. The wider the collection of referent images, the more the resultant narratives multiply and the more they reflect back upon the foundational text. In other words, the further out of the garden we flee, the more our gaze is directed back there. Selected events are retold and recombined to emphasize what I consider the predominant themes that have overgrown that carefully planted garden. The distortions as well as the parallels are essential to the spectator's altered incorporation of the original ideas—the ones that have been borrowed and intentionally (mis)used. Listen for the sultry siren song of Rita Hayworth, calling to us from the 1946 film *Gilda*. No matter how far we run, we are still that same disorderly woman. Her sly smile assures men that it is OK to look, to desire, because you can always Put the Blame on Mame.

The primary theme that I have played upon in the work is creation itself: God's creation of the universe, of the man, of the woman, of the laws of the Garden, that have in our culture taken on the force of natural law. The creation of the woman as a companion for the man is a theme that runs through much of our own popular culture.

Designing Women

By identifying the codes of contemporary American social and cultural ideologies found in both films and print ads from the '40s and '50s, one learns both how idealized images of people are constructed and how the people are positioned in the social hierarchy. Two American cultural icons combine to portray the woman from Genesis 3 in both her guises: Snow White and the Vargas pinup girl. As Mr. Disney's mother of us all, Snow White grows up to become the idealized wife of postwar America, depicted both in films and most stunningly in advertising. Popular images leave little doubt about what makes the woman "good," this wife-woman the deity might have created as the perfect companion for the man, once upon a time in a misty Garden. The solitary American woman is often pictured with equipment: refrigerator, stove, bathtub, and of course that serpentine instrument of housewifely delight, the Hoover hose vacuum cleaner. Thus, we have the category of woman set within her social context: the home, which is her companion while the husband and children are away. She is always smiling and never confounded by the way the machinery of her world operates.

She is the American girl, who instinctively knows how to clean, cook, and make a house a home; her lineage is reflected not only in advertisements but in that didactic tool: the feature-length cartoon. Walt Disney used Snow White to teach the young women who would grow up to clean those houses of the '50s how to whistle while they worked. If Snow White taught us anything, it was that it is as easy to keep house for seven as one. Clearly she is a woman who lives out the concept of woman from Genesis 3: She will work hard (remember those seven little boy-men on whom she practices her skills) and her desire will be for her husband—the prince.

From the other side of the tracks come the Vargas pinup girls, who tempt the American male to forget the rules of the game. With pale gold hair, blood red nails and lips, and a sinuous body, each one is a visual mix of the woman and the serpent. Dangerous but compelling, she exudes sexuality from the safe distance of the printed page.

The fantasy of the male being able to create for himself the perfect woman is transformed into a gothic warning in the *Bride of Frankenstein* (1935) and other cinematic dreams of technology aiding modern man's desire for what Shelley's monster shyly hopes will be created as a "friend for me." The man of science misuses the collective wonders of electricity and chemistry, and transplants in a vain attempt to elevate his abilities to the creative level of the divine. All he gets for his trouble is a monstrous imitation of a woman, perhaps all that his ego clay will permit him to shape. Elie Wiesel, a serious student of God's intentions, paints a cautionary midrash: The deity, even the deity, is doomed to failure in creating a perfect woman.

Taking the precaution to mold her from as innocuous a body part as a rib, Wiesel sighs, the woman is still rife with the faults God tried to avoid.

A third variation on the theme of male creating woman is found in the rash of films of men pretending to be women, and indeed in the cases of Dustin Hoffman (in *Tootsie*, 1982) and Robin Williams (in *Mrs. Doubtfire*, 1993) they are better at being women than women themselves. Of course there is also the comfort that they are still men underneath the latex and lashes. These women-men offer answers to Rex Harrison's despairing question to stodgy Colonel Pickering in *My Fair Lady* (1964), "Why can't a woman be more like a man?" First planted in the Garden, the dream of perfect companionship persists.

Out of the Garden has a simple structure, that of playing the traditional interpretations of Genesis 1-3 off against modern images in which the biblical tropes and themes are encoded. It will be clear from the mainstream interpretations that women were represented as either idealized objects of desire or as threatening forces to be tamed. Clearly these are not attempts to establish female subjectivity but rather reflect the search for male self-definition. Thus, popular films are said to belong to the patriarchy, leaving the female audience to identify with the male-as-subject and the female-as-object.

The Hanna-Barbera cartoon version (1991) of the book of Genesis marketed to a religious home market is an example of tradition as cliché. Today's media-savvy child will recognize the resemblance between Eve and Disney's Little Mermaid. Even *I* recognized the cartoon Adam as a caricature of that great male centerpiece, Arnold Schwarzenegger. In this larky recreation of the world according to video, the animals are cartoon quirky and cute; God's voice comes through the obligatory echo chamber; and the flaming cross at the end of the film reminds us that Genesis, in the ambitious plans of the video marketers, is "just the beginning." The calmly assured voice of Elie Wiesel from an educational video on midrash in the Bible (marketed by the way on the same religious cable channel as the Hanna-Barbera cartoon library) provides the erudite counterpart to the supersaturated paradise of Hanna-Barbera. Viewed by compliant spectators, one gets an immediate picture of a society which has formalized as its centerpiece the dominant and powerful male. Being forced to leave this garden of order would certainly be a shame—a calamity that, seen from the controlling perspective of the male gaze, is death-dealing and clearly the fault of the dis-orderly woman: the Vargas pinup who hides in the unconscious shadows of desire.

Into the Mall

Working within the principles of basic film theory, women are left with no active spectatorial position. Or so I thought until I lived for months with the images that became this multimedia exploration of the Garden story. The feminist interpretation of the woman reaching for the fruit in the Garden as positive, as reaching for knowledge, wisdom, pleasure is familiar to most readers of feminist analysis. But what happens after the woman eats of the fruit? Why have her sisters left the woman in the lurch, swallowing (and thus repressing) her new-found knowledge with the last sweet vestiges of the fruit? Why does she continue to be figured in visual and verbal interpretations alike as filled with shame and guilt at her deed? Why are both the woman and her companion so grieved at leaving the Garden? Why would this woman, willing to challenge the laws of the Garden, be downcast to be driven from the Garden of law and order?

The wonders of technology allowed me to play with two familiar visual images of Adam and Eve cast out of the garden. In the first, the couple, walking close together, share their shame, shoulders hunched, heads down. Their pale bodies form a stark contrast to the Edenic world which has grown dark and somber from their crime. *But wait.* If I raise the woman's head, if I rotate her arm until she is reaching out toward that new world, if I return the colors to bright sun-drenched colors of life? Could the woman not then be still the initiator she was while she was eating the fruit? Once I snapped off a luscious interpretation from the tree of tradition, I could imagine an Eve not bent from the weight of the existing cultural order. The tweaked image proves invaluable in subverting or creating alternatives to that order. Expulsion becomes escape.

The Eve eager to taste more of the world than was permitted to her is the artist, who must break through the transhistorical nature of traditional interpretation. The presumption that narrative interpretations apply equally across all time and instances leaves them immutable, inflexible, imprisoned within the patriarchal rules of the game. Reified images are poisonous fruit for the artist. Without demanding freedom from self-limitation, the artist is only a worker in someone else's garden. Reaching out for any fruit in any possible garden, even the fruit outside its recognized borders, is the work of the artist, undertaken by the Eve willing to play a disquieting role. Manipulating conventional visual images releases the potential of theorizing alternative readings or interpretations within any given text, visual or verbal. To deny that a spectator provides a *context* is to ignore that shifts in textual meaning relate to shifts in viewing situation. Just as feminists have searched for the woman in the text, one must look squint-eyed at visual images in order to effect cultural change. Just as suspicious readings have exposed the controlling codes in texts, so our new techno-toys allow us to reinscribe visual images, to escape the visual images that have grown so heartily in the garden of patriarchy.

In the final scenes of the film, I have nurtured a worldview that grew way out of the tree in the middle of that first Garden, transplanted into a landscape where the rules ripen and fall as easily as fruit from a tree. In our

Edenic world, rules are swallowed and gone, a dim memory that urges the woman, and man, to discover new trees, new gardens, new patterns. If the Garden is the organic canvas on which the artist imagines world, then Madonna and Michael invite us to dwell a while in a gender-free zone, where the confusion of male and female demands that the spectator regard the power of gender.

As the man said, "Genesis is only the beginning."

Alice Bach is assistant professor of Religious Studies at Stanford. She is executive editor of a new international journal, *BiblIcon* and editorial board member of *Semeia*. Her many articles and book reviews are now complemented by a book of literary and cultural criticism, *Seduction and Betrayal in Biblical Narratives* (Cambridge, 1997). She has completed the editing of a 29-minute film, which is the work referred to in this chapter: *Out of the Garden and Into the Mall: Eve's Journey from Eden to MTV;* and a reader entitled *Feminist Interpretations of the Hebrew Bible: The Mother of All Readers*. A well-known journalist and book reviewer, Bach has also written more than 20 children's books, among them two *New York Times* Best Books of the Year.

11

Musical *Mimesis* for Modern Media

J. Ritter Werner

Modern technology can combine lexical, musical, and gestural media into powerful, hybrid works of art that can memorialize thoughts, feelings, and physical actions. Can this technology incorporate these three elements in a balanced and effective way? It can if the producers of multimedia materials understand the various ways text, sound, and gesture have interacted throughout western history, and then, based upon that knowledge, avoid the pitfalls of the past, and re-present the recital tradition for contemporary audiences.

> "New art always forces us to see
> the art of the past differently."
> (Goldberg, 1995, p. 39)

Today music is a discrete medium of communication, often entirely disassociated from text or movement, whose purpose is to explore or move feelings. This pure or absolute state, however, is not the norm. For most of history, music has interacted with lexical and gestural media to produce powerful, hybrid works of art that not only communicate feelings, but also thoughts and physical actions. This multimedia approach probably results from two factors: that no single medium is capable of communicating the richness of experience, and that multimedia presentations facilitate memory.

Multimedia Presentations

Some of our most ancient narratives chronicle echoes of this multimedia experience. In the Book of Exodus, Miriam, the Jewish Polyhymnia, took up the timbrel and sang and danced with all the women of Israel to celebrate their deliverance near the Red Sea (Exodus 15.20-21). The *Shield of Heracles* by Hesiod includes a description of a bridal procession, accompanied by songs, torches, dancing, and instruments that enveloped a whole city with laughter and festivities. Both accounts from the perspective of communication were multimedia events, and they stir the imagination with delight and envy. Oh to experience such *joie de vivre!* However, there is also a sense of loss when silently reading these narratives. What were the sounds and the gestures? Unfortunately the original multimedia experience has been reduced to a written lexical medium that now lies silent and static.

Music, therefore, is not the only medium that suffers from excessive isolation. Our culture, at least since the Enlightenment, has reduced the rich, sonic, lexical medium to silent reading. However, unlike music, this silent form of the lexical medium dominates human communication. Many people treat it as *the* embodiment of intelligence and meaning with the capability to communicate anything and everything. Fortunately, this enlightenment is being questioned due, in part, to the invention and use of modern media which shun silent and static forms of communication.

In ancient and medieval times most people in the western world experienced words in their sonic form. The written medium was used primarily as a mnemonic device to aid performers in public recitals. Expressive dynamics, pitch inflection, and rhythmic variations were either added to a text according to unwritten oral conventions, or marked with secondary notational systems. These additions not only indicated various manipulations of sound, but sometimes indicated special gestures of the hands to help a performer remember the melodic contour of the text. This art of accompanimental hand gestures is called chironomy. The actual performance of a written text, therefore, was a multimedia experience, which included music and gesture.

Hebrew and Greek Traditions

In the Hebrew tradition this multimedia practice is documented in the *Mishnah*, and in the *Talmudim* of Palestine and Babylon. Rabbi Aqiva, who is still remembered on Yom Kippur as one of the 10 martyrs in the Hadrianic persecution in the year 135 A.D., always sang the Torah as part of his study (Avenary, 1963, p. 8). Rabbi Yohanan, who died in 279 A.D., once said, "Whoever reads Scripture without melody and recites traditions without song, of him Scripture says, 'And I have given him laws that are not good'" (Elbogen, 1911/1993, p. 382). Also according to the *Talmud*, teachers used chironomy to instruct their students in the correct delimitations of clauses found in Scripture. This practice remained in use until the 12th century, even after written accents were commonly added to the manuscripts (Avenary, 1963, p. 8).

In the Greek tradition documentation is also plentiful. Plato in his *Republic* makes a wonderful statement, "*harmonia* and rhythm must follow the words" (Barker, 1984, p. 130). The Greek term *harmonia*, which literally means "joining," refers to the proper singing of the high, low, and medium tones that follow the accents of the text (Aristotle, 1994, p. 347). The melody of a text therefore was embedded in the words with the rhythm. For

Plato, the lexical medium included two musical parameters: pitch-harmony and rhythm.

The pitch parameter was such an important element for the meaning of a text that a system of three extra-lexical marks was invented to insure proper performance of texts, when the oral pitch tradition became uncertain. This system was attributed to Aristophanes of Byzantium, and the Greeks called their accents *prosodia* (Latin is *accentus,* from *ad cano*), which means "song accompanying words" (Smyth, 1984, p. 37). The three accents, which are still in use in French, are the acute, the grave, and the circumflex.

Gestural media, which include mime, dance, and dramatic movement, were also associated with text and music in the Greek tradition, as we can see in this extended quotation of Hesiod:

> Memory...bore nine daughters [the Muses], all of
> like mind, the concern of whose hearts is song,
> and whose spirit is free of care, a little way
> from the highest peak of snowy Olympus. There
> are their gleaming dance-places and their
> beautiful homes.... And uttering through their
> mouths a lovely voice, they sing in praise of
> the customs of all and the noble practices of
> the immortals, uttering a most lovely sound.
> Then they went to Olympus, rejoicing in their
> beautiful voice, with undying song and dance:
> The dark earth rang about them as they sang
> their hymn, and a lovely clamor rose from
> beneath their feet as they went to their
> father. (Barker, 1984, p. 35)

The three dynamic forms of communication for the Greeks were not only linked, but were enfleshed and lived in one family. The mother was the Titan Mnemosyne, the daughter of Uranus and Gaia, and the personification of memory. The father was the Titan Zeus, youngest son of Chronus and Rhea, the sky god. Their children were nine daughters, the Muses, goddesses of poetry, music, drama, mime, history, dance, and astronomy, and "all intellectual pursuits" (Reid, 1993, p. 671). Their collective duty was to keep alive the memory of the immortals through poetic song and gesture. They also inspired mortals to do the same, as Hesiod also tells us, "For it is through the Muses...that there are singers...upon the earth.... He whom the Muses love is happy, for a sweet voice flows from his mouth" (Barker, 1984, p. 36). It is no wonder that Hesiod prays to them, "Hail, children of Zeus! Give me a lovely song" (p. 36).

This combining of text, music, and gesture into an ancient form of multimedia was common and central to both Hebrews and Greeks. Its purpose was to concretize memory, and/or to connect individuals to God or to the immortals. This boon to humanity, however, had limitations. Verbal thought was often shackled by poetic rhythm, and musical expression was subordinated to grammar and syntax. Gesture was often circular or repetitive. To overcome these limitations, the tight bonds between the three media were loosened. Prose with free rhythm grew and developed. Melodic invention with independent pitch manipulation replaced word-bound patterns. Linear movements in ritual and drama were emphasized over repetitive gestures.

Modern Traditions

This loosening process started in the ancient period, and picked up momentum in our first common millennium. As centuries passed, the connections between text, music, and gesture became more tenuous. Now, since the Enlightenment, the bonds are sometimes nonexistent. Literature is read silently. Drama and poetry are spoken, not intoned. Music is organized and energized instrumentally. Dance, which appears to be bound to music, is often not rhythmically connected to its sister art in performance.

Fortunately, important echoes of the ancient syntheses are still present. Sacred prose and poetry are chanted in Orthodox synagogues and churches and in various Roman Catholic rites. Text and tune or text and rhythm, as in the case of Rap, are loosely bound in popular music. Gesture continues to be strongly bound to text and music in various folk traditions.

In addition, descriptions of the ancient synthesis were the inspiration for the invention and development of opera and ballet, starting around 1600, when pastoral poems, music, and gestures were combined. For the Italians this meant a *dramma per musica*, consisting of a libretto, sung to the accompaniment of instruments, and presented theatrically (Ferguson, 1959). For the French this meant a *ballet de cour,* consisting of a series of accompanied dances, introduced by pastoral songs, and presented in a decorated hall (Bukofzer, 1947).

Of the two genres, the Italian is the more important due to the refinement of a type of solo song called *Monody*. The point of departure for its creation was the Platonic idea that "*harmonia* and rhythm must follow the words" (Barker, 1984, p. 130). Composers around the turn of the 17th century took this statement from the *Republic* very seriously, and started to compose melodic lines that mirrored the word accent, grammar, and rhetoric of the text. The melodies that were produced were very simple, and in some ways like the chant style used to sing scriptural passages and the Psalms in the Latin Roman Rite. There was one difference: These Monodies were accompanied by two instruments, one for the bass line, the other, usually a lute or a keyboard instrument, to add the harmony. It was this addition that proved to have far-reaching consequences. Composers gradually noticed that the accompaniment could be used to mirror the rhetoric of the text. This in turn freed them to compose more expressive and beautiful melodies. This division of labor between the two lines of music is a major watershed in music history. The association of instrumental accompaniment with the rhetoric of text enabled instrumental music to develop its own language-like rhetoric, while at the same time, the expressive characteristics of the art expanded dramatically (Georgiades, 1982). The only thing lost in the process was the importance of the text. "Music is the essential artistic medium in Opera" (Kerman, 1988, p. 214). The text became its servant.

The elusive ancient synthesis was once again lost with the passage of time. However, from the point of view of modern media, the development of music, as an expressive medium, was a real gain. By the end of the 19th century music had the power to define character, generate action, and establish atmosphere, with or without text or gesture (p. 215). It is no wonder, when the Lumière brothers had the first commercial projection of a silent film 100 years ago, that they hired a pianist to accompany the event (Randel, 1986, p. 305), or that the great master of musical characterization, Camille Saint-Saëns (1835-1921), who composed *Le Carnaval des Animaux,* and the opera *Samson et Dalila,* was the first to compose a score expressly for a film, *L'Assassinat du Duc Guise,* in 1908 (Harding & Fallon, 1980, p. 406).

With the joining of music to film the threshold to the media of motion was traversed. At first film was the only example, but, soon it was joined by regularly scheduled radio programming that included music. Next came the talkies, elaborate films with opera-like soundtracks. After World War II the media of motion exploded with the development of television networks, computers, video, cable, and digital recording technology (Hudson, 1987).

In 1923, the phrase "mass media" was coined to describe the growing numbers of people affected by these and other technical advancements (Simpson & Weiner, 1989, vol. 9, p. 439). In less than 50 years this phrase mutated into the term *multimedia*, since all the media of motion were being integrated into one, powerful tool of communication (vol. 10, p. 82). Now in the '90s, with interactive multimedia connected to the World Wide Web, the word "media" is often used as a singular noun with a singular verb on city streets. In the eyes and ears of contemporary users, all media is one.

We have come full circle. Modern technology is capable of combining lexical, musical, and gestural media into powerful, hybrid works of art that can memorialize thoughts, feelings, and physical actions. Can this technology incorporate these three elements in a balanced and effective way, and avoid the pitfalls of the past? My answer is yes, if the producers of multimedia materials develop a concept that I call "musical *mimesis* for modern media," and if we can expand the ancient concept of *harmonia* to include all facets of the multimedia art.

Mimesis

Mimesis is "a favorite word in classical Greek criticism for describing the relationship between a work of art and its object" (Stanford, 1967, p. 99). Aristotle opens his *Poetics* with a detailed discussion of *mimesis* by using it as *the* defining term for epic, tragedy, comedy, choral song, and instrumental music (Aristotle, 1958, p. 3). In his *Rhetoric* he adds sculpture to his list of mimetic works (Aristotle, 1994, p. 124).

The common translation for this word in reference to the arts is "imitation." That is what the early opera composers were doing when they invented *dramma per musica*, imitating the musical and dramatic descriptions of the Greek theater. For that reason they missed the mark and distorted the ancient synthesis of text, music, and gesture, allowing music to eclipse her two sister arts.

Other translations for mimesis can be "re-presentation" or "re-embodiment" (Stanford, 1967, p. 99). With these terms we come closer to describe what is needed. Both re-presentation and re-embodiment emphasize that art is a process of recreation, and that the thoughts, feelings, and physical gestures in a silent text are not fully experienced until they are performed. The question posed at the beginning of the chapter—"What are the sounds and gestures in a silent text?"—is not rhetorical in a multimedia context. Without sounds and gestures major portions of a text's message remain dormant. My pressing question becomes: "How to awaken the sounds of a text?"

First, review the recital tradition of texts in general and of biblical texts in particular. This tradition starts with the Bible, which was written with the understanding that it was part of a multimedia performance. The received text, therefore, can be analyzed for change of voice, described dynamics, word-sounds for mood, word order, sentence intonations, surface rhythms, tempo changes, repetition of words and sentences, and changes in rhetorical form (LaRue, 1970). Second, experience the continuing Orthodox recital traditions of Scripture. Third, study any setting of a particular text in any context: liturgical, operatic, folk, or popular.

After this review the next step is to compose a contemporary musical setting that is faithful to this tradition. This is not as difficult as it sounds, since all western musical styles spring from the same roots. The final step is to make sure that the setting does not overpower the other elements of the presentation. This is where expanding the ancient concept of *harmonia* can be very helpful.

Harmonia

The source for the Greek noun, *harmonia,* is a verb that means to fit or join together. As a noun it can refer to the joining of any two things:

pipes, pitches, or people. *Harmonia*, in Greek mythology, is the daughter of war-like Ares and the erotic and beautiful Aphrodite—Mars and Venus in the Roman Pantheon (Reid, 1993, p. 279). If ever there was a mismatched couple it was these two; yet, when they mated, they produced *Harmonia*.

There is an important insight in this ancient myth that can help us creatively work with mismatched media. The war-like and the beautiful must interact to produce harmony. In terms of text, music, and gesture the dynamics of each must be joined aesthetically. To bring this about, three principles need to be remembered during any production: (1) The total media experience must be unified. (2) There must be sufficient variety in each medium to sustain interest. (3) The polarity between unity and variety must be balanced (LaRue, 1970, p. 204). If these principles are successfully applied, harmony will be established, the art produced will be very powerful, and multimedia will become common and central in our communication of the Bible. As Walt Whitman said:

> If the time ever comes when iconoclasm does its extremest in one direction against the books of the Bible in its present form, the collection must still survive in another, and dominate just as much as hitherto, or more than hitherto, through its divine and primal poetic structure. (quoted in Atwan & Wieder, 1993, p. xxvii)

J. Ritter Werner is music director of the Multimedia Translations Project for the American Bible Society. He also composed the settings for the art/chant versions of "The Visit" and "A Father and Two Sons." He is a graduate of the College Conservatory of Music at the University of Cincinnati where he majored in organ and minored in musicology and music theory. Postdoctoral work took him to Canterbury Cathedral, England, to study under Allen Wicks. Werner is currently music director and organist at the Church of the Holy Angels, Dayton, Ohio. He belongs to the music faculty at Wright State University and holds a graduate degree in biblical studies from United Theological Seminary. He has just published the compilation and arrangement *Gregorian Chant: Music from Antiquity for Modern Liturgy.*

12

Multimedia Images:
Plato's Cave Revisited

Gregor Goethals

How do we integrate the visual arts—static and moving images—with written and oral texts in experimental translations of biblical stories? Even as artists and art historians in the American Bible Society project address this question, we must look critically at the imagistic context in which we work. Drawing upon recent art criticism, we examine the mystique of "Art" and the Romantic veneration of the "Artist" as seer. Revisions of these concepts open up opportunities for new emphasis on functions and contexts of images. Equally important is the recognition of popular culture's roles in meeting the need for public stories, icons, and rituals. As work on CD-ROM productions proceeds, two historical modes of visual communication emerge as models: the book and ritual. Neither one is entirely adequate as a model, but their histories suggest that each undergoes continuous transformation through technology and the human imagination.

Introduction

R. G. Collingwood may help the readers as well as authors of this collection of diverse essays with his observation that those who listen or read must know the question that is being addressed. So let me identify at once the question that has propelled the work of the graphic designers and art historians associated with the American Bible Society project: "How do we integrate the visual arts—static and moving images—with written and oral texts in experimental translations or transmediazation of biblical stories?"

While the question seems straightforward, many historical and cultural factors complicate it. Two are paramount. First, for centuries religious traditions influenced by the radical Protestant reformers have not known what to do with images at all. Even as groups found uses for biblical representations—in publications, biblical illustration, tracts—the pictures themselves have often been extremely sentimental, frequently disdained for their

229

lack of so-called quality. Over time the visual arts, uprooted from their liturgical contexts, moved into the mainstream of secular society. Now images
reign supreme, especially in what we think of as popular culture such as
film, television, advertising. Like the shadows in Plato's cave, ubiquitous,
constantly shifting images of the mass media provide pictures that entertain
us as we speculate about the real and unreal.

A second factor complicating our basic question is the cultural aura
surrounding "art" and "artist." The visual arts identified as "high culture"
have typically been devoid of conventional religious symbols. Relatively few
artists of the 20th century have used biblical subjects or produced works to
adorn liturgical spaces. Indeed, for many the practice of art itself has religious significance. Many persons claim that the act of painting, for example,
offers a spiritual fulfillment once associated with religion. Literary artists
and musicians have made similar observations. These claims become apparent in the aesthetics of the Enlightenment and Romanticism, and they have
continued into the late 20th century.

Aware of the disregard with which major artists have viewed churches'
attitudes and uses of images, designers and art historians on this project
strongly felt that we should keep these issues in mind. Moreover, each person has wanted to rethink issues related to religious symbolism and the visual arts. Our aim is to try to make changes both in philosophical perspectives and in the quality of work produced. Thus before taking up the major
question, I would like first to look critically at two well-entrenched ideas
that often cloud public perceptions. This will provide a context for the challenges we face and some of the processes developed in the course of our
work.

We shall, first, examine the mystique of "art" that has come under
scrutiny in recent years; several critical studies have opened up new perspectives and possibilities for those interested in religious symbols. Second, and
closely related to this, we will look briefly at changing views of the artist.
This is particularly important in light of the demands and expectations we
present to visual artists working on these projects. Thus, in focusing first on
"art" and then on the "artist" it will become clear, I believe, just how we are
flying in the face of popularly accepted concepts.

Finally, I shall speak about some specific uses of images in the multimedia project. Our team has proceeded very much like Abraham, described
by Paul in Hebrews 11.8-10: We have gone out by faith, leaving a familiar
terrain without knowing exactly where we were headed. We have encountered various limits, changing forms and functions, opportunities, unprecedented technological challenges and problems many of us had not faced—or
dreamed of. At the same time, some roles we first thought were new have
turned out, indeed, to be older ones performed by images in the past. Thus,
when possible, I want briefly at the end to point out certain analogies be-

tween past and present image-use as subjects for future inquiry. In this essay I have relied upon key studies which address a selective range of works.

Alternatives to "Art"

Early conversations among those working on the project identified some problems. It was clear that we wanted to avoid the kind of sentimental work associated with institutional religious art of the late 19th and 20th centuries. We were equally mindful of the pitfalls present in the so-called high culture scene across which various "isms" and aesthetic theories have for decades paraded. In the popular imagination, as well as among many artists and art historians, "art" has taken its place alongside religion, a great transcendent, mysterious, autonomous realm of being. It offers all followers—artists, critics, historians, ordinary museum visitors—similar comforts of salvation: a sense of well being, detachment from the world, a special calling that sets them apart from others. While our team was committed to bringing the highest standards of visual arts into the ABS multimedia experiments, we were not interested in a novelty-driven "art" product.

The writings of several art historians and critics turned out to be helpful as we began to sort out some of these issues and to think about the role of the visual arts and religious symbolism. Looking at the concept of "art," they have examined the mythologies associated with that term, mythologies that continue even now to flourish. Particularly useful were the writings of Hans Belting, Arthur Danto, James Ackerman, and Donald Kuspit.

Belting (1990/1994) traces the use of images as objects of veneration in early and medieval Christianity, pointing out a shift in the late Middle Ages from public to private image as ordinary persons acquired devotional pictures for themselves. "Individual citizens did not want an image different from the public one so much as they needed one that would belong to them personally" (p. 410). Eventually the private image became dominant, and here the character of "art" began to emerge.

By the late 16th century many reformers had emptied their churches of images, symbolizing "a purified, desensualized religion that now put its trust in the word." But, Belting adds, "the crowded walls of the picture cabinets in private houses, which did not interest Luther, testified to the presence of painting, of which key works (of genres and artists) were then being collected." These images took on a new role in representing art. Moreover, says Belting, paintings and sculpture retained by churches in Italy were "images with a double face, depending on whether they were seen as receptacles of the holy or as expressions of art." A unified concept of the image in which the aesthetic and holy were inextricably mixed was given up. "Art was either admitted to this area [religion] or remained excluded from it, but it ceased to be a religious phenomenon in itself. Within the realm of art, images symbolize the new, secularized demands of culture and aesthetic experience" (p. 458).

Thus in Italy, where the radical reformers had less impact, as well as in northern Europe, images were valued as works of art. Belting notes that earlier humanist writers, such as Leon Battista Alberti, "provided artists and connoisseurs with a text to refer to," and raised painting to the "status of a science among the 'liberal arts'" (p. 471). In addition, symbols from Greek and Roman mythologies were systematically selected and incorporated into the subject matter of "art." These new subjects, such as the gods and goddesses, had no reality of their own since they were drawn from classical literature. Even the older devotional images, however, which had at one time communicated a religious reality, were no longer "free of ambiguity." The label "art" was attached to images both sacred and secular (p. 472).

Thus the crisis of the image elaborated in great historical detail by Belting initiated a modern view of art. Emanuel Kant and philosophers of the Enlightenment further liberated aesthetic action and contemplation, essentially bestowing upon the arts an unprecedented epistemological and symbolic independence. The arts were channels of communication uniquely empowered to affect, inform, and indeed transform the human spirit. Indeed, the sacred and awesome became so closely associated with artistic creation that subject matter ceased to be the identifying characteristic of a holy object. Enlightenment philosophy reinforced the separation between the visual arts and their institutional functions within both church and state. Whereas medieval sculptors and painters rendered visible the symbols of the church, artists of the Romantic era were encouraged to embody their private visions of salvation. Aesthetic sensibility and creative action assumed overtones of religious contemplation. This view of art has continued into our own time, allowing us to lose sight of the social functions of images in legitimating institutional beliefs.

In another work Belting (1983/1987) continued to explore changes in the concept of art and art history. From this rich essay, I would like simply to highlight one or two points. As the visual arts became increasingly disengaged from the institutional patronage of church and state, artists eventually turned away from public images. Contemporary artists intensified the Romantic search for private religious symbols and meanings. Eventually this became part of the mythology of the "avant-garde." Belting writes: "The forward march of art becomes the responsibility of a cultural elite who feel entitled to define progress among themselves and who are nonetheless convinced that history will take up the rear" (p. 13).

Other historians of art have also questioned the concept of the avant-garde. Over two decades ago, art historian James Ackerman pointed out that in a society committed to novelty, such as we have today, the role of the avant-garde has become meaningless: "In a dynamic society committed to an expanding economy, technology, education, and welfare, continuing innovation is a condition of survival, and one that can be taken for granted. The artist, critic, and historian can afford to focus attention on problems of value and meaning" (Ackerman, 1969, p. 17). Amid the flux of novelty the question is not "What is new?" but "What is of value?" Ackerman has emphasized the need for contemporary artists to address the function of art and its responsibility for the communication of public, not private meanings. We have made art, he argues, into a functionless luxury, subject to manipulation in the marketplace in the same way as fashionable clothing. The museum has become an artificial environment, and the visual arts increasingly removed from a living culture (Ackerman, 1973, pp. 34-35). Other critics as well have called attention to the increasing isolation of art from the public sphere. Harold Rosenberg, for example, points out the many ways in which various media in contemporary society have taken over art's traditional social roles (1972, p. 209).

An early 20th-century modernist aesthetic envisioned "art" as a unified process which various epochs and styles had shaped. The so-called fine arts in particular served as a great portal to experiences of transcendent reality. During the latter part of the century, however, many assumptions of modern art have eroded. Mass media and the communications revolution have made us aware of disconnected, yet simultaneous forms of diverse cultures. Moreover, the lines between "high" and "popular" material culture have become considerably blurred. Philosopher-art critic Arthur Danto suggests that we may now be approaching the end of art as we have understood it in the modern era. Sketching the trauma which has, he says, beset painting with the advent of photography and film, Danto reasons that art has become essentially preoccupied with its own self-identity. As artists of the late 20th century became increasingly involved with the question "What is Art?" they moved steadily toward philosophy. Finally, art has become, he says, "vaporized in a dazzle of pure thought about itself" and remains solely the object of its theoretical consciousness (Danto, 1986, p. 111; 1987). This "end of art" however, does not mean that image-making will cease. Quite the contrary, the visual arts in all media and technologies may be freed from self-consciousness to serve and enhance human experience in a variety of ways (1986, pp. 217-18). For Belting as well, new insights may await artist and art historian as the diversity of art discloses itself "in its ever-changing roles and definitions in history" (Belting, 1983/1987, p. 45).

These discussions of changing concepts of art help to clear the air and stimulate individuals to think about the many ways in which images may function in today's world. Art historians and artists working on the multimedia project have sensed both a new freedom and a challenge. As we collaborate on the multimedia project, we want, on the one hand, to think about and explore in greater depth the previous uses of images in communicating stories and symbols. Cultural historian Johann Huizinga pointed out that the great art of the Middle Ages can be seen essentially as an "applied art," a term that may offend artists caught up in the claims of an autonomous art. What Huizinga was describing, however, was an art "wrapped up in life...not desired for its own sake, but to decorate life with the splendor which it could bestow" (Huizinga, 1956, p. 244). In this sense, we want to do all we can to bestow upon these biblical stories whatever splendor the visual arts can bring to them. On the other hand, we want to engage fully the ever-changing technology and to understand better how it has modified, or may modify, traditional forms of religious communication. To achieve this we need men and women who are also raising questions about the nature and function of the visual arts and about their social responsibilities as image makers.

Image of the "Artist"

During the Renaissance we began to see a shift in the image of the artist: The sole emphasis upon craftsmanship diminished, and other intellectual roles, such as humanist, poet, and thinker, became more prominent. Alberti, for example, trained in a university, signaled that the artist was no longer simply a master painter or stone carver but must be versed in mathematics, the classics, literature.

One of the most significant changes in the concept of the artist, however, came with Romanticism and the Enlightenment as "art" became an autonomous dimension of culture, set free from institutional authorities. As both religious and political patronage dried up, the artist was left to explore inner boundaries, visions, and fantasies. Indeed, the social mission of the artist shaped by Romanticism became that of a seer, one who looked within the soul's depths and discovered there the symbols that must be expressed. For many artists creative visual expression and religious imagination were fused; their personal visions become more important than conventional mythologies.

In the past, artists drew their subjects from a reservoir of shared meanings. But increasingly during the 19th and 20th centuries, the artist was left alone, seen essentially as an originator of myths and symbols. In addition, the individual artistic imagination, continually generating new, changing forms, now became a source of religious inspiration. Evidence of this appears early in the 19th century and continues into the late 20th.

Henry Fuseli, a painter and theorist, was active as a painter in England in the late 18th and early 19th century. In lectures given at the Royal Academy of Art we see some of the earliest expressions of this new individualism in the arts. Fuseli contended that individuality was more important than the rules of painting, generally established by the art academies. His critical departure from academic theory became clear in a discussion of subjects or the content of painting. Typically the word "invention" was used to describe the special formal interpretation an artist gave to subjects which were necessarily found in poetry, mythologies, or history. Fuseli re-directed the origination of symbolism to the mind of the artist. Could the painter discover subjects within the imagination "without having recourse to tradition or the stories of history and poetry?" (Wornum, 1848, p. 411). He answers decisively: "Why not.... Shall the immediate avenues of the mind, open to all its observers, from the poet to the novelist, be shut out only to the artist?" (p. 411). Fuseli wanted to liberate painters and give them the ancient prerogative of the poet—"that imaginative power by which the images of invisible or absent things are represented by the mind with the same energy of objects moving before our eyes" (pp. 412-415).

While Fuseli's ideas may have seemed revolutionary to some English academicians, they were flourishing in Germany, particularly in the thought and work of the painter Caspar David Friedrich. Indeed, in the course of the nineteenth century artists in Europe and America, rebelling against academic traditions, freely chose their own themes. Today, art students find it inconceivable that there was ever a time when symbols were given to artists, not invented by them. Such a shift in the source of symbolism, from the sphere of public myth to the private, inner world of the artist has had a profound effect on the ways in which we view image makers today, whether painter or film maker.

As artists assumed responsibility for creating their own symbolic world, their inner experience and imagination became a source of religious as well as formal revelation. Objects not necessarily understood as religious in content could be transformed in the mind of the artist. Ordinary subjects—landscape, everyday objects of still life arrangements, interiors—could be seen through the visionary eyes of the artist and thus become imbued with religious symbolism. Vincent Van Gogh has become a popularly recognized symbol of such an artist. Through his transformative vision all the world became radiant with iconic possibilities. The poet W. H. Auden observed that Van Gogh's pictures were religious because the painter "regarded nature as the sacramental visible sign of a spiritual grace which was his aim as a painter to reveal to others" (Auden, 1959, p. 40). Van Gogh himself wrote: "I want...to paint men and women with that something of the eternal which the halo used to symbolize, and which we seek to convey by the actual radiance and vibration of our coloring" (quoted in Auden, p. 40). Auden saw Van Gogh as the first painter consciously to attempt to produce a painting which would be religious without containing traditional religious iconography—"a parable for the eye." Communications would thus depend on a universal symbolism of color and form which reveals itself immediately to the senses without misinterpretation (p. 40).

Early in the 20th century two other painters, Wassily Kandinsky and Piet Mondrian, shared Van Gogh's concern for communicating universal religious truths. Unlike Van Gogh, however, these painters eliminated all representational elements, all traces of the real world. Convinced that spiritual reality is most adequately expressed in non-objective shapes and colors, they gradually developed an abstract visual language. Such abstractions, they believed, formed the basis of a universal visual language which could transcend cultural boundaries, revealing an absolute metaphysical reality. Kandinsky also drew parallels between music and color. Like music, abstract, non-discursive colors and forms could evoke powerful emotions, directly expressing the dynamic movement of the soul. For both Kandinsky and Mondrian art was revelatory, and they saw the role of the artist as an aesthetic mystic whose works might awaken the life of the spirit. Critical of the materialism they saw all around them, they viewed themselves and their work as part of a spiritual reformation.

Later in the 20th century a Protestant theologian, Paul Tillich, provided artists and critics with a theological basis for attributing religious significance to symbols they drew from within themselves. He believed that all subjects could be potential sources of revelation. Moreover, Tillich's references to art reinforced the view of the artist as witness to an individual, solitary journey of the spirit. Appreciative of artists whose work reflected experiences of anxiety and soul searching, Tillich described the creative process as heroic. Confronted by the abyss of life's meaninglessness, an artist faces and expresses this anxiety and searching. Like other existentialists of his time, Tillich attributed a saving dimension to the creative process itself, adding to the artistic mystique a unique capacity for apprehending spiritual truths (Tillich, 1964).

Recent art critics are less convinced about the special powers of the artist. Like writers we mentioned previously, philosopher and art historian Donald Kuspit (1994) studies the concept of the avant-garde and the mythologies embedded in it. Kuspit traces perceptions of the artist which arose in the late 19th century and which, he notes, are in "disrepair" but still very much present. During the early part of the 20th century the artist increasingly was seen as a kind of "Promethean adventurer, an individualist and risk taker in a sheepish society" (p. 1). Thus two great mythologies of the avant-garde emerged. One attributed a special perceptual power to artists as persons with both exceptional insight and sight. The other proclaimed them as "uniquely authentic in an inauthentic society" (p. 2). Both enable artists to be viewed as those individuals who, through their creative activity, are immediately engaged with some primordial order of being, generally inaccessible to ordinary people. Kuspit writes, "the artist is idealized for the transmutation of value—for the revolution in the sense of life—that his perceptual and personal authenticity effect and symbolize" (p. 2). Kuspit traces the changes he perceives between the early modern avant-garde and the "neo avant-garde" of the late 20th century, whom he characterizes as exceptionally narcissistic and pretentious, dependent upon publicity for survival.

The analyses of Kuspit and others enable us to detect an aesthetic gnosticism accepted by culture's elite and ordinary people alike. The artist plays the role of priest or shaman, visionary, and outsider. Within this intellectual climate it is not hard to understand why the great public symbols of today have arisen in popular culture, collectively shaping our rhythms of time and space through television and mass media. In this atmosphere we must learn to distinguish between artists of merit whose visions are attempting to correct or enlarge our shared, public symbols and those who are transient, noisy creatures of hype.

The American Bible Society Project

In roughly sketching some of the ideas swirling around the terms "art" and "artist," I have tried to present a cultural backdrop for work on the multimedia project. It may help explain why, as we approach artists and talk to them about the project, there has to be considerable clarification about what we are trying collectively to achieve. Generally we also spend some time explaining the nature and mission of the American Bible Society (ABS). Very often people, especially in the initial meeting, treat us as though we were evangelists laden with tracts and messages about the care of their souls. Even after we have begun to communicate, we typically have to explain to them that we are not looking for a re-hashing of trite, sentimental biblical symbols that seem quickly to rush to their minds.

In working with artists we want to be sure they understand that we are considering their work because they have distinguished themselves, for instance, as film makers, graphic designers, and musicians. At the same time, we have to make it clear that commissioned pieces are essentially rooted in the task of translations. While we have sought out artists who seem to be sensitive to narrative complexities and religious insight, the emphasis is upon biblical narratives, not their own personal spiritual visions—no matter how impressive these might be. This point is critical, since serious, gifted artists today often see themselves as the conscience of society and are indeed involved in great causes. Many are searching for shared symbols and attempting to correct myopic public visions about the "other"—however that is defined. Indeed, the freedom to critique and refine cultural symbols is something we have come to expect from artists. Some are exploring the boundaries of our society's symbols and have become our iconofiers and iconoclasts in a consumer-obsessed society. As individuals or connoisseurs we can applaud and support this work. The goal of the multimedia projects, however, has to be sharply focused.

The fact is that the visual arts in the multimedia work of the ABS are fundamentally accountable to the primary function of translation (or transmediazation) of biblical texts and the exegetical or study helps that accompany them. In this sense we are much closer to the medieval manuscript illuminators, glass workers, or sculptors who were given the subjects to work on. On the other hand, this limitation has unleashed in the past, and we hope now as well, great energies of artists and given new, vital shapes to traditional stories and symbols. For example, we know from the study of books that Irish monks, unaccustomed to the classical language of the human figure, transformed book illumination as they transposed their own native designs from metalwork into colors, lines, shapes of the printed page. Given the Gospel, these northern artists transformed its pages with unprecedented vitality and expression.

From art historical studies and, indeed, from our own experience we have discovered that, far from diminishing individuality, collaboration has enhanced the special roles and tasks of each participant. Art historian Edgar Wind observed that contrary to popular notions, exchanges between artist and patrons helped to spark great moments of artistic activity. Like other critics previously mentioned, he also believes that we remain susceptible to the Romantic fable of the artist dreaming in a garret, working only as the spirit moves. Fearing that we might disturb an artist's "inspiration," we have, he says, placed an excessive burden on the artist's personal choice. Wind uses the metaphor of a temple and its forecourt to illustrate the creative process artist and others share:

> When we treat art as sacrosanct we clearly refer to the temple and to nothing else: There the artist is necessarily alone with his genius. But in the forecourt he should not be left alone. And yet we leave him alone there as well, because we mistakenly extend to the porch the same veneration as belongs to the sanctuary. Even in the exercise of the artist's will, we think that no pressure should be brought to bear on him, for fear that it might disturb his inspiration, and so all his preliminary decisions must be made by him *in vacuo.* For whom, for what purpose or place he will plan a new work, or from what sources he should draw his themes—these are matters rarely suggested to him by an external assignment; as a rule they are left for him to imagine, to invent. (Wind, 1969, pp. 89-90)

We hope to attract artists and art historians to this project who understand the dynamics of interaction between tradition and novelty, between artist and sponsor. Our major concern is to find gifted artists in design, film, painting, computers who are open to collaborative work and who understand that this project is so large that no single vision is adequate to the task. Specifically, we are in search of artists interested in shaping old stories in a new way. New translations provided by a team of scholars are our given subjects. When they are invited to work on the ABS's multimedia translations, we expect visual artists to bring with them a passion for quality and an intense drive to explore collectively contemporary media and forms; thus new voices and visions are given to older, traditional symbols. Through shared imaging and imagining we hope that individual talents can be forged to create a whole, greater than any of its separate parts.

Experiments in Multimedia Images

To put the visual arts of the multimedia project in perspective, we have to remind ourselves that there is no time at which visual language is not, in some measure, a basis of communication for someone sitting before a monitor. We often forget, for example, that translated texts are visual and that shapes and lines of calligraphy or type may give a particular tone to the words they embody. Printed or electronic letters form words which communicate particular meanings to us. There is also, however, a visual syntax or ordering of the shapes of letters. The design, spacing, and colors of individual letters and combinations of characters can affect our perceptions of meaning. Moreover, the monitor's screen, a complex orchestration of sound and moving images, is the ever-present object to which the viewer responds. Diverse forms, from biblical texts to performers, all exist within a visual field.

In the initial phases, the translation and scholarly work on the exegetical material for the study are circulated to a team of artists and historians. The art historians' task is to search for visual representations of the biblical themes as they have been used over centuries. (See Figure 1) This means that we eventually build collections of materials taken from a wide range of

Used with permission of Gregor Goethals and Scala/Art Resource, NY.

© *1992 American Bible Society*

Figure 1: **Artists and art historians search for visual representations of biblical material, for example, this image of the Pantocrator.**

Figure 2: **The "mega-metaphor" or symbol structure of the mall, as used in the American Bible Society CD-ROM, *A Father and Two Sons.***

sources: architectural settings, panel paintings, free standing sculpture, prints, manuscripts, engravings—wherever the subject has appeared. We have also made every effort to explore non-Western traditions and folk art. Once assembled, a summary of the material is prepared and presented to a larger group of researchers.

This larger group consists of scholars and artists from a variety of disciplines. As film makers are chosen for particular translations, they are also brought into this group. Researchers and artists share their findings in an effort to arrive at what we began to call a "mega-metaphor," a large symbolic structure that could "house" or aesthetically accommodate various parts of the interactive design—translations, study helps, activities, and various special features developed for the CD-ROM. Following that, the different groups—artists, musicians, scholars—work independently, yet continue to circulate proposals for organizing and developing various parts of the program.

Let me give some examples. For the translation of "A Father and Two Sons" (Luke 15.11-32), we began to speculate about a space, a context in which teenagers (the original group for whom the translation was conceived) often meet, namely the mall. At the same time, to avoid triviality the mall concept had to be expanded and placed in a continuum of public spaces of the past where people might have gathered to hear stories or exchange ideas.

So, we worked backward in time collecting images of public spaces in the ancient world, such as the agora in Athens. We also selected images from contemporary urban malls in Los Angeles, San Francisco, New Orleans, and other cities. All of these became assets for the graphic designer to work with, manipulating them to form various screens and sub-sets of screens. (See Figure 2)

The selection of the assets and the preparation of screens for "The Visit" (Luke 1.39-56) brought up entirely different kinds of considerations. Since the passage being translated focuses on the relationship of two women and Mary's song, The Magnificat, we spent a long time discussing the mega-metaphor that might be appropriate for this translation. After searching and reflection we began to work with the nautilus shape as a form which could be manipulated in a variety of ways. The nautilus itself is a rich symbol, used in many cultural settings. (See Figure 3) In addition, the logarithmic spiral so vividly present in the nautilus is the basic growth pattern for all living things, as well as a principle of construction in humanly created forms such as the spiral stairway. In addition to the nautilus, however, we also

By Gregor Goethals. © 1994 American Bible Society

Figure 3: The "mega-metaphor" or symbol structure of the nautilus, as used in the American Bible Society CD-ROM, *The Visit.*

needed a more architectonic form to structure the compositions of the screens. To complement the curvilinear forms of the nautilus design we did photographic studies of a chapel located on the campus of the Harvard Business School. This is a circular chapel with an adjacent enclosed glass area which serves as a space for meditation. Together these geometric forms suggest the contour of a nautilus. Photographs emphasizing the structural supports of the meditative glass enclosure provided the geometric shapes that worked well with the more flowing design of the nautilus. (See Figure 4)

One of the title screens from the CD-ROM illustrates one way of combining elements. Screens like this also reveal the importance of layering images, a technique the designer used to harmonize different kinds of images into a montage. In the opening frames we also used specific paintings of the Nativity in order to set the translation of the meeting between Mary and Elizabeth in the larger context of the Nativity story.

Re-combining the visual assets and developing montages for screens has been the major work of the graphic designer. These screens then become, to a degree, comparable to the layout of a book. Yet, rather than a simple, plain, or light ground for printed words, the designer overlays images, shaping sequences of patterns as a background for the video translation as well as for texts. In this sense a screen is comparable to a page of an

Figure 4: A screen from the American Bible Society CD-ROM, *The Visit*, showing the combination of graphics and text for Mary's world.

illuminated manuscript where text and image are intertwined so that image reinforces text, and in the mind's eye the two are indivisible.

Trying to understand new ways to develop images and compositions from multiple resources—still and moving images, art objects, text—is the overarching task of the artists and art historians working on the project. How to relate past forms and functions of images to constantly changing technical innovation? How to develop new forms for traditional functions? Or how to discern new functions that may be emerging in contemporary imagistic media?

A brief glance backwards over the last several decades indicates that as both Protestant and Catholic religious groups developed electronic communication, they tended to use a charismatic figure as a focus for mass communication. Beginning with radio and continuing into television—from Charles E. Fuller's radio program "The Old-Fashion Revival Hour" to the telecast presentations of Fulton J. Sheen and Pat Robertson—the emphasis has been upon the persona of magnetic individuals. Although some electronic preachers, such as Pat Robertson, have over time produced elaborate patterns of programming—news, documentaries, commercials, culinary and financial advising, even an attempt at a soap opera—the centerpiece has been a charismatic individual. Some groups experimented in religious drama; various denominations simply broadcast religious services, but these were essentially linear, visualizations of varying forms of worship. In the ABS multimedia experiments we wanted to see how traditional models for communication might be modified by technology. Moreover, with the emphasis upon translation or transmediazation of the Bible, we deliberately sought to emphasize the Bible story itself rather than the charisma of the storyteller.

To help us in these experiments we have begun to explore two historical models of religious communication for multimedia space and design. Neither of these is fully adequate, but we may, nevertheless, use them selectively. One is the form of the book; the other is ritual.

Since we are working with translations of texts and study helps for them, the book comes naturally to mind as one model. While the print medium has for many been superseded by the electronic, the design and typography of books may serve as a springboard for artists working on the project. On the one hand, there is a history of the book which is centuries old and has undergone countless stylistic and technological revolutions. Embedded in this history is a storehouse of designs, layouts, figurative and nonfigurative, narrative and non-narrative visual forms which can become a reservoir for multimedia images. On the other hand, the book has also been a traditional means for communicating the gospel. Although understood at first only by an educated clergy, the massive books were used in the liturgy and ceremoniously elevated for the congregation and given a spatial presence. With the advent of printing and reproduction techniques biblical texts and images became accessible to ordinary people and are now circulated to millions.

If we think about the continuum of changing visual images and technological innovations and its function as a form of mass communication, the book has played an important role as a metaphor. One area for further study here has been suggested by Susan Ward, who is researching visual narrative in the art of the Middle Ages. In examining medieval techniques for remembering, scholars make us aware of the powers of the image that have been forgotten or moved off the horizon of modern consciousness. When we treat books as static, throw-away objects, we lose sight of the ways in which a passage or page, particularly in an illuminated manuscript, became a focus for religious meditation or an aid to memory. In addition, we frequently ignore the order in medieval books through which sequential pages, with varying combinations of calligraphy and images, formed the basis of a dynamic temporal and spatial experience. The turning of carefully orchestrated pages drew viewers into a moving stream of image and text. We have much to learn from such an ebb and flow of shapes, colors, and letters. In the planning of multimedia designs, we need to do further research on the function of images, particularly when they are used in conjunction with texts. At the same time, we clearly need other models as we design for interactive media.

In the history of Christendom, and indeed of most religious traditions, another form of communication may also be useful to us as a metaphor in exploring multimedia images: ritual. This model is abundant with various art forms and has been used by scholars for interpreting contemporary media such as television (Goethals, 1981). It allows for moving images—complex, intertwined art forms of dance, mime, song, and storytelling. In traditional and modern rituals we have a total sensory approach to human communication. Costumes, body adornment, and gestures contribute to visual narratives and symbols, the stories typically enacted in bounded architectural or natural settings. While we are uncertain about their nature, we may speculate that the first human multimedia experiences occurred among those early humans who left evidence of their rituals on the walls of caves, such as those at Lascaux.

One takes part in ritual action at particular times and in certain designated places; and in the course of ritual community beliefs are reinforced and individuals experience its transformative power. On these particular points the metaphorical connections may falter. Although we may to a degree interact with the computer, it is different from the human interaction of ritual. Moreover, ritual is a communal activity, while the interaction between an individual and the computer is a much more private, solitary engagement. More complicated still is the mixture of experience and psychological attitudes of those taking part in a ritual. Still, these qualifications which raise questions about the adequacy of the metaphor may also be a starting point for further study and exploration. The metaphor of ritual remains useful since its hallmark is participation; multimedia interactive capabilities may transform a person who simply views into one who reacts and participates in a process.

If we explore the ritual metaphor, we can interpret screen designs in different ways. It may function as a backdrop, a theater set against which actors move. In a CD-ROM the video window transforms the "page" into a context for drama, dance, or story-telling. The screen could also be seen as a portal, through which the participant enters other worlds. In describing those worlds the language of "reality"—"virtual" or "hyper"—may be modified and enriched by descriptions and analyses of ritual action. Ritual time and space take us out of ordinary temporal and spatial boundaries into extraordinary ones; through ritual we understand alternative concepts of time, space, and dramatic action. Anthropologists' observations on the dynamics and the spatial/temporal dimensions of ritual can be useful for multimedia experiments.

Anthropologist Victor Turner, for example, was among the first to observe that residual traces of traditional religious rituals are found in various forms of entertainment, as well as in high and popular arts. Drawing upon his fieldwork, he found the liminal or transitional phase of ritual especially important for understanding certain aspects of contemporary culture. While he considered this phase the essentially *anti-secular* component of ritual, he nevertheless argued that this topsy-turvy kaleidoscopic mixing of natural and supernatural, grotesque and benign, super reality and fantastic was dispersed into secular spheres. He coined the term "liminoid" to describe the symbolic activity that resembles but is not identical with liminal—particularly evident in entertainment, sports, games, theater, film, and the arts. Through our games and our arts we momentarily transcend social structures to play with ideas, visions, words, paint, and social relationships (Turner, 1974; 1977). Further analyses of such liminoid activity may be found in the research of Mihaly Csikszentmihalyi and his colleagues who did extensive interviews with athletes and performing artists in order to understand better this "anti-secular" element of self-transcendence (Csikszentmihalyi, 1975).

For Turner and others the self-transcendence of play is an important bridge between secular and sacred ritual. Indeed, play, or game, serves as a continuum of self-transcendence that moves from the heroic to participation in a divine game. Renaissance scholar and Commissioner of Major League Baseball until the time of his death, A. Bartlett Giamatti (1989) in his book showed how baseball provided an occasion for heroic self-transformation for both player and spectator. Building upon the work of Johann Huizinga (1950) theologian Hugo Rahner uses the metaphor of play to describe how all creation—past, present, and future—is caught up in a great cosmic game. Everything, he says, proceeds from the One who initiates the ultimate game, extending from the "round of the stars and atoms to the gravely, beautiful play" (Rahner, 1972, p. 12) of human beings. Rahner paints a vivid portrait of the "grave-merry" person who grasps the sobering, but liberating truth that life at all levels participates in a great cosmic game (p. 27).

We learn from ritual studies about extraordinary times and spaces which throughout human history have allowed ordinary people to escape the ordinariness of real time and space. In thinking about analogies to ritual, many questions emerge. One, for example, might be: "What kind of screen designs can enhance, but not overshadow the play of moving forms?" This is particularly important in light of current technology which allows only a very small-size video window. Even now, however, constant innovations in technology may completely change present design considerations. Attention to ritual studies, however, draws us not only to formal questions but also to those of function. For example, distinctions can be made between "representation" ("re-presentation"), a term we associate with images that narrate a story and "presentation," an immediacy or sense of presence associated with images and objects in a ritual context.

The ritual analogy might be explored in greater depth if we could develop ways to engage multiple, not single audiences. Originally, the American Bible Society selected teenagers as the focus group for their multimedia experiments. In our thinking we seemed to have followed the traditional commercial market in shaping the material for a certain age and educational level. While enormously successful in advertising and marketing consumer goods, the strategy of adjusting information for particular groups may forfeit the complexity that has characterized earlier art forms. A ritual model, for example, allows for a continuum of age, education, and belief that may include children and adults—those who see it as play and those who see it as an encounter with transcendent Being.

In the work that we have done so far, there is some degree of complexity as the viewer becomes better acquainted with the interactive features of the CD-ROM. For example, the works of art, mentioned earlier, which present a variety of visual interpretations of the biblical story may be accessed and studied individually. One can also move the images around to create a slide show as well as a text for it. Still, this does not satisfy the need for a complexity that will allow viewers over time to grow and move deeper into its form and content. To achieve this we need to be less bound to the psychology and techniques developed for a consumer society. We may need to refocus our studies and look at the work of anthropologists and historians who are trying to understand more about the levels of communication in ritual that appeal to different ages and backgrounds.

Conclusion

The task assigned by the American Bible Society to the multimedia translations group was to develop forms for communicating stories of the

Bible in contemporary cultural languages. The term "functional equivalent" has been used to describe contemporary forms analogous to ancient ones in their capacity to bring the biblical stories to life. Whether or not the work done so far should be called "translations" has been very much debated. The term "transmediazation" has also been used to describe these experiments. There are some who think that any deviation from the language of an original text is inadequate. On the other hand, growth of religious ideas has always been shaped by those who are trying to communicate sacred stories to an "other," which inevitably involves translation. Today the language of culture we must learn is imagistic, electronic, and constantly undergoing innovations. As we continue to work on these prototypes we need, in particular, to understand more about the relationships and different modes of communication inherent in image and word. Ironically advertising industries have done more than other institutions in researching these topics, and we can, above all, learn from them about the power of images.

The irony deepens when we realize that a secular society driven by marketing and consumerism has, perhaps inadvertently, successively appropriated certain religious forms of communication to serve its own ends. Pictures of athletes are transposed into icons that promote cereals and shoes. Those dissatisfied with traditional religious rituals fulfill ritualistic needs for an escape from time in entertainment and sports events, whose sacred times and spaces have been opened up to millions via TV. Collectively the images of popular culture shape our major mythologies and reinforce them through a host of secular liturgies and litanies. In short, those involved in the ABS project are working inside Plato's cave.

Within this image-saturated culture, however, there is the challenge to present stories, centuries old, in new languages. In a society whose values and myths are centered on personal success and self-aggrandizement, the biblical stories may become alternative narratives for our time. Further, if we explore more deeply the traditional forms—the book and ritual—through which biblical stories have been transmitted, we may understand better how to use and extend technological innovations. Over time these forms themselves have undergone transformations. If we can focus on their functions in human communication, we may adapt contemporary technologies in novel ways, continuing the transformative process which has historically characterized the relationship between religion and culture.

Gregor Goethals is a graphic designer and art historian. Her academic interests in both Art History and Philosophy of Religion led to graduate work at Yale and later to a doctorate at Harvard. Following that, the Rhode Island School of Design in Providence became an immeasurably rich environment for over 20 years. There, she became Professor of Art History, serving as department head and later as dean of Graduate Studies. Her books include *The TV Ritual:Worship at the Video Altar* (Beacon, 1981) and *The Electronic Golden Calf: Images and the Making of Meaning* (Cowley, 1991). Presently she is working on *Escape from Time: Ritual Dimensions of Popular Culture* and serving as art director for the American Bible Society's Multimedia Translations Program.

13

Programming Issues
in Multimedia Design

Reg Pettus

This chapter covers the process of defining user needs, customer objectives, and sponsor orientation issues in the development of multimedia applications. It also discusses issues such as design strategy, "technical" aspects of client and team management, and maximizing the talents of the project manager, graphics designer, testers, and software engineers.

The multimedia development process starts with the sponsoring agency or client who has a need. The client starts the whole process by recognizing that something has to be done and then assembling an internal core team to begin the process of satisfying that need. If they determine that the solution requires multimedia, then the team will focus on that resource area. This ultimately leads to the bringing in of a multimedia consultant or developer.

Client and Developer Relationship and Roles

The proper philosophy for developing highly effective multimedia applications and solutions includes a team approach—something both the client and the developer need to agree on from the very beginning. All members of the team must participate from day one throughout the development process. This approach minimizes transition problems between development phases and reduces possible miscommunication between members of the team. As a result, everyone on the team understands the critical assumptions, content requirements, and underlying objectives needed to develop a successful product. The team approach also extends to the client or sponsor personnel. Developers want them to "own" the final product as well. In fact, any developer should welcome a client's active participation throughout the development, training, and implementation processes. Clients must be aware of the effect each decision has on the development process, so that they can make well-informed decisions consistent with their overall goals. The team's goal is to ensure that the final product is one that the customer and end-user will be proud of.

Programming Issues in Multimedia Design

The field of multimedia development brings up many issues that all project teams find they must contend with as they build their titles. A major point that all members must keep in mind as they perform their functions has to do with the needs and expectations of the end-users. Also, we must look at sponsor objectives. In order for any project to be successful, these issues must be addressed in an aggressive and consistent manner.

Keeping all of the above issues in mind, let's look at the CD-ROM project we have just completed with the American Bible Society. The initial challenge was that readership of the Scriptures among young people was steadily going down. Considering the main mission of the ABS, this trend directly conflicted with its philosophy. So how do we help reverse this trend using proper programming techniques?

Programming Techniques: The Technical Aspects

To simplify terms and understanding, we first need to define the term "programming techniques." This term means the use of images, photographs, color, text, and video to convey an idea or an attitude. These elements, since they come together in the realm of the computer, should be considered as data. By considering them data, the concept of mixing, storing, and presenting the material will seem less like hocus-pocus and will also broaden the view of the developer.

The use of images and photographs as part of multimedia development follows the age-old saying "A picture is worth a thousand words." Also, there is never a "typo" in a picture. Pictures and images provide the environment with a way to expand the story being told and to do it without regard to any language barriers that may exist. In the early days of multimedia programming, images and pictures could only be shown in crude block-type renderings. Today we can "scan" images and pictures in such fine detail that it would be hard to see any block characteristics unless you "zoom in" to extremes. Images today can range from 16 colors to 16 million colors. The main factor in determining what palette or range of colors one uses is the type of system the end-user will use. Since many of the systems being sold today come with the ability to show 65,000 colors and higher, the trend is toward a higher color level.

Text has always made up part of our accepted mode of information exchange and, until now, was considered the primary mode. While in many areas it is still primary and will remain so for some time, in the realm of

Figure 1: **Screen from the American Bible Society CD-ROM, *A Father and Two Sons*. Note the integration of text and graphics.**

multimedia it functions as a cooperative asset. "Cooperative" means that text does not outweigh the other elements; neither does it have any less value in the overall scheme of things. Text adds value to images; it can explain pictures as well as supplement video. (See Figure 1) Early in the technology, text was relegated to be shown only in a straightforward and bland system font. But with more powerful machines and programs, the developer now has different fonts available as well as different sizes. At this point text can truly exercise its "adding" function.

Many saw video as the glamorous part of the multimedia development process. To many of us in the computer field, this medium represented the crowning glory of the multimedia environment. In the initial phases of the technology, users watched video on a separate video monitor since computer monitors at that time could not handle analog video input. Putting video on the computer screen was made possible by the advent of special cards that went inside the system. While effective, the price for these cards often ran higher than the cost of the system itself. Over the past few years, however, technologies have developed that now allow high quality video images to be shown on the system without any special cards or software.

In summary, these assets make up the main features and functions of serious multimedia programming. The effective use of these assets will determine the success of a program. Each one must be considered and designed with the human aspects of the end-user in mind. For instance, a video that cuts to a new scene every three seconds may work well with a young audience, but will give an elderly audience a splitting headache. Focusing on traditional pictures will work very well when presented to an older audience, while an iconic style will please the eyes of the younger generation.

Programming Techniques: The Human Aspect

Understanding the technical environment is only the beginning. In order to effectively use this technology, we must gain a detailed perspective of the typical end-user. This information will allow us to focus on what colors work best with a segment, what type of music fits the background and foreground of the program, or even what video style works best with an audience.

Going back to the ABS's multimedia program, let's examine its intended audience, the sponsoring organization, and the program itself with its final structures.

The primary user specified was between 16 and 18 years of age. The group initially set a church environment as the primary place of use, but also wanted to include the home setting. The church setting—a traditional Sunday School classroom—features the teacher normally delivering information in a "one-on-many" setting. This allows the teacher to manipulate the system for the entire class in such a way that the students explore the information as a group. At this level any discovery that occurs will usually happen at the group level. Another setting, a library or learning laboratory, allows the user to go through the program in a "one-on-one" mode. This is usually the most desirable because the interaction happens at the personal level and thus all discoveries by end-users are theirs and theirs alone. This level will also characterize the home environment.

The inquisitive nature of the end-user encouraged the graphic designers to use icons built from existing images and photographs. This creation style imparted a flexibility of time and space. The images allowed the feeling of a contemporary space that was not bounded by time. In the program *A Father and Two Sons*, the image model is a shopping mall. This mall gives the feeling of now, yesterday, and tomorrow. All of this is accomplished through images and blending. The mall concept gives our intended audience a comfortable cyberspace location to visit. (See Figure 2)

The color mixture for this program used a palette of 16 million colors. While we know that all 16 million are not used, the resulting resolution of 640 dots across the screen and 480 dots down using 256 colors for each screen gave us the best solution possible for the standard Windows® environment. This method allowed us to use screens that did not require any dependency on the palette of any other screen. If a screen requires a level of blue that no other screen in the application needs, it will not require any extraordinary programming since the overall palette can hold all the colors that any of the screens need. Otherwise a phenomenon known as "palette shifting" would occur. This happens when the program must load the new required colors into a limited palette just before the next image is shown, causing the old image to be briefly shown in the new color scheme and thus sometimes looking terrible.

In *A Father and Two Sons,* we focused on the use of reds (to give us warmth), along with gray tones and metallic blues to mentally move us through space and time.

The text gives us an opportunity to accent the information that the end-user is either seeing or hearing. To give our audience a good comfort level, we chose to go with a traditional black text on a white background. This model adds a paper and pencil feel to the program. For fonts we chose the standard Windows® system font and the Windows® Arial font. The system font is used in the "list" or selection boxes in the program. The Arial font is used in the "dialog" or informational boxes. We also chose to use a multiple color format for the text to give the end-user clues as to what terms

Figure 2: Screen from the American Bible Society CD-ROM, *A Father and Two Sons.*

and phrases contain "hyper-links" to deeper information. This flexibility in text presentation lets us adapt the text data to a look or feel consistent with the attitude of our audience.

Video can tell a story like no other medium can because it communicates through both sight and sound. This can occur at a multi-dimensional level where we can deliver sight information in a still and/or motion video format. We can also meld in vocal sounds and/or music. Video brings a great deal of power to the developer, as well as responsibility. With the youthful audience that was identified for the application, ABS felt that the video had to be fast moving and electric in nature. The design team chose an MTV style of presentation and asset attitude. Segments were edited in short pieces that usually lasted for two to five seconds per shot. This gave a continuously fresh look that was new and upbeat. Today's young audience feels that looking at an image for more than five to 10 seconds is boring and sluggish. While one would want a great deal of camera movement in this type of delivery, we had to keep it to a minimum because the video frame rate (normally at 30 frames per second) of the finished product would make it look too choppy.

In summary, each aspect of the development needs to focus on the end-users' expectations. Missing the mark on any of these points will jeopardize the effectiveness of the program and thus lower the level of information that would be retained by the end-users. So understanding the basics of the technology and getting a detailed look at our end-users allow us to work with the program in such a way as to mold it into something our audience feels is useful. If perceived as being useful, then it is perceived as satisfying a need.

Establishing User Need

A key point in the development process was to find a way to expose our audience to the Scriptures and to do so in a way that would compel that audience to find out more through further research in the Bible itself. Recognizing that youth today are video oriented and most are computer literate thanks to games like Nintendo and Sega, we knew that the main interface between them and the message had to be at a comfortable and "cool" level. Thus CD-ROM! But the challenge did not end with figuring out that youth quickly gravitate to multimedia. The hard part was giving them an internal reason to want to work with the content. This was done by getting their attention, allowing them to commit a segment of their time to explore the content, and to feel in total control of the environment. The need of the end-users must be a need that they perceive rather than a need thrust upon them. The initial need may be to just explore and discover information. Because they don't feel trapped, the end-user will often continue with the material until an outside force of some type intervenes.

@LEVEL1TOP = The Team

The team approach lies at the heart of our concept for doing multimedia application development. The team consists of many varied talents and skills molded together with a common goal of producing a quality and cost-effective multimedia product. The members of the ABS team came from all discipline areas of the development cycle. This included people from the sponsoring agency and other supporting entities. The members of the team should represent the functions needed for program completion. During the cycles of development, we can get a good idea of how labor intensive the process can be.

Application Project Manager

The overall responsibility for managing this team and attaining the required success lies with the project manager. As an application development vendor, we assign a project manager to each project effort. This person oversees all aspects of project development, implementation, and day-to-day operations, including documenting all phases of the project, developing a detailed flow of the application, and formulating the overall plan for review and approval. This plan naturally includes goals, budgets, securing and allocating resources, and the scheduling for each phase of the project. The project manager maintains an on-going dialogue between the customer's staff and the project team to ensure that this approved plan is being executed as defined and within cost objectives.

Development Team

Once the development phase starts, the project manager identifies members of the team who will take responsibility for defining the deliverables and implementation process. This subset of the main team consists of, for example, technical writers and computer specialists. This team, along with members of the customer's staff, develops and publishes any required user guides and installation documentation. They also define the installation process for the hardware and software and ensure that the ongoing support structure is consistent with the application implementation plan.

Project Team Functions

The application designer gives a sense of life to everyone's ideas and concepts. Usually trained in instructional design, this individual is commissioned to work on detail analysis and setting structures, as well as transferring concepts and strategy onto paper. Working with the total team, the designer develops an overall content and design strategy that fits the program and appeals to the end-user. Other duties include writing creative treatments, preparing application flowcharts, and setting system functions. The overall program structure is planned and laid out during this phase of program development. Flowcharts are created using the audience analysis, customer ob-jectives, and other data. The basic user interface is put into place at this time along with the basic programming structure agreed upon by the design team. During this phase the designer and the project manager work very closely with the client and the subject matter expert to produce an approved design document. This document serves as a source of information for all activity on the project. A designer also coordinates and communicates with various team members, supervises the writing process, and prepares a prototype sample for the team and client review.

The "Rembrandt" of the group, the graphic artist, must have a firm understanding of electronic art and its application. This point is critical con-sidering that the artist must be able to think in the realm of an electronic surface rather than a paper or canvas one. The artist also develops prototypes based on the initial ideas of the project team and works very closely with the designer and project manager to visualize concepts and to create graphic images, icons, and digitized images. Managing the screen files, assembling screen assets, and creating and maintaining project book and graphics docu-mentation also belongs to the artist's duties.

Writers make the information "come alive" for the end-user. They must be able to develop scripts and produce story boards that capture the viewers' minds as well as transferring to them a sense of exploration of the material. While a background in journalism helps, the ability to write for the "ear" or to write in a conversational tone is essential. Writers outline the application content, visualize the concepts needed, and then define the script and text specifications. They work closely with the designer and project manager as they write creative treatments and scripts.

The video team possesses an in-depth knowledge or experience in both audio and video production and participates in decisions that directly affect the "media" elements. Team members plan and schedule internal and exter-nal resources, scout locations, supervise freelancers, and coordinate and su-pervise the production process. If CD-ROMs are part of the product, they may also manage the disc replication process as they maintain production files that include scripts, shot sheets, editing decisions, and budget.

Programmers or "bit-twiddlers" build the command set that the appli-cation needs to run in an effective manner. While their training and experi-ence in programming is usually at the computer science level, a strong knowledge of DOS, OS/2, MAC or the Windows® environment is absolutely essential. This elite corps needs to be able to read design documents and flowcharts as well as understand what must happen for the end-user and thus design the testing strategy for the application. In building their code set they will follow established software standards and system-defined protocols, and establish and maintain the application source code document. Their magic then translates flowcharts and storyboards into the required authored format that the audience will interact with in the final product. Once complete, they will schedule the revision process with the testing, graphics, and design teams.

Testers are often part of the initial design team. They must have an intimate knowledge of the program, and the sooner they can be brought into the process, the better. These individuals help rectify any "bugs" or software issues early in the design process. The testers must first identify testing resources. These resources can be programmers brought in on a contract basis or a group of journalism majors from the local college or university. Working with the project manager, testers prepare a schedule for testing the application. One part of the process is to verify the application installation instructions; another is to proof graphics and text that occur both in the electronic and printed format. They review and test each area of the actual application to insure an error-free package. Testers identify any consistency issues and proof packaging quality. Once they find an issue or error, they must document these errors or concerns and then verify documented revisions. They will then work closely with the project manager and the authoring team to ensure corrections are complete.

The project manager uses a two step approach to final validation. Once the application is complete, the project manager reviews and tests the application and documentation, utilizing the developer's internal staff of quality assurance testers. All recommendations are documented and reviewed with the client and designer prior to making any changes. At the end of this test period, the client provides a sample audience of testers to review and validate the application. After this test is successfully completed, the application is validated by the developer and client and then classified as complete. After delivery, the program is added to the developer's product support list, and the developer provides on-going support as specified by the application plan.

Reg Pettus is founder and CEO of Pettus Media and Design, Inc. He and his team have provided award-winning multimedia development services since 1991 to the American Bible Society, IBM, Turner Educational Services, TRO Learning, and New Vision Production. Pettus has been a speaker at such conferences as Image World and the International Television Association.

From One Medium
to Another

───── ◯ ─────

Part III

Future Studies:

Accepting the New Challenges

Future Studies:
Accepting the New Challenges

This last section looks to the future. If multimedia translation presents a case study of moving from one medium to another, what will happen with the new media that lie on the horizon? What implications follow from those media? Without trying to cover every possibility, this section describes two aspects of the future: virtual reality and interactivity.

Gregory Shreve introduces virtual worlds and asks what they might do to our understanding of the Bible. If we can get inside the biblical world, how will this affect our faith response? Glorianna Davenport poses a similar question, but roots it in an examination of interactive, dynamic worlds —worlds currently available in the testing labs at MIT. Finally, Phil Mullins provides an introduction to the theory that might help us understand translating in these new worlds. What would an electronic hermeneutic predict? If literacy describes people's response to the world of print—the world that grounds our traditional understanding of biblical translation—can its electronic equivalent contribute to our understanding of moving from one medium to another?

14

From Scriptural to Virtual: Bible Translation, Hypercommunication, and Virtual Reality

Gregory M. Shreve

The translation of the Bible into a virtual medium must address four important areas. (1) Technology: The implication of different virtual environments for the virtual experience (for instance immersion versus window VR systems) must be explored. (2) Communication: In virtual environments the ability to communicate is augmented. Communication becomes hypercommunication as a variety of sensory modes (aural, tactile, visual) are integrated in a powerful message delivery system. (3) Translation: In hypercommunication the translation issues become quite complex because the cultural semiotics underlying aural, tactile, and visual information coded in the virtual environment must also be translated. There is the further complication of translating a primarily textual (scriptural) message to a multichannel virtual message. (4) Religion: The existence of virtual Scripture will be certain to evoke debate. There are questions which are bound to arise about the nature of a virtual religious experience and the implications of such experience for religious issues such as the quality of faith and the conduct of evangelism.

The phrase "virtual reality" evokes images of video games, of television exaggerations like *VR Troopers* and *VR 5*—including the lurid cybersex and cybervillainy of the movie *Lawnmower Man* (1992). The very idea of virtual reality sounds fantastic, like a science fiction story made real. Yet virtual reality is more than a current media fad; it is more than a mere speculation about far distant possibilities. Virtual reality (VR) is a current technology—practical applications exist now in architecture, in medicine, and in the military. While there certainly are entertainment applications, for example, the virtual "battle arcades" of the last few years, there are a host of serious applications already working.

The computer and media technologies to implement large-scale commercially viable virtual reality systems are in active research and development. Strides in computer imaging, sound processing, real-time graphics, natural language processing, motion sensing, and other technical fields are combining to produce a composite technology that will provide the foundation for a new form of communication. Given the exponential rate of the growth of hardware and software power, the large-scale commercial and social debut of virtual reality is imminent. I am convinced that we have not sufficiently considered the social and cultural implications of this new technology and the changes it will bring to the ways we communicate. Virtual reality communications and media will have significant, sometimes dislocating, social and cultural impacts. The purpose of this chapter is to examine only certain aspects of the sociocultural impact of virtual reality: the impact virtual media will have on communication, on translation, and, specifically, on Bible communication and translation. This is a daunting task, but if I can only describe the potential significance of VR (and its potential dangers) and raise the significant communication, translation, and religious issues, then I will have served the objective of this volume, which is to draft an intellectual map for the future of the American Bible Society's multimedia projects, a future in which virtual reality media will play an increasing role.

What is Virtual Reality?

Before embarking on an exploration of virtual reality and its impact on the communication and translation of the Bible, it is important to understand what a virtual reality is. Below are some definitions culled from the literature. Hugh Applewhite defined VR as the "experience of immersion into an intensely active computer simulation" (1992, p. 1). William Bricken of the Human Interface Technology Laboratory called it "broad bandwidth first-person participation in cyberspace" (1992, p. 9). Yet another definition, this one from Norman Goldfarb, claims that "virtual reality describes an interactive computer system that is so fast and intuitive that the computer disappears from the mind of the user, leaving the computer-generated environment as the reality" (1991, p. 114). Finally, John Latta of the 4th Wave Corporation says that virtual reality is "a human-computer interface where the computer and its devices create a sensory environment that is dynamically controlled by the actions of the individual so that the environment appears real to the participant" (1992, p. 112). These definitions all offer some intriguing ideas that I would like to group into concept categories:

1. Computer-generated contexts. The first category includes the idea of new computer-generated contexts or settings that are experienced by a human being. While this experienced setting resembles the physical world (e.g., "real" reality), it is not. The operative words in this context are "computer simulation," "computer-generated environment," "sensory environment," and "cyberspace."

2. Quality of human experience. The second category emphasizes the quality of the human experience of the context or setting generated by the computer. The salient ideas here are first-person participation, broad bandwidth participation (this means the experience is multi-sensory: touch, hearing, sight, taste, maybe even smell), immersion, and the realistic appearance of the computer-generated environment.

3. Bilateral experience. The third category of concepts emphasizes the fact that the experience of the artificial context or setting is bilateral. Individuals can act within the setting, and the setting will alter or respond to their acts. The significant notions here are interactivity, intensely active, and the dynamic control of the virtual environment by the actions of the participating individual(s).

Virtual reality is a rapidly developing technology to be sure, but it is still in its childhood. It is, as our trial definitions have indicated, some kind of environment (technology-generated) that provides human beings with enough artificially generated sensory cues that the individual engages in a sort of "willing suspension of disbelief" (Glenn, 1992, p. 62). The participant in the environment experiences sensory input that leads him or her to substitute, at least temporarily, virtual inputs for the physical sensory inputs of the empirical world. Steve Glenn of the SimGraphics Engineering Corporation has suggested that it is best to focus on the experience rather than on the technology when looking at definitions of VR: Virtual reality is an experience generated by a number of technologies. The experience is sufficiently realistic that the observer or participant believes that it is real (p. 62). Thus, a virtual reality Bible experience would be a computer-generated presentation or representation of a Bible scene or episode that a user would accept as real. Visitors to a virtual Bible scene might, for instance, really believe they were looking at, even participating in, the Last Supper.

The name "virtual reality" was first used by Jaron Lanier, the founder and chief executive officer of VPL Corporation. The word "virtual" is used with the same meaning it has in computer science when we speak of virtual memory, or in physics, when we speak of a virtual image. A virtual object or context is not real but is perceived and acted upon as if it were real. In computer science virtual memory is not RAM or core memory—it is disk memory used as if it were RAM. This virtual memory allows computers to act as if they had more working memory available to them than they really do. Today the term is used more and more to refer to three-dimensional realities that are computer-generated, viewed with head-mounted displays (stereo-viewing goggles), and manipulated with data gloves. These realities, while they do not yet approach the sensory resolution of empirical reality (they still appear cartoonish), will become more and more real-seeming. It will become easier and easier for visitors to such realities to accept them as real and to act in them as if they were real.

"Cyberspace" is a term created by William Gibson in his novel *Neuromancer* (1984). This term refers to a more expansive concept—it is a single artificial reality that could be experienced simultaneously by thousands of people world-wide. It is a possible application of virtual reality as a means of visualizing and navigating the global communications network that now links thousands of computers and millions of individuals through the telecommunications and e-mail networks—the Internet. I will want to return to this notion of simultaneous "cohabitation" of a virtual space when I discuss the implications of virtual reality for communication and, in line with our topic, for group-shared experience of a virtual Bible. Cyberspace will be a virtual place, computer-generated and maintained, where telecommunication can be implemented as face-to-face communication.

"Artificial reality," a term coined by Myron Krueger, was actually first used in 1984 and has been primarily superseded by the term virtual reality; this latter term is the one that hit the newspapers—*The New York Times* front page—in 1989 (Rheingold, 1991, p. 115). The primary emphasis of Krueger's concept was the synthetic nature of the reality, the ability to create a reality for which there was no real antecedent. That is to say, things are possible in the new environments that are not possible in the "real world." What this implies for communication is that the resources of the artificial reality to visualize the conceptual content of our messages will not be constrained by physical law, by distance, or maybe even by time or historical remove—but only by our ability to represent and display. These qualities have some significant impacts on the delivery of the Bible in a virtual medium; the mysteries and majesties of Bible events, which can only now be imagined by readers or seen in movies, could be directly experienced.

Virtual realities will become a medium, like television and movies, for representing messages that we, as human beings, wish to communicate. If one of the messages that we wish to communicate is the Word of God in the Bible, then it may be that we will wish to represent its events, its ideas, its personages, and its settings in ways which can be experienced as real. To the extent that virtual reality is used to communicate a message to those who experience it, there are communication issues to be resolved—e.g., what are the unique characteristics of a virtual medium? To the extent that the virtual medium is used to communicate the biblical message across languages and cultures, there is a translation issue to be faced. Finally, because of the unique character of the discourse to be translated and communicated in the virtual medium, there are significant religious issues that, at the very least, need to be debated.

Types of Virtual Reality Systems

Before continuing with a discussion of these issues, some introduction to the technology is in order. VR systems break down into three basic types (Glenn, 1992, pp. 63-64):

1. Immersion VR. These VR systems immerse or surround the participant in the virtual environment. One of the best examples of this is the University of North Carolina's architectural walk-through. The staff at UNC created a 3D computer representation of a building they were designing. Architects and future occupants were able to make a "walk-through" inspection wearing a pair of head-mounted goggles and using a treadmill. In this reality as you walk on the treadmill, you move through computer-generated hallways and rooms. As Glenn describes his experience, "If you look up, you see the building's ceilings, look left or right, you see walls, look down, you see the floor" (p. 63). In immersion systems participants *perceive* that they are in an alternate environment. In an "immersion" Bible this means that participants would be immersed in a detailed, multiple-sense, computer-generated context and would see and believe themselves to be on the steps of the temple with the money changers or at the Sermon on the Mount.

2. "Window" VR. In this form of VR users view and interact with the environment through a window or a viewport that is usually a set of displays or screens. The best examples of these kinds of systems are the flight simulators used by military and commercial aviation. Most use real-time computer graphics (about 10-60 frames per second) to simulate the movement of planes and other vehicles. This is a less intense experience of VR than immersion systems but could be also adapted for Bible communication. In "window" applications the events and landscapes of the Bible could be navigated or browsed in an extremely realistic way. Unlike the viewport represented by a movie screen or a television display, however, the users are able, to some extent, to dynamically control what is present on the screen. The sense of exploration and discovery is heightened by the users' ability to control what is found in the environment and by their ability to proceed differently through the experience each time they navigate it. Some sort of navigational control is necessary and, most likely, a metaphor for movement and navigation using the medium—a time machine.

3. Third Person VR. In such systems users view themselves within a virtual environment. Glenn describes the Mandala System from Vivid Effects, which captures a user's body movements and images and processes them with software to integrate them with stored computer images. Users view the composite images (their body image plus the synthetic images) on a display and can manipulate the virtual objects they see in the monitor with their physical hands and feet and input devices (pp. 63-64). In a VR Bible a third person system would allow a user to enter a biblical reality, but at one remove. As in immersion systems, there is contact and interaction with the virtual world, but the experience is less direct and immediate. It is not first, but "third person" experience.

During the development of VR Bible applications there will be an evolutionary path. Window Bible VR systems will come first. Operating primarily in visual and auditory modes, they have a less complicated technology. Window systems are also, in the semiotics of media, only an interactive step above film and computer-generated movies. Third-person VR applications will come next, expanding the level of interaction with the VR environment and the objects in it. Full-immersion systems will come last, exhibiting the greatest levels of user control and interaction in the virtual environment, responsiveness to user action, and the most complete range of sensory output.

Wearable versus Environmental

While we are on the topic of types of VR systems, two other ways of looking at VR should be mentioned. The one involves personal or worn technology that induces a virtual environment; the other technology is located externally, in the environment of the user. Wearable technology encumbers the user. It imposes limits on the user: The wires and sensors are physical constraints. As the miniaturization and personalization of powerful processors and the distribution of computing power continues, it is likely that we will carry, wear, or have implanted the devices we need to connect to distributed virtual computing resources. An alternative environmental technology does not encumber a user. In this mode the virtual reality is experienced without wearing any special instrumentation. The technology for perceiving the participant's actions is distributed throughout the environment using 3D displays and realistic sound generation. There may be also a mixture of wearable and environmental display (3D glasses plus 3D display). This kind of VR technology would feature virtual theaters for public VR or VR rooms in the well-equipped home occupying the place where our home theaters and Surround Sound© systems now reside. The well-equipped church of the future may have just such a room for virtual Bible lessons and study.

Key Parameters of VR Systems

When we examine the different kinds of VR technology, there are some key parameters that must be considered.

1. Degree of Realism. This is basically a measure of the quality of the sensory outputs provided by the VR system. In an immersion environment there must be (at least): (a) high quality images at high resolution and (b) realistic tactile feedback (the ability for the participant to perceive tactile "resistance" in the artificial environment when touching or pushing or lifting objects) (Latta, 1992, p. 113). There should also be other sensory inputs, including natural-seeming sound.

In a virtual Bible this would mean that it should be possible, if I am experiencing a virtual Sermon on the Mount, not just to see and hear the Sermon, but to feel the crowd as it "resists me" pushing my way to the front to hear the words that are to be spoken. Immersion systems call for the highest degree of realism because they call for the greatest suspension of disbelief. Some critical technical issues involved in creating and maintaining a sense of realism include (a) motion analysis or how well the system detects and interprets action; (b) the accuracy with which the system can measure and discriminate movements; (c) the sample rate/response rate, which is the time required for a VR system to register a user behavior, process it, and generate a response (Krueger, 1991); and (d) how well the system establishes and maintains a coherent virtual physics. Totally graphic creations in the virtual world must also perceive the participant and other objects in the graphic world and act in a consistent way. That is to say, the reality has to provide "sensory" and as-if "physical behavior" for the objects of the world as well as for its human participants. So if I throw a virtual ball against a virtual wall—or a moneychanger from the temple—there has to be a physics that makes it (or him) bounce. In a Bible VR participants would expect the physics of the real world; this would mean that one would have to respect the integrity of objects so that a person could not walk through walls or put their heads inside of objects (at least not without wanting to). However, given the nature of the biblical world, there are some persona who may perform actions that others cannot. Moses can part the Red Sea, but, I, the biblical VR tourist, cannot.

2. Level of Control. Realism is also influenced or enhanced by the level of individual control of the environment. The more apparent control a participant in a virtual reality has, the more likely the user will perceive that the environment is inhabited (or inhabitable), rather than merely a viewed external scene. Systems with high imagery and low control are essentially passive; systems with both imagery and high control are interactive and, so to speak, inhabitable. An example of this in Bible VR would be the ability to not just participate in a Bible scene such as the Sermon on the Mount in a programmed way (the experience always remains the same whenever I repeat it), but to determine, dynamically, by my own actions, how I proceed through the crowd, where I position myself among the listeners, and whether I speak to members of the crowd.

The issue of control is an important one in all VR, but it becomes a thorny issue from a religious and scriptural viewpoint in Bible VR. How much control will participants be given to alter events (even virtual ones) whose nature and sequence is historic, authoritative, and laden with religious meaning? I'll return to this issue later because, while a high level of control is desirable in many VR applications, e.g., VR adventure games, we need to consider what the level of control in Bible VR should be.

Some other technical issues involved with control are: (a) the ability of the system to parse complex gestures, motions, or discourse into constituent units for analysis and interpretation (for subsequent reaction); (b) the mode of action or control used by the VR participant—metaphoric gestures, magic hand movements, or natural language commands (Krueger, 1991, p. 142); (c) how the user is able to control movement and navigate in the virtual environment; and (d) how well the system is able to make assessments and interpretations of the interactions and user behaviors that take place within its scope (p. 120).

3. Sensory Environment. This parameter includes the range of the human senses that are stimulated by the VR system and the way the actions (motions, head position, angle of gaze) of the participant are detected and processed by the system. Smell and taste will be the last sensory modalities to be resolved by VR. Most of the advanced systems deal with sight, sound, and touch to greater or lesser degrees. The greater the range of senses stimulated, the more real the experience will be. If I walk through the market in Jerusalem I should be able not just to see and hear, but to feel and touch, to smell and to taste. The illusion of reality is created by the computer generation of sensory stimuli. The VR experience is an interplay between the human sensory systems, computer hardware, and software technology. In terms of their importance for creating artificial realities, sight and hearing dominate, followed by touch and other tactile senses, with smell and taste of lesser significance.

Vision and VR

In both window and immersion systems visual resolution is an issue because, as we said above, it affects the acceptability of the experience and the degree of realism. We also spoke earlier about sampling rate and response rate. The correlate of this, with respect to the visual system, is what is called "temporal resolution" or the number of virtual environment frames generated per second. Myron Krueger and George Trumbull have argued that a minimum temporal resolution of 60 frames per second is required for someone sitting passively and watching a Window VR. If there is movement of the head, hand, and body while viewing, then the frame rate has to increase dramatically. In Bible VR a 60 frame per second temporal resolution could suffice in window or third-person VR, but would not suffice in immersion scenes where, for instance, a participant might be expected to shoot an arrow, catch a bag of money, cast a net, or perform some other activity requiring the coordination of hand, eye, body, and virtual objects.

Human beings have developed color vision and stereoscopic vision over a long period of time. This highly developed sense provides a wide field of possibility for manipulating computer graphics in VR. Much of what occurs in VR graphic realities is dependent on the fact that vision is a dominant sense mode. Basically vision is able, as Krueger says, "to tyrannize the other senses" (1991, p. 125). Our visual experience (the way we process vision) establishes our sense of reality, for instance our orientation, distance, and perspective. We have certain "visual expectations" that VR can manipulate to create illusions (p. 126). One visual expectation is optical flow, the expectation associated with movement that one visual scene will merge smoothly into the next. Visual reality flows together as we move through it. VR needs to have sufficient resolution and speed to duplicate optical flow. But of course VR can also manipulate our optical experience. VR could, for instance, manipulate visual feedback so that we could appear to be taking giant steps, jumping over tall buildings, or wearing the "seven-league boots" of the fairy tales!

Regarding perspective, as we get closer to objects we expect them to get larger; as we move away from them they should appear smaller. VR systems could manipulate the visual expectation of perspective for some interesting but potentially disorienting visual experiences. By manipulating our visual expectations of flow and perspective we could create alternate experiences of physical space. Virtual space could be experienced differently than physical space. It would be possible in Bible VR systems to manipulate optical flow and perspective to allow us to see things from points of view impossible in physical reality, for instance, a Goliath's eye view of David and his sling, or a view of the gullet of Jonah's whale as we slide down it.

One of the visual issues in virtual reality is self-image. Typically, virtual participants need to see an image of their bodies, or some parts of them, usually a hand, in order to manipulate objects in the virtual environment. In a group experience of VR the participants need to see one another's whole body in order to interact naturally. (This implies that certain rules for communication such as those for linguistic and face-to-face interaction will still apply in VR.) In third person systems, it is usual for the full body to be used in the VR. In goggle-type immersion systems it is not unusual to see just the representation of a hand and some other parts of the body. After all, in real reality we don't usually see our full bodies face on.

Typically, in an immersion system you create the illusion of "being" someone or something else (Krueger, 1991, p. 127). The VR system can manipulate what you see of yourself and how you see yourself (virtual mirrors can also be embedded in the environment). In Bible VR the malleability of self-image raises the possibility of allowing VR users to take on biblical persona, or persona whose clothing, names, appearance, and VR identities are biblically accurate and appropriate. Once again, there are religious issues to be considered. Do we allow users to become biblical persona—Job, Moses, David, even Goliath? What are the implications of doing so and what controls should be or need to be placed on the actions they can take as such persona?

Tactile Feedback

Visual displays are a key to realism in the VR sensory environment. Another important element is the tactile feedback provided by tactile displays. A tactile display provides physical sensations such as touch and feel during the virtual session. In window VR systems or third person systems tactile displays are usually not used or required; they are more suitable for immersion systems. The display usually is part of a wearable technology using body position sensors and a variety of tactile stimulator devices. The stimulator devices can be used to generate sensations of resistance, texture, warmth, and other tactile sensations. These sensations are extremely important in adding to the degree of realism in the VR. When added to visual and auditory input the user can not only see and hear objects in the virtual environment, but touch and feel them.

Given the appropriate provision of tactile feedback we should be able to touch objects and have them resist us. They could be made to appear solid, rough, smooth, heavy, light, and so on. Various technologies for accomplishing such effects include electrical stimulation of opposing sets of muscles, exoskeletons that allow or resist body movement under software direction, artificial skins, and shape-memory alloys. An extremely interesting product is the "smart skin" being developed at the University of Pisa—an artificial skin with about the same thickness as human skin. It is made of a water-swollen conducting gel between two layers of electrodes that monitor the flow of electricity through the gel. As pressure deforms the gel the voltage on the electrodes changes; these changes can be communicated to another skin and cause a corresponding pressure change which can be communicated to a second participant's real skin.

In Bible VR, the implications of tactile feedback and tactile displays are the possibilities for heightening the realism of the experience by allowing users to handle objects, move obstacles, climb mountains, and so forth. We might be able to make users feel the heat from the burning bush, the rain falling on Noah's ark, even the pain of the crucifixion.

Sound and the Auditory Experience

Krueger argues that auditory experience is less crucial than visual experience for determining our sense of place. We are used to sounds, he argues, that are dissociated from our immediate physical environment, sounds from radio and television, for instance. For one thing, he argues, sounds are dynamic; they occur and are gone. We usually process them after the event that caused them has passed. Consider the slamming of a door, the ringing of a bell, and so on (1991, p. 139). Thus auditory expectations (like the visual expectations of optical flow and perspective) are less crucial than visual expectations in allowing us to act in and understand physical reality.

Nevertheless, sound does exist in physical reality and accompanies, or is a result of, a variety of actions. It would seem silly if we threw a ball through a virtual window and it was not accompanied by the sound of breaking glass. In VR, sound can be used to reinforce visual boundaries such as the limits of virtual objects (visualize a crashing sound when we bump into a virtual glass door). In VR, there will be a place for real-world sounds (bird song, thunder, wind, rain), music (following the tradition of movies!), and, of course, for speech.

With modern sound-processing techniques you can change the apparent origin of a sound, and sounds could be made to appear to come from any location. If there were several people in a VR context, techniques exist that would allow a person's sound and sound responses to follow him. NASA has a device called the "convolvotron" which can displace sounds and make them appear to be coming from different locations (p. 142). One person's speech could be displaced to another. Objects and physical structures could make sounds or talk, echoes could be created, a virtual plague of locusts could raise an awful din, the voice of God could speak from the burning bush, and so on. Another application of sound processing and displacement could be in a shared group experience of a Bible scene. Participants speaking different languages could be made to appear to speak the languages of the other participants by displacing the voice of an interpreter to the mouth of a speaker. This would be an entirely new mode of Bible translation as virtual interpreting. If the computer handles the interpreting, then such an experience would require, of course, more than just sound hardware like the convolvotron, but also significant speech processing capacity and machine translation. I will return to this notion of virtual interpreting later.

Speech and Speech Understanding

Speech sounds are relatively easy to produce; great advances have been made in the synthesis of speech; and human voices can be synthesized, or sampled and transformed, to produce extremely realistic speech. Speech synthesis is not the problem. Speech recognition is. Speech recognition is really understanding language. In VR, true speech recognition and natural language understanding will be extremely valuable. Speech recognition will be important for control of the environment because it will replace the requirement for gestures as a control language in immersion systems and reduce the number of elaborate controls in window and third-person systems. It will also be important as an addition to motion analysis and dramatic sensing; by monitoring the speech stream of interacting participants the system can derive information about the course of events, about the nature of events about to unfold, and about the nature of the interaction. Speech understanding will also be necessary for virtual interpreting.

Speech recognition and language understanding have been a goal of artificial intelligence research almost from the start. There are several related problems, but one of the most important ones is the problem of ellipsis since people are always leaving things out! We have an ability from context (physical and linguistic) to "fill in the blanks" and make sense of utterances. Consider the sentence:

"Chris is fixing dinner? Then let's stop by the drugstore!"

Understanding this pair of sentences requires background knowledge, some of it mutual knowledge shared by the participants. If I add that Chris is not a good cook and Chris's potential victims have eaten at the house before, then we can figure out the logic of this sentence by inferring that the guests will be buying antacids at the drugstore. Computer understanding of language is not just a matter of lexis and syntax and dictionary semantics. Language understanding is a complex matter of matching linguistic knowledge and world-knowledge (as well as other specialized knowledge). How could we solve the language understanding problem? Note that this is not just a VR problem, but a general artificial intelligence problem, that, if solved, could then be used in VR. There are at least two approaches to the language understanding problem: (a) provide the necessary background knowledge to the computer, requiring extensive programming and huge amounts of storage or (b) build a knowledge acquisition device to acquire and develop in the computer the same knowledge structures and understandings that we develop through experience.

The understandings a computer would have to develop would involve not only the attributes of people, events, objects, and processes, but also the physical and social interactions and temporal sequences they can be involved in. The computer needs to understand, for instance, what the temporal relationship is between a bad meal and an antacid and what the cultural relationship is between a drugstore and an Alka-Seltzer[©]. There are a great many conventionalized interactions and sequences (going to a restaurant, buying groceries, haggling for a carpet in a bazaar) that are almost like scripts (Schank & Abelson, 1977). The computer could store such scripts so that it could not only understand the dictionary meanings of words in text or discourse, but also infer the broader significance of the action sequences or stories (see Davenport, 1996) that coherent sequences of words and discourses refer to.

Of course, in an application such as a virtual Bible the computer would not need to know about every possible domain of people, objects, places, and scripts. The VR system would only have to have a knowledge of the operation of the world in which the experience occurs (the physical world of the Holy Land), of the cultures and customs of the inhabitants of that historical world, and a full knowledge of the biblical events to be displayed and to which participants are reacting. Because the virtual world will include speech and discourse, designers will also have to think about the kinds of speech conventions or speech scripts which will apply. When I enter the virtual world, will I expect to follow the cultural customs and scripts appropriate for ancient Jerusalem or those for Egypt under the pharaohs? What about scenes, say, the story of Cain and Abel, for which the cultural antecedents are unclear? Will we assume the communicative and interactive scripts of the VR participant as a default? What happens when the participants are from different cultures?

All human interactions, whether script-like or not, play out in physical and social contexts. Speech, sound, vision, and tactile sensation are all sensory outputs presented to a participant in a virtual reality as part of an artificially generated context; the user experiences the complex sensory output as a composite of world details. This composite changes as participants move or indicate that they want to change the environment. The set of outputs that exists at any one time and in which human action or interaction occurs is called a virtual context.

Context and VR

VR is basically a human inhabited and created space; it is, for the most part, human-derived. The scenes or contexts created in it are based on human expectations; the sensory outputs of the virtual environment are matched to the cognitive system of the user. The behavioral outputs of the user, in turn, control and determine subsequent system output. Unlike "real" reality, virtual reality is extremely malleable and responsive. There are an infinite number of possible states of the virtual reality. Any one state might be called a context or the logical equivalent of a visual frame.

The potential volume of input and output data for simulating reality and responding in ways "real" reality cannot is tremendous. The possible complexity of the artificial reality is infinite and beyond the capability of all processors, even the human brain. Generally we do not attend to all of the details of the environment that are potentially available to us. We usually only attend to those aspects of the environment that are pertinent to our task or to our reason for entering or engaging in a scene. Krueger mentions, for instance, that when we are crossing a street we pay attention to the details of the crossing task itself, the cars, the street, the lights and signs, and less attention to the inner workings of our bodies or the fact there is a stone gargoyle on the cornice of the building above us.

We attend to different elements of our environment. There is a selection from the overall environment of details to focus on and pay attention to. This selected set, based on attention and task, is a "pertinent context." The pertinent context is the currently active "state of the world" including physical environment, body state, and mental/task orientation to which the processing task must be devoted in a VR system. What is useful from a software point of view is that if a pertinent context can be defined and selected, it reduces the amount of possible information input and output that is relevant to the task-context and that needs to be tracked by the system. All the system needs to do is monitor whether the significant details of the context have changed and in what way (Krueger, 1991, p. 156). In the VR reality, the pertinent context includes (a) the participant's image; (b) any significant objects; (c) the background or scene; and (d) the visual and auditory transformations associated with the participant's movements (related to the current context and expected to be maintained during the context).

Only certain aspects of the participant's behavior are relevant to this virtual context since most of the display does not change on a moment-to-moment basis. When changes do occur they are derived from the previous display by transformations performed relative to the user's actions. This paradigm allows the reduction of input by filtering the potential input relative to the "virtual context and user behavior" relationship. The paradigm makes decisions relative to system response on this reduced input set, and generates output displays. For instance, in a virtual context of the Sermon on the Mount the computer does not need to be worrying about all possible contexts contained in the Bible, but only the physical settings, participants, objects, and other pragmatic features that belong in this context and that are being directly affected by the participant's current actions. This reduced set includes a great many but a finite and specifiable number of world details.

Contexts do not change randomly, but predictably in context-action chains, either because they are in some way "scripted" by human convention, or, in the present case, because a virtual world being presented, such as that of the Bible, is already specified in a narrative form. In such cases we already know what the general limits of context change can (or should) be. We have, literally, a mega-script within which we can embed lower-level scripts for more spontaneous user interactions and experiences—a huge multi-level net of contexts. We know basically what things are possible and which are not in the world we are representing. Context-action chains could be defined for a specified domain, even one as large and complex as the Bible particularly if the initial task of Bible virtualization is carried out in logical segments, for example by sections of the Old or New Testament.

Thus, a VR reality is actually a huge "context net" with every context connected to several, but limited number of adjacent contexts, which are in turn connected to others. Each context node associates with procedures for initializing, normal operation, and exit detection. Control consists of monitoring a participant's actions and either maintaining the current context, or transiting to the appropriate adjacent context. The context must be accepted as "real," but this does not mean that the world or context net portrayed has to be a real world; it might be a world in which we are allowed complete freedom of action and all things are possible. When we read fiction, fantasy, science fiction, even historical fiction, we participate in worlds that do not, or no longer exist. Thus "reality" need not be defined against the empirically or physically real, since artificial reality explores the concept of possible worlds. This is related to the notion of "linguistic co-presence" (Neubert & Shreve, 1992) that establishes a possible world in a text, that is, words appearing together create a mental set that evokes a world. Here "virtual co-presence" establishes a viable alternate reality, but the images are not evoked by words alone, but by a composite of all the sensory attributes of a real world such as sound, image, and sensation.

We can establish almost any kind of world we want. Thus, the world of the Bible could be established as an historical world or as a didactic world for Bible instruction. If it is presented as a didactic world, then the presence of, for instance, a virtual teacher-guide or some sort of artificial entity acting for the system is logical. In a VR context where the intent is to allow users free rein, to allow them to lose themselves in the illusion, such guides are reminders of the real world and would not be desirable. Some of you are already anticipating a danger here; in a virtual world where the user is not anchored in some way, one may be unable to draw the line between VR and the core reality. A user becoming lost in virtual space raises some important sociocultural issues. It could be possible, in VR systems of sufficient complexity, for the user to be unable to end the experience or, worse yet, to not want to end the experience. The specter of VR junkies raises its head.

Communication, Code, Language, and Translation in VR

When we have such real-seeming contexts, we will probably have a need for communication. People will want to inhabit contexts together, even if they are artificial ones. They will want to engage in interaction, and therefore there will be communicative, discursive, and textual forms occurring in and adapted to those environments. But what will be the nature of communication, language, and discourse in the virtual world?

At the University of North Carolina researchers have begun to work on what they call a "Virtual News Environment" or a virtual newspaper. This has led them to consider questions of what it means to say that VR is a new medium of communication. Many people have compared VR to older media. Krueger has envisioned it as super-television or film. Lanier compared it to a hyper-telephone, a new form of the English Commons or town meeting. But it is in fact more than these older media; Alan Kay called it a "metamedium" because it can simulate the details of other media, including media that cannot and have not existed physically (Biocca, 1993, pp. 16-17).

The big question is, what will be the conventions for virtual meta-communication? Current communication systems (television, telephone, newspaper) are being drawn together by the development and possible emergence of a common interface. For instance, the development of high definition television is facilitating the merger of television and computer. The national fiber optic communication system has an extremely high bandwidth, and at present only VR could consume the capacity of such a system. The question, again, is will we know how to use the huge capacity and power of VR communication when it emerges as a synthesis of older media? The conventions of the existing media will be the first conventions of the new metamedium. But as the unique capacities of virtual communication emerge, the metamedium will give birth to an extremely flexible, powerful, and responsive form of hypercommunication. It will develop its own conventions, modes of presentation, musical and visual styles, mechanisms of control and display, symbologies, and language forms.

While it is clear that technological developments are leading to the merger of existing media into the virtual metamedium, we might ask what the impetus is to create any kind of virtual reality. One motivation, according to Krueger, has to do with human-machine communication or the "encounter between human and machine":

> Humans are evolving slowly, if at all.... Computers are the most rapidly evolving technology in history.... [S]tudy of the interface should focus on the static qualities of the human, rather than on the transient issues of computer technology. The computer should adapt to the human, rather than the human adapting to the computer.... [T]he ultimate computer should perceive the human body, listen to the human voice, and respond through the human senses. (1991, p. xiv)

But, perhaps more importantly, VR has to do with our need to communicate more effectively with one another. Virtual reality is a form of communication in which the computer-generated reality, because of its responsiveness to control, is used to augment our ability to deliver messages. What we really want to do is to use the computer to augment our human-to-human communication, and to do that we need to have a prosthesis that is more sensitive to our needs than the current generation of computer interfaces. This sensitivity is precisely what VR provides, because by monitoring human behavior for control cues the machine can manipulate sensory output to communicate an environment to us. Or, just as importantly, it can use the sensory qualities of an environment to communicate. We, aware in turn of the dyadic relationship with the prescient environment, can manipulate it to communicate with others who enter the environment with us.

The context-set created and manipulated by VR, because it is all potentially controlled and controllable, allows every aspect of the artificial environment to carry meaning; thus there is great communicative potential. The power of the VR interface derives from the malleability of the multisensory interface it creates and allows us to manipulate. Regardless of whether the VR interface to the computer is worn or inhabited, VR allows us to interface to the computer and thus enhance our own ability to communicate with one another. This augmented communication is a new form of communication. It is hypercommunication, and existing forms of discourse and text will not remain unaffected.

I am interested in what will happen to language and language forms like discourse and text when communication occurs in the synthetic realities generated by VR systems. One of the interesting observations about the act, let us say, of telephoning is that there is an altered "sense of place." In face-to-face communication the act of communication is "located" in space; in a telephone call each participant is located in a different physical space, but the discourse is located in some shared information space defined by the link itself. Recent developments in VR will allow this shared information space to be visualized and for the participants in the communication to occupy it simultaneously. Imagine the power of a sermon or Bible lesson communicated, not by radio or television, or even face-to-face from the pulpit, but through VR. Each participant can share with the others a common experience in which image, sound, touch are used to communicate. This is not so difficult to conceive of. After all, if we look at the evolution of two-way communication devices there is a pattern of increasing immediacy in the interaction as we proceed from telegraph (textual interaction), through the telephone (speech interaction), through video-conferencing (image-speech interaction), and, finally the virtual conference (image-speech with sense of mutual presence). The sense of immediacy is provided by the computer's ability, via its control of our sensory environment, to provide us with a sense of "presence" in an environment other than the one we physically occupy.

As an example, consider how VR would affect interpreting services: the virtual interpreting mentioned earlier. A VR system could implement interpreting in several ways: (a) virtual participants and virtual interpreter inhabit a virtual space; (b) virtual participants with hidden virtual interpreter and transformation of auditory cues to "displace the interpretation" to the participants—this is possible since the computer can control the input and output to the participants and effectively make an appropriately transformed voice of the interpreter appear to come from the mouth of the other participant—and (c) virtual participants with natural language processing/interpreting of the interaction by the VR system.

This general model could be easily adapted for Bible translation and communication purposes. The scenario gives a whole new meaning to Bible translation. The Bible needs, of course, to be mono-lingually translated from a print medium to the virtual one; this whole essay up to this point has been about the broad implications of this translation. But there are also issues of translation in its more usual intercultural-interlingual transfer sense. As we bring the print medium into the virtual medium—the scriptural to the virtual—we will be able to bring the Word of God over in several forms. The words of the Bible can still be read as text in the virtual environment, but will be accompanied by non-text visual and auditory images. Imagine a virtual scene with virtual subtitling. The words could also be spoken by biblical characters, actors, guides, and narrators. There could, of course, be various blends of virtual text, dialogue, and narrated word. As virtual Bibles are communicated across languages, Bible translation will also have to concern itself with interpreting. It might be possible to implement multilingual virtual Bibles using the interpreting technology described above in systems adapted to recognize and adapt to the participant's cultural and linguistic background. As I enter the virtual environment, the system adapts to my communicative needs. As I approach the (virtual) village of Bethlehem, my hand touches the stable door and a voice narrates, in my language, the words of the Bible. Fellow travelers, also virtual tourists, hear those same words in their languages. As one of the magi passes by me to present his gifts, he speaks to me in German and my colleagues hear those words in Spanish. As I leave the scene, I say "good-bye" to them and they hear my German as Spanish. I hear their Spanish as German. Clearly, the virtual world will be a busy place for translators and, especially, for interpreters (who will need to inhabit the environment but be hidden in it) unless natural language understanding, speech recognition, and machine translation programs advance enough to allow the high response speed necessary for computers to do all of this work.

The purpose of using VR is to create what some have called "communication with realistic sensations" or what I have called "hypercommunication." The implications of VR are not just the sharing of virtual place but also the ability to use the computer-human interface to access computer power and therefore to create alterations in the virtual space in the fabric of the sensory illusion. We can use the power of language and of visual, auditory, tactile, spatial, and other codes in a powerfully dynamic way. VR expands the number of codes that we can use and the ways in which we can use them because VR uses the power of an almost infinitely flexible environment to communicate. In the VR environment thought can become not just speech, but action and multi-sensory manifestation. These new musical, iconic, and auditory hypercodes have not yet been established or conventionalized. New codes will have to be created, not just for command and control, but to most effectively utilize the VR resource at our disposal. Of course, we have already mentioned gestural languages for command and control, which have not yet been conventionalized. It is clear that language and speech will remain a primary form of human-machine and human-human communication in the environment. But it is clear that there will be many non-verbal codes possible as well, perhaps complex color codes, sound codes, and iconic codes, perhaps adopted in human communication simply because they are possible, flashy, and fun to use.

To illustrate what I mean, imagine a scene in which I am communicating with someone with whom I am angry; they are doing something that annoys me in the VR environment. The computer, sensing my mood, darkens the environment, perhaps virtual thunderheads gather on the virtual horizon and appropriately ominous music sounds. Reaching out with my hand I generate a circular image of the annoying person and put a line across it. So far not a word has been said, but much has been communicated.

Clearly there are several problems with this scenario. First, in many cultures the number of explicitly conventionalized non-verbal codes are few; to the extent that my choice of imagery, music, and icon is understandable we can use it in VR. I expect VR to lead to an explosion of meaning-packed virtual icons and sound bites used as parts of augmented discourse. But non-verbal codes, like linguistic ones, require translation; the cultural meanings of sounds, colors, and images are also culture-bound. The iconographies, musical symbologies, color codes, and other non-verbal sign systems developed in early VR will very likely be adopted wholesale from the culture that finances the research and development. Bible VR of necessity will adopt these early codes. As VR Bibles make their way out of the English-speaking and largely American consuming audience, all of these codes will require a special form of multimedia translation to be most effective (although one could continue the cultural imperialism of Hollywood and distribute them anyway!).

To summarize, while it is clear that there will be an elaboration of new non-verbal codes in VR, language and speech will retain their primary role. Language in VR will be used in at least three different ways:

- Communication with the VR system through natural language. This means escaping the limitations of gestural command language and entails powerful natural language processing.
- Communication with other participants, who are real people in virtual personae inside the virtual reality, as in VR "virtual conferencing."
- Communication with the VR system through artificial entities or with autonomous artificial entities within the VR system. For example, a Bible VR participant can communicate with a virtual apostle using language.

Participants and Intelligent Agents

The resolution of the design issues described earlier will help to create real-seeming environments. Yet, most environments that human beings are interested in visiting (outside of medical applications) are populated. VR can be populated by two kinds of communicative partners: other VR participants in a shared VR space, and intelligent agents controlled by the VR system itself. Now objects in the virtual world may be as complex as we can program them to be; one suggestion has been that the inhabitants of virtual worlds may be not just human beings in virtual form but also artificial entities.

Making artificial human beings with which communication can occur is a difficult and not yet surmounted graphic problem. It is hard to make them look and act real, and there is also the problem of imparting these complex entities with volition. But, because of the possible entertainment value as well as their value as controls to the computer (info-servants), there will be increasing interest in creating so-called intelligent virtual agents. In Bible VR intelligent agents can assume a great deal of importance. They can act as guides and teachers, and the Bible experience will be all the more real if we can speak to the characters in the environment. Some of the agents may be actual personages from the Bible, although these may always need to act in character. Other agents can be special tour guides or Bible teachers who accompany the visitor. How and whether agents are implemented depends partially on the metaphor being used to represent the experience, e.g., how the context is presented and the attitude with which the participants enter (or are allowed to enter) the experience.

VR, Interaction, and Cooperation

VR creates an illusory space in which remote participants can act and interact as though they are together. The effectiveness of VR as a communication medium depends on the strength of this illusion of being together. But the VR reality is an illusion and does not have the true "resistance" that physical reality does. It is malleable and capable of being shaped by its human participants to meet their communicative needs. For the first time the physical context (a simulacrum thereof) can be manipulated as a communicative tool. A myriad of questions are raised. Will this illusory space have rules, especially rules of interaction? Will the malleability of the virtual meeting ground require conditions and limits on the interaction? Will it ban unilateral alterations of the context? Will we be required to appear in our own characters rather than manipulating our appearance? Will we ban threatening manipulations of the environment? Will there be a necessity for the government to monitor VR interaction to inhibit virtual crime, assault, murder, and rape? How can we prevent sin, much less crimes in a Bible VR? Will there be a new pragmatics when the conditions of the context are under conscious control? That is, when we are in virtual communication can we be allowed to change some of the apparently physical and social conditions of the communication such as our gender, our appearance, or apparent beauty, dignity, and stature? What will be allowed in this new kind of communication?

The answer to such questions involves whether or not acceptability conditions develop for virtual communication and whether or not they become enforced by convention rather than by regulation. This is an extension of the principle of interactive cooperation, and cooperation with VR may take on a new meaning since all participants, unless limited by the system or by social convention, may alter significant elements of the virtual context at will. The question of acceptability also involves the development in a communicating community of standard and expected communicative habits. In this new form of communication, conventions must arise to control the potentially explosive possibilities of the communicative situation when it occurs in the "enhanced modes" possible in VR.

I speak of communication in the VR as augmented or hyper-communication because it uses the computer to augment the range and power of human communication. Yet the augmentation or bringing to bear of computational power cannot be simply an implementation of sheer power, a flashy display of computer graphics and electronic wizardry. VR cannot function as a communicative medium for most pragmatic purposes if it remains a "magic place" where anything is possible. After all, not all purposes and intents are served by a virtual acid trip. If I want to learn to fix my car through VR, I want the experience to be as organized and planned and predictable as a good Chilton's repair manual. Thus I perceive the development of all sorts of specialized VR text types, virtual media forms adapted for specific purposes, some persuasive (virtual advertisements), some instructional (virtual textbooks), some legal, some entertaining, and, of course, some religious.

Maxims of a Virtual Medium

To guide us in the development of the new forms of virtual media, Grice's (1975) maxims of textual communication may be useful:

1. Maxim of Virtual Quantity. "Make your contribution as informative as is required.... Do not make your contribution more informative than required" (p. 45).

In VR systems this maxim may be difficult to follow. Because VR is an augmentation of communicative ability a participant is literally able to call information down from the heavens like thunderbolts and present it in a variety of infinitely controllable perceptual modes. The temptation to create virtual "ultra-discourses" that are the virtual equivalent of verbosity is tremendous. We may have discourses that flood the senses and are difficult to decode. The principle of cooperation will require participants to discover mechanisms for communicating in an enhanced mode—choosing not all of the augmentations available (music, sound, tactile, visual) for communication, but only those necessary for the precise transmission of the message.

Since the communicative augmentations, like language, have communicative value only insofar as their interpretations are secure and their recipients know how to decode them, the problem of mutual knowledge in intercultural situations will still rear its head. How to translate the augmentations? The greater the cultural difference the greater the difficulty in using visual or auditory icons to enhance communication. Is this a new field of enterprise for the virtual intercultural communicator? Even in monocultural situations the accepted signs for certain visual and auditory meanings in the new virtual communication will not have been established. What will the "virtual words" be for indexing virtual experiences? What new discourse strategies will emerge for opening, ending, and continuing augmented conversation? New words and linguistic structures may develop for controlling the virtual environment, as control and command structures, for instance. There may also need to be ways to distinguish our conversation with other participants in the environment from our conversation with the reality itself, and with artificial entities inhabiting the environment.

    2. Maxim of Quality. "Try to make your contribution one that is true" (p. 46).

    Elsewhere (Neubert & Shreve, 1992), we have talked about texts as creating virtual worlds in which possible states of affairs exist. Pragmatic texts are almost always factually true; many other texts are true only relative to the possible world represented in the text. In the infinitely malleable virtual reality what is the truth? Truth will depend on communicative function and the relationship of the message to a defining social interaction. VR realities will resemble texts in that they will eventually develop types related to particular social relations and needs. Pragmatic virtual reality forms will adhere to factual truth. Simulations for training purposes, for instance, will model "real, empirically possible" situations. But, of course, there will be fiction, virtual poems, virtual newspapers, and virtual campaign speeches! Here truth will be judged relative to the state of affairs presupposed by the text, the social interactions they serve, and by the participants' orientation to the VR reality.

    Like texts, VR contexts will capture the power of co-presence. But unlike texts, the mental images associated by linguistic co-presence can be given sensory manifestation. Thus the ability to tell the truth as well as to lie and deceive is very great. There is more reason to worry about virtual campaign speeches than about virtual cults and the potential misuses of virtual Bibles.

    3. Maxim of Relation. "Be relevant" (p. 46).

    In his third maxim Grice admonishes us to "be relevant." As with the maxim of quantity this admonition presents some problems in VR. While the maxim of quantity is a reference to the quantity of information and VR's potential for flooding the input channels, the maxim of relation instructs us to present our communication in such a way that our reader or hearer can pick out what is important or primary from what is secondary, tertiary, or merely trivial.

    Devices will have to emerge in VR that function to help the reader wade through the flood of information, like headlines for a newspaper article. We will need virtual markers and comments to delineate the "relevance structure," the new from the old information, the significant from the unimportant. The important semantic relations or threads of the virtual discourse will need to be traced. New coherence-generating devices operating parallel to language will need to develop. For instance, in a virtual conversation it will be possible for the computer to visualize the contents of our speech. If I am, for instance, talking about the repair of a particular device, what will be the mechanism to direct the participant's attention to the visualization I have just instructed the machine to produce and keep hovering in the virtual air? Will it be a linguistic cue, an auditory cue, a visual cue? Or will it be a gesture from the producing participant?

In Bible VR this is a particularly interesting issue since many of the Bible contexts which will first be translated will be instructive ones such as parables. What mechanisms will we use to appropriately direct Sunday School students' attention to the relevant details instead of having their attention wander off to focus on a virtual bee buzzing about the Good Samaritan's head (a bee we will not want to delete because the illusion of reality is in the details!)?

4. Maxim of Manner. "Be perspicuous" (p. 46).

Grice also instructs us to "be perspicuous." This means that, in addition to taking into account the previous maxims, VR systems have to develop mechanisms for achieving clarity, brevity, and orderliness. VR communications will develop conventional forms that will be adapted to their communicative function and the intentionalities of the communicative situation. As VR communications specialize to carry out specific intents such as entertaining, informing and narrating, they will have interactional aims just like texts have. Specific forms for achieving specific goals will develop. Will these forms be culture-bound like the textual differences between culture/speech communities?

VR as Augmented Text

It is clear from my discussion that VR realities will have much in common with texts. Like texts, they will be ways of transmitting knowledge through coded messages. In VR those coded messages can be transmitted through a multiplicity of parallel and immediately controllable sensory channels. New coding systems will develop and be used, and virtual realities will be "densely coded." Like texts, VR realities will develop conventional scripted forms and we will use them as goal-oriented mechanisms for achieving our objectives. They will be created to fulfill purposes and meet goals. This fundamental fact will have a major impact on the development of these new communicative forms that will be partly linguistic and partly not. Speech and writing will be used simultaneously, because writing could be visually experienced. A form of writing can be displayed in the reality on, or over objects, or hovering in the air, hidden until invoked by a command such as, "Computer, what is this object called in Hebrew?" These speech/graphic messages can be mixed in a bewildering variety of ways with images, objects, sounds, holographs, and sensations.

While I think it is clear, and have maintained up to this point, that speech will remain the primary communicative mode in the VR and that it will retain its discourse and text-like qualities in the main, it will undergo transformation as the visual and other perceptual modes of the VR impinge upon it. Speech will become, for instance, more telegraphic, perhaps requiring the development of new linguistic signals indicating, say, the imminent invocation in the virtual air of a hovering image to illustrate a just-uttered concept. New codes, and conventions for their usage, will be a natural result of the development of the new medium.

VR realities will develop text-like qualities, with characteristic intentionality, acceptability conditions, situationality, informativity, coherence and cohesion mechanisms, and intertextual relations (Beaugrande & Dressler, 1981). Acceptability conditions (what conventions users understand and accept) will arise and will reflect specific social and interactive structures (have "situationality" in Beaugrande's terms) even if many of the new situations will never have existed before. New social structures and combinations may form that we have not predicted, especially involving interaction with artificial entities. Finally, especially in those cases where the VR realities have pragmatic purposes such as training, persuasion, and advertising, there will be specific coherence mechanisms to create a coherent virtual experience and cohesive devices for maintaining the coherence of the reality "at the surface of the experience."

Virtual cohesion will be the generation of synthetic sensory cues to maintain the integrity of the virtual experience (the virtual equivalence of lexical and grammatical cohesion). Virtual coherence will be the maintenance of underlying goal-orientation, adherence to social scripts, schemes, and plans. This will be particularly important in a medium where temporal and physical relationships, physical appearances, and contexts may alter or be altered at will. Virtual coherence will function, as textual coherence does, to establish a conceptual structure that is not random, but structured in such a way as to carry a sensible message in the medium. All communication is propositional. Except for the backgrounds and objects that serve primarily as props, there will be in VR the possibility to present the propositional structure with augmented speech using, for example, image and sound. What will be the devices equivalent to the coherence markers of a text that support the transfer of conceptual relations? As people experience a virtual communication, they need to be able to uncover the propositional structure. The mechanisms for indicating it will be partly linguistic (because speech will still be a primary carrier), but also may be derived from other possibilities of the virtual environment. The specific devices used, though still mostly linguistic, may be enhanced by visual collocations and image systems and specific visual or sensory cues that will link to word systems, for instance, to create "experience systems" that structure the VR and give the VR a particular texture in the textual and not the tactile sense.

As experience accumulates in VR communications, certain forms will emerge and establish expectations in their "experiencers," creating an intertextual element for VR that will define its typological structure. Ultimately, as people live greater portions of their lives in VR, the mechanisms for linking speech with other sensory "invocations" of the VR will develop into a conventionalized repertoire and become a permanent part of a new form of augmented discourse.

VR and the Bible: Religious Issues

It is clear from the points so far covered that the implementation of the Bible in a VR medium entails technical issues; communication issues involving the nature of code, language, and text; and inter-medium and inter-lingual translation issues. However, because of the nature of the text involved, religious issues must also necessarily arise. I am not a theologian, but I would like to conclude the discussion by raising some issues for others to debate and to resolve. The questions I would like to raise involve the following: (a) Is the "Scriptural" quality, to the extent we can agree what that is, of the Bible affected by the translation to the virtual medium? (b) What is the effect of the virtual move on the authority and perceived mutability or immutability of the Scriptures? (c) What is the impact of the virtual move on the nature and quality of faith? and (d) What are the sociocultural impacts of virtual Scriptures on evangelism and its ethics?

Scriptural to Virtual

One of the problems we face in creating the virtual Bible is defining and deciding what qualities of the Bible must be preserved. While I cannot hope to enumerate all of these qualities, I will enumerate enough to communicate my point, including the fact that (a) the Scriptures are venerated by a group or groups who believe them to possess divine authority; (b) they have the ability to engender, create, or build belief or faith in their readers; (c) they are the basis of a large body of secondary literature, commentary, and interpretation; (d) they are a sociocultural foundation of ritual behavior and social organizations (churches); and (e) they have an historical existence and may exist in numerous versions with continuing debate over the validity of those versions.

All of these Scriptural qualities will have an impact on the move to virtual form. The virtual transformation of the Bible will not escape the influence of what it means to be Scriptural. There are two primary issues to be dealt with here. First, what will be acceptable in a virtual Bible can only be determined against the five criteria listed above. The groups who authorize the transformation, interpretations, ritual behavior, and view of the evolution and status of the text they currently use will create a set of criteria that will determine what they will allow and not allow in the virtual world. The whole notion of "fidelity" in the translation to the virtual ultimately resides, practically speaking, not in the source text, but in the perceptions and evaluations of the groups authorizing and using the translation.

I would like to raise the following issue. Is the move to the virtual environment in itself a violation of the "Scriptural" nature of the Bible? Is there some intrinsic character of virtuality that is inimical to the Bible as Scripture (e.g., as a written text)? Mind you, this is an issue we face when we make biblical films and videos, but it is an issue brought much more starkly into the foreground because of the possibility that users can act, interact, and precipitate change in a text that is essentially regarded as authoritative and to some extent less mutable than others.

Authority and Mutability

The Bible, as a religious text, is imparted with an authority derived both from its sacred origin and from the veneration with which it is regarded by believers. In translation theory authoritative texts have long been treated in a way different from more pragmatic texts. Translators have oriented themselves toward the author or authors of the text and viewed the source as less liable to change. Virtual artists converting the Bible to virtual form may have to orient themselves less to their audience and more to their source text to avoid crossing the line from virtual Bible to virtual Bible entertainment. Once this line is crossed, it is difficult to imagine where the process of mutation would stop.

Earlier I spoke of one characteristic of virtual reality, the high level of interaction between the user and the virtual environment. The virtual environment may be infinitely more malleable and capable of change. Religious, historic, and other authoritative texts brought into the virtual environment can be significantly altered—at least there is the possibility of alteration. Now the question arises, "When does the user's interaction with the virtual Scripture breach the authority of the text?"

The virtual environment implies mutability; a singular characteristic of the virtual environment is that it is capable of response. In a "free" virtual environment, which I will define as one in which the users are free to elaborate their own virtual experience, there are very few controls. Through dramatic sensing and its ability to respond to our verbal and gestural commands, we can alter the sequence of contexts and events we view. We can change the nature of the story we are living and alter its endings. There is no foreordained course of events. This seems to contradict the character of Scripture. The very mutability that endows the virtual environment with its tremendous communicative appeal also allows the sacred text itself to be, perhaps, inappropriately shaped. Now, there are solutions to this. First, it is possible to create virtual Bible experiences with limits on the level of control. That is, the environment can allow changes of certain kinds: whom I talk to, how many loaves I eat, how I make my way through the crowd at the Sermon on the Mount. But I cannot prevent the miracle itself from happening. Note that the problem here is not a technical one; it is a problem of meaning and action. What are the limits of action in the virtual Bible space given the religious semantics the publishers of the virtual Bible wish to maintain? The limits can only be decided with reference to the software developer's doctrines and dogma (or lack thereof). These limits may be freer or stricter depending on the denomination or corporation involved.

Virtuality and Faith

One of the characteristics of the Scriptures is that they are the foundation of faith. They have an effect on their readers, in some cases to plant and nurture religious belief. What is the nature of the faith engendered by virtual experience? When one reads a text of the Bible there is a certain amount of hard work involved. That is, one must paint the scenes and images in the mind and imbue the words read with meaning. When miracles such as the parting of the Red Sea or the raising of Lazarus are depicted, we cannot see these miracles; we must imagine them, and then, more importantly, believe in them on that basis alone. A theologian once said that it is a good thing that there are not miracles every day because then we would not need faith to believe in them. This remark has some pertinence to the virtual experience. When I enter a virtual Bible, it is possible for me to directly experience in full multi-sensory mode the miracles I had to take on faith before. We make the power and majesty and mystery of Bible events into a class of dramatic special effects. Our virtual participant may be very susceptible to the sensory power of these virtual miracles. It may become much easier to impress, to engender belief, and to convert. But aren't there some hard questions to be asked? What is the nature of this belief? My sister, who toils in God's vineyard in Charleston, South Carolina, once told me, "People are hungry, they are hungry for faith, for something to believe in." My question is, if we give them the virtual Bible, is this fast-food faith—faith candy—for the impressionable, for those who want the Technicolor© and Surround Sound© experience of God?

This is only one possible interpretation; another view might be that the vehicle is unimportant, that if the message is the same ("Jesus Christ is our Lord and Savior") then it doesn't matter how the faith is engendered. I do not know the answer to this question; I don't know if there is real faith and some sort of virtual "quasi-faith." But the developers of virtual Bibles need to think about this question and its possible answers.

Evangelism

Some groups of believers and denominations will shy away from virtual reality and the virtual Bible. They will view the whole technology as a perversion, as another mask offered by Satan to obscure the Word. Other denominations, including many in the mainstream, will immediately see the tremendous didactic impact of virtual Bible lessons, of virtual Sunday school. And such applications, if properly monitored and controlled, can certainly have tremendous impact. Virtual parables come to mind as a relatively easy, instructive, and socially useful Bible VR application.

There are enough individuals and groups, however, who will see the tremendous influence and power that early and effective VR applications can bring. Virtual reality Bible scenes can be a tremendous tool for influencing large groups of people and attracting them to join churches and contribute money. There is evangelism, an old church tradition, and televangelism, perhaps a more dubious church tradition. Virtual evangelism will be a thousand-fold more compelling, convincing, and effective—and open to abuse by charlatans and false prophets. To the extent that the evangelizing group is socially, morally, and religiously responsible, there is no particular problem with virtual evangelism. To the extent that a group is opportunistic, essentially irresponsible, mostly immoral, and interested more in power and profit than faith and good works, then there is an extreme danger.

Conclusion

Bible VR is an imminent reality. The technology to present Bible events and stories exists now, and will develop quickly enough so that in a decade there will be intensely realistic sensory environments with natural language control populated by artificial entities and co-inhabited by fellow believers. The virtual environment augments our ability to communicate with one another and enhances the ability of the Bible publisher and communicator to transfer the Word of God. The power of virtuality brings both promises and pitfalls. There is the possibility to reach quite effectively many people raised in the electronic generation, to teach the young, and to equip the missionary. The danger is that cults and false prophets, interested in power and profit, may utilize this new tool to their own benefit. As the American Bible Society creates an intellectual map for the next two decades I beg it to consider both the potentials and the pitfalls of the new virtual world that is being created.

Gregory Shreve is professor of Modern and Classical Languages at Kent State University and founder/director of the Institute for Applied Linguistics. In 1993 he held the Karl Brugmann Chair of Linguistics and Translation at the University of Leipzig, Germany, where he lectured on the future of translation and interpreting in an age of new electronic media and virtual reality. A general editor of the monograph series "Translation Studies" and co-author of the book *Translation as Text*, he is a leading American proponent of empirical translation studies and computer assisted translation.

15

Stories as Dynamic
Adaptive Environments

Glorianna Davenport

Stories are invitations to understand ourselves, our community, and the world around us. During a live conversation or performance, an active feedback loop exists between an audience and a teller of tales. The greatest benefit of the feedback loop is that it allows for personalization and individual learning. In computational modes of storytelling, the designer can promote feedback as a natural extension of the story situation by careful development of the story modules, by attention to the voice of the audience, and by introducing visible content frameworks. In some experimental works, strategies of "narrative guidance" and "society of audience" are juxtaposed in order to insure a more cohesive story experience.

We live in an age where what is new and innovative tends to obscure connection and continuity. Nonetheless, the age old principles of human storytelling remain essential to the ways in which we humans grow in our understanding of the world and of our own experience in that world. If we look at story across a range of invention—spoken language, performance, written language, print, movies, and television—we discover that new technologies have successively traded the dynamics of interaction with a teller for increased audience size and cultural longevity. What distinguishes the computational media from past forms of mass media is the potential of introducing audience feedback and personalization into the experience.

The behavior of a dynamic, machine-based system is governed by complex instruction sets that are authored by many people and contained within a box called a computer. Unlike the literary and graphic traditions, which focus on intuition and subjective craft, computing is a young science that takes most of its cues from mathematics, particularly the mathematics of transformation. While progress in building more flexible media-capable hardware and software has increased dramatically over the past decade, new story forms that are both engaging and sensual are just beginning to emerge.

Interactive media—as I understand the term today—implies that, in collusion with the viewer, the computer is exerting some dynamic control over run-time sequencing of the media content.

A Trail of Bread Crumbs

Few people would question that the Bible contains powerful stories that have provided generations of readers with a measure of our own morality and mortality. How can media make these stories more accessible and compelling? Attempts to transcode biblical stories into motion pictures often fail because the cinematographic representation does not transport the audience back in time. In movies, any flaw in continuity or cohesion due to an inappropriate detail in the set, the cast, the performance, the direction, or the editing, encroaches on the viewer's suspension of disbelief. In contrast to the movies, missionaries on radio and television work in a less error prone lecture format. However, while the translation from family elder or pulpit to a one-way television channel extends the potential for audience numbers, it lacks the personalization and feedback that live discussion enjoys.

The discussion style associated with the teaching of biblical texts suggests a very compelling but technically difficult model for new technology. However, the idea of actively associating ideas and leaving a trail which someone else can share has been a goal of hypertext systems for many years. It is in fact plausible that the Old Testament, while not explicitly discussed by Vannevar Bush, Douglas Englebart or Ted Nelson, did provide the tradition on which hypertext was modeled. In fact, Vannevar Bush's vision of hypertext (Bush, 1945) included the notion of "memory traces," traces which illuminated both the history of a single scholar's exploration, and the collaborative path of many scholars, through a library. The astronomical growth of material available on the World Wide Web attests to the powerful backbone of a standard file address protocol and the hypertext link. As individual researchers browse electronic materials, they can perform the function of an editor: evaluating the relative value of materials; discarding the irrelevant; collecting and connecting the relevant; attaching informed commentary to selected materials.

In addition, the Bible provided the computational community an exemplary non-linear text. Few people read the Bible from first page to last, without pausing. Rather, individual scholars, at every level of knowledge, take particular themes or stories and deconstruct them in order to understand their symbolism and extract their lessons. In a recent conversation with my sister Suzy Brooke, who has spent many hours reading and studying the Bible, we discussed trails formed by two themes of particular interest to her. The first concerns the theme of leadership and the separation of the stories of leadership from the exposition of laws in the Old Testament. Her trail began in Exodus where Moses looks up from his work, tending sheep, to discover a burning bush. As Moses approaches the burning bush, God reveals himself to Moses, the shepherd, commanding him: "Don't come any closer. Take off your sandals—the ground where you are standing is holy" (Exodus 3.5 Contemporary English Version).

Suzy paused to explain that shoes were, at the time, a rare article of clothing and connoted human authority. She suggested that by taking the shoes off, Moses is putting aside personal selfhood, and accepting God whose name is "I AM THAT I AM" (Exodus 3.14). Now barefoot, Moses can walk with those he will lead without flaunting authority. Most of us will find this lesson compelling at some level. But it is the expert, the scholar who can lead us along the leadership trail. Suzy's bread crumb trail takes us through many scenes which allude to the difficulty of moving a generation out of slavery into freedom. Skipping Numbers and Deuteronomy, we arrive at Joshua who is able to make progress in the Law. What interests Suzy, as she moves into Kings, is how the notion of healing begins to emerge in parallel with governance by Law.

Current Technology and Non-Linear Storytelling

How well does current technology support non-linear storytelling? In the CD-ROM version of *Society of Mind*, we are introduced to Marvin Minsky as a lecturer as well as a seminal writer on the subject of how we think (Minsky, 1994). *Society of Mind* is formatted as an augmented book, replete with indexes and video lecture segments. The Minsky cut-out, who talks to us as we request his presence, helps make many of the ideas of *Society of Mind* more accessible. The navigation is consistent and fun, which makes our exploration enjoyable. However, what the experience of *Society of Mind* lacks is the society of audience, people gathering together to share insights which have awakened their thinking.

Bush's concept of hypertext included a human dynamic that is not fully functional in *Society of Mind* or in most CD-ROM titles. The concept of memory traces requires that the machine be cognizant of the bread crumb trail and, over time, make inferences linking it dynamically to other trails. The ultimate goal of the dynamic process, which allows us to explore, learn, edit, talk, test, and explore some more, is emergent knowledge. The bread crumb trail is built out of what others give us by way of knowledge and connections. It was this richness that Vannevar Bush felt could be captured by electronic hypertext.

Today, a vision of content links has been augmented by the programming of "social agents" which can search for similarity between large feature sets and generate on-the-fly a composite path, based on the exploratory roamings of many individuals. Agent-makers might choose to extract feature sets that reflect a specific special-interest community, as in *Firefly*, a commercial version of HOMR or Helpful On-Line Music Recommendations (http://ringo.media.mit.edu/ringo/ringo.html). Under this approach, trends discovered within a community are repackaged as editoral expertise, which can be used to steer individuals through the larger information space. As the source and scope of the editorial voice changes, the development of social and intellectual groups may also evolve.

Bush recognized that a trail of bread crumbs served a powerful editorial function, and that a system could leverage common knowledge in order to grow new knowledge. Thus the electronic medium can be used to shape new societies, societies of people who have shared not only a text but the process of understanding that text.

Out of the Box into a Theatrical Space

What other forms might a transcoding of biblical stories take? One possibility would be to develop adaptive models of stories within the context of immersive participatory environments—both in the box and out of the box. Here I will review some story models we have built that include facilities for inter-player communication, and a clear and unique sense of navigating through place.

Two years ago, Larry Friedlander and I attacked the problem of creating a responsive physical environment (Davenport & Friedlander, 1995). In a collaboration with 20 Massachusetts Institute of Technology (MIT) students, we mounted a show entitled "The Wheel of Life." The audience experienced the environment as either "explorers" or "guides." The central idea was to create a collaborative interchange between the two players. In 13 weeks of rapid development and prototyping, we evolved three worlds: Water, Earth, and Air.

"Water" was instantiated in a 40-foot-high fishbowl-shaped translucent scrim on which images were rear-projected. (See Figure 1) By entering the space, an explorer initialized the story. Flung to the bottom of the sea by an enormous hand, the explorer found himself surrounded by singing fish, including a huge muslin-covered-rebar walk-in whale with a brilliant pink mouth. A guide encouraged the explorer to strike up a conversation with the whale using a compendium of visual and whispered cues. If the explorer could get the whale to sing, he was rewarded with a joyful rite of passage.

The story of "Earth" was inspired by Percy Bysshe Shelley's poem "Ozymandias." The "lone and level sands" were contained in a large rectangular enclosure replete with broken columns, an arch, and the ruins of a wall. Sensors detected and indicated the movements of the explorer. As the explorers entered this space, they were advised that through a process of discovery they could help restore these wastelands to life. Explorers were led from task area to task area by emphatic changes in the lighting and messages from a guide. In one interaction, the guide triggered short snippets of poetry, such as "it is the East and Juliet is the sun," which played in

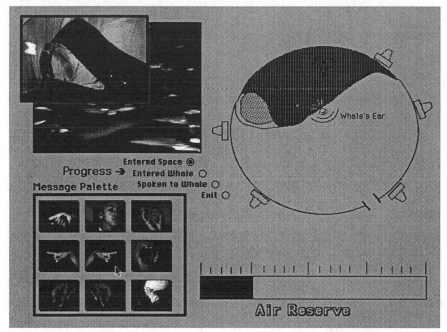

David Tames. © MIT Media Lab

Figure 1: Details from the virtual reality experience, "Water," in which the player questions a whale for clues. The images are rear-projected on a translucent scrim.

small monitors buried within the columns of the arch. If the explorers deduced that these were disguised instructions to stand on the designated points of a pressure-sensitive compass set into the floor, their insight was rewarded.

The experience of "Air" took place in a large inflatable mylar spaceship that was caught in a red nebula. Five rag-tag crew members were distributed around the circumference of the ship. An explorer was encouraged to awaken them from their trance-like red state into their active blue state. Unless the explorer could transform all, the ship did not stand a chance of surviving. In order to free the crew, the explorer had to discover pressure sensitive spots in front of the monitors and had to activate these sensors in the correct order. True to an MIT fantasy, the guide had to master the concept of a video game before providing useful information to the explorer.

When one creates an unusual story, one learns a lot about what did not work. For instance, it was more difficult than we had expected for some explorers to situate the story—a small percentage of disoriented explorers never quite "got it." Temporally, because of the demands of audience size and throughput, we had to limit visitors to 10-minute explorations of each of the three "worlds," rather than letting them take whatever amount of time they wished. Structurally, all of the interactions were simple and task-oriented, and therefore lacked some of the magic that complex rule-based transformations or other heuristics might have been able to provide. Nonetheless, on the whole "The Wheel of Life" was very well-received. The immersive participatory environment was lively and fun, and it inspired many researchers to explore content in a new way.

Transformational stories require us to understand the psychology of the audience. Why should I want to become involved in an interactive story? Certainly not in order to click buttons, select icons, read menus or scroll bars. Rather, I choose to participate in an interactive story to have an experience. The interface must be an integral narrative element of the story.

Two More Stories

The problem of creating an engaging experience in which the viewer can participate has other pitfalls. In particular, the first person role of "viewer as pilot" must be resolved against available limits in the story plane. Recently at MIT, we created two stories to learn more about how we can balance story, system, and audience control.

In *Dogmatic*, a virtual reality piece by Tinsley Galyean, a viewer is free to look around a space from a given position in the story space (Blumberg & Galyean, 1995). The story consists of five scenes. To insure that the viewer acknowledges the plot point in each scene, the story is based around what we call a directable character. In this case, a dog is the directable character and is also the antagonist; the audience is the protagonist. The idea behind a directable character is that it can operate on high level behaviors. Therefore, if a story requires the participant to look in a particular direction, the story could send a directive to the dog to stand in front of you and bark for example. Throughout this noire story, the viewer feels that they are in control, until they are not any more! (See Figure 2)

Lurker suggests another model for dynamic storytelling. It runs on the World Wide Web, and was designed with two objectives in mind (Morgenroth & Davenport, 1995). The first requires that the story promote a style of "thinking" in the minds of the participants; the second, that the story be experienced by a community of participants. Six audience members are chosen to participate each time the game is played. Each player receives e-mail and takes on another identity: a rat or a monkey, for example. Each player and all the characters in the story have home pages on the Web. The *Lurker* story involves the disappearance of one member of the hacker community; as a lurker, you, the audience, receive a call to arms to help the hackers find the lost member of their group. As the story evolves, the lurkers are faced with challenges that engage them in conversations with their fellow voyagers.

The "society of audience" model provides a particularly promising avenue for exploration because it takes advantage not only of a new distribution channel but also of new ways of community building. The separation between fictional characters and audience in *Lurker* makes the interaction between real characters feel intimate and immediate; however, the separation must be conceptually structured or it could trigger some confusion on the part of the audience.

The Look and Feel of Things to Come

In thinking about transcoding biblical stories, one needs to consider that the new medium is as much graphical as it is informational. While I cannot go into the developments with regard to relational grammars and automatic layout here, I can say that work in these fields has evolved in the past few years and is important in the creation of dynamic stories.

In the world of infinite zoom, an effect inspired by Charles Eames and Philip Morrison in *The Powers of Ten* and implemented by Muriel Cooper and her students in the Visible Language Workshop at MIT, any piece of information has a home if you know its spatial relationship to other points of interest (Morrison, Morrison, and Eames, 1982). A modeled world could be all-encompassing and arranged as a stack or as a set of conceptual relationships, again a bread crumb trail.

When mapped to diverse texts, libraries, or cinematic story elements, dynamic graphical cues will become part of the language of interactive story. As we wander through the woods and fields in our first person reverie, spatial metaphor allows us to visualize the trace of our wandering, creating thereby a tool for non-linear access to a larger, more consequent story base.

© *MIT Media Lab*

Figure 2: **Scenes from the virtual reality experience, "Dogmatic," with the directable character of the dog.**

Glorianna Davenport serves as an associate professor of Media Technology at the Massachusetts Institute of Technology where she directs the Interactive Cinema Group at the Media Laboratory. Trained as a documentary film-maker, Davenport began working in interactive media in 1980. Her research includes developing prototypes for interactive media and tools which support creative development of these stories. She is currently completing a book, *1001 Electronic Story Nights*, which focuses on narrative models for interactive media.

16

Media Ecology and the New Literacy: Notes on an Electronic Hermeneutic

Phil Mullins

This essay discusses the ways in which contemporary North American society is becoming a computer-mediated culture. Online literacy is replacing the literacy of print. Hypertextually organized, multimedia experience is becoming the norm which supplants many of the values of book culture. Integrated, interactive electronic media are shifting many of the pretextual notions that inform human meaning-making. As our tacit expectations and habits of thought are reconstituted, our suppositions about religious meaning also will shift. This essay provides a preliminary effort to chart the contours of such changes.

A Media Ecosystem

Media are not passive conduits of information, but active shapers and massagers of messages. To fully apprehend the character of the world they bring us, we must see them as an ecosystem: interacting, shaping, and re-presenting our experience. We are, of course, no longer supplied solely by natural media—in fact, the majority of our information about the world is technologically constituted to some degree. This fact makes investigations of media's shaping effects or ecology important. (McDaid, 1991, p. 204)

We have been preoccupied, ever since Marshall McLuhan made "media" a household word, with the much sexier world of broadcast television. It was TV that was creating the global village full of couch potatoes with minds to match. It was TV that dramatized politics. It was TV that created a special channel to reenact rhapsodic sexual foreplay on a round-the-clock basis. Thus bemused, we failed to notice that the personal computer had presented itself as an alternative to the printed book and the electronic screen as an alternative to the printed page. Furthermore, in the last three or four years, that alternative page has been

301

enhanced so that it can present and manipulate images and sounds almost as easily as words. (Lanham, 1993, pp. ix-x)

John McDaid's comment offers an accessible contemporary metaphor with which to explore some of McLuhan's important but sometimes enigmatic pronouncements that seek to illumine the subtle power of media technologies. Media form an ecosystem within which we dwell, and we need to attend to and care for the cultural media ecosystem, just as we might think about devoting human energy to understanding and actively shaping the fate of a particular natural ecosystem. We ignore media ecology at our peril.

The North American media ecosystem is technologically structured and dynamic. As the system shifts, it powerfully recasts what might be termed the pretextual dimensions of human life lived within it. Because it reshapes our dispositions and our skills for making meaning, it recontours what we think. The second quotation, from Richard Lanham, suggests a venue within which to think concretely about such recontouring at the end of the 20th century. In the '60s, the oracular McLuhan mesmerized those who worked to understand contemporary culture, producing extraordinary, sustained interest in television and the broadcast media. Meanwhile, the computer has become a common tool that only recently has begun to be recognized by scholars as a major vehicle for communication. Lanham, Jay David Bolter, George Landow and others argue convincingly that the computer is likely an epoch-making device that, like the printing press, will be increasingly more important in the transmission, preservation, and transformation of culture. Much contemporary cultural criticism uses the ambiguous term "postmodern" to stand for what seems to be the ambience of our time. Perhaps a more apt neologism would be computer-mediated culture. Such a term as "computer-mediated culture" signals that computer-mediated communication is now a decisive factor modifying the dispositions and skills that dominated in the culture of print and the book.

In this essay I can only hint at, rather than argue for, the appropriateness of this term and the periodization it implies. Others have certainly analyzed the emerging cultural environment in ways somewhat similar to my account. McDaid's periodization is similar: "Because the conversion to digital form and our dependence on computers are the defining characteristics of true electronic environments, I would like to follow Baudrillard (1983) in suggesting the term *digitality* (to parallel *orality* and *literacy*) as the shorthand descriptor for this emerging paradigm" (1991, p. 206). Bolter's two major books (1984, 1991) also defend the claim that the computer is an epoch-making device and that we have entered a new culture of electronic reading and writing. Landow (1992b) explores the way in which much poststructuralist/postmodernist literary theory finds embodiment in the arena of digitized electronic communication.

Extending McDaid's media ecosystem metaphor, emerging culture can be thought of as a hypertextual or hypermedia ecosystem. Lanham's final sentences above hint at what this means. The computer is becoming a major reading and writing environment; it is our access to integrated, interactive media. In this essay I attempt to think carefully about such integrated, interactive media.

Hypertext as Semantic Artifact and Cultural Phenomenon

When a technology is as pervasive and as profoundly shaping as print has been, it is often difficult to perceive the full extent of its entitlements and exclusions. Its formations and empowerments seem simply natural and right. When a new tool emerges, however, the conflict engendered by its emergence can illuminate previous obscured relations. (Kaplan, 1991, pp. 14-15)

Even a brief experience of reading and writing in a hypertext environment denaturalizes and demystifies the culture of the book. (Landow, 1992a, p. 203)

Both Nancy Kaplan and Landow are attuned to the rough transitional qualities of the contemporary period in places like North America where computers and computer uses have proliferated. The mental habits of print culture have, until recently, been so deeply rooted and tacit that they seemed (and, in fact, have been) natural and normal. We don't notice, until we are unsettled by experience with the computerized or digitized media, how much we have taken for granted. Always the pretextual dimensions of human meaning-making are broad in scope, but transitional periods offer a peculiar vantage point from which to focus on some of our established and our forming habits of thought. Here I am most interested in the dispositions that are slowly taking shape in the emerging electronic culture. But it is possible to grasp these only by thinking comparatively about what Kaplan calls the "entitlements" and "empowerments" of earlier print culture whose grip on us is now loosening. An initial foray to uncover our changing dispositions can begin with a perhaps simplistic analysis of computers and computer generated communication artifacts.

What Do Computers Do?

Computers are electrical devices that can store enormous quantities of information in digitized form and randomly retrieve such information almost instantly. Today computers can digitize both aural and visual information, including alphabetic symbols. Computers, of course, also can be linked together in networks (local and wide area). Given the right tools and skills appropriate to the electronic environment, the computer user has a capacity to manipulate digitized information in an unprecedented way. The technological features of networking, the digitization of different media, compact storage, and especially quick random access make possible integrated, interactive media as a cultural phenomenon. In the culture of the next century, it seems reasonable to expect that our hearing of meaningful sounds, viewing of pictures, and reading of language will increasingly be integrated in communication artifacts generated by, accessed through, and exchanged with the digital computer.

In addition to hardware and software components of integrated, interactive media, the social and political dynamics must nurture and give definitive shape to the development of a computer-mediated culture. Kaplan puts it this way: "As the material instantiations of discursive practices, tools or technologies necessarily embody ideologies and ideological conflict" (1991, p. 14). Historically-oriented students of technology such as Arnold Pacey warn about the dangers of assuming that technical innovations alone transform human values and pretexts (1983, pp. 13-34). Some hypertext theorists seem much more attuned to social and political dimensions of the shift to a culture in which human consciousness is shaped by the importance of integrated, interactive electronic media. Kaplan is among the more sensitive theorists, as are Stuart Moulthrop (1991) and Myron Tuman (1992a; 1992b).

Discussions about integrating media are, of course, not new in cultural history. Many treatises on theater, illuminated manuscripts, opera, and program music often show an interest in integration. The computer deals with digitized information and that means that an extraordinary control over integration is possible. It is arguable that any integrated artifact that is "art" is inevitably "interactive" insofar as it provokes reaction. But this is certainly the minimalist case of interactivity and moves too far into philosophical abstraction to pursue here.

Interactive Artifacts and their Cultural Significance

As an integrator of digitized media, the computer produces interactive artifacts which we can understand in several different ways or at several different levels. The simplest model for conceiving and thinking about interactivity often seems to underlie many technical discussions of "hypertext" and "hypermedia." Digitized information can be aggregated and the blocks or modules can be tied together in multiple ways. Thus, technical discussions of hypertext and hypermedia often speak of information nodes and associative links as, for example, in Conklin (1987, p. 18), Jonassen (1989, p. 7), and Schneiderman & Kearsley (1989, p. 3). The discussion of hypertext and hypermedia provided by these figures are all rather sober and practical treatments; this tends to be the norm among computer scientists and others involved in technical research on hypertext.

Reasonably early in this history those whom I would dub academic humanist hypertext theorists began participating and offering papers that were not technical treatments so much as they were social, historical, and cultural analyses of the implications of hypertext. Particularly those interested in literary theory or engaged in using the computer to teach college composition often became interested in the cultural aspects of hypertext. With the growth of the Internet and the World Wide Web, interest in, as well as writing about, hypertext (i.e., hypertext and hypermedia) has greatly expanded. Some of this is in print, but much of it is only electronically accessible. Carl Mitcham (1994) organizes his discussion of philosophy of technology by distinguishing engineering philosophy of technology from humanist philosophy of technology. A similar conceptual division between the technical hypertext theorists and the humanist hypertext theorists is a very useful orienting device. My comments will follow more the work of the humanists whose reflection on the cultural implications of hypertext for religion is just beginning.

Clearly such reflection should be a part of concrete projects such as the American Bible Society (ABS) Multimedia Translations Project. This endeavor should not be simply concerned with technical problems or even simply "multimedia translation" problems; it must also consider what I term broader cultural/consciousness problems. Surely it is a serious misreading of the contemporary cultural shift to construe the implications of the ABS multimedia project in terms only of making the Christian Scripture accessible to the MTV generation. Some exposure to humanist discussions of cultural implications of hypertext certainly makes this clear. As the pages that follow will suggest, humanist discussions are rich (sometimes wildly imaginative and, as Tuman warns, sometimes "oversold," 1992b, p. 78), diverse, and confusing, because so much often is drawn into their orbit.

Hypertext and Hypermedia

Random access is an especially important capacity of the computer as a tool for accessing digitized data. It allows the computer user to move almost instantaneously in hypertext from one node to another via the link. In the case of digitized alphabetic writing, what appears on the screen can be set up as an entryway to a few or many other documents which have some relevance; a node has within it branches to other nodes and the user must select one of these. As Michael Heim notes, the computer is a practical but not a logical requirement for hypertext and hypermedia: "I define hypertext as nonsequential writing with free user movement. It has nothing to do with computers logically; it has to do with computers pragmatically, just the way large numbers and large bookkeeping schemes have nothing to do with the computers logically but, rather, pragmatically" (1993, p. 33).

In addition to "hypertext" or "hypertextual organization," "hypermedia" is a common term today. Although it now is used interchangeably with "hypertext," "hypermedia" points to the fact that, since different media can be digitized, the arrangement of nodes and links can thus provide a "multimedia" experience. Although I will most frequently use the term "hypertext" in these comments, I refer more generally to the kind of organization and presentation made practically possible via the digital computer; I thus include what in earlier literature was broken out as "hypermedia" and today is sometimes referred to under the rubric of "multimedia."

From a phenomenological perspective, hypertextual artifacts accessed by the computer can be thought of as networks or webs of information. The web is a collection of nodes in some linked relation whose complexity can vary. A network can take on a structure with a beginning, middle, and end to imitate a printed document. But to think about an electronic web in these terms fails to recognize the peculiar potential of the electronic environment. The physical character of printed documents requires that some parts of the document immutably precede others, although there is no necessary reason the reader must negotiate a printed document in this order. Electronic writing releases readers and writers from an immutable order, although not from the project of ordering as a component of meaning-making. Although electronic documents are frequently termed "nonsequential" writing, as Landow points out, this in fact means such documents are "multisequential" (1992b, p. 70): There are many possible paths for a reader/user to take in or through (but "through" does not imply exhaustive completion) a hypertextual electronic environment. The reader/user of hypertext chooses or selects what is to be negotiated; electronic texts most frequently are thus, at the level of the engaged reader or user, an interest-shaped permutation of a larger body of information.

The Discomforts of Electronic Meaning-Making

In the past, cultures using earlier writing technologies have generated a great deal of thought about, and emphasis upon, responsibilities for textual coherence and order; such thought is addressed, however, to writers rather than readers. Contemporary culture lives in the wake of such thought and many questions about coherence and order in an electronic environment remain yet unresolved. We live in a transitional period like the age of the incunabula, the first 50 years after the development of the printing press and an interesting time of experimentation and social learning when the potential of the letterpress was being discovered. Some practices of the scriptorium carried over into the new era; some carried over briefly but were soon discarded (Hindeman, 1977). This pattern may persist in the present transition.

Certainly, computer-mediated communication makes coherence, from a writer's perspective, a more local concern. Individual modules must cohere, but the responsibility for broader orderings seems to rest largely with the reader/user of an electronic network. Thus, a shift of responsibility occurs in the transition from the late stage of print culture. This implies that an electronic environment for reading and writing raises some questions with respect to our established ideas about making an argument or case, especially in the broader sense. Not only philosophers, but also literary scholars interested in changing suppositions about narrative indeterminacy and closure have begun to examine such questions (Kolb, 1994; Douglas, 1994).

Many people who make meaning in hypertextually organized electronic space are presently self-conscious about the constructive role they play in negotiating materials available in the space. Print readers have somewhat similar constructive responsibilities, but the immutable and finite physical qualities of printed documents have allowed less self-consciousness about the reader's role. What happens, when making meaning with the help of a computer, is that things unmistakably appear and disappear on the screen in response to reader initiative; decisions about where to go next cannot be easily avoided by simply allowing an ordering imposed by the writer to prevail.

The electronic reader or user as a self-conscious, interested driver may also become rather acutely aware of (and even wary about, as I discuss below) how much lies at his or her fingertips in the larger electronic environment. At least, as the early hypertext theorist and visionary Ted Nelson imagines it, the whole world could be, hypertextually, at one's fingertips. Nelson speaks of the "docuverse" (1992, p. 53) of all literature:

> The real issue is literature—all literature. The problem is to create a unifying and principled basis for the interconnection of everything that everyone says, to maintain the integrity of each document, and yet allow everything to be deeply interconnected. So the issue is one of *grand hypertext*, as I call it, and of the literature of tomorrow, and of how to create a conceptual framework satisfactory for indefinite growth. (1992, p. 54)

Nelson's utopian plan is, of course, not a reality, but it does point to the larger fabric of computer-mediated communication that has important bearing upon thinking about hypertext and the mental habits of computer users. Perhaps most interestingly, Nelson's scheme reincarnates an Enlightenment dream in the heady psychological environment of cyberspace. Ironically, this dream has surfaced at a time in which cultural critics, such as Lyotard (1979/1984, p. xxiv), have proclaimed metanarratives—including those of the Enlightenment—no longer credible.

Experiencing Hypertext (1)

Experience with hypertextually organized resources occurs in contemporary culture as we use the computer in two ways or places; both work to reshape our earlier culture's mental habits. The more obvious case might be dubbed discrete hypertext, designed software that runs on individual personal computers or a local area network. The interactive CD-ROM products produced by the ABS's multimedia project provide a clear example of such discrete hypertext or discrete hypermedia. It certainly appears that more and more discrete hypertextual products, some identified as educational and some as entertainment, will soon appear on the market.

Such discrete commercial hypertextual software falls into two broad categories: "content" oriented and "process" oriented. If content oriented, a piece of hypertext illumines a topic. Process-oriented hypertext software, frequently advertised as a "tool" of some sort, allows users to create a web whose content is up to the user. Process-oriented hypertext originally helped programmers construct complex programs. The commercial software *Storyspace* (created by Bolter and others) is an example of process-oriented hypertext software; the package is sometimes used as a writing tool that uses the nesting capability of hypertext to teach students how to produce prose that moves from one topic to another. Some process-oriented software allows users to produce read-only hypertext products treating particular topics; later users cannot substantially modify them. Other process-oriented software allows users to produce hypertext that later users can substantially modify.

Of course, many content-oriented discrete hypertext products have appeared in specialized domains such as those of institutional (and academic) religion. For example, Bible study has prompted a spate of hypertext products in the U.S. Landow discusses one of these, *CD Word*, an electronic, multiple translation Bible. He offers two speculations:

> Will electronic versions of the Bible, like *CD Word*, that seem to be essentially democratizing similarly desacralize the Scriptures? They have the potential to do so in two ways. First, by making some of the scholar's procedures easily available to almost any reader, this electronic Bible might demystify a text that possesses a talismanic power for many in its intended audience.
>
> Second and more fundamental, the very fact that this hypertext Bible enforces the presence of multiple versions potentially undercuts belief in the possibility of a unique, unitary text. (1992b, p. 64)

Landow (a Brown University Victorian literature specialist) reflects in his rather naive comments how little he understands about the use of the Bible in religious communities and the relationship of that use to biblical scholarship. Nonetheless, Landow does at least begin to articulate questions about the Bible and electronic culture that need both refinement and serious attention. Others have dug deeper into the matter (Boomershine 1993a, 1993b; Fowler, 1993; Goethals, 1990, 1993, 1996, in press; Harley, 1993; and Mullins, 1990, 1993, 1996a, 1996b).

More interesting than the discrete hypertext product Landow has encountered (i.e., *CD Word*) are the more explicitly interpretative ventures in biblical study. In addition to the products produced by the ABS's Multimedia Translations Project, a fascinating simple example is the collection of eight computer-accessed case studies available under the title *Easy Greek Case Studies: Soul Journey for Inquiring Adults*. The cases focus upon contemporary issues in Roman Catholic and Protestant churches (for example, authority, the role of tradition and innovation, and the role of women). Each case puts the resources of Scriptural and historical studies at the disposal of the student interested in examining the issues.

Experiencing Hypertext (2)

Hypertextually organized resources are also accessible in contemporary culture on the Internet. We can distinguish this type of hypertext or domain for hypertextual experience from discrete hypertext by terming it "global hypertext," a term pointing to the broader base or scope of hypertextually organized materials. Certainly today, with the proper interfaces on the World Wide Web, hypermedia experience opens for the electronic reader with a shocking scope and brilliance. Global computer networks consist, of course, of local computers with local storage linked together. Such a collectivity, with its browsers and search engines, works rather like discrete hypertext with "horizontal" organization like the World Wide Web or in menus ("vertical" organization) on the many gophers found on Internet.

Certainly the emergence of the larger electronic world of globally linked computers differs from the kind of tethered world, the heritage of the Enlightenment, with a finite number of appropriate classificatory schemes within which to locate ourselves and our experience, which most in North America, until recently, were socialized to expect.

I have commented at greater length elsewhere (Mullins, 1996a, 1996b) on possible impacts of information proliferation. Heim quips about "the artificial information jungle" (1993, p. 104) that spreads over the world, noting that "cyberspace without carefully laid channels of choice may become a waste of space" (p. 105). Paul Saffo, a director at the Institute for the Future in Menlo Park, California, recently commented that "only half of the information revolution has been delivered to us: the access, and the volume.... The other half is reducing the flood to a meaningful trickle" (quoted in Mellinger, 1995).

In this section, I have sketched some phenomenological and cultural parameters within which to think about hypertext and hypermedia. It should be clear that our meaning-making experience in the emerging hypermedia cultural ecosystem stretches and modifies some important notions and practices that are normative or natural in print culture.

Rethinking Literacy

It would be comforting, for example, to be able to depend on the basic definition of literacy as "the ability to read and write," but the meanings of *reading* and *writing* are themselves unstable. Even worse, their meanings have shifted in the past and may shift again in the future, precisely in response to technological change, so that questions concerning the impact of technology on literacy can quickly become circular: How do we study the impact of a new technology on literacy when our understanding of literacy is itself shaped by an existing technology, often in ways that are not fully conscious? (Tuman, 1992b, p. 2)

Tuman's logical conundrum pointing to the changing character of "literacy" offers a second point of departure for reflecting upon some of the rhythms in the emerging hypertext cultural ecosystem. Historical thinking forces the recognition that "literacy" is not one thing but many. Tuman shows the ways in which "reading" and "writing" are socially and technologically constituted. In history, particular kinds of communication tools and societal arrangements fit seamlessly together, and those who dwell in a particular socio-technical world come to learn its lessons and accept its logic.

Tuman persuasively argues that, at the present, western notions of literacy are moving beyond the ideals and practices that dominated in an industrial society. Although all of its specific contours remain unclear, we are developing "online literacy" (1992b, p. 22), which reflects the fact that the computer has become a basic tool in a service economy in which information is central. But the transition now being effected is not smooth. Like Kaplan and Landow, Tuman believes that the transformation of industrial print culture leaves the present a time of nostalgia, struggle, and confusion. Those who are candid admit that it is not clear what literacy is becoming and therefore, Tuman suggests, it is appropriate to "problematize literacy":

> What remains difficult is to know what specific changes in the practice or the nature of literacy to expect, and, perhaps more importantly, to decide how we are to feel about them. So many discussions in this area lead in the direction of gauging the impact of computers on standards of literacy: Will they make us more or less literate? But, as we have seen, our sense of what it means to be literate is likely to shift in the very process of analysis, with the result of our arguing at cross purposes. The only solution here is to problematize literacy, to look more carefully at precisely what it is we have achieved through the technology of print and how such achievements may be affected by emerging electronic technologies. (p. 15)

In this section, I want to "problematize literacy" by highlighting the emergent cultural images of texts, readers, and writers seen against the backdrop of some of the powerful carry-over images of industrial print culture. To do this, of course, requires the recognition that any understanding of "text," "reader," and "writer" are so interwoven that they presuppose each other. I begin with a discussion of "text" but necessarily absorb into it quite a number of ideas about "readers" and "writers."

Recontextualizing Text

> More than any other term crucial to this discussion, *text* has ceased to inhabit a single world. Existing in two very different worlds, it gathers contradictory meanings to itself, and one must find some way of avoiding confusion when using it. (Landow, 1992a, p. 42)

Today the notion of "text" is very broadly applied even outside of discussions about the computer. In some hands, everything can be a "text." Bolter argues that within the expanding cultural sense of text, especially in computer-mediated communication, one must remember that a text functions symbolically, that is, as a sign rather than perceptually:

> The danger, then, is not that the computers will supplant books, but rather that the computer will not be allowed to fulfill its promise as a new writing system and provide us with a new kind of book. To fulfill its promise, the computer must not be used merely to provide video games. Like all earlier forms of literacy, computer literacy is semiotic.... The digital computer reconfirms the dichotomy between perception and semiosis as two aspects of mind, and it comes down firmly on the side of semiosis. The immediate perception of the world is not open to the computer. Like all writing systems, the computer must work through signs in order to represent, classify, and operate on perceived experience. (1991, p. 224)

Bolter could have philosophically articulated his intuition in a sounder fashion if he had followed C. S. Peirce and refined his thinking about signs rather than relying upon an absolute distinction between signs and percepts. For Peirce, humans always engage in semiosis (even when perceiving) but on different levels. Sandra Rosenthal summarizes Peirce's semiotic position thus: "Indeed, for Peirce, sensuous recognition and conceptual interpretation represent two ends of a continuum rather than an absolute difference in kind" (1983, p. 313). Nevertheless, in a more general way, Bolter makes a philosophically interesting plea that virtual reality technology, the next turn in computer-mediated communication, makes us take very seriously.

Clearly, Bolter lines up against virtual reality technology as it presently is discussed:

> A simulated world, a world of pure perception, can serve to counterpoint daily work in the world of signs. But it should be obvious that virtual reality cannot in itself sustain intellectual or cultural development. It must always be the "other" world which we visit from time to time.... The problem is that virtual reality, at least as it is now envisioned, is a medium of percepts rather than signs. It is virtual television. The world of useful work is a world of reading and writing, and yet at least some developers of virtual reality want to bypass or even deny such symbolic communication. (1991, p. 230)

Sarah Sloan raises the same kind of question about virtual reality technology and narrative: "Virtual realities throw into confusion the boundaries between the inside and outside of texts. The virtual world and its participants merge into a seamless collaboration" (1994, p. 26). Bolter's distinction between semiosis and pure perception is a practically useful distinction (even if not philosophically sound), and those designing multimedia software should bear in mind that a text's ability to maintain symbolic distance, that is, to be recognized as symbolic, importantly shapes how it is treated or "read." When one allows a multimedia text to slip into the level of pure perception, one settles for a certain kind of meaning that is quite different from the richly orienting kinds of meaning that the canonized texts of earlier cultures had. Interestingly, Heim (1993) does not, like Bolter, orient his discussion of virtual reality around the difference between semiosis and perception. But Heim does suggest that society will need to develop ways to preserve the contrast between virtual and real worlds, noting that virtual reality technology ought to make us more mindful of human solicitude, human mortality, and the temporal character of human life.

New Meanings for "Text" and The Rebirth of Rhetoric

At least for intellectuals, the line between a "metaphoric" and a "literal" sense of "text" is becoming slippery, and using the computer as an environment for communication certainly further broadens cultural associations for "text." The "integrated" character of digitized media combines sound, moving pictures, and alphabetic symbols. The preeminence of words, which was a part of book culture, has been superseded. Speaking of the era of print, Lanham offers the following satirical jab at the narrowness of print culture's vision: "In a literate culture our conception of meaning itself—whether of logical argument or magical narrative—depends on this radical act of typographical simplification. No pictures; no color; strict order of left to right then down one line; no type changes; no interaction; no revision" (1993, pp. 33-34). Lanham additionally suggests that integrated media brings with it a fundamental reorientation of the sensorium:

> Concomitantly with the explosion of the authoritative text, electronic writing begins a complete renegotiation of the alphabet/icon ratio upon which print-based thought is built. We can detect this foregrounding of images over written words most clearly in the world of business and government communications, but it is happening everywhere. When the rich vocal and gestural language of oral rhetoric was constricted into writing and then print, the effort to preserve it was concentrated into something classical rhetoricians called *ecphrasis*, dynamic speaking-pictures in words. Through the infinite resources of digital image recall and manipulation, ecphrasis is once again coming into its own, and the pictures and sounds suppressed into verbal rhetorical figures are now reassuming their native places in the human sensorium. (1993, p. 34)

Lanham welcomes a rebirth of rhetoric in its richest sense. In an era of digitization, the act of "writing" can employ anything which can be digitized. Linguistic signs no longer have priority in communication. You can now "write" by stringing together provocative images, audio, and conventional written language. Each of these venues may have its special grammar and rhetoric, but now hybrid grammars and rhetorics are imaginable. Of course, you cannot necessarily spin out syllogisms in audio or video or a mixture. But you can make or design unfolding meaning.

Actually, with the advent of digitization, western culture is only rediscovering this larger sense of "writing" that was an important part of the tradition before printing. The work of scholars who study illuminated manuscripts richly documents this "writing." Robert Calkins' criticism of the narrowness of much of art historical scholarship nicely suggests the dynamism of the medieval book:

> Art historians tend to examine miniatures as paintings—as isolated images to be arranged like photographs or excised folios in a row in order to demonstrate stylistic affinities and development, or like canvasses hung on a museum wall, to be contemplated in isolation in their own right. Only passing attention is paid to their context in the book or their relation to the text they illustrate; and almost none to their placement on the page and their relation to such secondary decorations as may accompany them, such as decorative borders, and to the sequence in which they reveal themselves as one turns the page. In its proper environment—as part of a book—an illuminated page is rarely seen one at a time, for it usually is seen in conjunction with its facing folio. That is the way a book presents itself to the viewer, and frequently the designers of a book took this presentation into account.... [A] medieval book is not a static object as one sees it in exhibition cases, presenting only two folios at a time to the viewer. It possesses a fourth dimension, for it requires a sequential experience, like music which unfolds and flows through time, or like a building around and through which one must circulate to fully receive successive impressions of the relationship of its exterior volumes and interior spaces. As the context of the text reveals itself through time, building the narrative by word, sentence, and paragraph, so time is a factor in turning the pages so that the layout of the page and the sequence of illustrations and decorations of the divisions unfold ad seriatim. (1984, p. 16)

Calkins' more general treatment of illuminated books (1983) as well as his detailed discussions of particular manuscripts (1986) offer other insights about the construction of what we are now beginning, in the age of digitization, to term "integrated" media.

The Collectivity of Texts in Computer-Mediated Culture

The emergence of the computer as a reading and writing tool restores to cultural notions of "text" some of the earlier sense of weaving, but now the threads constituting the warp and woof are digitized. The images of the woven and weaving used in connection with digitized media serve not only to point to the union of sound, video, and written language. Hypertext theorists have taken such images to point to other aspects of digitized communication. Moving in the direction suggested by Nelson's "docuverse," figures like John Slatin portray hypertext as "an embodiment of intertextuality"

(1988, p. 115; Harley, 1993, p. 177). Reading on the computer requires that you focus at a given locus at any particular moment. But given the speed of computers, what is before you on the CRT at a given moment always promises extension to other material.

Heim points out that the "hyper" in "hypertext" refers to another dimension of text beyond the focal, as in mathematical physics, where "hyperspace" refers to space which has more than three dimensions (1993, p. 30). In the electronic environment, "other" material thus seems also present or potentially so, and this presence makes it lose its separateness. The boundedness that seemed natural in the world of the book and print documents seems no longer so natural. Landow speaks of both the way in which hypertext "blurs the end boundaries of the metatext, and conventional notions of completion and a finished product do not apply" (1992a, p. 59) and of the way in which hypertext creates an "open-bordered text, a text that cannot shut out other texts" (p. 61). Not only the boundedness among texts but also that between self and world is relaxed as we step deeper into an era of computer-mediated culture. What seemed in the culture of print to be a clear division between the internal and the external (Descartes' *res cogitans* and *res extensa*) seems less clear or at least less foundational in a world of electronic texts.

Of course, Cartesian and Enlightenment thought has for two decades been under siege in the academy. Lanham suggests that notions of canon, a non-interactive view of writing, and a largely Cartesian metaphysical scheme for conceiving text and reader are bound up together:

> The traditional idea of an artistic canon brings with it, by the very "immortality" it strives for, both a passive beholder and a passive reality waiting out there to be perceived, the best that has been thought, said, or painted perhaps, but unchangeable in its perfection, a goddess we can adore but never ask out to play. (1993, p. 38)

Part of the decline of the self-world dichotomy is an interesting experimentation with new post-Cartesian and post-Romantic images of the self, some of which intimately connect person and computer. Cyborg images abound in contemporary popular culture. Many but not all of these are dystopian. Scholars, too, play with cyborg images, trying them on as metaphors to live by; in this regard, Donna Haraway's (1990) now famous cyborg manifesto comes to mind.

Slatin is correct in suggesting that in a computer-mediated culture any particular text can be conceived as a "collectivity of texts" bound up with one another and mutually constituting one another (1988, p. 115). In book culture, the relation among texts was often conceived in literary terms. The educated reader, for example, was expected to appreciate that the poetry of T. S. Eliot drew into its orbit, through a staggering array of allusions, many other literary works. Good writers were recognized as good readers in print culture. Literary theory in the late age of print sometimes spoke of works of literature as the product or outgrowth of earlier literature. This sense of the relation of that which is written has been pushed a step further in the era of electronic writing.

Electronic Linking: Its Partisans and Detractors

Sometimes electronic authors and electronic magazines vividly point to the sense in which, for any textual articulation, other articulations are integrally constituting, as does a recent article by Kaplan (1995) at a WWW site, an article that is a hypertextual discussion of hypertext. Two of the most interesting longer works in this vein are the *Storyspace* "version" of Bolter (1991) and the electronic version of Landow (1992a). In the electronic texts, both authors call attention to the ways in which they differ from the printed books.

The Kaplan article actually incorporates substantial portions of some of the authors she relies upon and/or with whom she is in dialogue. This extended electronic linking practice provides, on one hand, a refreshing change from the normal scholarly habit of providing the written equivalents of sound bites and potshots. According to Landow, hypertext promises to end the print practice of introducing other authors into a text only to make them appear highly attenuated (1992a, p. 67). On the other hand, electronic texts that offer a very complex pattern of linking with extended nodes inevitably diminish the sense the book or print reader had of what is primary and what is secondary.

About the reader's experience of hypertextual annotation of a text, Landow says that "electronic linking immediately destroys the simple binary opposition of text and note that founds the status relations that inhabit the printed book" (1992a, p. 65). Some commentators such as Heim focus on the link as the truly culturally significant component of hypertext but are not, like Landow, ready to see the link as liberating. Heim suggests if the link or "jump gains dominance over logical steps, hypertext literacy may epitomize the postmodern mentality" (1993, p. 39) with which he associates a certain orientation to trendy, quickly changing meaning. Heim indicates there is, deeply embedded in hypertext, a certain hubris:

> Hypertext emulates a divine access to things. Although God does not need to jump, the hypertext user leaps through the network of knowledge in something like an eternal present. The user feels intellectual distances melt away. Empowered by hypertext, however, the human victory over time and space is merely symbolic. Human users remain on the level of symbols, as they are not really gods and do not see things in a simultaneous present all at once. Total information is the illusion of knowledge, and hypertext favors this illusion by letting the user hop around at the speed of thought. (p. 38)

While this seems too harsh a criticism, it touches again upon what I above identified, in connection with Nelson's "docuverse," as the aspect of hypertext theory that is a great Enlightenment dream in a postmodern era.

Landow counters the claim that electronic texts diminish our sense of what is primary by suggesting that hypertext simply overcomes the "univocality" of print: "Whenever one places a text within a network of other texts, one forces it to exist as part of a complex dialogue" (1992a, p. 63). In a similar vein, Bolter suggests "a text as a network has no univocal sense; it is a multiplicity without the imposition of a principle of domination" (1991, p. 25). He argues hypertext has "no canonical order" and, further, that it is "topographic writing":

> In place of hierarchy, we have a writing that is not only topical: We might also call it "topographic".... Electronic writing is both a visual and a verbal description. It is not the writing of a place, but rather a writing *with* places, spatially realized topics. Topographic writing challenges the idea that writing should be merely the servant of spoken language. The writer and reader can create and examine signs and structures on the computer screen that have no easy equivalent in speech. The point is obvious when the text is a collection of images stored on a video disk. (p. 25)

An Intertexual Ethos

Extended experience with reading and writing in the electronic medium will perhaps provide a growing intertextual ethos among electronic writers and readers. To put it as Landow does, there will emerge a new sense that centering is central to text and reading and, further, where there is a center a periphery cannot be far behind:

> Hypertext linking situates the present text at the center of the textual universe, thus creating a new kind of hierarchy, in which the power of the center dominates that of the infinite periphery. But because in hypertext that center is always a transient, de-centerable virtual center—one created, in other words, only by one's act of reading that particular text—it never tyrannizes other aspects of the network in the way a printed text does. (1992a, p. 66)

Nevertheless, any practical sense of intertextuality as textual riches ready-to-hand is certainly in part an illusion. Clearly it requires human time and energy to go through another linked text of any length; one can quite easily get lost or lose interest along the way in a network of electronic nodes. In addition, networked computers frequently foul up linking arrangements for reasons that likely will prevail in a less than ideal world.

A deeper cultural sense of intertextuality may promote, in emerging culture, a more reasonable appraisal of texts and writers than prevailed in an era strongly influenced by Romantic aesthetics because it situates them in a context. Hypertext theorists frequently address moving beyond Romantic suppositions governing our sense of what reading, writing, and the written are (as these are reinforced by print). Tuman (1992b, pp. 52-81) rather soberly argues, however, that some largely Romantic notions still remain embedded in the ideas of many advocates of hypertext, especially those who celebrate hypertext as a new genre for literature, for instance as interactive fiction (Douglas, 1994; Bolter, 1991, pp. 121-146). Tuman's trenchant criticisms should make those interested in hypertext theory do periodic reality checks:

> The basic problem of hypertext is not the technical limitations.... The problem rather lies in the fervor of its champions, many of whom, for all their deconstructive, postmodern rhetoric, seem beguiled by their own nostalgia for print literacy. These are readers and writers who themselves are both deeply trained in print literacy and fervently opposed to its own hierarchical structures. What they seek, therefore, is a new literacy practice, one that will at once destroy all the authoritarian aspects of the old (including the notion of fixed authors and texts) and yet retain the essential parameters and feel of what they have always known (including new kinds of cooperative authors and new kinds of open-ended texts). As a result hypertext is oversold as a new kind of text (although not really a text at all) that allows for a new kind of open-ended author (who turns out to be not really an author). (1992b, p. 78)

Certainly Bolter, as well as some other theorists, recognize that the issue of Romantic suppositions is really part of larger questions about the nature of literature and the place of authority which digitized media open up:

> As long as the printed book remains the primary medium of literature, traditional views of the author as authority and of literature as monument will remain convincing for most readers. The electronic medium, however, threatens to bring down the whole edifice at once. It complicates our understanding of literature as either mimesis or expression, it denies the fixity of the text, and it questions the authority of the author. The author is no longer an intimidating figure, not a prophet or a Mosaic legislator in Shelley's sense. The author's art is not a substitute for religious revelation, and authors do not lay down the law. The electronic author assumes, once again, the role of a craftsman, working with defined materials and limited goals. In constructing an electronic text as a network of related episodes, the author comes to emphasize the formal qualities of art, rather than the inspiration that transcends form. And as the Greeks understood, a sense of form is a sense of one's limits. (1991, p. 153)

Proliferation of Information

It is not clear, however, that situating a text in a context of texts—especially in a world drowning in information—necessarily means that readers and writers will acquire greater historical sensitivity. Those socialized in a more fully electronic culture may be mindful of the debts (i.e., influence or relationship) one text has to another without necessarily connecting texts to place and time of origin. It seems likely that historical sensibility was in part nurtured by book culture. The separateness of works promoted linking to temporal and social location in a way that neither a predominantly oral culture nor a culture deeply committed to the computer as a communication tool can support. To put it as Landow does, "text" in the new electronic context becomes not merely a "unique type embodied in a single object" but it is "a type as a complex set of variants" (1992a, p. 56). Nevertheless, Landow argues that proliferation of hypertext will enhance historical sensibility: "The evidence of hypertext, in other words, historicizes many of our most commonplace assumptions, thereby forcing them to descend from the ethereality of abstraction and appear as corollaries to a particular technology rooted in specific times and places" (p. 33). I suspect that this may be the case for those socialized largely by the late culture of the book, especially academics in the 20th century, the true heirs to Romantic notions about writing. But I doubt that historical sensibility will be reawakened by hypertext for persons in a culture in which electronic reading and writing are more dominant socializing factors. In the final analysis, the whole notion about what constitutes "historical sensibility" (or "translation"—even "multimedia translation") is deeply shaped by the literacy of print.

The proliferation of information in the emerging computer-mediated culture is a serious matter affecting human meaning-making (Mullins, 1996b). Tuman shows that, in the emerging sense of "literacy," the problem of locating what you are interested in becomes central: "The problem of filing and retrieving—of finding what one wants—all of a sudden moves out of the background of literacy, and the whole field of information technology, with its new terminology, takes on a new importance" (1992b, p. 19).

In an environment of excess, information becomes a commodity to be consumed or not consumed. In an environment of excess with sophisticated technological tools, perhaps the general approach to knowledge will change. Meyrowitz suggests that:

> Our advanced technological stage allows us to hunt and gather information rather than food. Like hunters and gatherers who take for granted the abundance of food "out there" and therefore only hunt and gather enough to consume immediately, we are increasingly becoming a "subsistence information society." (1985, p. 317)

A "subsistence information society" is one in which people thoroughly assimilate and self-consciously carry with them very little available information, even though there seems to be so much information, and it seems so readily available:

> Rather than engaging in long-term storage of knowledge in their memories or homes, many people are beginning to believe that information is available "out there" and that individuals do not need to stockpile it. Our children sing "we don't need no education," and even many scholars have begun to steer away from collecting and storing in their minds the long, linear arguments of literacy that linked new discoveries to old and that pointed to the future. Instead, the computer is increasingly used as an abundant jungle of bits and pieces of "data" (albeit, a jungle created and stocked by us). Some data are hunted, gathered, and analyzed when an appetite for correlations arises. The connections found are often consumed and digested immediately without being painstakingly linked to other knowledge and ideas. (p. 317)

As Tuman points out, our whole set of descriptive and evaluative terms for thinking about knowledge and cultural lore is presently being recast. Tuman rather aptly characterizes Landow as an "acclaimed literary historian" deeply socialized by book culture who therefore finds it natural "to see students using computers as an infinite reserve shelf to gain the interdisciplinary knowledge of the interconnectedness of British literature, history, and art that many traditional scholars lack" (1992b, p. 80).

Those who work on the ABS multimedia translations of sections of the Bible are perhaps also engaged in an endeavor to produce an infinite (or at least a rich) interdisciplinary reserve shelf. Later generations, however, may be puzzled by what is included, particularly material historical in orientation. After all, book culture nurtured historicist orientations to Scripture. Until recently, much higher criticism of the Bible was rather narrowly committed to interpreting texts in terms of an "original" or an early context. Ironically, biblical literalism also seems to arise from an orientation to text that the culture of the book subtly promotes (Mullins, 1996b). Bolter offers a perspective similar to that briefly outlined here:

> It is no accident that the age of printing became obsessed with assigning authorship and verifying texts. Such scholarship, called "textual criticism," began in the Renaissance and reached its zenith in the 19th century. The goal of this exacting scholarship was to determine letter by letter what Plato, Euripides, or the Church fathers "really" wrote: to apply the standards of printed accuracy to the manuscript tradition of ancient and medieval. Textual criticism set out to establish a little canon for each author. (1991, p. 152)

The Meaning of Canon

A deeper sense of intertextuality may also make it more difficult for some or any texts to play a paradigmatic function in culture as, for example, the Bible did in some places and stages of the development of the western tradition. In the best sense, the canons of earlier cultures provided a paradigmatic function. To put matters somewhat theologically, canons testify as authentic witnesses and anchor traditions that employ writing. But the paradigmatic role of the canon simultaneously causes a problem because the paradigmatic also excludes. Contemporary culture, with its extraordinary sensitivity to inclusions and exclusions, is deeply divided about the worth of canons (and perhaps also profoundly confused about the function of canons). Clearly, much of the hypertext literature argues that canons are destabilized in a hypertextual cultural ecosystem. The electronic reading and writing medium does not offer very effective ways, as did print and manuscript culture, to enforce choices. Bolter describes this aspect of computer accessed texts in terms of the contest between author and reader which should be seen in historical perspective:

> The computer therefore makes visible the contest between author and reader that in previous technologies has gone on out of sight "behind" the page. The author has always before had the upper hand, although each previous technology of writing allowed for a different kind and degree of control. With the purely linear presentation of the papyrus roll, neither author nor reader had many choices.... Gradually the structure became externalized through the development of the paged book, marginal notes, use of various scripts, and other techniques culminating in modern printed typography.... In general, authors in the age of print have exerted their authority in subtler, but still effective ways. The electronic medium challenges all such attempts to circumscribe the reader's participation. (1991, pp. 154-155)

The destabilizing of canons results from the interactivity of digitized media. Bolter describes the already emerging scenario rather matter of factly:

> In the world of electronic writing, there will be no texts that everyone must read. There will only be texts that more or fewer readers choose to examine in more or less detail. The idea of the great, inescapable book belongs to the age of print that is now passing. (p. 240)

At the least, it seems likely that a step deeper into electronic culture will shift the present polarized discussion regarding canons. Great and inescapable books, even sacred texts like the Bible, have heretofore depended in part for their status upon the physical discreteness and stolidity of texts (which existed in print culture and its predecessors), upon a reasonably weak cultural sense of intertextuality, and upon the self-perceptions, as passive receptors (common in print culture), of those who use them. These factors should become clearer as they fade from the scene. The case with sacred texts or, better stated, what makes and sustains status as Scripture, is a complex matter. This is obvious to anyone who has studied historically the formation and development of a religious tradition. Sometimes literary critics and those who study media seem rather naive about what Gamble (1985, p. 46) terms the "textualization of tradition." Among important recent scholarly work on the nature and function of Scripture from a cross-cultural perspective, Graham (1987) emphasizes the ways in which orality has and continues to be very significant in scriptural traditions across the world. Similarly, Smith (1993) shows the multiplicity of "Scripture" across traditions and the historical or changing character of a community's relation to its Scriptures. He emphasizes the importance of Scripture in shaping lives (i.e., what I have above termed the "paradigmatic" function). Smith also notes the ways in which the pluralism of the contemporary world offers peculiar opportunities self-consciously to reconstruct our notions of Scripture so that something of its paradigmatic role will continue in religious communities. An important project for those with interest in the efficacy of Scripture in emerging culture would bring together the cross-cultural interest in Scripture represented by figures like Smith and Graham and the analytical work on digital communication.

The question of destabilization of canons promoted by the electronic medium for reading and writing raises, for some, a large but unanswerable question: Is hypertext primarily an opportunity rather than a threat? It certainly is not clear that it must be a threat but neither is it clearly only a boon, as some hypertext theorists contend. Perhaps Robert Fowler correctly suggests that the electronic medium reminds readers/writers that persons and the politics of a community establish canons and that the process of recentering is—and should be—ongoing:

> Nonetheless, centers are crucial; humans cannot live for long without a center. The danger, perhaps, is the fixed and permanent center, imposed tyrannically. Hypertext, however, offers the possibility of a shifting center, a "multicentered" or "infinitely recenterable" textual universe, with the center to be determined by an empowered, liberated reader. Centers come and go; the act of establishing a center, however, is an ongoing necessity, to be repeated again and again. (1993, pp. 161)

The Reader Is Writer and the Writer Is Reader

> The figure of the hypertext author approaches, even if it does not entirely merge with, that of the reader; the functions of reader and writer become more deeply entwined with each other than ever before. This transformation and near merging of roles is but the latest stage in the convergence of what had once been two very different activities. (Landow, 1992a, p. 71)

As long as you keep (this) text in the electronic medium, you may also change it as you see fit and hand the changes on to others. You may want to indicate that you have changed the text. On the other hand, you may not, but then your readers will probably falsely assume that the original author was responsible for the text you wrote. All readers should be aware that anything in the text may have been added by someone other than the original author. But of course, this caveat applies in a Borgesian way to the previous sentence as well. (Moulthrop, 1994, p. 313)

Root metaphors for the written text and the human activities of reading and writing have, until recently, come from common experience with handwriting, typewriting, and print. The previous section suggested that some of these root metaphors have begun to change and that new pretextual suppositions appropriate to a hypermedia ecosystem are taking shape. Although notions of text, reading, and writing cannot be pulled apart, I want somewhat to shift attention in this section to the activities of reading and writing by considering yet another image of the digital text. When Bolter claims a text accessible on the computer has "no canonical order" (1991, p. 25), he is making the same claim that Moulthrop makes when he calls hypertext simply "distributed textuality" (1989, p. 266). This image of text as "distributed" calls attention to the fact that writers can offer and readers must choose a variety of particular realized constructions. Electronic writers count on active readers, and readers have nothing to read unless they act. In this sense, because it is "distributed," a textual network is an opportunity waiting for human interest and skill to concatenate a particular permutation. Any particular permutation is a preeminently occasional creation or discovery which reflects the participation of the interested reader.

Contemporary society uses distributed databases for many tasks. For the more general purpose of modeling communication, Moulthrop draws, in speaking of "distributed textuality," on the icon of the database. He adapts the technical language and conceptual milieu used to understand databases (e.g., "distributed") in a curiously apt way. From an implementation standpoint, database records use some indexed memory structure so that they can be later located and manipulated as desired. Bolter's claim for the "topographic" character of writing on the computer complements Moulthrop's database imagery. Both suggest the dimensional qualities of a reader's sense of the text and textual work in the culture that is emerging: Digital text and work with digital text is imagined in terms of space much more than in terms of time. Digital text or "distributed textuality" form a set of topics regarded as places or memory locations, which can be selectively combined.

Print, of course, already had spatialized notions of text and textual work. Even in the ancient world, spatializing served to enhance memory, as is pointed out in Carruthers' illuminating discussion of ancient memory which includes the following comment on the tablet or writing space metaphor:

In addition to demonstrating that pre-modern scholars thought of re-membering as a process of mentally visualizing "signals" both of sense objects and objects of thought, this metaphor also shows that the an-cients and their medieval heirs thought that each "bit" of knowledge was remembered in a particular place in the memory, which it occupied as a letter occupies space on a writing surface. (1990, p. 29)

Only a small step separates notions of digitized text as "distributed" resources that require assemblage by users from notions of readers as figures whose activity may include writing. Readers of digitized text may have the option and even be invited to add to or realign what they assemble. The second quotation opening this section playfully suggests the way in which a cultural transition into notions of reader-as-writer seems to be occurring. This passage appears at the beginning of the electronic "version" of Bolter (1991). As Moulthrop notes, this is a copyright notice that hints at the ways in which our ideas about authority and proprietorship are being challenged and transformed in the era of electronic writing (1994, p. 313). It assumes the powers readers have to alter what they receive and puts them on notice to give up some pretextual notions about authorship common in the culture of the book. Of course, not all hypertexts allow readers to alter the network that they originally come to. Some hypertexts are read-only, as opposed to read-write, but it seems likely that more and more electronic materials may allow and even promote the role of reader-as-writer. Michael Joyce distin-guishes "exploratory" from "constructive" hypertexts and his distinction turns on just this point (Joyce, 1988, p. 11; Kolb, 1994, p. 324).

Moulthrop comments that Bolter's copyright notice points to the "re-cursive playfulness" of the electronic medium:

Perhaps even the author-function who warns you about multiple author-ship is other than the one countersigned "Jay David Bolter." Welcome to the text-as-rhizome, where every apparently stable or atomic division of expression can break down to reveal a subtext, some less-that-primal scene of writing. (1994, p. 313)

Lanham also recognizes that reading and writing on the computer not only make text malleable but, in doing so, also change the tacit attitudes of read-ers and writers toward texts, making such attitudes much more flexible: "The intrinsic motival structure of electronic text is as comic as print is serious" (1993, p. 38). As Tuman points out, the playful qualities of elec-tronic text fit seamlessly with the greater sensual richness of integrated digi-tal media; integrated digitized media, sensuous and playful, represent a re-jection of the aesthetics of print. Although there is loss in the demise of the aesthetics of print, there is also a recovery of cultural possibilities in which "reading and writing, experiences of students using computers may well take on a more traditional aesthetic character, with a parallel narrowing of what has been a chasm between literacy and fine arts education" (1992b, p. 127).

Perhaps undermining the rigidity and excessive gravity projected by print will be a positive cultural change felt in the attitudes of readers. However, not all hypertext theorists interpret the playfulness of electronic text as altogether benign and a welcome relief. Tuman suggests that the likely significance for the reader of the cultural shift to hypertext is a rather fundamental change in the nature of reading literature. Additionally, he resists the tendency to identify hypertext as a new kind of text, and thus he remains at odds with figures like Moulthrop who speak of "distributed textuality." He claims "in the midst of all the enthusiasm about hypertext it is too easy to overlook the fact that it is fundamentally a system for retrieving digitized information" (Tuman, 1992b, p. 78). Tuman criticizes other theorists like Slatin for proclaiming that hypertexts are extended books:

> Hypertexts are not really texts at all, not documents prepared by authors to convey a distinct world view to readers; they are systems for storing and retrieving information, in much the same way that an online version of the Library of Congress catalogue is a system for shelving and subsequently locating library materials. (p. 75)

Tuman argues for a more mundane and restricted notion of hypertext, one that he believes will, in effect, preserve some book culture notions about texts because such notions, in turn, will preserve some of the valued activities associated with literature and literary education:

> The central question for hypertext is...whether literacy education in an age fully acculturated into hypertext and online reading will keep such a traditional reading experience at the center of instruction; or put in another way, whether the academic discipline that concentrates on critical and aesthetic reading and writing, instead of information retrieval and report generation, will remain at the center of liberal education.... Is it possible for the ascendancy of hypertext to do anything but push literacy in the direction of information management? (p. 78)

Tuman makes a good case that economic factors will push culture into greater and greater reliance on hypertextually organized digitized materials, and that our development and habituation of online literacy skills will proceed apace. If he is correct about this, it may make little difference whether or not one insists that hypertext is a new kind of text (as some theorists do) or primarily a retrieval system for digitized information. As a theorist, Tuman senses important losses (perhaps more than other hypertext theorists) in the shift from print literacy. Put in another way, he is less confident that the new literacy brings overwhelmingly positive changes. Perhaps his sense of loss is greatest in discussing the change in print culture (actually, high literary print culture) reading experience treated below.

According to Tuman, extended experience with hypertext may make readers unable temporarily to suspend disbelief, and this has been central to appreciative reading of literature in book culture. That is, sensitive reading of literature has been based heretofore upon a reader's ability to take a text seriously as a coherent expression of another person who invokes a coherent world. The reader must transcend his or her own situation in order empathetically to dwell in a fictional world:

> At the center of print literacy has been a single notion of reading, that of one's sustained, close involvement with one text. The task of reading has entailed our understanding this text as the projection of the author's imagination; what we understand in reading is the author's projection of a possible world. Central to print reading is the ability (and willingness) of readers to delay fulfilling their own immediate needs...so that they could participate in...the imaginary world projected in the text—in reading as in play, we forego the demands of the present to live by some other, imaginary rules. (p. 75)

Hypertext reading, however, "denies such an approach to reading by removing the experience of another from the center of the text (which other? which text?) and by giving the reader the real, not just ludic, capacity to change the text" (1992b, p. 76).

I doubt it is possible, as Tuman claims, to have readers who fail altogether to find the experience of another person in texts. Reading or, more generally, semiosis at the level of language, presupposes intentionality. Allowing the reader to become a writer and assigning the reader the task of assembling what is to be read thus cannot fully succeed in "removing the experience of another from the center." Such new habits may mean that the experience of the reader is at the center along with projected experience of another. This is a shift from the culture of the book in which the experience of the reader remained hidden. Socialization in a culture heavily reliant upon electronically accessed hypertext may make readers recognize that the experience of another is not on the surface. Tuman implies hypertext is solipsistic, but surely this is an exaggeration. Literature does depend upon suspending disbelief, but so too does theater, film, and intelligent human response to any symbol. There is a relationship between the "natural" or everyday domain of human practices and the "transnatural" or transnormal domain of human practices which artistic and religious communication relies upon (Polanyi & Prosch, 1975). Tuman's analysis does not seem to have adequately probed the epistemic and aesthetic issues embedded in reading artistic and sacred texts.

The Playfulness of Electronic Media

Although Tuman's account of the fate of the hypertext reader seems somewhat hyperbolic, his analysis does point to some serious and deeply embedded questions about expectation and trust that are bound up with the transition from print culture's pretextual notions of the roles of reader and writer. The playfulness of electronic media will hopefully not slide into a larger loss of faith in the written electronic word. Moulthrop's "recursive playfulness" and a helpful attitudinal destabilization of the printed word are, in the final analysis, parasitical upon cultural attitudes which regard the written word as faithful, as capable of articulating human solicitude.

Some deconstructionist talk about "play" and the "play of signs" seems little more than a happy-faced nihilism. As I discuss below, I believe that it remains an important cultural task to work out a careful new understanding about how the truthful continues to be a part of digitized discourse. But I remain somewhat troubled by the way in which some commentators present "digital playfulness." Bolter's copyright notice and Moulthrop's praise of it celebrate the Borgesian, undependable elements. When does one cross the line between play and irresponsibility? Communication does have moral dimensions and we cannot altogether ignore them in the name of liberation from the hierarchies and the Apollonian elements of print culture. Finally, it is also disturbing to hear so frequently that the culture of print has no play. As Tuman points out, "print too has its games—puns, anagrams, riddles, and the like—but they have a minimal sensual component" (1992b, p. 127).

Certainly, the new ludic mode invited by digitized media often appears in the posture of electronic writers. Informality prevails in fluid writing; electronic writing, and especially that done on the Internet and in networked classrooms, acquires a dialogic quality because redaction and response are easy and can become central activities:

> Texts can be readily moved and copied and, depending on the software used, a multitude of "typed" comments and responses can be attached, creating a situation where the original text begins to be seen less as the primary focus of concern and more as the occasion for an extended dialogue among interested parties. (p. 89)

But the underside of malleable text is a suspicious disposition toward texts. Wise readers don't quite know how much to trust what surfaces on the Internet, but this is also true of many printed documents. The institutional structures that developed in print culture which led to trust in the book and printed word (and even beyond basic trust to silly notions that books always speak authoritatively) barely exist in cyberspace. But such institutional structures are slowly arising.

The playfulness of electronic writing also connects with the fact that digital writers are very self-consciously readers and recyclers of what has been already written. In this sense, a culture shaped by electronic writing resembles a primary oral culture: Much is or can be recycled. Electronic writers are folk for whom keeping files of florilegia is easy. The writing of others, as well as one's own words, can be easily manipulated and sent forth again. The resources available to mine electronically are thus more irresistible than resources available in print. Cutting and pasting, organizing in modules whose order is now recognized as less than eternal, "publishing" such material in one of the several ways the electronic environment offers—these are the activities of electronic writing, and they make writers less self-important than the process of writing in the culture of the book. These are activities that move in the direction of merging the reader and writer roles, as the quotation from Landow opening this section indicates. Relaxation of the distinction between reader and writer brings with it some of the changes identified in the previous section as the fragmentation of canons:

> If the distinction between author and reader were indeed eliminated, one would also have to discard any sense of textual identity or hierarchy, at least in absolute terms. Since the hyperdocument would always be in flux, it could not be constituted as a series of discursive stabilities but would in actual fact represent a smooth space constantly reconfigured by lines of flight. (Moulthrop, 1994, pp. 305-306)

Moulthrop's figure of a "smooth space constantly reconfigured" is a geometric figure. The activity of writing in the electronic medium is highly interactive, and thus, as Moulthrop puts it, the conjoint writing project, the hyperdocument, is never really complete. The written is no longer a stable point as it appeared in print culture, but it is an emerging trajectory.

After Thoughts: Facing the Music on the CRT

> What, if anything, are we in danger of losing—or conversely, what might we gain when students in large numbers and eventually people throughout society begin "writing," not just by linking items in a database or conversing online, but by integrating words with pictures, moving as well as still, and sounds? (Tuman, 1992b, pp. 116-117)

> The seemingly straightforward question "Should we care about the transformation of literacy" quickly leads to a series of probing, troubling questions about our individual and collective attitudes toward where we have been, where we are now, and where we seem to be heading. Print literacy is an expression of the best and the worst of the intellectual dimension of modern, industrial culture, just as online literacy seems to promise (or threaten) us with the best and the worst possibilities of a postmodern, post-industrial world. (pp. 117)

Perhaps more than most who have thought hard about the cultural importance of hypertext and hypermedia, Tuman has a sense both of the loss and the opportunities which digitized media are bringing. We must care about the transformation of literacy and face those troubling questions about our past and our future that Tuman and others recognize as now becoming visible as we move more decisively into a computer-mediated culture. The discussion that follows in this final section attempts to gather up several of the themes treated above concerned with human meaning-making in a hypermedia ecosystem. I have argued that both our thinking about and our performance in the process of meaning-making is shifting as we move away from a culture dominated by print. What bearing do such changes have upon human religiousness and religious meaning? Since this chapter appears as part of the background study of the ABS's Multimedia Translations Project, I focus my effort to draw together previous discussions around this issue.

Making Meaning in an Electronic Culture

In a culture dominated by print one could objectify and think of meaning as fully external, as determined and present in the printed text waiting to be extracted. But such a non-relational way of approaching meaning does not seem plausible in a world in which a reader clearly acts self-consciously to generate whatever is to be negotiated and identified as meaningful. In an electronic environment, the meaningful has a fluidity about it. The meaningful appears and disappears and shifts. Meaning in an electronic environment arises from a relation between elements that an interested party brings together at a particular time. Only with difficulty can meaning be construed as in some sense final and outside a temporal frame. It is more difficult to imagine meaning as absolute (the last word) or unequivocal in a context where one node leads inevitably to another. With regard to the temporary nature of closure in an electronic environment, Landow thus summarizes the new ambience: "In contrast to print technology, which foregrounds the physical separateness of each text, hypertext reifies the connections between works and thus presents each work as fundamentally connected to others" (1992b, p. 71).

Meaning in an electronic context also has a known participative quality concerned with directing human attention to bear upon a focal interest. Human beings are more clearly creatures with attention and attention span in an electronic culture; meaning is bound up with attention, but there is much latitude about that to which persons can attend. Given the enormous communicative opportunities available in an electronic web of some scope—or Nelson's "docuverse" (1992, p. 53)—we cannot help but recognize that choice and responsibility are central to meaning-making. But to emphasize choice and responsibility is not just a move to "subjectivize" meaning and meaning-making. The dualisms subjective/objective and internal/external are frameworks that seem to work more naturally for discussing meaning in the culture of print where texts occupy space and cannot shift before your eyes. The objects of computer-mediated communication are clearly creations or constructions of attentive subjects, but they are also authentic discoveries. They are not less real or less significant because we participate in their coming to presence, and such objects are always potentially present and interesting for other subjects.

These shifts in the cultural sense of meaning will inevitably have some bearing upon the appropriation of what can be described as the transcending and transforming communicative artifacts which traditionally have offered comprehensive levels of meaning—that is, religious meaning. It seems likely that the tendency to objectify and reify meaning in sacred texts, a move frequently made in religious communities in the last century of the era of print, will not prosper in the culture shaped more profoundly by the computer as a communication device. Objectifying and reifying habits of thought were present in late print culture in North America in both fundamentalist biblical literalism and in so-called higher criticism of the Bible (Mullins, 1996b). Wilfred Cantwell Smith calls fundamentalism a "modern aberration" that confuses what he terms transcendence and the mundane concrete. Fundamentalism "treats the Scripture in one's hand almost as if it determined the absolute, rather than *vice versa*" (1993, p. 235). Smith points to the fact that biblical literalism effectively captures the transcendent in the Christian text rather than imagining the transcendent as in some way broader and yet manifest in Scripture. The framework of plausibility that could entertain such a reversal of the longer history of many traditions owes a debt to print which fixes and externalizes texts in a way never possible before print. Interestingly, a curious sort of literalism about the sacred text occurs also in much higher (often called "scientific") biblical criticism that was, until recently, largely historicist in orientation. Such scholarship sought diligently to find the meaning of the text in an original or earliest social context. Such "original" meaning was affirmed as of primary importance. This orientation toward original meaning should be understood in terms of the character of print culture or at least its proliferation of texts. In such an environment of proliferation, the matter of linking text, even sacred text, with a concrete historical first context could appear as the proper approach to meaning.

It seems likely that the problematizing of meaning in sacred text which has occurred in the last century will be less a problem in a cultural environment shaped more definitively by hypermedia. Book culture nurtured historical consciousness, but a culture in which hypermedia is important may not sustain this emphasis. At the least, electronic alternatives to the book will make less plausible a narrow sort of historicism. Those socialized in an electronic writing environment find a pluralistic orientation toward meaning normal. A critical self-consciousness about the meaning-making process emerges in an electronic writing environment. Such self-consciousness insists upon the recognition that a text, even a sacred one, is more than simply the presence of an author. At the least, there is awareness that the reader's own imagination and interests are present and important in meaning-making.

Issues of Canon

In a culture in which computer-mediated communication is significant, several factors resist the objectification of textual hierarchies or canons which were so prominently a part of book culture (Fowler, 1993). In the first place, the way in which meaning-making works in an electronic environment constantly pulls materials together rather than allowing, as in the case of printed volumes, material to have independent standing. One attends to the center (on the screen) but this links with much that is not present but can become focal. There is an infinitely re-centerable quality in an electronic environment for meaning-making. Given the potentially vast scope of possible linkages in an electronic web, a conceptual emphasis upon connection or inclusion emerges rather than one upon disjunction or exclusion. Relationships or potential relationships become tacitly presupposed. But the kind of emphasis upon relation in an integrated, interactive environment puts texts together on a horizontal plane rather than in a hierarchy.

Many religious communities have long had established sacred textual traditions that set the canonical off from the non-canonical. In western culture, earlier communication technologies have had significant impacts upon the ways in which the sacred text was received in a community and a culture. The relation of the canonical to the non-canonical has in part been established by the technology through which the religiously meaningful texts were created. The decorated Bibles of manuscript culture evoked an awe that mass produced paperback Bibles cannot. But mass produced paperbacks literally and metaphorically contribute to notions that the Bible is accessible and even transparent. Paperbacks, because of sheer numbers, help make the canonical sacred text recognizable or identifiable. They thereby reinforce the canonical/noncanonical distinction.

It remains unclear how the new electronic writing environment will affect the idea of canon as it operates in religious literature. Already in late print culture, the class roughly termed popular religious literature included much more than the canonical sacred text. It included all sorts of study aids, inspirational material (some of it audio and/or video taped), and devotional literature. Within particular subcultural communities, some of this literature acquired near canonical status insofar as its use became very popular and even normative. Recently, the contours of popular religious literature have expanded, adding computer-accessed resources. "Religious literature," electronic or print, indeed forms a market exploited with all the skill that resourceful capitalists can muster in North America. The appetite for what sells under the rubric "religious literature" is voracious. A recent newspaper article on the 1993 trade show of the Christian Booksellers Association indicated that annual Bible sales are more than $400 million. There are now available 450 English versions of the Bible including "niche Bibles" produced for specialized audiences such as athletes, women, pregnant women, environmentalists, and recovering alcoholics, to name a few (White, 1993).

Perhaps because of the seeming immutability and physicality of the printed word, western culture for some time had a tendency to think of language, especially written religious language, as having a rather narrow informative function. Sam Gill, an expert in native American religion and culture, argues that this tendency has created a narrowness in the study of religion:

When asking the "meaning" of a sign or sign event that principally performs as act to change the world, if meaning is equated with a semantical-referential sense, comprehension and intelligibility are nearly impossible. The study of religion has commonly put itself in just this position. (1987, p. 162)

Gill also suggests that more attention needs to be paid to the performative aspects of signs if there is to be recognition of richer notions of religious meaning: "Signs occur to perform—that is, to affect others, to manipulate the world, to create results. Indeed, even the aspect of signs that informs is but a type of performative function" (p. 162).

Gill's work, which is indebted to J. L. Austin and speech act philosophy, as well as to the work of C. S. Peirce on semiotics, raises an important point related to my earlier criticisms of Bolter's view of virtual reality. There I pointed also to Peircian semiotics, which I find a rich perspective that emphasizes the ways in which signs produce an ongoing cycle of effects in a community. Peirce's ideas in part lie behind what I term below an orientation to meaning as process. Peirce's semiotics is, however, anchored in his philosophical realism. I suggest in this section that computer-mediated communication can provide culture with a richer sense of meaning, but that this potential will be fulfilled only if we rediscover ways to speak of truth and reality.

In a communicative environment in which the computer plays a major role, it seems very likely that more performative notions of the sign will become accepted as the norm. This is perhaps already present in the skepticism that attends the reception of many messages in contemporary culture. It frequently seems sensible to ask self-consciously what effect is trying to be created in me (receptivity toward a product, sympathy for a political candidate, for example) in a consumer society awash with information. But a deeper sense of the power of signs to produce effects does not necessarily need to lead to cynicism.

Authority, Truth, Reality

A culture more deeply shaped by integrated, interactive digitized media is one in which inhabitants will acquire more relational, participative, and performative tacit suppositions that inform meaning-making. It seems likely that such an environment will need to develop new ways to think about authority, truth, and reality. It must clarify how these matters bear upon communicative artifacts that function to provide religious meaning. These concerns about authority, truth, and reality are, of course, philosophical issues and not particularly new ones. They have been part of the ongoing great conversation in western history that took place as media ecosystems evolved.

Neil Postman contends that "every epistemology is an epistemology of a stage of media development" (1985, p. 24). The suggestion that these philosophical issues need renewed discussion is to say no more than emerging electronic culture needs to work out its epistemology more carefully. During the age of print, much of the conversation about religious authority and truth has revolved around, in diverse combinations, three poles: powerful and sometimes autocratic religious institutions, enlightened (reasoning) individuals, and a sacred text proclaimed and regarded (often naively) as sufficient. Already it is clear that a conversation so oriented misses the mark. Inhabitants of computer-mediated culture will likely not be satisfied to approach questions about authority and truth quite so immodestly as thinkers in print culture have. They will hesitate to grant an institution, a reasoning subject, or a sacred book the privilege of decreeing, in the universal mode, what is and ought to be. Experience with interactive, integrated electronic media cultivates the sense that human signifying activity is continual and infinitely rich; notions about authority and truth must in some way incorporate this processive element. Simple ideas about correspondence lack dynamism and lose credibility in a non-print world. Truth may be more concerned with understanding and respecting the relationality of elements and the fecundity of the process than with correspondence. In such a world one must discover and clarify how loyalty and commitment, being true, fit within an orientation to meaning as process. One must discover ways in which truth is inevitably a corporate and tradition-grounded enterprise, even as it also is a transforming enterprise. In sum, it seems extraordinarily important that a culture reliant upon digitized media learn anew how to speak of truth as it resides in signs (i.e., in a community's use of signs). The electronically mediated, malleable, and sensuously rich sign is not a threat. But neither can it be much of an opportunity until the veridical potentials of such signs become clearer to the inhabitants of a culture in which such signs proliferate.

Questions about truth and authority in a social environment shaped by computer-mediated communication connect closely to questions about the nature of the real. A culture that relies upon digitized communications (as a primary context for meaning-making) needs a clear and philosophically sophisticated sense of what reality is. Questions about the real take on a new urgency in computer-mediated culture. In the culture of print, reality was most frequently identified with the external and the tangible, while high praise also went to human socially constructed realities. This bifurcated way of mapping the cosmos seems less apt in a world in which the computer can offer such richness, brilliance, and pliability—Albert Borgmann's fitting summary terms for what the computer brings. He, however, finds the world produced by the computer very likely to be a world of only disposable and discontinuous experience; it is then a specter which he terms "hyperreal" (1992, p. 118). Although Borgmann's skepticism about the potential of the computer runs too deep, he does suggest, in a way similar to my argument, that contemporary society in the early phase of computer-mediated culture needs to rediscover realism. He speaks of the "eloquent reality" of "focal things" that have "commanding presence, continuity with the world, and centering power." Such things "warrant themselves" (pp. 119-120).

In an era of print and of fixed and visible words, philosophical talk of the real often seemed to emphasize the word and human capacities for using and creating with language. But it appears that computer-mediated culture needs an ontological geography that more carefully delineates the reality of abstract entities, while at the same time helping humans remember their own socio-temporal and natural locations and possibilities. Heim speaks of certain important "hooks on the reality anchor" (1993, p. 136) that he thinks appropriate in a culture in which virtual reality technology is important. His "hooks" are human mortality, the carryover between past and future in the human world, and human care (pp. 136-137). I am suggesting something similar but perhaps with a greater emphasis upon the natural and social, that is, historical, cultural, and tradition-situated ecology of human life. In any event, a sufficiently rich understanding of the real can serve as an important support for human efforts to discern meaning, particularly religious meaning, in computer-mediated culture.

Phil Mullins teaches in an interdisciplinary humanities program at Missouri Western State College in St. Joseph, MO, bringing together topics in philosophy, religious studies, and cultural history. He earned his Ph.D. at the Graduate Theological Union, Berkeley, with a dissertation treating the thought of Michael Polanyi. Recent professional papers and articles have focused on topics in philosophy and on cultural changes brought by the computer. Since 1991, he has edited *Tradition and Discovery*, the journal of the Polanyi Society. He is active in the American Academy of Religion and the Polanyi Society and has been the recipient of numerous grants from the National Endowment for the Humanities.

From One Medium
to Another

Postlude

From One Medium to Another

Ronald W. Roschke

As a summary document, this chapter attempts to create a portrait of the "state of the art" with specific reference to issues in communication theory, translation, arts, technology, and the Bible. Viewing this material alongside the American Bible Society's work in multimedia translation enables us to use this ongoing project as a laboratory for considering these topics. Finally this chapter describes an agenda for further research and reflection and comments on how the results of this Symposium might influence the future course of biblical multimedia translation.

An American Bible Society Symposium

The 17 chapters that make up the American Bible Society's (ABS) Symposium on multimedia translation point us toward an amazing future that already appears on the horizon. My assignment was to react to this material and to the discussion which the authors had over the course of the two-day Symposium. Here, I will attempt to create a portrait of the "state of the art" with specific reference to issues in communication theory, translation, arts, technology, and the Bible.

There are two overall impressions that I have from the Symposium. First, I sense that the electronic landscape is far more complicated than I had previously imagined. The emergence of a culture built around electronic texts will profoundly shape new understandings of the Bible, literacy, narrative, truth, reality, and roles of "author" and "reader." Entirely new ways of processing information will appear, and other ways of thinking about and handling knowledge will become strangely problematic in ways in which we never encountered them before. But for all this strangeness, these chapters also reveal a surprising familiarity and continuity with the past. We might actually discover that the Bible and communities of faith built around it have been "multimedia" for a long, long time.

Communication

Paul Soukup's chapter invites all of us to start paying more attention to the relationship of message and audience. He illustrates how, early in the era of mass media, much of the research and reflection on electronic hermeneutic thought of messages as if they were a kind of "magic bullet" which could be shot into a mass audience, where the message would automatically accomplish its intention. Only later did theorists and researchers become more sensitized to the active role of audiences and begin to reflect on how electronic audiences participate and evaluate the information they are receiving from the mass media.

But why this shift? I suspect that it is a reflection of the media shift that our culture was going through in these years, as the pre-understanding of print culture slowly evolved into our more contemporary notions of electronic culture. Scholarship went through a transition just as the culture did. The world of print and print culture seduced western civilization for centuries into ignoring many important aspects of communication. The emerging electronic culture is helping us to be sensitized again to realities that for centuries we have forgotten.

Long ago, when language passed out of face-to-face conversations and communication first went into writing, then into manuscript, and yet later into print, the immediacy of language slowly was forgotten. Surrounded by manuscripts and books, people began to imagine that communication was a "thing" and language was an "object." Think of how writing takes the dynamic interchange that happens in conversation and turns it into something that can be manipulated, held in your hand, stored on a shelf, sent through the mail. Karen Blixen's marvelous book *Out of Africa* (1938) includes a story about how she once wrote down a statement for Jogona, a man who worked for her. Jogona was unable to read or write. His statement was prepared for presentation to the District Commissioner in a case involving a shooting accident on the farm. When she finished taking down the statement, Blixen presented the document to Jogona for his verification. Blixen says that Jogona gave her "a great fierce flaming glance":

> Such a glance did Adam give the Lord when He formed him out of the dust, and breathed into his nostrils the breath of life, and man became a living soul. I had created him and shown him himself: Jogona Kanyagga of life everlasting. When I handed him the paper, he took it reverently and greedily, folded it up in a corner of his cloak and kept his hand upon it. He could not afford to lose it, for his soul was in it, and it was the proof of his existence. Here was something which Jogona Kanyagga had performed, and which would preserve his name forever: The flesh was made word and dwelt among us full of grace and truth. The importance of the account was not lessened but augmented with time, as if to Jogona the greatest wonder about it was that it did not change. The past, that had been so difficult to bring to memory, and that had probably seemed to be changing every time it was thought of, had here been

caught, conquered, and pinned down before his eyes. It had become History; with it there was now no variableness neither shadow of turning. (p. 124)

This is what happens when words get written down and printed. And this objectification of language becomes so normative for us that we cannot help but think of language in this way. The electronic flux of communication helps to turn language "objects" back into linguistic events, and in this transformation the role of the audience becomes much more intense.

This brings us to a second insight about communication. Electronic culture will make us more aware that all communication is interactive. Perhaps we tend to think that it is electronic technology that is creating interactive communication, but these essays help to demonstrate that interactive communication has a long history. In fact, this ought to have been obvious all along! If you are going to communicate, you are by definition already involved in being interactive. Books are interactive, not just computers. A book sitting as an object on a shelf does not "do" anything. It is only really a book when you begin to pick it up and read it and relate to it; then it serves as communication. And in reading you begin to enter into dialogue with a book.

As members of the Symposium watched Alice Bach's film, we gave a good illustration of how audiences create meaning. The film elicited giggles and reactions from those of us watching. Think about going to a movie and how you and those around you together create the meaning of that event. That is interactive communication. But it can just as easily happen in book discussion groups or living room conversations. In fact, every performance of a text is a new creation that creates new meaning.

A third insight: Language is always being created anew. Descriptive translation studies, introduced to us in these pages by José Lambert and Patrick Cattrysse, may encourage us to wonder whether perhaps all communication is not really translation. Translation is needed when you have a message that is somehow "locked up" and needs to be "unlocked" in order to be understood. But that is exactly what goes on in every communication, because all communication flows out of consciousness. Each of us lives in our own "virtual reality," our personal, private consciousness. But that consciousness is a "bubble" in which each of us is totally isolated. I cannot let you into my consciousness, and you cannot let me experience yours directly. I may see an object or see the color blue, and you may see it as well, but I don't know what your blue is like. You don't know what mine is like. I need to somehow translate my consciousness into your consciousness. Thus, in translation we are actually doing something which is a part of every act of communication.

Art

What is "new" in electronic text is the reintegration of sight and sound elements back into communication. Art, then, bears a unique and important relationship to electronic text and electronic hermeneutic. Since hermeneutics came into being through the creation and analysis of written texts, an electronic hermeneutic would need to reflect upon what happens to "text" when sight and sound are added to it.

In creating the first three interactive video translations of the New Testament, the multimedia translations team of the ABS had to struggle with imaging the text. This struggle has included a variety of issues to be decided and selected:

- Translation of the ancient story into a contemporary visual story line.
- Selection and design of the interactive "world" in which the translation or transmediazation is embedded.
- Selection and design of accompanying graphics.
- Translation of linguistic elements of the written text into visual images or the decision to leave linguistic elements unrepresented by visual images.

Electronic texts are also sound events. An electronic hermeneutic needs to account for the way in which sound modifies communication as we pass from written text to communication event.

Here, too, the ABS multimedia translations team has had to contend with several different acoustic issues:

- Translating the Greek into a spoken English text.
- Determining how that text will be heard; for example, as speech, as chant, as song.
- The quality of that voice, its inflections and tone.
- The nature of the music and its relation both to the original text and the visual images which now accompany it.
- The presence of a soundscape in creating an interpretive horizon.
- The possibility of the use of silence and its meaning.

Although the inclusion of sight and sound creates new challenges for multimedia translators, the essays in this volume indicate that art is both an "old" and a "new" element in biblical texts and translations. For centuries, stained glass and chant existed alongside a manuscript tradition. In biblical languages accents occurred as musical intonation rather than as stress, as in modern English. Biblical language was thus always a musical reality, and in this way multimedia returns us back to our biblical roots. Once again, our print orientation blinded us to many important elements of the biblical texts.

Elizabeth Keen's essay and visuals on ballet marvelously illustrate how dance combines the "old way" of tradition with "new" innovation of gesture.

Synchronic tropes, which have been used for centuries along with classical positions and movements, are modified by new gesture, as when, for instance, Balanchine has the younger son in *The Prodigal Son* pound his thigh to show rebellion.

Gregor Goethals' paper also demonstrates that while multimedia texts radically open the visual dimensions of biblical communication, they really do nothing more than return the community of faith back to our ocular roots. Print orientation blinded biblical scholarship to icon and art. Goethals's keen analysis of how the role of artist has changed through history is echoed in the collaborative electronic approaches described by Reg Pettus.

There are a great many theoretical problems that will need to be resolved as we make our way into an electronic hermeneutic. The interaction of sight and sound in semantic space is filled with difficult and thorny challenges. Here are just a few of the issues that we will need to address:

- How is information processed aurally/orally? How is information processed visually? How do these processes relate to the traditional hermeneutics of writing?

- What new possibilities and problems are created by placing a linguistic track beside audio and video tracks in multimedia texts? How can translators, writers, and artists use the reinforcement and the interference patterns of these complex relationships to create meaning effects? Paying attention to oral communication, in which sight and sound are already wed to semantic content, will provide many clues for creating an electronic hermeneutic.

- What is happening to traditional canons of art and music criticism as text is wed with sight and sound? How do changes in the means of production alter the rules by which meaning is created?

We need to recognize the importance of this moment. The electronic revolution means for us the recovery of an ancient synthesis of information and experience. Long ago in oral culture, information was visual and auditory and experiential all at the same time; communication was music, song, dance, gesture all together. For a millennium now, these elements have been divorced from each other. Now they are coming back together again. In a multimedia world, textual scholars will need to learn how to speak and move through the arts. This will prove to be both a challenging and exciting aspect of our work in the decades ahead!

Technology

Those who attended the conference discovered an exciting world with incredibly broad horizons opening up. Glorianna Davenport's glimpse of the Reality Engine and Gregory Schreve's impressive demonstrations of virtual reality help us to sense how electronic landscapes are going to continue to develop and unfold.

These new technological advances will challenge many established linguistic and textual notions and will create new problems and possibilities for biblical studies. Not the least of these developments will be an unavoidable shift in how we think of narrative. Up to this point, I have always experienced narrative as being "led through a story," having someone else leading me. If electronic technologies begin to give me, the "reader," control of that, I do not know what will eventually happen to our notion of narrativity. Perhaps narrative as we know it will simply disappear. It is hard to overestimate the cultural implications of such a shift! But I do find some new intriguing ideas, when Davenport implies, for example, that an index is really a narrative. This is a very creative and engaging metaphor. It suggests that in indexing a database, for example, I am giving an information system a "narrative" by which it can be understood. And if that is the case, could it also be true that a narrative is an index? And if a narrative is an index, then perhaps there may be multiple ways of organizing biblical materials. A diachronic "stringing" of them together may be only one arrangement. What happens if we begin to think of new kinds of narratives, new kinds of indices by which to take biblical elements and allow users to come up with new ways of combining them? That is a radical departure from what we are used to thinking about, but the new technologies may really encourage us to think that way.

When it comes to technology I think that we are going to need to talk about the issue of control more and more. Who is in control? What are the parameters of control? How does control happen? But again, this is an "old/new" reality. If communication has always been interactive, then it must also be true that the control of communication has been interactive as well. Even in highly hierarchial cultures, people have participated together in the interactive creation of meaning. For some that has meant saying "No" to a text. Sometimes one could say "No" to a text publicly, and sometimes one had to say "No" to a text very, very silently or just simply resist it. This has really constituted part of our textual history all along.

I think another reality that will become increasingly important in electronic culture is the matter of economics. There is a new economic imperialism with which all of us must deal. Economics plays a vital role in the production of film, television, and our own biblical multimedia translations. Multimedia texts are expensive and complicated to produce. But even more, I am convinced that economics is the new gatekeeper for the information age, replacing the academy and the university just as those institutions replaced the church at the time of the Reformation era and the advent of the print revolution. Economic factors will need to become an increasingly important part of our analysis and discussion.

Part of this new economic reality must be tied to a resolute conviction about continuing to fuse scholarly reflection with the production of materials and prototypes. This firm conviction on the part of ABS needs to continue to be affirmed into the future. It has been absolutely essential in this project that those who are doing theory also create hands-on programs that finally end up in the marketplace. Translation studies show us that we need to fuse together theoretical issues, research issues, and production issues; all of them need to be together, and people need to be working in all three areas simultaneously.

Bible

During the Symposium, the papers in this volume generated some lively discussion about faithfulness. What does it mean to be faithful to a sacred text? How will communities of faith be faithful to their traditions and faithful to God's Word in an electronic world? These are new questions and issues biblical scholars must address. Yes, we sense that faithfulness is an issue, but faithfulness to what? We who are involved in biblical studies need to continue to define what it is we are actually translating. Are we translating the words that are written down on a page? Are we translating the sound of a text as it may have been spoken in ancient communities of faith? Is it the experience of the story as it may have been told before it went into writing? Each or any of those, or all of them, may actually be part of the reality of the Bible. But what you choose as your starting point will determine whether you have produced a faithful translation or not.

Regular worship attenders know and can think of experiences in which they have sat in a community of faith, hearing somebody read word for word the text of a faithful translation; because some readers do not know the first thing about public speaking, they slaughtered the text. There was no silence, no pregnant pauses. The words were all there, but was it a faithful translation? Or, does faithful translation require that attention be paid to sound? And if it requires that, does it not require an attention to gesture, to color, to movement, to all kinds of realities that have been closed off to us for centuries because we have been so immersed in print culture? Yes, we want to be faithful, but we may have to radically broaden the notion of what that faithfulness might include.

This Symposium was at one and the same time exhilarating and scary. We are about to enter a strange new world far different from anything that has come before. And some of this new world feels like an echo from the past. Much of it seems foreign and uncharted. Those who took part in this Symposium had a chance to look into this landscape.

Ronald Roschke is pastor of Grace Lutheran Church in Boulder, CO. He is a pastor of the Evangelical Lutheran Church in America and has served congregations in Kansas and New York City. He has been a member of the multimedia translations research team of the American Bible Society since its inception in 1990. His major area of focus in the multimedia project is theory development and electronic hermeneutic.

References

Ackerman, J. S. (1969). The demise of the avant-garde. *L'Arte, 6,* 4-17.

Ackerman, J. S. (1973). Judgments of value. In J. D. Farquhar (Ed.), *Studies in art history: Presented at the Middle Atlantic Symposium in the history of art, 1971-73* (pp. 34-35). College Park: University of Maryland.

Allen, F. L. (1931). *Only yesterday.* New York: Harper & Row.

Applewhite, H. L. (1992). Position tracking in virtual reality. In S. K. Helsel (Ed.), *The technology, research and business of virtual reality* (pp. 1–8). Westport, CT: Meckler.

Aristotle. (1958). *On poetry and style* (G. M. A. Grube, Trans.). New York: Bobbs-Merrill.

Aristotle. (1994). *The art of rhetoric* (J. H. Freese, Trans.). Cambridge, MA: Harvard University Press.

Ashton, J. (1994). *Studying John: Approaches to the fourth gospel.* Oxford: Clarendon.

Atwan, A., & Wieder, L. (Eds.). (1993). *Chapters into verse.* New York: Oxford University Press.

Auden, W. H. (1959). Calm even in the catastrophe. *Encounter, 12,* 37-40.

Avenary, H. (1963). *Studies in the Hebrew, Syrian and Greek liturgical recitative.* Tel-Aviv: Israel Music Institute.

Babington, B., & Evans, P. W. (1993). *Biblical epics: Sacred narrative in the Hollywood cinema.* Manchester: Manchester University Press.

Bakker, M. (1995). Vertalen in Cratylië. In H. Bloemen, E. Hertog, & W. Segers (Eds.), *Letterlijkheid, woordelijkheid* [Literality, verbality] (pp. 15-36). Antwerpen: Fantom.

Balanchine, G. (1954). *Balanchine's new complete stories of the great ballets.* (F. Mason, Ed.). Garden City, NY: Doubleday.

Balusubramanian, V. (1994). *State of the art review on hypermedia issues and applications* [On-line]. Available: http://www.zgdv.de/www/zgdvuig/papers/multimedia/hypermedia_ review/index.html

Barbiero, D. (1991, January-February). Jenni Lukac: Votive shrine. *Art Papers, 64.*

Barker, A. (1984). *Greek musical writings.* New York: Cambridge University Press.

Barnouw, E. (1970). *The image empire: A history of broadcasting in the United States*. (Vol. 3). New York: Oxford University Press.

Barr, J. (1961). *The semantics of biblical language*. Oxford: Oxford University Press.

Barth, K. (1968). *The epistle to the Romans* (E. C. Hoskyns, Trans.). Oxford: Oxford University Press. (Original work published 1918)

Barthes, R. (1975). *S/Z* (R. Miller, Trans.). London: Cape. (Original work published 1970)

Baudrillard, J. (1983). *Simulations*. New York: Semiotext(e) Inc.

Beaugrande, R. de, & Dressler, W. (1981). *Introduction to text linguistics*. London: Longman.

Bebbington, D. (1989). *Evangelicalism in modern Britain: A history from the 1730s to the 1980s*. London: Unwin Hyman.

Belting, H. (1987). *The end of the history of art?* (C. S. Wood, Trans.). Chicago: University of Chicago Press. (Original work published 1983)

Belting, H. (1994). *Likeness and presence: A history of the image before the era of art* (E. Jephcott, Trans.). Chicago: University of Chicago Press. (Original work published 1990)

Betti, E. (1962). *Die Hermeneutik als allgemeine Methodik der Geisteswissenschaften*. Tübingen: Mohr (Siebeck).

Biocca, F. A. (1988). Opposing conceptions of the audience: The active and passive hemispheres of mass communication theory. In J. A. Anderson (Ed.), *Communication yearbook/11* (pp. 51-80). Newbury Park, CA: Sage.

Biocca, F. A. (1993). Communication design in virtual reality. In S. K. Helsel (Ed.), *VR becomes a business* (pp. 16–37). Westport, CT: Meckler.

Blixen, K. (1938). *Out of Africa*. New York: Random House.

Blumberg, B. M., & Galyean, T. A. (1995). Multi-level direction of autonomous creatures for real-time virtual environments. *Computer Graphics-Proceedings 1995, 47-54*.

Blumhofer, E. L. (1993a). *Aimee Semple McPherson: Everybody's sister.* Library of Religious Biography, 5. Grand Rapids, MI: Eerdmans.

Blumhofer, E. L. (1993b). *Restoring the faith: The Assemblies of God, Pentecostalism and American culture.* Urbana and Chicago: University of Illinois Press.

Bolter, J. D. (1984). *Turing's man: Western culture in the computer age.* Chapel Hill: University of North Carolina Press.

Bolter, J. D. (1991). *Writing space: The computer, hypertext, and the history of writing.* Hillsdale, NJ: Erlbaum.

Bonnell, J. S. (1935). The Bible and the blind. *Bible Society Record, 80*, 154-155.

Boomershine, T. E. (1993a). Biblical megatrends: Towards a paradigm for the interpretation of the Bible in electronic media. In H. C. Kee (Ed.),

The Bible in the twenty-first century (pp. 209-230). Philadelphia: Trinity Press International.

Boomershine, T. E. (1993b). Response to R. Harley, "New media: The potential and the problems." In H. C. Kee (Ed.), *The Bible in the twenty-first century* (pp. 179-184). Philadelphia: Trinity Press International.

Borgmann, A. (1992). *Crossing the postmodern divide.* Chicago: University of Chicago Press.

Bourdieu, P. (1994). *Raisons pratiques: Pour une théorie de l'action.* Paris: Seuil.

Bratcher, R. G. (1995). Current trends in translation. *The Bible Translator, 46*(4), 439-444.

Bricken, W. (1992). A formal foundation for cyberspace. In S. K. Helsel (Ed.), *The technology, research and business of virtual reality* (pp. 9–35). Westport, CT: Meckler.

Brockway, M. (1995). Notes for *Prodigal son.* [Video]. Nonesuch Records.

Brookman, P. (1992). The Politics of hope: Sites and sounds of memory. In *Sites of recollection: Four altars and a rap opera* (pp. 14-42). Williamstown, MA: Williams College Museum of Art.

Brown, M. E. (1994). *Soap opera and women's talk: The pleasures of resistance.* Thousand Oaks, CA: Sage.

Brown, R. E., Fitzmyer, J. A., & Murphy, R. E. (Eds.). (1990). *The new Jerome biblical commentary.* Englewood Cliffs, NJ: Prentice-Hall.

Buffum, H. (1926). *A radio station for Jesus.* [sheet music] Topeka, KS: Anderson Printing & Music.

Bukofzer, M. F. (1947). *Music in the Baroque.* New York: W. W. Norton.

Bultmann, R. (1960). Is exegesis without presuppositions possible? In S. M. Ogden (Ed.), *Existence and faith: Shorter writings of Rudolf Bultmann* (pp. 289-96). New York: World Publishing, Meridian.

Burke, D. G. (1993). Translating Scripture into electronic media. *The Bible Translator, 44*(3), 101-111.

Burke, D. G., Wosh, P. J., & Goostree, L. (1992). The Bible in the twenty-first century: Confronting the frontier. In W. Forker (Ed.), *The future agenda: Festschrift for John Templeton* (pp. 16-38). Edinburgh: Hanover Press.

Busch, E. (1976). *Karl Barth: His life and letters and autobiographical texts* (J. Bowden, Trans.). Philadelphia: Fortress Press. (Original work published 1975)

Bush, V. (1945, July). As we may think. *The Atlantic Monthly* [On-line]. Available: http://www.csi.uottawa.ca/~dduchier/misc/vbush/as-we-may-think.txt

Calkins, R. G. (1983). *Illuminated books of the middle ages.* Ithaca, NY: Cornell University Press.

Calkins, R. G. (1984). *Programs of medieval illumination*. The Franklin D. Murphy Lectures 5. Lawrence, KS: University of Kansas, Spenser Museum of Art.

Calkins, R. G. (1986). Literal sequence and the decorative crescendo in the Drogo Sacramentary. *Gesta, 25*(1), 17-23.

Campbell, R. (1981). *The Bible on film: A checklist, 1897-1980*. Metuchen, NJ: Scarecrow Press.

Cantril, H. (1940). *The invasion from Mars: A study in the psychology of panic*. Princeton, NJ: Princeton University Press.

Carey, J. W. (1989). Mass communication and cultural studies. In J. W. Carey, *Communication as culture: Essays on media and society* (pp. 37-68). Boston: Unwin Hyman.

Carruthers, M. J. (1990). *The book of memory: A study of memory in medieval culture*. Cambridge: Cambridge University Press.

Catechism of the Catholic Church. (1995). New York, London, Toronto, Sydney, Auckland: Doubleday.

Cattrysse, P. (1990). *L'adaptation filmique de textes littéraires: Le film noir américain*. Unpublished doctoral dissertation, Leuven.

Cattrysse, P. (1992a). Film (adaptation) as translation: Some methodological proposals. *Target, 4*(1), 53-70.

Cattrysse, P. (1992b). *Pour une théorie de l'adaptation filmique: Le film noir américain*. Bern: Peter Lang.

Cattrysse, P. (1994a). Pour une approche intersystémique du cinéma. In J. Müller (Ed.), *Towards a pragmatics of the audiovisual* (Vol. 1, pp. 61-75). Münster, Nodus Publikationen.

Cattrysse, P. (1994b). The study of film adaptation: A state of the art and some "new" functional proposals. In F. Eguiluz (Ed.), *Transvases culturales: Literatura, cine, traducción* (pp. 37-51). Vitoria: Universidad del País Vasco.

Cattrysse, P. (1996). Descriptive and normative norms in film adaptation: the Hays Office and the American film noir. *Cinémas. Journal of Film Studies, 6*(2-3), 167-188.

Chamberlain, L. B. (1935). Supplying the blind with the Bible. *Bible Society Record, 80*, 155-157.

Coakley, S. (1988). *Christ without absolutes: A study of the christology of Ernst Troeltsch*. Oxford: Clarenden Press.

Cohen, S. J. (1992). The prodigal son. *Choreography and Dance, 2*(3).

Collins, W. A. (1981). Schemata for understanding television. In H. Kelly & H. Gardner (Eds.), *New directions for child development: Viewing children through television. No. 13* (pp. 31-45). San Francisco: Jossey Bass.

Conklin, J. (1987). Hypertext: An introduction and survey. *Computer, 20*(9), 17-41.

Courtine, J.-F. (1990). *Suarez et le système de la métaphysique*. Paris: Presses Universitaires de France.

Croatto, J. S. (1984). *Hermenéutica bíblica: Para una teoría de la lectura como producción de sentido*. Buenos Aires: La Aurora.

Csikszentmihalyi, M. (1975). Play and intrinsic rewards. *Journal of Humanistic Psychology, 13*(3), 41-63.

Culpepper, R. A. (1983). *Anatomy of the fourth gospel: A study in literary design*. Foundations and Facets. Philadelphia: Fortress.

Danto, A. C. (1986). *The philosophical disenfranchisement of art*. New York: Columbia University Press.

Danto, A. C. (1987). *The state of the art*. New York: Prentice Hall Press.

Davenport, G. (1996). Stories as dynamic adaptive environments. In R. Hodgson, Jr. & P. A. Soukup (Eds.), *From one medium to another: Basic issues for communicating the Scriptures in new media*. New York and Kansas City: American Bible Society and Sheed & Ward.

Davenport, G., & Friedlander, L. (1995). Interactive transformational environments: The wheel of life. In E. Barrett & M. Redmond (Eds.), *Contextual media: Multimedia and interpretation* (pp. 1-25). Cambridge, MA: MIT Press.

Deemer, C. (1994). *What is hypertext?* Available: http://www.teleport.com/~cdeemer/index.html

De Mille, A. (1991). *Martha: The life and work of Martha Graham*. New York: Random House.

Douglas, J. Y. (1994). "How do I stop this thing?": Closure and indeterminacy in interactive narratives. In G. P. Landow (Ed.), *Hyper/text/theory* (pp. 159-188). Baltimore: Johns Hopkins University Press.

Dowdy, A. (1973). *The films of the fifties: The American state of mind*. New York: Morrow.

Eco, U. (1979). *The role of the reader: Explorations in the semiotics of texts*. Bloomington: Indiana University Press.

Elbogen, I. (1993). *Jewish liturgy* (R. P. Scheindlin, Trans.). New York: Jewish Theological Seminary of America. (Original work published 1911)

Eliot, T. S. (1975). The function of criticism. In F. Kermode (Ed.), *Selected prose of T. S. Eliot* (pp. 68-78). New York: Harcourt, Bracc, & Jovanovich and Farrar, Straus, & Giroux.

Even-Zohar, I. (1978). The position of translated literature within the literary polysystem. In J. S. Holmes, J. Lambert, & R. van den Broeck (Eds.), *Literature and translation: New perspectives in literary studies* (pp. 117-127). Leuven: Acco.

Even-Zohar, I. (1979). Polysystem theory. *Poetics Today, 1*, 287-310.

Even-Zohar, I. (1990). Polysystem studies. *Poetics Today, 11*(special issue).

Farrar, F. W. (1886). *History of interpretation*. New York: E. P. Dutton.

Farrer, A. (1967). *Love almighty and ills unlimited*. London: Collins and Fontana.

Ferguson, D. N. (1959). *A history of musical thought.* New York: Appleton-Century-Crofts.

Finnegan, P. (1990). Reviews. *Sculpture, 9,* 76.

Fiske, J. (1987). *Television culture.* London: Methuen.

Forshey, G. (1992). *American religious and biblical spectaculars.* Westport, CT: Praeger.

Fowler, R. M. (1993). The fate of the notion of canon in the electronic age. *Foundations and Facets Forum, 9*(1-2), 151-172. Available: http://ccat.sas.upenn.edu/jod/texts/fowler.canon

Frank, A. P. (1994). Forum: Übersetzung - Translation - Traduction. *Target, 6*(1), 67-80.

Frei, H. W. (1992). Review: *Karl Barth* by Eberhard Busch. In *Types of Christian theology* (pp. 147-163). New Haven, CT: Yale University Press.

Fry, E. McG. (1987). Faithfulness—A wider perspective. *United Bible Societies Bulletin, 148/149,* 41-60.

Gadamer, H.-G. (1959). Vom Zirkel des Verstehens. In H.-G. Gadamer, (1985). *Hermeneutik II: Wahrheit und Methode: Ergänzungen. Register* (pp. 3-23). Gesammelte Werke, Band 2. Tübingen: Mohr (Siebeck).

Gadamer, H.-G. (1960). *Wahrheit und Methode: Grundzüge einer philosophischen Hermeneutik.* Tübingen: Mohr (Siebeck). [(1975/1991). *Truth and method* (1st ed./2nd rev. ed.) (J. Weinsheimer & D. G. Marshall, Trans., Rev.). New York: Crossroad.]

Gadamer, H.-G. (1961). Zur Problematik des Selbstverständnises: Ein hermeneutischer Beitrag zur Frage der Entmythologisierung. In H.-G. Gadamer. (1985). *Hermeneutik II: Wahrheit und Methode: Ergänzungen. Register* (pp. 121-132). Gesammelte Werke, Band 2. Tübingen: Mohr (Siebeck). [On the problem of self-understanding. In H.-G. Gadamer. (1976). *Philosophical Hermeneutics* (pp. 44-58). (D. E. Linge, Trans.). Berkeley: University of California.]

Gadamer, H.-G. (1962). The philosophical foundations of the twentieth century. In H.-G. Gadamer. (1976). *Philosophical Hermeneutics* (pp. 107-129). (D. E. Linge, Trans.). Berkeley: University of California.

Gadamer, H.-G. (1963). Die phänomenologische Bewegung. In H.-G. Gadamer. (1987). *Neuere Philosophie I: Hegel-Husserl-Heidegger* (pp. 105-146). Gesammelte Werke, Band 3. Tübingen: Mohr (Siebeck). [The phenomenological movement. In H.-G. Gadamer. (1976). *Philosophical Hermeneutics* (pp. 130-181). (D. E. Linge, Trans.). Berkeley: University of California.]

Gadamer, H.-G. (1964). Die Marburger Theologie. In H.-G. Gadamer. (1987). *Neuere Philosophie I: Hegel-Husserl-Heidegger* (pp. 197-208). Gesammelte Werke, Band 3. Tübingen: Mohr (Siebeck). [Martin Heidegger and Marburg Theology. In Gadamer, H.-G. (1976). *Philo-*

sophical Hermeneutics (pp. 198-212). (D. E. Linge, Trans.). Berkeley: University of California.]

Gadamer, H.-G. (1965). Vorwort zur 2. Auflage. In H.-G. Gadamer. (1985). *Hermeneutik II: Wahrheit und Methode: Ergänzungen. Register* (pp. 437-448). Gesammelte Werke, Band 2. Tübingen: Mohr (Siebeck).

Gadamer, H.-G. (1966). Mensch und Sprache. In H.-G. Gadamer. (1985). *Hermeneutik II: Wahrheit und Methode: Ergänzungen. Register* (pp. 146-154). Gesammelte Werke, Band 2. Tübingen: Mohr (Siebeck). [Man and language. In H.-G. Gadamer. (1976). *Philosophical Hermeneutics* (pp. 59-68). (D. E. Linge, Trans.). Berkeley: University of California.]

Gadamer, H.-G. (1967a). Aesthetik und Hermeneutik. In H.-G. Gadamer. (1987). *Kleine Schriften II: Interpretationen* (pp. 1-8). Tübingen: Mohr (Siebeck). [Aesthetics and Hermeneutics. In H.-G. Gadamer. (1976). *Philosophical Hermeneutics* (pp. 95-104). (D. E. Linge, Trans.). Berkeley: University of California.]

Gadamer, H.-G. (1967b). Goethe und Philosophie. In Gadamer, H.-G. (1987). *Kleine Schriften II: Interpretationen* (pp. 82-96). Tübingen: Mohr (Siebeck).

Gadamer, H.-G. (1967c). Über die Ursprunglichkeit der Philosophie. In H.-G. Gadamer. (1986). *Kleine Schriften I: Philosophie. Hermeneutik* (pp. 11-38). Tübingen: Mohr (Siebeck).

Gadamer, H.-G. (1968). Klassische und philosophische Hermeneutik. In H.-G. Gadamer. (1985). *Hermeneutik II: Wahrheit und Methode: Ergänzungen. Register* (pp. 92-117). Gesammelte Werke, Band 2. Tübingen: Mohr (Siebeck).

Gadamer, H.-G. (1969). Hermeneutik. In H.-G. Gadamer. (1985). *Hermeneutik II: Wahrheit und Methode: Ergänzungen. Register* (pp. 425-436). Gesammelte Werke, Band 2. Tübingen: Mohr (Siebeck).

Gadamer, H.-G. (1972). Nachwort zur 3. Auflage. In H.-G. Gadamer. (1985). *Hermeneutik II: Wahrheit und Methode: Ergänzungen. Register* (pp. 449-478). Gesammelte Werke, Band 2. Tübingen: Mohr (Siebeck).

Gadamer, H.-G. (1975). Selbstdarstellung Hans-Georg Gadamer. 11.2.1900 (abgeschlossen 1975). In H.-G. Gadamer. (1985). *Hermeneutik II: Wahrheit und Methode: Ergänzungen. Register* (pp. 479-508). Gesammelte Werke, Band 2. Tübingen: Mohr (Siebeck). [On the origins of philosophical hermeneutics. In H.-G. Gadamer. (1985). *Philosophical apprenticeships* (pp. 178-193). (R. Sullivan, Trans.). Cambridge, MA: MIT Press.]

Gadamer, H.-G. (1976). *Philosophical hermeneutics* (D. E. Linge, Trans.). Berkeley: University of California Press. (Original work published 1967-1972)

Gadamer, H.-G. (1979). Rationalität im Wandel der Zeiten. In H.-G. Gadamer. (1987). *Neuere Philosophie II: Probleme. Gestalten* (pp. 23-46). Gesammelte Werke, Band 4. Tübingen: Mohr (Siebeck).

Gadamer, H.-G. (1986a). Aesthetic and religious experience. In R. Bernasconi (Ed.), N. Walker, (Trans.), *The relevance of the beautiful and other essays* (pp. 140-153). Cambridge: Cambridge University Press. (Original work published 1967-1980)

Gadamer, H.-G. (1986b). Zwischen Phänomenologie und Dialektik. In H.-G. Gadamer. (1985). *Hermeneutik II: Wahrheit und Methode: Ergänzungen. Register* (pp. 3-23). Gesammelte Werke, Band 2. Tübingen: Mohr (Siebeck).

Gadamer, H.-G. (1986-1987). Erinnerungen an Heideggers Anfänge. In F. Rodi (Ed.), *Dilthey-Jahrbuch/4* (pp. 13-26). Göttingen: Vandenhoeck und Ruprecht.

Gadamer, H.-G. (1987). *Neuere Philosophie I: Hegel-Husserl-Heidegger.* Gesammelte Werke, Band 3. Tübingen: Mohr (Siebeck).

Gadamer, H.-G. (n.d.). Témoignage et affirmation. In E. Castelli (Ed.), (1972), *Le Témoignage* (pp. 161-165). Paris: Aubier.

Gamble, Jr., H. Y. (1985). Christianity: Scripture and canon. In F. M. Denny & R. L. Taylor (Eds.), *The holy book in comparative perspective* (pp. 36-62). Columbia: University of South Carolina Press.

Garafola, L. (1989). *Diaghilev's ballet russes.* New York: Oxford University Press.

Gardener, H. (1983). *Frames of mind: The theory of multiple intelligences.* New York: Basic Books.

Georgiades T. (1982). *Music and language.* New York: Cambridge University Press.

Gerbner, G., Gross, L., Morgan, M., & Signorielli, N. (1986). Living with television: The dynamics of the cultivation process. In J. Bryant & D. Zillman (Eds.), *Perspectives on media effects* (pp. 17-39). Hillsdale, NJ: Erlbaum.

Giamatti, A. B. (1989). *Take time for paradise.* New York: Summit Books.

Gibson, W. (1984). *Neuromancer.* New York: Ace Books.

Gill, S. (1987). *Native American religious action.* Columbia: University of South Carolina Press.

Glenn, S. (1992). Real fun, virtually: Virtual experience amusements & products in public space entertainment. In S. K. Helsel (Ed.), *The technology, research and business of virtual reality* (pp. 62–69). Westport, CT: Meckler.

Goethals, G. (1981). *The TV ritual: Worship at the video altar.* Boston: Beacon Press.

Goethals, G. (1990). *The electronic golden calf: Images, religion, and the making of meaning.* Cambridge, MA: Cowley.

Goethals, G. (1993). Response. In H. C. Kee (Ed.), *The Bible in the twenty-first century* (pp. 185-191). Philadelphia: Trinity Press International.

Goethals, G. (1996). Revision: New forms for traditional texts. *Religion and Education, 23*(1), 34-37.

Goethals, G. (in press). Escape from time: Ritual dimensions of popular culture. In S. Hoover & K. Lundby (Eds.), *Media, religion and culture: Rallies, rituals, resistance.* Newbury Park, CA: Sage.

Goldberg, V. (1995, April 9). Looking at the poor in a gilded frame. *The New York Times,* Section 2, p. 39.

Goldfarb , N. M. (1991, September 30). Virtual reality: The state of the art. *MicroTimes,* 114-116.

González, J. (in press). Archaeological devotion. In L. Bloom (Ed.), *Gender and race politics in visual culture.* St. Paul: University of Minnesota Press.

Graham, M. (1991). *Blood memory.* New York: Doubleday.

Graham, W. A. (1987). *Beyond the written word: Oral aspects of scripture in the history of religion.* New York: Cambridge University Press.

Grice, P. (1975). Logic and conversation. In E. P. Cox & J. L. Morgan (Eds.), *Speech acts* (pp. 41-48). New York: Academic Press.

Grondin, J. (1994). *Introduction to philosophical hermeneutics* (J. Weinsheimer, Trans.). New Haven, CT: Yale University Press. (Original work published 1991)

Gutt, E.-A. (1992). *Relevance theory: A guide to successful communication in translation.* New York: United Bible Societies.

Hagedorn, F. L. (1991). Why multimedia translations: An American Bible Society perspective. *United Bible Societies Bulletin, 160/161,* 20-26.

Hall, S. (1980). Encoding/decoding. In S. Hall, D. Hobson, A. Lowe, & P. Willis (Eds.), *Culture, media, language* (pp. 128-139). London: Hutchinson.

Haraway, D. (1990). A manifesto for cyborgs: Science, technology, and socialist feminism in the 1980s. In L. J. Nicholson (Ed.), *Feminism/postmodernism* (pp. 190-233). New York: Routledge.

Harding, J., & Fallon, D. M. (1980). Saint-Saëns, Camille. In *The new Grove dictionary of music and musicians* (vol. 16, pp. 400-407). Washington, DC: Macmillan.

Harley, R. M. (1993). New media for communicating the Bible: The potential and the problems. In H. C. Kee (Ed.), *The Bible in the twenty-first century* (pp. 161-178). Philadephia: Trinity Press International.

Harpold, T. (1991). *Hypertext and hypermedia: A selected bibliography* [Online]. Available: http://www/lcc.gatech.edu/faculty/harpold/papers/ht_bibliogr aphy/indcx.html

Hastie, R. (1981). Schematic principles in human memory. In E. T. Higgins, C. P. Herman, & M. P. Zanna (Eds.), *Social cognition: The Ontario Symposium* (Vol. 1, pp. 39-88). Hillsdale, NJ: Erlbaum.

Hastorf, A. H., & Cantril, H. (1954). They saw a game: A case study. *Journal of Abnormal and Social Psychology, 49,* 129-134.

Hatch, N. O. (1989). *The democratization of American Christianity.* New Haven, CT: Yale University Press.

Heidegger, M. (1959). *Unterwegs zur Sprache.* Pfallingen: Neske.

Heidegger, M. (n.d.) *Wegmarken.* Gesamtausgabe, Band 9. Frankfurt: Verlag Klostermann.

Heim, M. (1993). *The metaphysics of virtual reality.* Oxford: Oxford University Press.

Helsel, S. K. (Ed.). (1992). *The technology, research and business of virtual reality.* Westport, CT: Meckler.

Hermans, T. (1985). Introduction. In T. Hermans (Ed.), *The manipulation of literature: Studies in literary translation* (pp. 7-15). London and Sydney: Croom Helm.

Hermans, T. (1991). Translational norms and correct translations. In K. van Leuven-Zwart & T. Naaijkens (Eds.), *Translation studies: The state of the art: Proceedings of the first international James S. Holmes Symposium on translation studies* (pp. 155-169). Amsterdam and Atlanta, GA: Rodopi.

Hertzog, H. (1944). What do we really know about daytime serial listeners? In P. F. Lazarsfeld & F. N. Stanton (Eds.), *Radio research, 1942-1943* (pp. 3-33). New York: Duell, Sloan, & Pierce.

Hindeman, S. (1977). Cross fertilization: Experiments in mixing the media. In S. Hindeman & J. D. Farquhar (Eds.), *Pen to press: Illustrated manuscripts and printed books in the first century of printing* (pp. 101-211). Baltimore: University of Maryland Press and Johns Hopkins University Press.

Holmes, J. S. (1972; reprint, 1975). *The name and nature of translation studies.* Amsterdam: Translation Studies Section, Department of General Literary Studies.

Holmes, J. S., Lambert, J., & van dan Broeck, R. (Eds.). (1978). *Literature and translation: New perspectives in literary studies.* Leuven: Acco.

Hönig, H. G., & Kußmaul, P. (1982). *Strategie der Übersetzung: Ein Lehr- und Arbeitsbuch.* Tübingen: Narr.

Horst, L. (1987). *Pre-classic dance forms.* Princeton, NJ: Princeton Book Company.

Hudson, R. V. (1987). *Mass media.* New York: Garland.

Huizinga, J. (1950). *Homo ludens: A study of the play-element in culture.* Boston: Beacon Press.

Huizinga, J. (1956). *The waning of the middle ages.* Garden City, NY: Doubleday.

Jenkins, H. (1992). *Textual poachers: Television fans and participatory culture.* New York: Routledge.

Jensen, K. B. (1991). When is meaning? Communication theory, pragmatism, and mass media reception. In J. A. Anderson (Ed.), *Communication yearbook/14* (pp. 3-32). Newbury Park, CA: Sage.

Jonassen, D. H. (1989). *Hypertext/hypermedia.* Englewood Cliffs, NJ: Education Technology.

Joyce, M. (1988). Siren shapes: Exploratory and constructive hypertexts. *Academic Computing, 3,* 10-14, 37-42.

Kaplan, N. (1991). Ideology, technology, and the future of writing instruction. In G. E. Hawisher & C. L. Selfe (Eds.), *Evolving perspectives on computers and composition studies* (pp. 11-42). Urbana, IL: National Council of Teachers of English.

Kaplan, N. (1995, March). E-literacies: Politexts, hypertexts, and other cultural formations in the late age of print. *Computer Mediated Communications.* Available: http://sunsite.unc.edu/cmc/mag/1995/mar/kaplan. html

Kee, H. C. (Ed.) (1993). *The Bible in the twenty-first century: American Bible Society Symposium papers.* Philadelphia: Trinity Press International and American Bible Society.

Kennedy, G. A. (1984). *New Testament interpretation through rhetorical criticism.* Chapel Hill: University of North Carolina Press.

Kerman, J. (1988). *Opera as drama* (rev. ed.). Berkeley: University of California Press.

Kisiel, T. (1986-1987). Die Entstehung des Begriffsfeldes Faktizität in Frühwerk Heideggers. In F. Rodi (Ed.), *Dilthey-Jahrbuch/4* (pp. 91-120). Göttingen: Vandenhoeck und Ruprecht.

Kisiel, T. (1988). The missing link in the early Heidegger. In J. Kockelmanns (Ed.), *Hermeneutic phenomenology* (pp. 1-40). Washington, DC: University Press of America.

Kisiel, T. (1989). Why the first draft of *Being and Time* was never published. *Journal of the British Society of Phenomenology, 20*(1), 3-23.

Kisiel, T. (1993). *The genesis of Heidegger's* Being and Time. Berkeley: University of California Press.

Kolb, D. (1994). Socrates in the labyrinth. In G. P. Landow (Ed.), *Hyper/text/theory* (pp. 323-344). Baltimore: Johns Hopkins University Press.

Koller, W. (1972). *Grundprobleme der Übersetzungstheorie: Unter besonderer Berücksichtigung schwedisch-deutscher Übersetzungsfälle.* Bern: Francke.

Koller, W. (1979). *Einführung in die Übersetzungswissenschaft.* Heidelberg: Quelle & Meyer.

Koner, P. (1989). *Solitary song.* Durham, NC: Duke University Press.

Kosuth, J. (1993). Interview with Joseph Kosuth in *Installation Art. Art & Design, 30,* 95.

Krueger, M. W. (1991). *Artificial reality.* Reading, MA: Addison-Wesley.

Kuhn, T. S. (1967). *The structure of scientific revolutions* (2nd ed.). Chicago: University of Chicago Press.

Kümmel, W. G. (1972). *The New Testament: The history of the investigation of its problems.* (S. M. Gilmour & H. C. Kee, Trans.). Nashville, TN: Abingdon. (Original work published 1970)

Kuspit, D. (1994). *The cult of the avant-garde artist.* Cambridge: Cambridge University Press.

Lacy, C. (1977). *The word carrying giant: The growth of the American Bible Society (1816-1966).* South Pasadena, CA: William Carey Library.

Lamb, C. (1968). Introduction. In K. Muir (Ed.), *Othello.* London: Penguin Books.

Lambert, J. (1989). La traduction, les langues et la communication de masse: Les ambiguïtés du discours international. *Target, 1*(2), 215-237.

Lambert, J. (1991). Shifts, oppositions and goals in translation studies: Towards a genealogy of concepts. In K. van Leuven-Zwart & T. Naaijkens (Eds.), *Translation studies: The state of the art: Proceedings of the first international James S. Holmes Symposium on translation studies* (pp. 25-37). Amsterdam and Atlanta, GA: Rodopi.

Lambert, J. (1994). Ethnolinguistic democracy, translation policy and contemporary world (dis)order. In F. Eguiluz (Ed.), *Transvases culturales: Literatura, cine, traduccíon* (pp. 23-36). Vitoria: Universidad del País Vasco.

Lambert, J. (1995a). Translation, systems and research: The contribution of polysystem studies to translation studies. *Traduction Terminologie Rédaction: Études sur le texte et ses transformations, 8*(1), 105-152.

Lambert, J. (1995b). Van de nul-vertaling tot het niet-vertalen: Nog eens een andere kijk op vertaalbaarheid en op de vertaalproblematiek. In H. Bloemen, E. Hertog, & W. Segers (Eds.), *Letterlijkheid, woordelijkheid* [Literality, verbality] (pp. 167-177). Antwerpen: Fantom.

Lambert, J. (in press a). Le discours implicite sur la traduction dans l'encyclopédie. In M. Ballard & L. D'hulst (Eds.), *La traduction à l'âge classique.* Lille: Presses universitaires de Lille.

Lambert, J. (in press b). Language and translation as general management problems: A new task for education. In C. Dollerup (Ed.), *2nd Language International Conference, Elsinore June 1995.*

Lambert, J. & Robyns, C. (in press). Translation. In R. Posner, K. Robering, & T. A. Sebeok (Eds.), *Semiotik: Ein internationales Handbuch zu den zeichentheoretischen Grundlagen von Natur und Kultur* [Semiotics: An international handbook of the sign-theoretic foundations of nature and culture]. (2 vols.). Berlin and New York: de Gruyter.

Landow, G. P. (1992a). *Hypertext: The convergence of contemporary critical theory and technology.* Baltimore: Johns Hopkins University Press.

Landow, G. P. (1992b). Hypertext, metatext, and the electronic canon. In M. C. Tuman (Ed.), *Literacy online: The promise (and peril) of reading and writing with computers* (pp. 57-94). Pittsburg, PA: University of Pittsburg Press.

Lanham, R. A. (1993). *The electronic word: Democracy, technology, and the arts*. Chicago: University of Chicago Press.

LaRue, J. (1970). *Guidelines for style analysis*. New York: W. W. Norton.

Latta, J. N. (1992). When will reality meet the marketplace? In S. K. Helsel (Ed.), *The technology, research and business of virtual reality* (pp. 109–141). Westport, CT: Meckler.

Lawrence, F. (1976). The horizon of Vorhandenheit. In *Believing to understand: The hermeneutic circle in Gadamer and Lonergan* (pp. 13-55). Unpublished doctoral dissertation, University of Basel, Switzerland.

Lawrence, F. (1990). *Critical realism and the hermeneutical revolution*. Unpublished paper contributed to a living Festschrift for New Testament scholar Ben Meyer.

Limón, J. (1959). *Letter to Pauline, Betty, and Lucas on the occasion of the 10th anniversary of the* Moor's Pavane. New York: José Limón Dance Foundation Archives.

Lindlof, T. R. (1988). Media audiences as interpretive communities. In J. A. Anderson (Ed.), *Communication yearbook/11* (pp. 81-107). Newbury Park, CA: Sage.

Lorenz, C. (1987). *De constructie van het verleden: Een inleiding in de theorie van de geschiedenis*. Amsterdam: Boom Meppel.

Lowery, S., & DeFleur, M. L. (1983). *Milestones in mass communication research: Media effects*. New York: Longman.

Lukač, J. (1992). *Image/object/memory* [Exhibition Catalog, The Hand Workshop]. Richmond: Virginia Center for the Craft Arts.

Lull, J. (1980). The social uses of television. *Human Communication Research, 6*, 197-209.

Lull, J. (Ed.). (1988). *World families watch television*. Newbury Park, CA: Sage.

Lyotard, J.-F. (1984). *The postmodern condition: A report on knowledge* (G. Bennington & B. Massumi, Trans.). Minneapolis: University of Minnesota Press. (Original work published 1979)

Malina, B. J. (1993). *The New Testament world: Insights from cultural anthropology* (Rev. ed.). Louisville, KY: Westminster and John Knox.

Mandelstam, N. (1980). *Hope against hope: A memoir* (M. Hayward, Trans.). New York: Atheneum. (Original work published 1970)

Mander, J. (1992). *In the absence of the sacred: The failure of technology and the survival of the Indian nations*. San Francisco: Sierra Club Books.

Mandler, J. M. (1984). *Stories, scripts, and scenes: Aspects of schema theory*. Hillsdale, NJ: Erlbaum.

Martin, T. M. (1981). *Images and the imageless: A study in religious consciousness in film*. London: Associated University Presses.

McDaid, J. (1991). Toward an ecology of hypermedia. In G. E. Hawisher & C. L. Selfe (Eds.), *Evolving perspectives on computers and composition studies* (pp. 203-233). Urbana, IL: National Council of Teachers of English.

McLuhan, M. (1962). *The Gutenberg galaxy: The making of typographic man*. Toronto: University of Toronto Press.

McPherson, A. S. (1923a, May). Sister McPherson's sermons on phonograph records. *The Bridal Call,* 31.

McPherson, A. S. (1923b, July). Converting the world by radio. *The Bridal Call,* 15, 18.

McPherson, A. S. (1923c). *This is that*. Los Angeles: Echo Park Evangelistic Association.

Meeks, W. A. (1983). *The first urban Christians: The social world of the apostle Paul*. New Haven, CT: Yale University Press.

Mellinger, M. (1995, March, 2). *Global information technologies*. Public Address at Missouri Western State College, St. Joseph, MO.

Mesa-Bains, A. (1992). *Domesticana: The sensibility of Chicana Rasquache*. Unpublished paper.

Meyer, B. (1989). *Critical realism and the New Testament*. Allison Park, PA: Pickwick.

Meyrowitz, J. (1985). *No sense of place: The impact of electronic media on social behavior*. New York: Oxford University Press.

Minsky, M. (1994). *First person: The society of mind*. [CD-ROM]. New York: The Voyager Company.

Mitcham, C. (1994). *Thinking through technology: The path between engineering and philosophy*. Chicago: University of Chicago Press.

Moores, S. (1993). *Interpreting audiences: The ethnography of media consumption*. London: Sage.

Morgenroth, L., & Davenport, G. (1995). *LURKER: A thinkie for the society of audience*. Unpublished paper, MIT Media Lab.

Morrison, P., Morrison, P., & The Office of Charles and Ray Eames. (1982). *Powers of ten: About the relative size of things in the universe*. New York: Scientific American Library.

Moulthrop, S. (1989). Hypertext and "the hyperreal." In *Hypertext 89 Proceedings* (pp. 259-267). New York: Association for Computing Machinery.

Moulthrop, S. (1991). The politics of hypertext. In G. E. Hawisher & C. L. Selfe (Eds.), *Evolving perspectives on computers and composition studies* (pp. 253-271). Urbana, IL: National Council of Teachers of English.

Moulthrop, S. (1994). Rhizome and hypertext: Liberation and complicity in art and pedagogy. In G. P. Landow (Ed.), *Hyper/text/theory* (pp. 299-319). Baltimore: Johns Hopkins University Press.

Moulthrop, S. (1995). Getting over the edge. Home page [On-line]. Available: http://raven.ubalt.edu/staff/moulthrop/

Mullins, P. (1990). Sacred text in an electronic era. *Biblical Theology Bulletin, 20*(3), 99-106.

Mullins, P. (1993, November 23). *Multimedia as a theoretical tool.* Paper presented at annual meeting of Society for Biblical Literature, Washington D.C. Available: mullins@griffon.mwsc.edu

Mullins, P. (1996a). Imagining the Bible in electronic culture. *Religion and Education, 23*(1), 38-45.

Mullins, P. (1996b). Sacred text in the sea of texts: The Bible in North American electronic culture. In C. Ess (Ed.), *Philosophical perspectives on computer-mediated communication.* Albany, NY: SUNY Press.

Myers, K. A. (1989). *All God's children and blue suede shoes: Christians and popular culture.* Westchester, IL: Crossway Books.

Negroponte, N. (1994). *Being digital.* New York: Knopf.

Neill, S., & Wright, T. (1988). *The interpretation of the New Testament 1861 to 1986.* Oxford: Oxford University Press.

Nelson, T. H. (1992). Opening hypertext: A memoir. In M. C. Tuman (Ed.), *Literacy online: The promise (and peril) of reading and writing with computers* (pp. 43-57). Pittsburg, PA: University of Pittsburg Press.

Neubert, A., & Shreve, G. (1992). *Translation as text.* Kent, OH: Kent State University Press.

Newcomb, H., & Hirsch, P. (1984). Television as a cultural forum: Implications for research. In W. Rowland & B. Watkins (Eds.), *Interpreting television* (pp. 58-73). Beverly Hills, CA: Sage.

Newmark, P. (1981). *Approaches to translation.* Oxford: Pergamon.

Nida, E. A. (1952). *God's word in man's language.* New York: Harper.

Nida, E. A. (1964). *Toward a science of translating, with special reference to principles and procedures involved in Bible translating.* Leiden: Brill.

Nida, E. A. (1969). Science of translation. *Language, 45,* 483-498.

Nida, E., & Taber, C. R. (1969). *The theory and practice of translation. Helps for Translators,* 8. Leiden: Brill.

Ong, W. J. (1982). *Orality and literacy: The technologizing of the word.* New York: Methuen.

Ong, W. J. (1992). Communications media and the state of theology. In T. J. Farrell & P.A. Soukup (Eds.), *Faith and contexts: Selected essays and studies 1952-1991* (pp. 154-174). Atlanta, GA: Scholars Press. (Originally published in 1969 in *Cross Currents, 19,* 462-480.)

Pacey, A. (1983). *The culture of technology.* Cambridge, MA: MIT Press.

Peirce, C. S. (1955). Logic as semiotic: The theory of signs. In J. Buchler (Ed.), *Philosophical writings of Peirce* (pp. 98-119). New York: Dover.

Pöggeler, O. (1963). *Der Denkweg Heideggers* (1st ed.). Pfullingen: Neske.

Pöggeler, O. (1983). Nachwort. In *Der Denkweg Heideggers* (3rd ed.). Pfullingen: Neske.

Polanyi, M., & Prosch, H. (1975). *Meaning*. Chicago: University of Chicago Press.

Postman, N. (1985). *Amusing ourselves to death: Public discourse in the age of show business*. New York: Viking Penguin.

Poythress, V. S. (1988). *Science and hermeneutics: Implications of scientific method for biblical interpretation*. Foundations of Contemporary Interpretation, 6. Grand Rapids: Zondervan.

Pushkin, A. (1983). *Complete prose fiction*. Stanford, CA: Stanford University Press.

Pym, A. (1992). *Translation and text transfer: An essay on the principles of intercultural communication*. Bern: Lang.

Rader, P. (1925, December 25). The announcer. *National Radio Chapel Announcer*, 3.

Rahner, H. (1972). *Man at play*. New York: Herder & Herder.

Randel, D. M. (1986). *The new Harvard dictionary of music*. Cambridge: Belknap Press of Harvard University Press.

Reid, J. D. (1993). *The Oxford guide to classical mythology in the arts, 1300-1990's* (Vol. 2). New York: Oxford University Press.

Rey, A. (1995). *Essays on terminology* (J. C. Sager, Trans., Ed.). Benjamins Tranlations Studies, 9. Amsterdam and Philadelphia: Benjamins. (Original work published 1975-1988)

Rheingold, H. (1991). *Virtual reality*. New York: Simon & Schuster.

Ricoeur, P. (1976). *Interpretation theory: Discourse and the surplus of meaning*. Fort Worth: Texas Christian University.

Ricoeur, P. (1980). *Essays on biblical interpretation*. Philadelphia: Fortress.

Roberts, D. F. (1971). The nature of communication effects. In W. Schramm & D. F. Roberts (Eds.), *The process and effects of mass communication* (Rev. ed., pp. 347-387). Urbana: University of Illinois Press.

Robinson, J. M. (1959). *A new quest of the historical Jesus*. Studies in Biblical Theology, 25. London: SCM.

Robinson, J. M., & Cobb, Jr., J. B. (Eds.). (1964). *The new hermeneutic: New frontiers in theology: Discussions among continental and American theologians*. New York: Harper & Row.

Rosenberg. H. (1972). *The de-definition of art*. New York: Horizon.

Rosenthal, S. (1983). Meaning as habit: Some systematic implications of Peirce's pragmatism. In E. Freeman (Ed.), *The relevance of Charles Peirce* (pp. 312-327). La Salle, IL: Monist Library of Philosophy.

Sanders, E. P. (1977). *Paul and Palestinian Judaism: A comparison of patterns of religion*. Philadelphia: Fortress.

Schank, R., & Abelson, R. (1977). *Scripts, plans, goals and understanding: An inquiry into human knowledge structures*. Hillsdale, NJ: Erlbaum.

Schmidt, S. J. (1991). *Grundriss der empirischen Literaturwissenschaft.* Frankfurt/M: Suhrkamp.

Schneiderman, B., & Kearsley, G. (1989). *Hypertext—hands on!: An introduction to a new way of organizing and accessing information.* New York: Addison-Wesley.

Schramm, W. (1971). The nature of communication between humans. In W. Schramm & D. F. Roberts (Eds.), *The process and effects of mass communication* (Rev. ed., pp. 1-53). Urbana: University of Illinois Press.

Shakespeare, W. (1968). *Othello* (Edited by K. Muir). London: Penguin Books.

Sheehan, T. (1976). *Hermeneia* and *Apophansis*: The early Heidegger on Aristotle. In F. Volpi (Ed.), *Heidegger et l'idée de la phénomenologie.* Phenomenologica, 108. (pp. 252-271). Dordrecht: Kluwer.

Silva, M. (1990). *God, language, and scripture: Reading the Bible in the light of general linguistics.* Foundations of Contemporary Interpretation, 4. Grand Rapids: Zondervan.

Silva, M. (1994). Contemporary theories of biblical interpretation. In *New Interpreter's Bible,* (Vol. 1, pp. 107-124). Nashville, TN: Abingdon.

Simpson, J. A., & Weiner, E. S. C. (1989). *The Oxford English dictionary* (2nd ed.). Oxford: Clarendon Press.

Slatin, J. M. (1988). Hypertext and the teaching of writing. In E. Barrett (Ed.), *Text, context and hypertext: Writing with and for the computer* (pp. 111-129). Cambridge, MA: MIT Press.

Sloan, S. J. (1994). Close encounters with virtual worlds. *Educators' Tech Exchange, 2*(1), 23-29.

Smith, W. C. (1993). *What is scripture?* Minneapolis, MN: Fortress Press.

Smyth, H. W. (1984). *Greek grammar.* Cambridge: Harvard University Press.

Snell-Hornby, M. (1988). *Translation studies: An integrated approach.* Amsterdam and Philadelphia: Benjamins.

Soares, J. (1992). *Louis Horst: Musician in a dancer's world.* Durham, NC: Duke University Press.

Sophocles. (1947). *The Theban plays: King Oedipus, Oedipus at Colonus, Antigone* (E. F. Watling, Trans.). Baltimore: Penguin.

Soukup, P. A. (1983). *Communication and theology: Introduction and review of the literature.* London: World Association for Christian Communication [reprint: London: Centre for the Study of Communication and Culture, 1991].

Stackhouse, S. (1994). *The Moor's Pavane: Notes on the characters, casting and scenes.* Manuscript, Dance Notation Bureau.

Stanford, W. B. (1967). *The sound of Greek.* Berkeley: University of California Press.

Stock, B. (1983). *The implications of literacy: Written language and models of interpretation in the eleventh and twelfth centuries.* Princeton, NJ: Princeton University Press.

Stodelle, E. (1984). *Deep song: The dance story of Martha Graham.* New York: Shirmer Books.

Stoerig, H. J. (1963). *Das Problem des Übersetzens.* Darmstadt and Stuttgart: Goverts and Wissenschaftliche Buchgesellschaft.

Stout, H. S. (1991). *The divine dramatist: George Whitefield and the rise of modern evangelicalism.* Grand Rapids, MI: Eerdmans.

Strauss, L. (1970). A giving of accounts with Jacob Klein. *The College Annapolis and Santa Fe, 22*(1), 1-5.

Taper, B. (1960). *Balanchine: A biography.* New York: Harper & Row.

Tatman, M. R. (1925). God's Saturday night. *The Midnight Cry, 12*(3), 1-3.

Terry, W. (1975). *Frontiers of dance: The life of Martha Graham.* New York: Crowell.

Thielman, F. (1994). *Paul and the law: A contextual approach.* Downers Grove, IL: InterVarsity.

Thomas, K. J. (1994). Criteria for faithfulness in multimedia translation (and related audio components). *Bulletin of the United Bible Societies, 170/171*, 43-48.

Tillich, P. (1964). *Theology of culture.* New York: Oxford University Press.

Toury, G. (1978). The nature and role of norms in literary translation. In J. S. Holmes, J. Lambert, & R. van den Broeck (Eds.), *Literature and translation: New perspectives in literary studies* (pp. 83-100). Leuven: Acco.

Toury, G. (1980). *In search of a theory of translation.* Meaning and Art, 2. Tel-Aviv: Porter Institute for Poetics and Semiotics.

Toury, G. (1986). Translation: A cultural-semiotic perspective. In T. A. Sebeok (Ed.), *Encyclopedic Dictionary of Semiotics/2* Approaches to Semiotics, 73. (pp. 1111-1124). Berlin-New-York-Amsterdam: Mouton-de Gruyter.

Toury, G. (1995). *Descriptive translation studies and beyond.* Benjamins Translation Library, 4. Amsterdam and Philadelphia: Benjamins.

Tuman, M. C. (1992a). First thoughts. In M. C. Tuman (Ed.), *Literacy online: The promise (and peril) of reading and writing with computers* (pp. 3-15). Pittsburgh, PA: University of Pittsburg Press.

Tuman, M. C. (1992b). *Word perfect: Literacy in the computer age.* Pittsburgh, PA: University of Pittsburgh Press.

Turner, V. W. (1974). Liminal to liminoid, in play, flow and ritual: An essay in comparative symbology. *Rice University Studies, 40*(3), 53-92.

Turner, V. W. (1977). Variations on a theme of liminality. In S. F. Moore & B. G. Myerhoff (Eds.), *Secular ritual* (pp. 36-52). Ithaca, NY: Cornell University Press.

Vermeer, H. J. (1971). *Einführung in die linguistische Terminologie.* München: Nymphenburg.

Vermeer, H. J. (1983). *Aufsätze zur translationstheorie.* [mimeograph]. Heidelberg.

Vinay, J.-P., & Darbelnet, J. (1958). *Stylistique comparée du français et de l'anglais: Méthode de traduction.* Paris: Didier.

Vogler, C. (1992). *The writer's journey: Mythic structures for screenwriters and storytellers.* Studio City, CA: Michael Wiese Productions.

Voskuil, D. N. (1990). The power of the air: Evangelicals and the rise of religious broadcasting. In Q. T. Schultze (Ed.), *American Evangelicals in the mass media* (pp. 69-95). Grand Rapids, MI: Zondervan.

Waard, J. de, & Nida, E. A. (1986). *From one language to another: Functional equivalence in Bible translating.* Nashville: Nelson.

Ward, M. (1994). *Air of salvation: The story of Christian broadcasting.* Grand Rapids, MI: Baker Book House.

Wellek, R. (1942). The mode of existence of a literary work of art. *Southern Review, 7,* 735-754.

Westerholm, S. (1988). *Israel's law and the church's faith: Paul and his recent interpreters.* Grand Rapids, MI: Eerdmans.

White, G. W. (1993, July 15). Publication of the Bible goes forth and multiplies: Versions targeted at specific groups helps push sales above $400 million. *Atlanta Constitution,* p. F1.

White, R. A. (1994). Audience "interpretation" of media: Emerging perspectives. *Communication Research Trends, 14*(3), 1-32.

Williams, R. (1988). Suspicion of suspicion: Wittgenstein and Bonhoeffer. In R. H. Bell (Ed.), *The grammar of the heart: New essays in moral philosophy and theology* (pp. 36-53). San Francisco: Harper & Row.

Wilss, W. (1977). *Übersetzungswissenschaft: Probleme und methoden.* Stuttgart: Klett.

Wind, E. (1969). *Art and anarchy.* New York: Random House, Vintage Books.

Wornum, R. N. (Ed.). (1848). *Lectures on painting by the royal academicians: Barry, Opie, and Fuseli.* London: Bohn.

Wosh, P. J. (1994). *Spreading the word: The Bible business in nineteenth-century America.* Ithaca and London: Cornell University Press.

Wyatt, J. (1994). *High concept: Movies and marketing in Hollywood.* Austin: University of Texas.

Ybarra-Frausto, T. (1987). Sanctums of the spirit: The *altares* of Amalia Mesa-Bains. In *Grotto of the virgins* [Exhibition Catalog] (pp. 1-9). New York: Intar Latin American Gallery.

Ybarra-Frausto, T. (1991). Chicano movement/Chicano art. In I. Karp & S. D. Levine (Eds.), *Exhibiting cultures: The poetics and politics of museum display* (pp. 128-150). Washington, DC: Smithsonian Institution Press.

Zimmermann, J. H. (1968). *Public relations: Promotions and publicity—service to the Bible cause, 1931-1966: ABS Historical Essay # 17, Part VI-I.* Unpublished typescript, American Bible Society, New York.

Index

The American Bible Society Multimedia Translation Series

Out of the Tombs: Mark 5.1-20

Based on scholarly biblical research and quality video production, the American Bible Society's multimedia CD-ROM program Out of the Tombs: Mark 5.1-20 and the 9-minute video of the same name are available from ABS.

The CD-ROM program allows the user to gain historical background of the passage through short video documentaries and performances, maps, text, audio narration, art images, and musical selections. The user can access six video versions of the story from Mark 5.1-20. One can journey through the program at a comfortable pace and engage in activities such as the keeping of a journal, creation of a slide show, and the production of a script from which to film a video of the story.

Among its many awards, "Out of the Tombs" (video) captured the Golden Eagle Award from the Council on International Nonthreatrical Events (CINE) in 1992. "Out of the Tombs" CD-ROM was awarded the Gold Plaque at the Intercomm Festival in 1996.

A Father and Two Sons: Luke 15.11-32

Traditionally known as the Prodigal Son, this parable of Jesus is brought forward in time through a video translation of the text and an accompanying multimedia CD-ROM program. Both video and CD-ROM versions of "A Father and Two Sons" are available from the American Bible Society.

Accompanied by a comprehensive user's guide, the video is nine-minutes long and contains an original composition by recording artist Rory Block. The song "A Father and Two Sons" is also heard on Rory Block's album, "Angel of Mercy," available where cassettes and CDs are sold.

381

The multimedia CD-ROM program of the same name allows the user to view three different video versions of the parable, as well as explore the contextual background of the biblical story through the use of video and text. The user also can produce responses to the story by writing a video script, producing a slide show, writing a poem, and creating a new translation. A resource center provides artwork, maps, music, and films based on Luke 15.11-32.

In 1994, "A Father and Two Sons" (video) won the top award at CINE—a Golden Eagle, while the CD-ROM version was honored with a Silver Award at the Houston International Festival in 1996.

The Visit: Luke 1.39-56

"The Visit" is a journey into the biblical story of Mary's visit to her cousin Elizabeth as recorded in Luke 1.39-56. At a time when women seldom traveled alone, Mary courageously visited her elderly cousin Elizabeth to assist during Elizabeth's time of pregnancy. For her part, Mary received a blessing for her own unborn son, Jesus. In her joy, Mary sings the Magnificat or Song of Praise to God and remembers all of the great things God has done for the oppressed through the ages. The recurring images of the spiral or nautilus symbolize new life and the strength and leadership of women throughout biblical and modern history.

Composed and performed by Women of the Calabash, "The Visit" is one of an exciting series of video Scriptures from the American Bible Society. This 8-minute translation of Luke 1.39-56 is available with a discussion guide from the American Bible Society.

The multimedia CD-ROM program also called "The Visit" allows the user to view different video versions of the parable, as well as explore the contextual background of the biblical story through the use of video and text. The user also can produce responses to the story by writing a video script, producing a slide show, writing a poem, and creating a new translation. A resource center provides artwork, maps and music based on Luke 1.39-56.

Following the honors garnered by its two predecessor videos, "The Visit" (video) was given the Golden Eagle in 1994 by CINE. In 1995, the National Educational Media Network gave the Bronze prize to "The Visit" CD-ROM.

To order the any of the videos ($9.95) or the CD-ROMs ($39.95), call the American Bible Society at 1-800-32-BIBLE.